Anglo-French attitudes

Anglo-French attitudes
Comparisons and transfers between English and French intellectuals since the eighteenth century

Edited by
CHRISTOPHE CHARLE,
JULIEN VINCENT AND JAY WINTER

Manchester University Press
Manchester and New York

distributed exclusively in the USA by Palgrave

Copyright © Manchester University Press 2007

While copyright in the volume as a whole is vested in Manchester University Press, copyright in individual chapters belongs to their respective authors, and no chapter may be reproduced wholly or in part without the express permission in writing of both author and publisher.

Published by Manchester University Press
Oxford Road, Manchester M13 9NR, UK
and Room 400, 175 Fifth Avenue, New York, NY 10010, USA
www.manchesteruniversitypress.co.uk

Distributed exclusively in the USA by
Palgrave, 175 Fifth Avenue, New York,
NY 10010, USA

Distributed exclusively in Canada by
UBC Press, University of British Columbia, 2029 West Mall,
Vancouver, BC, Canada V6T 1Z2

British Library Cataloguing-in-Publication Data
A catalogue record for this book is available from the British Library

Library of Congress Cataloging-in-Publication Data applied for

ISBN 978 0 7190 7537 7 *hardback*

First published 2007

16 15 14 13 12 11 10 09 08 07   10 9 8 7 6 5 4 3 2 1

Typeset in Sabon by
Koinonia, Manchester
Printed in Great Britain
by Bell & Bain Ltd, Glasgow

This book is dedicated to the memory of
Pierre Bourdieu (1930–2002)

Contents

Contributors	*page*	ix
Figures and tables		xii
Acknowledgements		xiii
1 Introduction: new directions in the history of intellectuals in Britain and France JULIEN VINCENT		1

Part I Towards a reflexive history of intellectuals

2 The intellectuals: a prehistory JEAN-PHILIPPE GENET	25
3 British exceptionalism reconsidered: Annan, Anderson and other accounts STEFAN COLLINI	45

Part II An Anglo-French Republic of Letters?

4 The Royal Society and the Académie des sciences in the first half of the eighteenth century PASCAL BRIOIST	63
5 The English in Paris DANIEL ROCHE	78
6 The French Republic of Letters and English culture, 1750–90 LAURENCE W. B. BROCKLISS	98

Part III Cultural transfers

7 Reading revolution: towards a history of the Volney vogue in England ALEXANDER COOK	125
8 Mid-nineteenth century 'moral sciences' between Paris and Cambridge DAVID PALFREY	147

Part IV The internationalisation of intellectual life

9 Literary import into France and Britain around 1900: a comparative study BLAISE WILFERT	173

10 The commerce of ideas: protectionism versus free trade in the international circulation of economic ideas in Britain and France around 1900   JULIEN VINCENT   194

11 The Ibsen battle: a comparative analysis of the introduction of Henrik Ibsen in France, England and Ireland
   PASCALE CASANOVA   214

Part V Intellectuals, national models and the public sphere

12 French intellectuals and the impossible English model (1870–1914)   CHRISTOPHE CHARLE   235

13 An English crisis in French thought? French intellectuals confront England at the time of Fashoda and the Boer war
   CHRISTOPHE PROCHASSON   256

14 Homosexual networks and activist strategies from the late nineteenth century to 1939   FLORENCE TAMAGNE   271

15 Ironies of war: intellectual styles and responses to the Great War in Britain and France   JAY WINTER   284

16 Conclusions and perspectives   CHRISTOPHE CHARLE   299

Index   311

Contributors

PASCAL BRIOIST is *maître de conférences* at the University of Tours. He has published *Espaces maritimes au XVIIIe siècle* (Neuilly-sur-Seine: Atlande, 1997); (with Hervé Drévillon and Pierre Serna) *Croiser le fer: Violence et culture de l'épée dans la France moderne (XVIe–XVIIIe siècle)* (Seyssel: Champ Vallon, 2002); and *La Renaissance 1470–1570* (Neuilly-sur-Seine: Atlande, 2003).

LAURENCE W. B. BROCKLISS is Professor of Early Modern French History at the University of Oxford and a fellow of Magdalen College. He works on the history of education, science and medicine in early modern France and Britain and has a general interest in the history of European ideas. His publications include *The Medical World of Early Modern France*, ed. with Colin Jones (Oxford: Clarendon Press, 1997); *A Union of Multiple Identities: The British Isles, c.1750–c.1850*, ed. with David Eastwood (Manchester and New York: Manchester University Press, 1997), and *Calvet's Web: Enlightenment and the Republic of Letters in Eighteenth-Century France* (Oxford: Oxford University Press, 2002).

PASCALE CASANOVA is research associate at the CNRS-EHESS (Centre de Recherche sur les Arts et le Langage). She teaches at the University of Geneva and is a literary critic in Paris. Besides articles on literary history and world literary exchanges, she is the author of *The World Republic of Letters* (Paris: Le Seuil, 1999 and Cambridge, MA: Harvard University Press, 2005), and *Beckett l'Abstracteur* (Paris: Le Seuil, 1997).

STEFAN COLLINI is Professor at the Faculty of English at the University of Cambridge and a fellow of the British Academy (2000). His publications include *Public Moralists: Political Thought and Intellectual Life in Britain 1850–1930* (Oxford: Oxford University Press, 1991); *English Pasts: Essays in History and Culture* (Oxford: Clarendon Press, 1999); he edited Matthew Arnold's *Culture and Anarchy and Other Writings* (Cambridge: Cambridge University Press, 1993); *Economy, Polity, and Society: British Intellectual History 1750–1950* and *History, Religion, and Culture: British Intellectual History 1750–1950*, ed. with Richard Whatmore and Brian Young (Cambridge: Cambridge University Press, 2000).

CHRISTOPHE CHARLE is Professor of Modern History at the Université of Paris-I Panthéon-Sorbonne. He is a member of the *Institut Universitaire de France* and

Director of the Institut d'Histoire Moderne et Contemporaine (CNRS/ENS). His publications include: *Naissance des 'intellectuels' (1880–1900)* (Paris: Minuit, 1990); *A Social History of France in the Nineteenth Century* (Oxford: Berghahn 1993; French edition 1991); *La République des universitaires (1870–1940)* (Paris: Le Seuil, 1994); *Les Intellectuels en Europe au XIXème siècle* (Paris: Le Seuil, 1996, 2nd edition 2001); *Paris fin de siècle, culture et politique* (Paris: Le Seuil, 1998); *La Crise des sociétés impériales (1900–1940), essai d'histoire sociale comparée de l'Allemagne, de la France et de la Grande-Bretagne* (Paris: Le Seuil, 2001); and *Le Siècle de la presse 1830–1939*, Paris: Le Seuil, 2004).

ALEXANDER COOK is a research fellow at the Centre of European Discourses, University of Queensland. He specialises in the study of intellectual history in Europe and its colonies, and contemporary cultures of public history. His publications include: *Gold: Forgotten Histories and Lost Objects of Australia* (Joint editor, Cambridge: Cambridge University Press, 2001); 'The use and abuse of historical re-enactment: thoughts on recent trends in television history', *Criticism*, 46.3 (Spring 2005); 'Sailing on the ship: reenactment and the quest for popular history', *History Workshop Journal*, 57 (2004); and 'The art of ventriloquism: European imagination and the South Pacific', in *Cook and Omai: The Cult of the South Seas* (Canberra: NLA Press, 2001).

JEAN-PHILIPPE GENET is professor of Medieval History at the Université of Paris-I- Panthéon-Sorbonne and director of the Laboratoire de Médiévistique Occidentale de Paris (LAMOP) (CNRS/Paris-I). His publications include *La Genèse de l'État moderne: culture et société politique en Angleterre* (Paris: Presses Universitaires de France, 2003); *Le Monde au Moyen âge: espaces, pouvoirs, civilisations* (2nd expanded edition Paris: Hachette Supérieur, 2004). He edited *L'Etat moderne, le droit, l'espace et les formes de l'Etat* (Paris: Éditions du CNRS, 1990); *L'Etat moderne, genèse: bilans et perspectives* (Paris: Éditions du CNRS, 1990) and, with Günther Lottes, *L'Etat moderne et les élites: XIIIe–XVIIIe siècles: apports et limites de la méthode prosopographique* (Paris: Publications de la Sorbonne, 1996).

DAVID PALFREY is a British Academy Postdoctoral Fellow at Robinson College, Cambridge. He completed his Ph.D. at the University of Cambridge on 'The Moral Sciences Tripos at Cambridge University, 1848–1860' in 2003. His current research is on European intellectual contexts for English law (*c.* 1825–40).

CHRISTOPHE PROCHASSON is *Directeur d'études* at the Ecole des Hautes Etudes en Sciences Sociales. His publications include *Les intellectuels, le socialisme et la guerre, 1900–1938* (Paris: Le Seuil, 1993); (with Anne Rasmussen) *Au Nom de la Patrie: Les Intellectuels et la première guerre mondiale, 1910–1919* (Paris: La Découverte, 1996); *Les Intellectuels et le socialisme, XIXe–XXe siècle* (Paris: Plon, 1997); *Paris 1900: essai d'histoire culturelle* (Paris: Calmann-Lévy, 1999); *Saint Simon* (Paris: Plon, 2005); and the *Dictionnaire critique de la République*, ed. with Vincent Duclerc (Paris: Flammarion, 2002).

DANIEL ROCHE is Professor at the Collège de France and director of the *Revue d'Histoire Moderne et Contemporaine*. He has published *The People of Paris: An Essay in Popular Culture in the Eighteenth Century* (Berkeley: California University Press, 1987; French edition 1981); *France in the Enlightenment* (Cambridge, MA: Harvard University Press, 1998; French edition 1993); *The History of Everyday Things: The Birth of Consumption in France, 1600–1800* (Cambridge: Cambridge University Press, 1998; French edition 1997) and *Humeurs vagabondes* (Paris: Fayard, 2003).

FLORENCE TAMAGNE is *maître de conférences* in Modern History at the University of Lille III. Her main publications are *History of Homosexuality in Europe: Berlin, London, Paris 1919–39* (London: Algora Pub., 2004) and *Mauvais Genre: une histoire des représentations de l'homosexualité* (Paris: EDLM, 2001). She also contributed to *Gay Life and Culture* (London: Thames & Hudson, 2006).

JULIEN VINCENT is a Junior Research Fellow at Wolfson College, Cambridge, and a research associate at the Institut d'Histoire Moderne et Contemporaine (CNRS/ENS). His publications include 'The Sociologist and the Republic: Pierre Bourdieu and the Virtues of Social History', *History Workshop Journal*, 58 (2004); and 'L'économie morale du consommateur britannique en 1900', in A. Chatriot, M.-E. Chessel et M. Hilton (eds), *Au Nom du consommateur* (Paris: La Découverte, 2005).

BLAISE WILFERT is *agrégé répétiteur* at the Ecole Normale Supérieure (Paris) and research associate at the Institut d'Histoire Moderne et Contemporaine (CNRS/ENS). He completed his doctoral dissertation on *'Paris, la France et le reste… Importations littéraires et nationalisme culturel en France, 1885–1930'*, at the University of Paris-I Panthéon-Sorbonne, in 2003. His publications include 'L'oblat qui voulait être roi. George Saintsbury critique', *Romantisme*, 121 (2003); and 'Cosmopolis ou l'homme invisible: les importateurs de littérature étrangère, 1871–1914', *Actes de la Recherche en Sciences Sociales*, 144 (2002).

JAY WINTER is Professor of Modern European History at Yale University. His publications include: *The Great War and the British People* (Cambridge, MA: Harvard University Press, 1985); *Sites of Memory, Sites of Mourning: The Great War in European Cultural History* (Cambridge: Cambridge University Press, 1995); and *Capital Cities at War: Paris, London, Berlin 1914–1919*, ed. with J.-L. Robert (Cambridge: Cambridge University Press, 1997). He was co-producer, co-writer and chief historian for the PBS series 'The Great War and the Shaping of the Twentieth Century', which won the Emmy award in 1997. He has recently published, with Antoine Prost, *Penser la grande guerre, essai d'historiographie* (Paris: Le Seuil, 2004).

Figures and tables

Figures

4.1 Professions of the members of the Académie des sciences in 1750	65
4.2 Articles published by French authors in the *Philosophical Transactions* (1699–1750)	71
4.3 Fields of interest of the Members of the Académie des sciences in 1750	72
4.4 Themes of the French articles in the *Philosophical Transactions* from 1700 to 1750	73

Tables

4.1 Structure of the two institutions	66
5.1 Movement of foreigners	83
5.2 Professions and social status of foreigners in Paris	84
6.1 Calvet's web: biographical profile	100–1
6.2 Books by British authors in Calvet's library	104
6.3 Medical books with British authors owned by Calvet (by date of publication)	105
8.1 The internal structural composition of moral sciences/ *sciences morales* as an academic field	153
10.1 National origins of the books reviewed in French and English economic reviews	205
10.2 Distribution of the national origins of books reviewed in the *Economic Journal* and the *Economic Review*	207
12.1 The two groups of Anglophile authors	238–9

Acknowledgements

This book arose from a Franco-British colloquium under the title 'British and French Intellectuals: Comparisons and Transfers', held in London at the Institute of Historical Research and the Institut Français on 2nd and 3rd March 2001. Several participants at the colloquium enriched our collective reflections, although they did not contribute to this book. The editors are particularly grateful to the late Pierre Bourdieu, as well as to E. H. Green, Marian Hobson, Eric J. Hobsbawm, Jeremy Jennings, Michael Kelly, Philippe Minard, Morag Schiach, Jean-François Sirinelli, Steven Smith, Gareth Stedman Jones and Christian Topalov, for their participation in the proceedings and debates. The colloquium was made possible thanks to the support of the School of Advanced Studies of the University of London, the Institut d'Histoire Moderne et Contemporaine (CNRS/ENS), the Ecole Normale Supérieure Lettres et Sciences Humaines, and the Bureau du Livre of the French Embassy in London. David Fennbach has translated chapters 4, 5, 9, 11, 12, 13, 14 and 16 from the French. Finally we are grateful to Arline Fernandez and Fanny Madeline for help with the index.

Christophe Charle
Julien Vincent
Jay Winter

1

Introduction: new directions in the history of intellectuals in Britain and France

JULIEN VINCENT

Pierre Bourdieu, who appeared in dialogue with Eric Hobsbawm at the closing session of the colloquium from which this book is drawn, had no illusions about this type of international gathering, full of goodwill and diplomatic subsidies, but intellectually unadventurous, offering only a poor opportunity for making any genuine progress in the subject under discussion. In 1995, in an interview devoted to the comparative history of sociology and history and the relations between the two disciplines, he explained:

> It may even be that this undertaking [of comparative history] is tremendously hard, and could only be conducted with any success by a genuinely collective effort. This would need an adequate social organization. We might think that the international colloquia that are so popular today would be perfectly appropriate. But in fact, if we want to go beyond a vague verbal consensus around a catch-all notion ('elites', 'royalty', 'power', etc.) of the 'Spanish inn' kind, we come up against social obstacles that at this point seem almost insurmountable.[1]

If Pierre Bourdieu did agree to speak at a colloquium that was both international and funded by the French Embassy, it was because he was aware of the preparatory discussion that preceded it and our concern to escape from the 'Anglo-French inn' syndrome, never mind the Spanish kind. This discussion bore on the difficulties of any 'genuinely collective work' between historians of England and France, as well as on the issues involved at this time in a comparative history of intellectuals. The present book reflects this discussion which aimed at identifying and developing new directions in the history of intellectuals in England and France. It also marks the completion of a series of works on the history of intellectuals and intellectual history in the eighteenth and nineteenth century, published in both France and Britain over the last twenty years, several of which are available in English.[2] While situated in a continuing flow of such works, it also signals a more recent turn in the reflections of historians in both countries. A swift comparison with the tables of contents of earlier collective works is enough to show, in fact, that if several contributors to this volume have been working on the subject for many years, new names mark the emergence of a new generation of historians working to extend this. Particularly original in our approach are two choices, one methodological and the other chronological. In the first place, the comparative *and* relational approach to which this book gives pride of place corresponds to the development of research on the history of intellectuals.[3] It marks a break with the limits of the national approach that prevailed until the early 1990s, and aims to neutralise certain biases specific to comparativism by a study of 'cultural transfers'. Second, as against the majority of recent studies focused on the twentieth century, the analyses here focus on the eighteenth and nineteenth centuries, up to the aftermath of the Great War.[4] By covering in this way more than two centuries (what Jean-Philippe Genet calls in his contribution the 'prehistory' of intellectuals), we explore the deep foundations for the emergence of intellectuals before they were given this name. Each of these choices requires explanation.

Comparisons and transfers

The perspective of this book aims to stress three major developments in British and French historiographies that are important for the area of research we are concerned with here and for its further development.

A reflexive turn

The first may be described as a reflexive turn, in both social and intellectual history, on both sides of the Channel. We have sought to indicate the importance of this by opening this book with two chapters with a reflexive aim – the first by the French social historian Jean-Philippe Genet, the second by the English intellectual historian Stefan Collini. For social historians, this means undertaking a critique of sociohistorical reason, i.e. placing their own categories for apprehending the past in historical perspective, in reaction against the too-often-anachronistic uses that have been made of these. In this way, social historians have made the history of words, concepts, statistical tools, territorial and chronological divisions – in other words of all the forms for delimiting the real that have been inherited by their discipline – into a preliminary of their research, and sometimes a new centre for it.[5] From the standpoint of the present book, it is important to note that this work of critique and reflexive historicisation of the categories of social history is comparable in many respects to the work undertaken on traditional categories of the history of political thought by Quentin Skinner and other intellectual historians associated with the Cambridge school. These last have strongly criticised the belief in the immediacy of signification of texts of the past and in the perennial nature of philosophical problems and traditions.[6] By replacing the history of concepts by a history of the *uses* of concepts, they have encouraged intellectual historians to take a reflexive turn.[7] These various developments, which could be summarised as an all-round critique of the Whig approach to history, have been often described in the English-speaking world, though more rarely in France, as a 'crisis' of history, even a real 'revolution in historical fashion'.[8] If their effect can be felt in almost every field of historical research, and has given rise to a copious flow of ink, all that matters for us here is to emphasise their consequences for the history of intellectuals.

The most important and most evident fact is that this reflexive turn has made possible a break with two major traditional kinds of definition of intellectuals and their place, in social development and the public space as well as in the market for ideas. These definitions are discussed at length in Stefan Collini's critical chapter on Noel Annan and Perry Anderson. The definitions at issue are on the one hand theorising and functionalist, i.e. a priori definitions that place the intellectual in a pre-established vision of social, political and intellectual history; and on the other hand, definitions claiming empiricist provenance, adapted to a single particular case and ruling out in advance any comparison with other cases. In contrast to these definitions that are either too general or too descriptive, the reflexive approach to the history of intellectuals grounds itself in a history of the very categories upon which any account of the various figures of political, moral or cultural authority can be based.[9]

It is appropriate to make clear here the reason why we have chosen to make use of the substantive noun 'intellectual', anachronistic as it is when applied to the eighteenth and early nineteenth centuries despite other terms being available, such as 'intelligentsia', 'cultural authority', 'public moralist', 'man of letters', '*savant*', '*Gelehrte*', 'political intellectual', 'critical/organic intellectual', and so on. While each of these terms has its particular advantage, our view is that none of them adequately expressed our desire to refer to several things simultaneously and without omitting any of them: the social history of the conditions of intellectual life, the cultural history of representations of the intellectual, the political history of their public influence, and finally the intellectual history of their contribution to scholarship and knowledge as well as to political thought and literature. This ambition, all the same, compelled us to use the term 'intellectual' in a perhaps unaccustomed sense. Behind the assertion, often encountered, that the notion of intellectual is unusable for England in the eighteenth and nineteenth centuries, lies the implicit assumption according to which it is only possible to speak of intellectuals once a certain number of preliminary historical or theoretical conditions are fulfilled, whether those specific to France at the time of the Dreyfus Affair, or else those that Gramsci defined.[10] The reflexive history of intellectuals, on the contrary, enables us to postulate that the figure of the politically committed Dreyfusard *intellectuel* of 1898 is only one particular case within a broad field of possibilities.[11] In speaking of 'intellectuals', our aim is not to stress one particular figure of symbolic authority in relation to others (and especially not that of the Dreyfusard *intellectuel*), but rather to indicate that the unstable and contested character of the definition and role of intellectuals is the very motor of their history.

The figure of the intellectual was indeed the object of continuous dispute on both sides of the Channel during the entire period in question here. In each country, intellectuals sought to define themselves against their particular context, some as professionals or experts who could deploy their monopoly of intellectual competence, others as a 'committed' group claiming a moral or political authority in public debate, others again as cultural producers contributing to knowledge or art. The reflexive approach challenges historians by claiming that, unless they concern themselves with these struggles over identity, they run the risk of continuing them by constructing in their turn, and most often unconsciously, a historiography of intellectuals in which the various possible definitions and approaches of the history of intellectuals – social, political, cultural or intellectual history – are opposed to one another, whereas they actually correspond to different facets of the same object. This is not the familiar complaint of the historian who wishes previous histories had been less narrow in focus. Indeed the temptation to censure the previous splintering of many fields of history must especially be resisted here, and this for two main reasons. First, historians are dependent on the way in which collections of institutional archives or personal papers have been constituted, both at a national and at a local level, and the tendency of historians to privilege intellectual biographies, prosopography or monographs on various intellectual groups or institutions largely derives from this material organisation.[12] Second, historians are intellectuals themselves, and their focus on one or another aspect of the history of intellectuals at the expense of others is partly a reflection of their own position, disposition and ideas in this respect. It is also an indicator of the constraints of their audience, and of the nature and variety of acceptable or fashionable subjects and methods available for research at any given time. Differences in historiographic styles – in political culture, but also in the nature of available archives, at both a national and international level – all combine to explain the absence of an integrated approach to the history of intellectuals at the same time as they echo the conflicts of this history. By taking these differences as a subject for research, the reflexive approach can be said to delineate the contours of a new definition of the historian as an intellectual, claiming that the discussion of national peculiarities ought to take place, not in a strictly national, but in an international sphere of historical debate.

The critique of exceptionalism

The second historiographical development that needs mentioning here, and indeed derives from the first, is the critique of the idea of exceptionalism in comparative history. The origin of this lies partly in a critique of theories of modernisation, but it has also found applications in many fields of history, and has particularly been at the centre of debates on the idea of a European history. In Germany it has led, via the critique of the notion of *Sonderweg*, to raise in a new way the question of the failure of the Weimar Republic and the difficulty of democratisation.[13] In France this debate has focused on the question of the demographic regime, the particular path of the industrial revolution, and the early date at which immigration became important.[14] In the United Kingdom, the critique of the idea of a particular English way, traditionally presented as a *political* exception in relation to Western Europe, but equally as an English *cultural* exception, and thought of in terms of notions of Enlightenment and intellectuals (or intelligentsia), has now to be placed in the context of the upsurge of 'European history'.[15] John Pocock, a historian of New Zealand origin, was one of the first and principal critics of this European perspective on British history in the early 1970s, a time when the entry of the United Kingdom into the EEC could raise fears that British history would be rewritten in such a way as to obscure its non-European aspect.[16] In a series of articles that have achieved classic status, he reproached the European perspective on British history for admitting under the counter a truncated definition of Britishness, arising from too strong a focus on the twin notions of 'normal way' and 'exception'. It is revealing that Pocock, one of the most eminent historians of British political thought, who for almost half a century has done so much to rethink intellectual history, is not a historian of intellectuals as a social group. Is not the history of intellectuals typically French? In fact, the notion of intellectual or intelligentsia in social history, in the same way as for example the notion of 'industrial revolution' in economic history or that of 'Enlightenment' in intellectual history may be perceived as a powerful reserve of interpretations in terms of normality and exceptionalism, always based on an at least implicit comparison with Britain's European neighbours. In this perspective, just as England can be deployed as a model for understanding the industrial revolution in France, so can France of the Lumières or the Dreyfus Affair appear if need be as either the normal or the exceptional case in relation to which the British case is defined, to the detriment of its Atlantic and Antipodean dimensions. It remains true that the critique of the categories of 'normal path' and exception, far from questioning European comparative history as such, has rather contributed to making its ambitions more precise. In the first place, it has enabled the existence of a genuine tradition of figures of the intellectual and the cultural authority to be recognised in nineteenth-century England, in which Stefan Collini signals the difference with the so-called 'French' model by speaking of 'public moralists'.[17] In the second place, it has led to showing the unity of European intellectual history by rejecting the idea that certain nations supposedly represent more than others a 'normal path' in the march of ideas. John Pocock has himself questioned the hypothesis of a 'normal path' of intellectual history, by criticising the idea of the absence of an English Enlightenment. This traditional thesis would in fact seem to presuppose that the notion of Enlightenment is appropriate only to the existence of an anti-clerical project and French-style *philosophes*. In this book, we extend this critique of the idea of a 'normal path' not only to the history of intellectuals, but also to intellectual history. Laurence Brockliss relativises the impact of British science and the philosophical spirit on French provincial scholarship in the second half of the eighteenth century. In the same way, I suggest that the idea of an English and Austrian 'marginalist revolution' in economics, in relation to which the French school would form an exception, is also a normative construction that the historian has to challenge. Finally, Pascale Casanova emphasises, on the basis of a comparative study of the reception of Ibsen, the very different meanings, depending on the English, Irish and French contexts, of what might appear in the late nineteenth century as a 'realist' turn affecting the entirety of European literature.

History of 'cultural transfers' and entangled history

Even if we do subscribe to the critique of the idea of British 'exception' or 'normality' as formulated by John Pocock and others, we do not think that such critique must necessarily lead to renouncing a European perspective on history. It is true that by highlighting the Anglo-French space we are forced to abandon certain research perspectives that Pocock proposes. For example, whereas he suggests a new way of understanding the notion of Britishness as a space of national cultural struggles and English hegemony, Pascale Casanova is the only writer to tackle explicitly here the question of relations between English and Irish intellectuals.

Likewise, and though Christophe Charle raises research propositions in this sense in his concluding chapter, we have not sought to re-read the history of intellectuals in the 'imperial' or 'Commonwealth' perspective proposed by the champions of the 'new British history', or by those of 'connected', 'shared' and 'entangled' histories.[18] Our emphasis on *English* and *French* attitudes should by no means be seen as a disregard for Britishness, or for provincial France, or indeed for the rest of the world. In the present collection of essays, however, these are mainly viewed through the eyes of English and French intellectuals, and in a cross-Channel rather than in a cross-regional or imperial perspective. Our reflection is inspired by the debate on comparative history that was launched in the 1990s by Michel Espagne and Michael Werner.[19] Starting from a critique of the comparative cultural history of European countries that is complementary to that of John Pocock, these authors embarked on a reflection, conducted chiefly by German and French historians, on the importance of a history of 'cultural transfers', to complete and correct the comparative approach. European cultures, for Espagne and Werner, risk being hypostatised as soon as it is forgotten that their very existence as *national* cultures results from their insertion into an *international* cultural space, in which cultural transfers are constantly deployed in order to construct the boundaries defining a cultural Other. The German case is paradigmatic for this process, since it was against French cultural domination that Herder, then Goethe, conceived the idea of a 'legitimate' German culture starting with translation of the great classic texts of antiquity.[20] This model, however, is equally applicable to intellectuals in the Anglo-French space, and it can be developed and made more complex on the basis of case studies showing the diversity of these types of cultural transfer. This is attempted in several chapters of the present book, where this notion undergoes various applications depending on the period under consideration and the intellectual contexts. Some authors, such as Blaise Wilfert, insist on the ambiguity of reference to nationality in these cultural transfers, something that generally leads to calling 'national' only those that have managed to impose their conception of legitimate culture in the country in question. Others emphasise the importance of the social conditions of international circulation of ideas, which conditions their reception in shifted contexts (Pascal Brioist, Alexander Cook, Pascale Casanova, Florence Tamagne). Jay Winter shows, on the basis of an analysis of certain literary texts on the Great War, how the difference in educational systems and formative experiences has its influence on habits of thought. Other authors, proceeding from the same considerations, insist on the limits of these cultural transfers. Certain chapters thus envisage a case in which the degree of adaptation of foreign works to the national context is so great that one may doubt whether anything at all has really been 'transferred'; here it is more appropriate to speak of an instrumentalisation of the language of nationality for the purpose of an ad hoc cultural construction (Daniel Roche, Christophe Prochasson). Emphasis on the importance of the notion of cultural transfer should not in fact lead to seeking out intellectual exchanges where these do not exist, as Laurence Brockliss suggests. Conversely, as Christophe Charle underlines, one must be able to recognise the existence of cultural transfers where historiography has tended to obscure them, and stress that these transfers are not unambiguous but on the contrary the object of conflict between different actors who claim the status of legitimate commentators on cultural difference.

Apart from a desire to restrain the sometimes distorting effects of comparativism, our decision to privilege the study of cultural transfers is also linked to another concern. We wanted the approach proposed to the book's contributors to itself promote a form of transfer – historiographical and methodological, in this case – between historians of England and historians of France. The reader will notice that intellectual history, in this volume as well as in historical production as a whole, is more a speciality of the English, whereas the social history of intellectuals is rather the work of the French (a fact that Christophe Charle returns to in the Conclusion). The variety of possible approaches in intellectual history and the history of intellectuals, however, is expressed here through cleavages that are not merely 'national'. Daniel Roche's contribution offers a 'concrete history of abstraction', the chapters by Pascal Brioist and David Palfrey a comparative history of the institutions of intellectual life, Blaise Wilfert and myself a history of the social conditions of intellectual life, Christophe Prochasson and Jay Winter a cultural history, and Alexander Cook and Pascale Casanova an intellectual history that examines the gaps between production and reception. Finally, at the same time as it enables the social history of intellectuals to be kept in tandem with intellectual history, the study of transfers offers the possibility of not restricting oneself to a single type of intellectual history at the expense of others. The present collection thus embraces both the history of political thought and literary history, two registers of thought closely linked, even though subsequent disciplinary specialisations have artificially divided them.

Anglo-French attitudes: comparisons and transfers between English and French intellectuals since the eighteenth century

As Stefan Collini's chapter on Noel Annan and Perry Anderson illustrates, the reflexive historian of intellectuals tends to be critical not only of so-called 'empiricism' but also of normative theories of the role of public intellectuals. This partly explains why, whereas the history of intellectuals draws on an already long-established tradition of theoretical work, inspired by both sociology and philosophy as well as by political and literary theory, we have deliberately chosen to draw a line under this, preferring to restrict ourselves to the more modest methodological considerations mentioned above. To attempt a new theoretical formulation of an already old historiographic theme would in fact have brought us up against the most firmly anchored aporias in the history of intellectuals, starting with the belief in the need for a pre-existing theory in order to write the history of intellectuals. The most typical risk in the kind of historiography represented in this book is in fact to sin by excess of intellectualism, this most often consisting in reproducing quite uncritically a vocabulary, habits of thought, a dissection of the object and an identification of 'pertinent' questions that have been constructed by the very people who are to be studied.

Towards a reflexive history of intellectuals

The solution we have chosen, instead of turning towards 'grand theory', is rather to turn towards the 'prehistory' of intellectuals, and invite a medievalist, Jean-Philippe Genet, to reflect on what Jacques Le Goff called as far back as 1957 'intellectuals in the Middle Ages'. This places our object right from the start in an anthropological perspective, transferring us to an epoch in which, as he says, nothing enables political society in England and France to be convincingly distinguished. Confronting various supposed characteristics of intellectuals with the test of the *longue durée*, Genet concludes that very few of these are specific to the early modern or modern epoch. He warns therefore against two kinds of anachronism that are particularly dangerous in the history of intellectuals: those that consist of projecting a present situation on to the past, as well as those that consist of attributing to one epoch a situation that is in fact much older. Neither the question of the social identity of intellectuals – self-considered or defined in functional terms by their position in the division of labour – nor that of their cultural authority or their influence in the public sphere, is specific to the eighteenth and nineteenth centuries. The divergence in religion and systems of education, which began to take shape from the sixteenth century onwards, informs a social group that at first does not display any notable differences between one side of the

Channel and the other. It is thus in the course of the period under consideration that English and French intellectuals became 'national'; and any study seeking to give pride of place to the subsequent period has thus to show the manner in which a national organisation of intellectual life was constructed and consolidated.

We begin our study at the moment of what Paul Hazard called the 'crisis of the European conscience', linked with the rise of English science in the late seventeenth century, and end it in the early twentieth century. This chronological perspective offers several advantages. First of all, the absence of a marked specialisation of intellectual life during the greater part of the period considered here requires that problematics used by historians of the twentieth century such as Jeremy Jennings or Julia Stapleton, who privilege the question of the political role of intellectuals, are not artificially transposed.[21] We have thus alternated chapters which may have been grouped under more traditional headings: chapters devoted to the conditions of intellectual life (Brioist, Brockliss, Roche), to the history of political thought (Cook, Palfrey, Vincent, Charle, Prochasson), and to literary and cultural history (Wilfert, Casanova, Tamagne, Winter). This also enables the scope of two traditional divisions made in intellectual history and the history of intellectuals to be relativised: first of all that of the French Revolution, often described as a transition from the Enlightenment to Romanticism, and second that of the late nineteenth century, and particularly the epoch of the Dreyfus Affair, which saw the emergence of the substantive-noun 'intellectual' in the sociopolitical vocabularies of Britain and France, and in the broader European context as well.[22] This reading that stresses political breaks could be opposed by a different reading emphasising the continuity of the *language of nationality*, one of the unifying themes of this book.[23] Finally, our Anglo-French perspective – which will have to be qualified by crossing it with other points of view – also enables us to observe the transition from a kind of intellectual condominium over Europe, based on the prestige of English science and French letters and the advance of the public space, to an increasingly European and even transatlantic intellectual life, in which Germany, Italy, Russia, Central Europe, the Americas and other emerging nations challenge this ancient hegemony.

The Anglo-French Republic of Letters in the eighteenth century
At the end of the seventeenth century, with the establishment of absolutist royal power in France and the Glorious Revolution in England, the French and English together dominated Europe, intellectually as well as militarily and politically. Was the eighteenth century for the English and French intellectuals one of a joint domination over Europe? Would it

be correct to date back to this era the image of a French model strongly influenced by Court and State, as against an English model that is private and self-organised? Were Anglo-French exchanges as intense as those that the history of ideas traditionally describes, using the examples of Montesquieu, Voltaire, Gibbon and Hume? Three articles here seek to reply to these questions. They must be understood in the context of the new historiography of European Enlightenments as illustrated by the works of Knud Haakonsen, Peter Harrison, John Gascoigne, John Pocock, Richard B. Sher, B. W. Young and others.[24] This historiography has reacted to prevailing, French-centred, accounts of *the* Enlightenment by stressing the contribution of Protestantism to it, particularly in England. Our chapters complement these intellectual histories by looking, in a way that is inspired by the French historiographic tradition represented by Roger Chartier and Daniel Roche, at the role of intellectual sociability and at the social conditions of intellectual life.[25] This could have been done by looking at the role of women in intellectual life, as Dena Goodman and, more recently, Antoine Lilti have done.[26] But, while these authors have generally confined themselves to the French context of salons, our contributors look at the international relations between English and French intellectuals. Their study of the circulation of men, books and ideas gives due insistence on various quantitative indicators and on collective biography. But they also highlight one aspect of French and English intellectual life which had already been identified by Germaine de Staël in *De l'Allemagne* as a crucial difference with the less centralised German intellectual life. They show that, in the eighteenth century, Anglo-French intellectual exchanges were still largely based on personal relations and closely knitted social networks, not just on the circulation of ideas within an abstract Republic of Letters.

Pascal Brioist undertakes a comparison between two key institutions of intellectual life in London and Paris, the Académie Royale des sciences and the Royal Society, at a moment of 'English crisis' in French thought stimulated by the impact of the Baconian and Newtonian paradigms on European science. Brioist shows that the difference, noted already by contemporaries, between a French Académie made up of pensioners maintained by the King, and an English club with no constraint or privilege, placed no brake on the circulation of people, books and ideas. Far from presenting an obstacle to exchange, these differences between two institutions, each adapted to their respective society and political regime, facilitated a dynamic of mutual stimulation between two social universes in which science was treated differently. In England this was still produced largely by the aristocracy and gentry, and presented to London society; in France, on the other hand, it was the work of doctors, professors and other members of the Third Estate.

Daniel Roche, starting from the question of cultural transfers between English and French intellectuals in the eighteenth century, leads to a more general reflection that he undertook with Jean-Claude Perrot some years ago, on the material conditions of abstraction, and asks what was genuinely 'intellectual' in the experience that an English philosopher might gain from a visit to Paris. Focusing on the case of travellers who, like Adam Smith, David Hume or Arthur Young, used their visits to France as a privileged ground for the elaboration of their own thought, he shifts this process of formation of ideas back into its material and social universe. The difficulty here is that the historian has to escape the pitfalls of those literary conventions specific to travel accounts, which prevent the reality of the 'intellectual' encounter between English and French from being grasped. What was the concrete experience of English philosophers visiting Paris in the second half of the eighteenth century? What hotels did they stay at, and why? How did they spend their time in France? Did they mix readily with the local population, and how? Daniel Roche's reply to these questions is paradoxical. Apart from a few exceptional cases such as Arthur Young, these travellers seem to have been surrounded by what George Sand called a 'British fluid', making them insensitive to their environment. Even when they did seem to integrate well into local society – such as David Hume, who became a real favourite of the Paris salons – this was in actual fact by virtue of their ability to embody pre-existing stereotypes of the English philosopher, rather than because of any new dialogue that was undertaken. Roche thus emphasises the ambiguity of the vague notion of Anglophilia (or Francophilia), which may be political but not philosophical, scientific but not political, sociable and not scientific.

Laurence Brockliss continues the sceptical course opened by Daniel Roche, examining the received idea according to which the second half of the eighteenth century was supposedly a period of intense cultural exchange between France and England. If the fashion for English philosophy and the English philosophers – whose importance in terms of intellectual exchange, moreover, Roche sharply tones down – was lively enough in the Paris salons, the same cannot be said for the provincial audience of the Lumières. Brockliss uses the case of Esprit Calvet's (largely male) 'web' in the French Midi to show that contemporary British thought actually aroused only a very limited curiosity or intensity of exchange. Few members of the 'web' visited England, and few could read English. Even their libraries, as Brockliss shows, reflected above all British culture prior to 1750. If the impact of English science was indeed very strong in France between the end of the seventeenth century and 1750, as Pascal Brioist shows, this culture was scarcely renewed – at least within 'Calvet's web' – in the second half of the century, an epoch of French cultural hegemony. Brockliss emphasises the role of the language of nationality in the intellectual exchanges of this time. He shows how discourse on science and British culture was never exempt from more general considerations on the philistinism of British scholars, who may have been very rich, but were reputedly unable to distinguish genuinely interesting pieces on their extravagant journeys in quest of antiquities, and were often viewed with distrust by these provincial Academicians, who were generally Catholic and hostile to the Protestantism of the British.

Both the common points and differences of perspective between the contributions of Brioist, Roche and Brockliss contain valuable lessons. While Brioist stresses the importance of the sites of intellectual exchange (circulation of people, books and printed matter, as well as correspondence), the other two authors dwell on the fact that these contacts were not always moments of genuine exchange, but often the sites of a lack of understanding or a failure of dialogue. Whereas Brioist and Roche show the closeness of Paris and London sociabilities in the age of Enlightenment, Brockliss highlights the gaps between these cultural capitals and provincial science, as well as the resistance of learned culture towards the philosophical Lumières. In sum, these three chapters show the value of a history of intellectuals that places the history of ideas together with that of the material and social conditions of their distribution. The first reason for this is that these two histories, if linked, do not share the same tempo. Thus the success in the fashionable world of Paris of a British intellectual figure such as David Hume does not enable any conclusion to be drawn as to the impact of British ideas. The practices of internationality, such as the fact of welcoming foreign intellectuals or translating their works, were thus sometimes actually components of an intellectual closure of the national space, as is also indicated in the contributions bearing on the late nineteenth century. The second reason is that these practices of internationality were nonetheless for intellectual communication between England and France. At the same time as the intellectual sociabilities of the two countries developed along different lines, the rules of intellectual discussion became more international, as Brioist shows in relation to the sciences.

Cultural transfers

Any study of the difficult circulation of ideas and modes of thought between England and France in the eighteenth and nineteenth centuries must necessarily consider a certain number of themes that Jean-Philippe Genet mentions in his contribution: the contradictory political developments, the deep differences between the educational and cultural systems, religious differences, and finally the fact that, in crossing the Channel and passing from one social group to another, ideas are inevitably divorced from their original context and have to be acclimatised into a new network of beliefs and a new culture. These themes guide the articles of Alexander Cook and David Palfrey, another common point here being their emphasis on the continuity of certain important debates of the early nineteenth century with those of the previous century. Palfrey shows evidence of the legacy of Condorcet on English and French debates on moral science, while Cook relativises the notion of 'Romanticism' to understand the intellectual context of post-Revolutionary France and England. Cook also tackles the question of Anglo-French transfers by drawing on the case of Constantin François de Volney, a French philosopher who was also one of the main reference points for English radicals at the start of the nineteenth century. He first of all locates Volney in his French context, before broaching the delicate question, previously examined by E. P. Thompson, of his partial reception and reinterpretation by English radicals. Volney, according to Cook, should be seen in the context of a French philosophical tradition devoted to the construction of a moral science designed to replace the superstitions of religion and reconcile men with natural law. But, whereas the French Volney was a moderate and liberal writer, the Volney of the English radicals was far more of a Jacobin. Cook thus shows to what degree the language of nationality – the fact that the reception of 'foreign' ideas in a country is often accompanied by a discourse on the nationality of these ideas – played a major role in the reception of Volney's book *Les Ruines, ou Méditation sur les révolutions des empires*, both making for a more radical reading of it on the part of its champions, and limiting its impact on the part of its opponents. The same theme reappears in several other essays and is explicitly discussed by Christophe Charle and Blaise Wilfert.

Palfrey takes up the history of Anglo-French moral sciences tackled by Cook, but considers the more 'conservative' standpoint of the Académie des sciences morales et politiques of 1832, and the 1848 moral sciences tripos at Cambridge. Placing these debates on the nature of the moral sciences in the context of institutional conflicts of the time, he shows how François Guizot, founder of this Académie under the July monarchy, moved from an optimistic and reforming notion of the moral sciences as seen also in Condorcet and Volney, to a more conservative conception that he saw as inspired by the 'English' political ideal. Paradoxically, it was this 'Anglicised' version of the French moral sciences that was acclimatised in Cambridge by readers of Guizot, in complete opposition to the 'Frenchified' and radicalised version that had been appropriated by radical English readers of Volney a few years earlier.

The internationalisation of intellectual life

The following section focuses on the internationalisation of intellectual life in the late nineteenth century. To what extent can intellectuals be compared to stockbrokers in a globalising economy? Did the internationalisation of intellectual life entail more protectionism or more free trade in the commerce of ideas? Blaise Wilfert and myself, both drawing inspiration from Bourdieu's ideas on the 'social conditions of the international circulation of ideas', tackle the question of the circulation of economic ideas and literary works through the prism of translations and reviews of foreign books. We offer quantitative analyses that in each case stress the largely 'protectionist' character of the two cultural ensembles in question. We both recall that intellectual translations and imports, whether undertaken by writers and literary critics or by economists and social reformers, often correspond to strategies designed to modify the balance of forces within their own national intellectual field. The history of cultural transfers, far from being the object of a distinct history, thus offers a perspective on the entirety of production within an intellectual field such as literature or political economy. Finally, we underline how the internationalisation of intellectual life that seems to have marked the late nineteenth century, far from promoting cosmopolitanism, was one aspect of a broader normative language and ensemble of practices designed to construct the national. Wilfert stresses the development of a group of 'free traders' in literature, based on a dense network of semi-professional translators, publishers and specialised collections. For my own part, I criticise the idea that Germany was the main source of inspiration for British economists in the late nineteenth century. This perspective, in fact, would mean remaining blind to the ambiguity of the definition of an 'economist' before 1914, and to the exchange between English and French social reformers.

Pascale Casanova writes in a similar perspective, which she has largely contributed to theorising in previous publications, but focuses here on the question of the comparative reception of various works.[27] Her contribution is anchored in a critique of comparative literature, which she sees as often reduced to a comparativism between works which sacrifice the comparative history of their reception, and consequently of the intellectuals who read and circulate them. Taking the particular case of Henrik Ibsen, she emphasises how markedly his reception, so different in Paris, London and Dublin at the turn of the century, reflected the specific literary issues at stake in these three cultural capitals. While the French were divided between the 'naturalist' Ibsen of Antoine and the 'symbolist' Ibsen of Lugné-Poe, the English, behind George Bernard Shaw, made Ibsen into a social realist adapted to Fabian socialism, while James Joyce used Ibsen to found a new 'national' Irish literature by opposing him to the neo-Romanticism of W. B. Yeats.

Intellectuals, national models and the public sphere

By the end of the nineteenth century, discourses about the nation had become a central part of the public role of intellectuals and a condition of their influence. While intellectuals were certainly consumers as well as producers of national models and stereotypes, they also knew how to undermine these models and stereotypes when needed. The internationalisation of intellectual life, while making the language of nationality both more complex and more central, also changed profoundly the nature of the relations between English and French intellectuals. One important aspect of this change after 1870 was the omnipresence of Germany. This breaks through the couple relationship that was characteristic of the earlier period, and brings it into a kind of 'ménage à trois'.

Christophe Charle modifies the traditional analyses of Claude Digeon, centred on the idea of a 'German crisis of French thought', and reminds us of the persistence of the English background in French intellectual debate even after 1870. Finding within Anglophile discourse a division into two groups, close to that found among French economists that I describe in my own contribution, Charle distinguishes two opposing currents among French intellectuals in the late nineteenth century: on the one hand a liberal group that saw a largely imaginary England as a political and social model, and which dominated Anglophile discourse until around 1900; on the other hand a younger group, issuing from the educational elite of the Ecole Normale Supérieure, whose analyses in the 1900s were focused around questions of nationalism and social democracy – the very themes that Elie Halévy was subsequently to take up in the latter volumes of his *History of the English People*.

The approach proposed by Christophe Prochasson considers intellectuals from the standpoint of cultural history, focusing on constructions of the image of the Other as anchorage points for the construction of national identities. Linda Colley has already admirably shown the effectiveness of this for the eighteenth-century British identity, even if she took scant interest in the role of intellectuals in this process.[28] Prochasson emphasises how in the years before 1914 everything operated in a 'triangle of comparisons' in which Germany, France and Great Britain played almost interchangeable roles, enabling a French commentator to say that the imperial ideas of Seeley were in actual fact German ideas expressed in English. Prochasson shows how, behind the fluctuations from phases of Anglomania to phases of Anglophobia which followed changes in the international political situation, the same cultural constructions still persist. Thus the repulsive figure of the nationalist Englishman that appeared at the time of the Fashoda crisis and the Boer War was very close to that subsequently applied to Germany during the Great War. He points out that this versatility of representations of the Other was based on certain continuities – thus the English were empiricist, religious, taken up with morality but also with commerce – this particularity being equally capable of serving as model or anti-model according to context.

Florence Tamagne completes our picture of literary circulation and cultural transfers from the particular perspective of homosexuality. This offers several advantages in relation to more traditional approaches to intellectual history that often focus on types of knowledge or discourse, as well as to a history of intellectuals that often privileges those biographical characteristics most closely linked with their career and trajectory in society. Homosexuality, far from being restricted to a private sexual practice, is in fact a specific space in which speech is often coded, readable only with difficulty if at all, and swings between euphemism and provocation. To investigate homosexual intellectuals in the late nineteenth and early twentieth centuries, at a time when France and Great Britain were among the most liberal societies, thus makes it possible to establish the persistence of forms of intellectual life that recall earlier eras, with the writers finding themselves under the constraint of a moral censorship and authoritarian power. This was particularly true in both France and Great Britain, as here, in contrast to the German case, the defence of homosexual rights was based first of all on the intellectuals. The existence of international homosexual networks functioned in fact, in this period, as a subculture and a specific space for cultural transfers and political demands that were formulated as a function of the rules specific to each of the two countries.

Jay Winter pursues ideas developed in Prochasson's essay by tackling the question of 'irony' in English writers. French writers, for their part, scarcely ever show such irony in their descriptions of the war. The irony of Jean Giraudoux in *La Guerre de Troie n'aura pas lieu* is here the exception that proves the rule. Winter invites us to consider irony not just as a mere literary figure, but as a genuine attitude of mind which he explains by a relation to life strongly marked, in the English case, by their vision of sport. This difference between national 'structures of feeling' partly translates that in the educational systems of the French and English formations, as well as the gap in the social recruitment of the two intelligentsias, both finding expression in their experience of the War. What Winter has elsewhere called the retrospective 'futility' and absurdity of the 'European civil war' could not have the same sense for French intellectuals who, even if pacifist, believed they had to fight to free their invaded country and overthrow the last aristocratic and monarchical regimes of Europe.[29] There can be no doubt that during the 1930s English intellectuals came in their turn to see themselves charged with a liberating and international mission in the face of the threats of the fascist regimes, whether they were conservative and imperialist or supporters of anti-fascism and socialism.

In recent years, historians of all countries have become increasingly interested in the complex relationships between the national public sphere and the international transfer of ideas, discourses or cultural forms. To the extent that this has been a common concern, this has not led them to unite in their methods and interpretative frameworks. For example, Pierre Bourdieu's call for a study of intellectuals that confronts discourses to objective positions in intellectual 'fields' and to the social conditions of cultural authority has been influential among French historians in the last two decades. British historians, by contrast, have moved away from the once-appealing sociological approach to 'national intelligentsias' and have turned instead to a study of linguistic contexts and ideological borrowings. Comparisons and transfers have played an essential part in the arguments of both champions and critics of these approaches on both sides of the Channel.[30] This phenomenon is certainly not new. But, while comparisons and transfers have been used and may still be used today to exaggerate national differences and sharpen intellectual antagonisms, this present collection suggests not only that they have been a common intellectual attitude of English and French intellectuals, but that they may also provide a ground for historiographical rapprochement.

Notes

1 P. Bourdieu, 'Sur les rapports entre la sociologie et l'histoire en Allemagne et en France', *Actes de la Recherche en Sciences Sociales*, 106–7 (1995), 119–20.

2 The most important of these for the approach pursued here include R. Chartier, *The Cultural Origins of the French Revolution* (Durham, NC: Duke University Press, 1991), and S. Collini, *Public Moralists, Political Thought and Intellectual Life in Britain, 1850–1930* (Oxford: Oxford University Press, 1991). The more numerous French works on the history of intellectuals are mostly not translated into English, though a general overview is given in J. Jennings, *Intellectuals in Twentieth-Century France: Mandarins and Samurais* (London: Routledge, 1993).

3 See, in particular, M. Trébitsch and M.-C. Granjon (eds), *Pour une histoire comparée des intellectuels* (Bruxelles: Complexe, 1998), and J.-F. Sirinelli and M. Leymarie (eds), *L'Histoire des intellectuels aujourd'hui* (Paris: Presses Universitaires de France, 2003).
4 See, for example, M. Cornick, *Intellectuals in History: The Nouvelle Revue Française under Jean Paulhan, 1925–1940* (Amsterdam: Rodopi, 1995); D. Drake, *Intellectuals and Politics in Post-War France* (Basingstoke: Palgrave, 2001); S. Hazaaresingh, *Intellectuals and the French Communist Party: Disillusion and Decline* (Oxford: Clarendon Press, 1991); P. Ory and J.-F. Sirinelli, *Les Intellectuels en France de l'Affaire Dreyfus à nos jours* (Paris: Armand Colin, 1986); J. Stapleton, *Political Intellectuals and Public Identities in Britain since 1850* (Manchester: Manchester University Press, 2001); and the contributions to 'The Role of Intellectuals in Twentieth-Century Europe', ed. J. Jennings, special issue of *European Legacy*, 5:6 (2000).
5 Examples of this approach include: L. Boltanski, *Les Cadres: la formation d'un groupe social* (Paris: Minuit, 1982); G. Stedman Jones, *Languages of Class: Studies in English Working-Class History 1832–1982* (Cambridge: Cambridge University Press, 1983); R. Chartier, 'Le monde comme représentation', *Annales ESC*, 44 (1989), 1505–20; P. Joyce, *Visions of the People: Industrial England and the Question of Class* (Cambridge: Cambridge University Press, 1991); P. Bourdieu, 'The Force of Representation: Notes on the Idea of Region', in *Language and Symbolic Power* (Cambridge: Polity Press, 1991), pp. 220–8; P. Bourdieu and L. J. D. Wacquant, *An Invitation to Reflexive Sociology* (Cambridge: Polity Press, 1992); C. Topalov, *Naissance du 'chômeur'* (Paris: Albin Michel, 1994); D. Wahrman, *Imagining the Middle Class: The Political Representation of Class in Britain, c. 1780–1840* (Cambridge: Cambridge University Press, 1995); M. Offerlé (ed.), *La Profession politique XIXe–XXe siècles* (Paris: Belin, 1999); A. Desrosières, *La Politique des grands nombres: histoire de la raison statistique* (2nd edition; Paris: La Découverte, 2000); C. Jones and D. Wahrman (eds), *The Age of Cultural Revolutions: Britain and France 1750–1820* (Berkeley: University of California Press, 2002); N. Racine and M. Trébitsch (eds), *Intellectuelles: du genre en histoire des intellectuals* (Bruxelles: Complexe, 2004).
6 Q. Skinner, 'Meaning and Understanding in the History of Ideas', *History and Theory*, 8 (1969), 3–53.
7 J. Guilhaumou, 'De l'histoire des concepts à l'histoire linguistique des usages conceptuels', *Genèses*, 38 (2000), 105–18.
8 G. Noiriel, *Sur la 'crise' de l'histoire* (Paris: Belin, 1996); J. Harris, *Private Lives, Public Spirit: Britain 1870–1914* (London: Penguin, 1993), p. vii; see also G. Stedman Jones, 'The New Social History in France', in Jones and Wharman (eds), *The Age of Cultural Revolutions*, pp. 94–105.
9 C. Charle, *Naissance des 'intellectuels' 1880–1900* (Paris: Minuit, 1990); F. M. Turner, *Contesting Cultural Authority: Essays in Victorian Intellectual Life* (Cambridge: Cambridge University Press, 1993).
10 See the introduction to L. Goldman, *Dons and Workers: Oxford and Adult Education since 1850* (Oxford: Clarendon Press, 1995).

11 C. Charle, *Les Intellectuels en Europe au 19ème siècle* (2nd edition; Paris: Le Seuil, 2001); 'L'histoire comparée des intellectuels en Europe: quelques points de méthode et propositions de recherche', in Trébitsch and Granjon (eds), *Pour une histoire comparée*, pp. 39–59.
12 On this question, see S. Collini, *English Pasts: Essays in History and Culture* (Oxford: Oxford University press, 1999), p. 119 and Part 2.
13 D. Blackbourn and G. Eley, *The Peculiarities of German History: Bourgeois Society and Politics in Nineteenth-Century Germany* (Oxford: Oxford University Press, 1984); see also S. Berger, 'Social History vs Cultural History: A German Debate', *Theory, Culture and Society*, 18:1 (2001), 145–53.
14 J. Dupâquier (ed.), *Histoire de la population française*, vol. 3, 1789–1914 (Paris: Presses Universitaires de France, 1988); M. Lévy-Leboyer and F. Bourguignon, *L'Economie française au 19ème siècle, analyse macroéconomique* (Paris: Economica, 1985); G. Noiriel, *Les Ouvriers dans la société française, 19ème–20ème siècles* (Paris: Le Seuil, 1986) and *Le Creuset français, histoire de l'immigration en France 19ème–20ème siècles* (Paris: Le Seuil, 1988).
15 The rich literature on English intellectuals as an exception can be followed through Perry Anderson, 'Components of the National Culture', *New Left Review*, 50 (1969), 3–57; John Hall, 'The Curious Case of the English Intelligentsia', *British Journal of Sociology*, 30:3 (1979), 291–306; and M. S. Hickox, 'Has There Been a British Intelligentsia?', *British Journal of Sociology*, 37:2 (1986), 260–8.
16 J. G. A. Pocock, 'British History: A Plea for a New Subject', *Journal of Modern History*, 47:4 (1975), 601–21; 'The Limits and Divisions of British History: In Search of an Unknown Subject', *American Historical Review*, 87:2 (1982), 311–36; 'History and Sovereignty: The Historiographical Response to Europeanisation in Two British Cultures', *Journal of British Studies*, 31:4 (1992), 358–89; 'Enlightenment and Counter-Enlightenment, Revolution and Counter-Revolution: A Euroskeptical Enquiry', *History of Political Thought*, 20:1 (1999), 125–39.
17 Collini, *Public Moralists*, pp. 2–3.
18 See the collection titled 'The New British History in Atlantic Perspective' in *American Historical Review*, 104:2 (1999). For a discussion of *connected, shared* and *entangled* histories, see M. Werner and B. Zimmermann, 'Penser l'histoire croisée: entre empirie et réflexivité', *Annales Histoire Sciences Sociales*, 1 (January–February 2003), 7–36, especially 8–9.
19 M. Espagne and M. Werner, *Transferts: Les relations interculturelles dans l'espace franco-allemand (18ème–19ème siècles)* (Paris: Editions Recherche sur les civilisations, 1988); M. Espagne, 'Sur les limites du comparatisme en histoire culturelle', *Genèses*, 17 (1994), 112–21.
20 On the 'Herderian Revolution', see P. Casanova, *The World Republic of Letters* (Cambridge, MA: Harvard University Press, 2004), chapter 2.
21 T. W. Heyck, *The Transformation of Intellectual Life in Victorian England* (London: Croom Helm, 1982); J. R. Jennings and A. Kemp-Welch (eds), *Intellectuals in Politics: From the Dreyfus Affair to Salman Rushdie* (London: Routledge, 1997); J. Stapleton, *Political Intellectuals and Public Identities in*

Britain since 1850 (Manchester: Manchester University Press, 2001).
22 Charle, *Les Intellectuels en Europe*, chapter 6.
23 On the continuity of the language of 'national character' between 1750 and 1914, see R. Romani, *National Character and Public Spirit in Britain and France, 1750–1914* (Cambridge: Cambridge University Press, 2002).
24 J. Gascoigne, *Cambridge in the Age of the Enlightenment* (Cambridge: Cambridge University Press, 1989); K. Haakonsen (ed.), *Enlightenment and Religion: Rational Dissent in Eighteenth Century Britain* (Cambridge: Cambridge University Press, 1996); P. Harrison, *'Religion' and the Religions in the English Enlightenment* (Cambridge: Cambridge University Press, 1990); J. G. A. Pocock, 'Enlightenment and Counter-Enlightenment'; R. B. Sher, *Religion and University in the Scottish Enlightenment* (Edinburgh: Edinburgh University Press, 1985); B. W. Young, *Religion and Enlightenment in Eighteenth-Century England: Theological Debate from Locke to Burke* (Oxford: Clarendon Press, 1998).
25 D. Roche, *Le Siècle des lumières en province: académies et academiciens provinciaux, 1680–1789* (Paris: Mouton, 1978), 2 vols, and Chartier, *The Cultural Origins*.
26 D. Goodman, *The Republic of Letters, a Cultural History of the French Enlightenment* (Ithaca: Cornell University Press, 1994); A. Lilti, 'La femme du monde est-elle une intellectuelle? Les salons parisiens au XVIIIe siècle', in N. Racine and M. Trébitsch (eds), *Intellectuelles: du genre en histoire des intellectuels*, in which other interesting essays on women intellectuals are included.
27 Casanova, *The World Republic of Letters*.
28 L. Colley, *Britons: Forging the Nation 1707–1837* (New Haven: Yale University Press, 1992).
29 A. Prost and J. Winter, *Penser la Grande Guerre: Un essai d'historiographie* (Paris: Le Seuil, 2004).
30 See, for example, on the British side, Stedman Jones, 'The New Social History in France', and P. Anderson, 'Dégringolade', *London Review of Books*, 2 September 2004, and 'Union Sucrée', *London Review of Books*, 23 December 2004; on the French side, see, for example, S. Cerutti, 'Le *linguistic turn* en Angleterre: Notes sur un débat et ses censures', *Enquêtes*, 5 (1997), 125–40, and Noiriel, *Sur la 'crise' de l'histoire*.

Part I
Towards a reflexive history of intellectuals

2

The intellectuals: a prehistory
JEAN-PHILIPPE GENET

At first sight, to entitle a book *Anglo-French Attitudes: Comparisons and Transfers between English and French Intellectuals since the Eighteenth Century* is to court danger. First, its subtitle roots it in a tradition of comparative historical research which, according to Marc Bloch, was inseparable from a long-term perspective.[1] Second, it calls for an interdisciplinary approach that is viewed with mistrust by many historians and social scientists.[2] Finally, it challenges a paradigm of national history that is still dominant, with the consequence that — to take but one example, though a most telling one — there is still a strong tendency among professional historians to restrict the application of the phrase 'European history' to the period since the signature of the Rome treaty in 1957.[3] Meanwhile, the concept of 'cultural transfer' has come to be seen by some scholars not only as a more secure route[4] to the in-depth study of the characteristics of 'national' or 'proto-national' culture,[5] but also in many respects as an alternative to national comparisons.[6]

A further difficulty is the fact that the comparison here is focused on England and France. The two countries have developed distinct historiographic traditions,[7] and though these have had close contact in the past, since the Second World War this contact has undergone a slow decline. It is impossible to study this development in depth here, as it deserves a full study of its own in the wider context of Anglo-French cultural relations. But to restrict myself to some impressions on the French side, it is notable that the French government has systematically encouraged and promoted cooperation with Germany, with the creation of the French Historical Mission in Göttingen having a powerful impact on French historiography; the number of theses devoted to German subjects has increased sharply, and the number of chairs occupied by specialists of German history in French universities has also increased. On the other hand, the French government has refused to create a French Historical Mission in Britain, and the number of specialists in British history (that is, having done their doctoral research on this subject) occupying a chair in French universities is minimal. To say the least, this situation does not improve mutual understanding,[8] though the situation in Britain is fortunately much more satisfactory as regards British specialists in French history. Yet the problem of intellectuals has been at the forefront of both historiographies for some time, even if in each case it has been restricted to the national space.

The main problem here, however, is not with methodology, but with the historical 'object' of the volume itself. As Christophe Charle has observed, the substantive noun 'intellectual' is of fairly recent origin, in France at least,[9] probably going back no further than the late nineteenth century. But historians have employed it freely to define a historical construct for which a medieval ancestry has been claimed. One eminent medievalist, Jacques Le Goff, has used the word to describe the new culture generated by the educational revolution which saw the emergence of the urban schools and their transformation into universities, first of all in Bologna, Paris and Oxford, and then in most of Europe.[10] More recently, Jacques Verger has criticised the choice of the term 'intellectual', proposing instead *les gens de savoir* as a French translation of the German *Gelehrten*.[11] Nevertheless, I think that there is in such a denomination something quite different from the idea of 'knowledge' which Jacques Le Goff had in mind, and the pride of those members of universities whose various alumni became popes and who were soon to monopolise Bishoprics and positions of power and influence in both State and Church, is better explained by their strong feeling of being the intellectual guides of Christian society. As Jacques Le Goff points out, quoting Aquinas, these medieval scholars felt justified in claiming an exalted position since it was their task to establish the truth and keep it unaltered and unblemished, through the exercise of human reason at its most efficient, now boosted by the virtuoso practice of logic and philosophy.[12] True, Aquinas had to concede that lawyers, physicians, and many 'artists' as well, did not consider themselves primarily as virtuous defenders of truth, but rather 'merchants of science' engaged in a trade 'perfectly comparable to other trades',[13] but this leaves untouched the exalted position of the theologians and the artists engaged in academic careers.

Both the comparative method and the usefulness of the term 'intellectuals' are discussed in the general introduction to this volume. In this chapter, I shall recall some well-known but useful facts in order to provide a long-term approach to the problem of the intellectuals, suggesting that trying to follow these through the changing conditions of social and political communication over the centuries helps illuminate the central characteristics of the group as such.

In search of medieval intellectuals

The first point I should like to make is that France and Britain each have a long history behind them, and in both national spaces intellectuals, whoever they turn out to be, have a common ancestry, revitalised at different stages. The national approach is therefore not the only 'natural' one, and for certain periods it is even unnatural, as we shall see. However, caution is necessary, because there was no medieval term approaching the modern concept of 'an intellectual', something which provides Christophe Charle with the opportunity to theorise a clear delineation between two categories, the 'self-styled intellectual' (for instance, those who came to the forefront with the Dreyfus Affair), and the 'sociological intellectual' who may be recognised as such by professional and educational standards, and can be subjected to quantification.[14] But not having the word in medieval texts does not preclude the existence in medieval societies of men having the functions and characters of 'intellectuals'. We must be very cautious with the words we choose to use when doing comparative history. When we consider the medieval origins of the modern state, for example, we must be aware that the word 'state' is probably one of the words used by European historians with the most varying set of connotations.[15] French historians, for example, are prone to conceptualise the European modern state in a way which, German historians might object, underestimates the modernity and the potentials of the Empire, or, Italian historians might argue, of the city-states – or simply of towns – as laboratories of political modernity.

Let us go back to Jacques Le Goff's definition and try to see if we can reconcile it with Charle's. It is effective enough in so far as it is based upon a division of labour, but then we run the danger of considering all educated clerics as intellectuals. In fact, even if we exclude lawyers, we are left with a growing population of students and scholars. But if the men who flocked to the Montagne Sainte-Geneviève to hear Pierre Abélard's lectures were no doubt clever and ambitious young men, anxious to discover and disseminate the truth, when their numbers increased and the schools diversified their teaching, these scholars fell into distinct groups with different roles in society. Most students had to restrict their ambitions to a simple rectorship in a country parish; on the other hand, many did receive better rewards, such as canonships in collegiate or cathedral churches, these benefices often implying judicial, administrative or financial work for the benefit of State or Church. Some became laymen (technically, they were clerics while students) and married, becoming schoolmasters or, in the fifteenth century, bureaucrats. True, many of these students, at least those who had teaching or pastoral duties, may fall into Charle's category of 'sociological intellectual', which may in turn be considered to coincide more or less with Jacques Verger's *gens de savoir*. The problem lies with the 'self-styled' intellectuals: do they have an equivalent before the eighteenth or nineteenth century?

Another definition, that proposed by Pierre Bourdieu, may prove useful here: he characterises the intellectuals as 'professionals in the handling of symbolic goods'.[16] 'Handling' may not be a precise translation of the French *manipulation*, but I should be inclined in any case to discard the automatically pejorative connotation conveyed by the French word. Therefore, if we consider the medieval period, we can decide to use the word 'intellectual' to designate those using both reason and knowledge to produce, interpret and adjust symbolic goods through constant reinterpretation. But in the Western medieval world, the Church was endowed with a supreme authority which conferred on it a monopoly in all such production and handling. All clerics shared the responsibility of transferring at least a part of these symbolic goods from the world of the learned (*clerici*) to that of the illiterate (*laici*);[17] but that responsibility was greatly enhanced and extended when the Church, in the aftermath of the so-called Gregorian reform, directly established its power over each Christian, a power resting on the unavoidable necessity for each individual, whether prince or slave, man or woman, warrior or peasant, to submit himself or herself to the spiritual guidance of the institutional Church as represented by the *ordo clericalis*, and try to achieve salvation. Indeed, the development of the schools from the late eleventh century onwards was only a by-product of this clerical 'revolution', since to supervise and shepherd a growing population whose every individual member had to be reached, convinced (and therefore educated) and controlled by able and efficient agents implied the existence of an army of priests, pastors and preachers. The parochial clergy and, soon, the members of the mendicant orders as well, had therefore to be provided with as solid and uniform a knowledge of the basic tenets of the Christian religion as possible.[18] To fulfil their mission, these men believed they had to establish, beyond dispute and discussion emanating from the *ordo laicorum*, the truth of the Christian religion as defined and interpreted by the Church, and had to be able to reject as heretical those who refused to conform or accept their teaching, thereby severing them from the *Ecclesia*.[19]

This process implied a substantial transformation of many of the tenets of the Christian religion: a much-increased dominance and control of the whole ecclesiastical structure by the Papacy, the enforcement of a strict distinction between the *ordo clericalis* and the *ordo laicorum*, the centrality of the Eucharist, the reorganisation of the Mass this implied, the new stress on communion and aural confession and the innovation of Purgatory (and here, too, we encounter again Jacques Le Goff's seminal work[20]), with its incalculable number of consequences. This new theology was engineered by the masters of the greatest and most prestigious school of medieval Christendom, that of the cathedral of Paris, which in due course became the University of Paris. But to impose such changes these masters had to be endowed with a new kind of authority: it is precisely in the complex elaboration process of this *auctoritas* that the modern notion of the *auctor* emerged.[21] Those theologians whose authority was guaranteed and reinforced by their affiliation to the school of Paris were of very different regional and intellectual backgrounds; but their voice was heard throughout Europe, and through the transfer effected by members of the clergy it helped to shape the mind and the religiosity of everyone. Not that they were unanimous: protracted and ebullient debates took place among them, often going too far and having to be censured by the Papacy. The extraordinary vitality and inventiveness of the theological (and soon philosophical) disputes of the eleventh and twelfth centuries is due to these men, in whom we may recognise the equivalent of Charle's self-styled intellectuals: a group of men – Peter Lombard, Petrus Comestor, Albert the Great, Aquinas, Duns Scotus to mention the most illustrious – whose books continued to be read for centuries. But is it possible to apply the word 'intellectual' to a professional (i.e. authorised, that is, endowed with *auctoritas*) trader in symbolic goods who was only the spokesman of a hierarchical organisation? In other words, was their commitment to truth superordinate to their commitment to the Church?

Spontaneously, the twenty-first-century reader would say 'no' and rather preserve the word for the heretics, or at least a certain category of heretics (that is, the learned ones) who, by opposing the Church, appear as the exact opposite of professional. In applying to the greatest of the Paris art and theology masters the word 'intellectual', we fall into one of the pitfalls of applying a modern word to a medieval category, which in fact occupied in its own society a situation opposite to that of the modern intellectual. Samuel Chandler's linking of intellectual and heretical precisely points to this possible inversion. But anyone familiar with the history of medieval universities knows that medieval scholars, trained by the Church for the Church, did use with considerable freedom the tools they had forged in importing Greek and Arabic thought, science and methods, thus reintroducing philosophy and the philosophical approach in Latin Europe.[22] By doing so, they went so far as to incur strict condemnation from the ecclesiastic authorities they were supposed to serve.[23] Even Aquinas's propositions were for a time condemned; and Siger de Brabant, William of Ockham, Master Eckhart and John Wyclif were each in their own right brilliant masters who nonetheless incurred the wrath of ecclesiastical censors. The intellectual was therefore a creation of the *Ecclesia*, in so far as he soon escaped the strict control of his creator and in the process created much of what was to be for centuries the prerequisites for the existence of intellectuals: a common language (in this case scholastic Latin), a public space (the lecture room), basic technologies of communication, oral or written (the system of *quaestiones*, and the spread of manuscript copies of texts in large quantities, using sophisticated devices such as the *pecia*), and, most of all, a position of authority in his field (Pierre Bourdieu's *champ*) of action.

The turning point of the fourteenth century

But this brings us to a second stage, in the early fourteenth century, and the emergence of a second type of intellectual. The mutation of medieval education had given birth as early as the twelfth century to the semantic absurdity of the *laicus literatus*: literally, the 'lettered illiterate', if we take into account the new meaning of *laicus* from the eleventh century onwards to designate someone who was not a clerk in the double sense of this later term, a cleric and a clerk, that is a literate man.[24] It thus became technically possible for educated members of the *ordo laicorum* to handle symbolic goods with the virtuosity and techniques that were previously the preserve of the schoolmen. And, in due course, the authorial role which had been assumed by university masters was extended to laymen. Dante is here the most obvious example, and he is also the first layman whose works were commented upon in the scholastic manner, which means they were thought to be invested with an authority second only to Aristotle and the Bible or their commentators.[25] Moreover, public lectures commenting on Dante's work were first delivered not in universities, but through lectureships endowed by city authorities, the first of these being given by Giovanni Boccaccio himself in Florence in October 1373, in the church of San Stefano di Badia.[26] However, Dante was exceptional in his impressive command of both Latin and the Tuscan vernacular, as well as in his close familiarity with scholastic techniques, apparently acquired in the Florence school of the Preachers. Italian humanists were to follow his lead in the careful construction of the interrelated notions of author and authority and, following Dante, Petrarch and Boccaccio, also assumed a public role, best exemplified by Petrarch's coronation as Poet Laureate in Rome in 1341. From the early fourteenth century, we can follow the development of Italian humanism which was soon to constitute a new paradigm of European culture and give birth to a new type of intellectual, eventually replacing the university master with the 'self-styled intellectual', though the culminating example of this was not an Italian, but Erasmus. This second stratum of European intellectuals, through a lengthy and complex process, transformed itself and lost in the process its strictly humanistic character: it provided a renovated Latin language, a wider spectrum of intellectual interests,[27] and an entirely new concern for the importance and use of vernacular languages, notably Italian and (later on) French. They thus laid the cornerstones for the construction of the *République des Lettres*, which connected and integrated at a European level: intellectuals operating within national public spaces where these existed, but gaining an additional authority from their international position.

These considerations are not leading us away from our subject – English and French intellectuals. They simply emphasise the importance of the European and non-national element in the figure of the intellectual. England and France, moreover, were not at the time separate entities: the English elite were French-speaking until the beginning of the fifteenth century at least, and some of the poets we shall go on to mention were personal acquaintances. The English occupation of France, as well as the captivity of eminent Frenchmen (such as Charles, Duke of Orleans, a remarkable poet in his own right), provided the occasion for close intellectual contact. But it is true that these common European elements were slowly absorbed and transformed to shape the figure of a third type of intellectual, operating, as we have said, within a national public space. The appearance of these proto-'intellectuals' may be traced in both France and England in the course of the fourteenth century. Like the Italian humanists, they were first and foremost 'authors' in the full, 'modern' sense of the word; but even if they had some Latin (and some even wrote excellent Latin), they preferred to use the vernacular, although they were not all laymen. Probably, the literary work which in the two great Western kingdoms marks the establishment of the poet as an 'authoritative' voice, addressing his public on matters of social, sexual and political morality hitherto reserved to the learned discussion of clerics, is the *Roman de la Rose* of Guillaume de Lorris, continued by Jean de Meung (of Guillaume we know nothing; Jean may have been a student, probably in Bologna, and later became a cleric), a tremendous success both in France and in England, as the number of surviving copies show. Though they derived many of their techniques and exposition (narrative, allegory and so on) from the abundant literary production of the second half of the twelfth century and the thirteenth, they abandoned the anonymity which had characterised earlier poets and intentionally assumed a position of authority. This is obvious in France, with poets such as Guillaume de Machaut, Eustache Deschamps, Christine de Pisan or Alain Chartier,[28] but the phenomenon is even more striking in England, with the so-called Ricardian poets[29] – Chaucer, Langland and Gower, to name only the most famous, where it coincides with the affirmation of English as a national language.[30] By this time, lay authors could themselves write on spiritual and religious subjects without arousing the Church's anger or fear.[31] All these writers, or rather 'authors', spoke for the political society as a whole, though no one has hired them for such a purpose, which was largely self-attributed. The poet who has conquered authorial status (the socially unacceptable Langland may be seen here as an exception, though he tries to reach a similar result by giving clues to his identity, having his character *Will* speak as the real author) is recognised as a public speaker, laying the foundations of what will gradually become the modern intellectual: neither a professional handler of symbols for the Church, nor a heretic, but an intellectual in his own right.

To assess the impact of such a transformation is possible through studying the contents of private 'libraries', known to us either by surviving manuscripts (especially when these bear marks of ownership) or by wills and inventories. The number of manuscripts still extant today with works of the three above-mentioned English poets is quite remarkable, as it is for Hoccleve and Lydgate in England and Alain Chartier in France in the following century. Lydgate offers a good example, since he derived his 'authority' both from his personal status as a Benedictine monk at Bury St Edmunds and from his association with the Court and the Lancastrian princes. All this points to the existence of a 'public sphere', though the borrowing of this phrase from Jürgen Habermas may sound misleading, since Habermas seems to think that the 'bourgeois public sphere' was the successor of the 'representative publicness' which it therefore supplanted, 'the representation of courtly-knightly publicity [which] attained its ultimate pure form at the French and Burgundian Courts in the fifteenth century'.[32]

This vision is too simplistic, however, giving far too much importance to the Courts, and neglecting the considerable abilities and openness of the citizens of the great merchant towns and members of the aristocracy, including the *petite noblesse*, the gentry and the professionals, who all had access to books, not to mention theatrical performances and the like. These social groups were eager to gather information on what was going on in the wider world: the fifteenth-century collection of the Paston Letters contains several newsletters giving news of the battles in the War of the Roses and from the Court. The importance of newsletters is striking when we read the English chronicles of the period, though their origin and conditions of production are not always clear: it is only from the end of the sixteenth century onwards that we have evidence of a systematic production, handled by professionals who were paid substantial sums for regular manuscript copies of their letters. In fifteenth-century England, nonetheless, it is clear that the City of London and London society were the driving force behind many historical and literary productions, and, if adverse circumstances limited the importance of Paris during most of the fifteenth century, the French capital occupied a situation more or less comparable to that in London both in the fourteenth century and again in the sixteenth.

The appearance and development of a general public, both ecclesiastical and lay, the birth of authorial status, the multiplication of books and the large circulation of written texts are but a part (albeit an important one) in what can be termed the communication system of a given society, and the strategies of individual actors in this system (and among them authors) depend on the specific system of each country in order to adapt themselves to the institutions which delineate its structure. I shall mention briefly just two examples. Without the existence of a good system for copying and publishing books in large numbers, the dissemination of manuscripts would have been impossible: the production of books, at first a quasi-monopoly of the monastic *scriptoria*, had already been relocated in towns with universities (with the creation of the *stationarius* and, in the most important of these at least, Paris and Bologna, the innovative system of the *pecia*); soon, shops appeared in most great towns which catered to a lay readership, and these bookshops and booksellers, with all the connected trades ('lymnours', scribes and copyists, painters etc.), paved the way for the printed book, its production and distribution. London, a smaller town than Paris in the later Middle Ages, offered fewer opportunities for 'publishing', and the start of printing in England was belated and slow: English authors had to develop different strategies to adapt to the 'bespoke' trade of London booksellers.[33] However, the poems of Chaucer, Gower, Hoccleve – and even more strikingly, Lydgate – were copied in the London shops in many manuscripts for members of the gentry or of the London elite. Another example of the importance of institutions for the system of communication is that of the Courts. The relatively small part played by the Court in England markedly contrasted with its dominance in France and Burgundy, but this had a paradoxical effect: the public stance of the French poet was more easily restricted to a courtly stage and audience and to the King's entourage, and no French poet of this period could claim an equivalent position of public moral authority to the Ricardian poets, despite their remarkable literary success. The strategies of poets such as Eustache Deschamps, Christine de Pisan and Alain Chartier were each markedly different. Christine, probably the most successful in the end, being widely read and even often translated into English, was in a difficult situation at Court as a widowed mother, and chose to produce, in a workshop she herself controlled, '*de luxe*' manuscripts that she dedicated personally to the princes (the dukes of Burgundy, Orleans, Berry and Bourbon) in the hope of handsome rewards, hardly the best route to a wide circulation of her texts. Chartier, who was a well-paid official, faced no such hardship, and the distribution of his works was quick and intensive, while Deschamps's poems, widely known and duly appreciated by courtiers who collected his poems, followed still another pattern[34] and survive in a relatively smaller number of manuscripts. Success and fame at Court was not an automatic road to success in the book trade.

However, the success of this first wave of 'national proto-intellectuals', if I may be allowed to use this phrase, did not last. The use of the vernacular restricted their audience to a national public space of still ill-defined identity, and the balance of political and religious forces within this public space was unstable, to say the least. They depended too much on the conditions of communication in their respective societies, while the rise of the absolute monarchy and the new religious atmosphere generated by the Reformation and Counter-Reformation left few opportunities for them to develop, at least in relatively strong monarchies such as the English and the French. The sweeping success of the Italian humanists, whose reformed Latin and classical references invaded one chancery and school after another, creating a new set of standards which asserted the dominance of a renovated Latin language over national idioms and reduced national public spaces to a quasi-provincial status: the most formidable 'intellectual' of the early sixteenth century was Erasmus, and the prestige of Sir Thomas More was largely won abroad, first as the radical author of *Utopia* and the translator of Lucian, printed in Paris or elsewhere on the Continent, then as the saintly Catholic rebel whose complete works were issued by the Louvain printers. This observation leads to the third point I want to emphasise. Since the chronological span of the present volume starts with the eighteenth century, by which time national cultural and political spaces were firmly established, many of the points I have dealt with until now have only a distant impact on the subjects debated, precisely because after the middle of the fifteenth century these 'national proto-intellectuals' had disappeared for the reasons mentioned above. If we take the example of England, some of them were remembered, especially Chaucer, and the Chaucer revival of the sixteenth century precisely chose to highlight his role as founder of the national idiom; but the political conditions of the time made the emergence of a new Chaucer impossible.

Divergent paths of the sixteenth century

In fact, it is probably at this time, during the second half of the sixteenth century, that the two political societies and cultures began to differ deeply. To sum up briefly what is a long and complicated story, one could say that England was successful in appropriating international humanism to create a national humanism, whereas France, due to the Wars of Religion, failed utterly – Montaigne being the admirable but isolated exception. France had to wait until the restructuring of the national literary stage under the aegis of the Bourbon monarchy[35] to see the emergence of an organised and well-structured 'literary field', a structure in which political power plays an important role. Christian Jouhaud[36] has charted the transformation of this structure, the transition from a *politisation de la littérature* to a *littérarisation de la politique*, which gave birth to the *gens de lettres* and the philosophers of the French Enlightenment, who fully deserve to be considered as 'intellectuals'. When Voltaire launched his attacks on the judicial establishment in the Calas and Sirven cases, he was able to challenge French institutions because he enjoyed in the public space a carefully constructed status of authority which made the set of philosophical and ideological references he used an acceptable alternative to the set of religious and political references on which both the *parlements* and the royal government operated, opposing a universal conception of humanity to the barbarous cruelty of unfair and vitiated judgements, substituting a moral tribunal for the justice of men. Most of Voltaire's references ultimately derived from authors such as Bayle or Locke, but they needed his mediation: Bayle wrote as an exile, and Locke was a foreigner. It was Voltaire's commanding position of intellectual authority which gave these ideas their full weight in French public opinion.

In England, on the contrary, the movement was earlier, and in a quite different direction. It was not without great difficulties. At first, the nationalisation of humanism did not succeed and it is highly significant that, though twice offered a professorship at Cambridge and despite long and repeated stays in England, Erasmus chose to go back to the Continent. Thanks to the far-reaching reform in the teaching of grammar conducted by successive masters of Magdalen school and the innovations of John Colet, among many other reasons, humanism was on the whole successfully and relatively quickly appropriated by the English system of education; but the philological and critical skills of English humanists placed them in a dangerous position in the religious battles which were fought under Henry VIII and his two first successors. The early Tudor Court, the natural stage for the humanists' careers to bloom, was a place full of danger, with its politico-religious intrigues and paranoia fuelled by a doubtful legitimacy. Several prominent humanists were executed or exiled. But it is possible to say that with the reign of Elizabeth an English humanism came into being. It benefited from the patient and careful elaboration of a strong national identity by erudite experts, while France was still embroiled in the torments of the Wars of Religion. Leland and Bale for literature, John Foxe for religion, Raphael Holinshed, John Stowe and William Camden for history, Richard Hakluyt for geography and discovery – to name but a few of these men – erected a base upon which everything else could be built. But the English public space and literary field presented from the start four characteristics which made them quite different from their French counterparts.

First of all, the Court or, more generally speaking, the royal entourage and the members of the governing circles, never achieved the dominance and the cohesion they had in France. The City of London always remained a powerful element, not only as an economic and political power, but also as a cultural and social centre, with the presence in London of Parliament, the Inns of Courts and the main courts of justice – their respective sessions and terms brought members of the provincial elites regularly to town. However, these elites remained in the 'country' most of the time: the debate as to the impact of the alienation of 'Court' from 'country' on the causes of the English Revolution is not transferable to the other side of the Channel.[37] Paris, though still larger at this time, never achieved a position similar to that of London, overwhelmed as it was by the failure of the *Ligue* and the *Fronde*. It is therefore quite understandable that the field in which the mixture of literary skill, assertion of authority and criticism of prevailing political and social conditions made the authors closest to the proto-intellectuals of the late fourteenth century was, until the Civil War at least, that of the stage, a danger fully realised by the censors who kept a close watch over the London theatres. This characteristic is closely linked with the second one: the strong and early centralisation of English political society, with a similar structure in all parts of England (not Britain, of course, since Wales, Ireland and Scotland had their own structures). French society, on the contrary, was atomised into provincial entities, whose regional languages were not seriously challenged until the reforms of the Revolution. This is why the Bourbon kings, and above all Louis XIV, had to create a new type of political centralisation around the royal Court, which formed a truly national public space after the failure of the *Fronde*. In due course, the emergence of the *parlements* as rallying points of opposition to absolutism and the development of provincial academies, together with the rebirth of Parisian political and cultural life in the salons as a counterpoint to the dominance of Versailles, led to a weakening of the central control of the Court and the royal government, offering new opportunities for enterprising individuals (such as Voltaire) to devise new strategies of public communication.

Even more important for us is a third point, the discrepancy in the structural situation of religion in the two societies. In England, despite the fear of heresy generated by the success of Wycliffism and Lollardry, lay participation in religious life was a long and well-established tradition.[38] It may have been the same in France, but the political divergences of the sixteenth century created a gap between the two nations. Though the Edict of Nantes secured a limited freedom for Protestantism, even this proved too much, and its revocation by Louis XIV led to the persecution and exile of the Protestants. Religious matters basically remained in France the preserve of the Catholic Church and were confined to a strict orthodoxy, largely through the agency of an absolute monarchy[39] for which homogeneity of religious views appeared a necessity: the fate of Jansenism, despite its strong appeal to many members of the intellectual elite, offers a good example.[40] In England, debate on religious matters (despite the reluctance of Tudor and Stuart monarchs) remained a central element in the public sphere of discussion. It was not without its dangers and it involved a continuous struggle, but under Elizabeth I the Puritans were successful enough in securing the patronage of a number of ministers and members of the Royal Council that they could publicise their views, except the most extreme, which had to be printed in the Netherlands and smuggled back to England. Even the Catholics, though officially considered little else than outlaws, managed to have their books copied or imported. This pluralism is well exemplified by the situation in the English Parliament, where people of different religious sensibilities coexisted. At all events, after the Glorious Revolution England offered opportunities for religious debate and discussion on a scale totally unknown in France. Political society had thus become in England a society in which the religious choices and opinions of men searching in the depth of their own conscience for truth and faith were an essential component of political as well as cultural life. This element existed in France as in most other European countries, but not to the same degree, and so religious preoccupations and conceptions could not have the same impact on public life and intellectual debate in France that they had in England. This difference had far-reaching consequences; we can follow it over several centuries, and it may be felt even today.

Last, the two systems of education had become quite different, with the recovery of Oxford and the rapid growth of Cambridge from the late fifteenth century onward, maintaining a strong position for English universities, while the Inns of Court, at first strictly professional, soon became a third component of the higher education system, well integrated into a general structure which provided general education to the upper classes while making them fit to rule their dependents and inferiors, and at the same time maintaining the traditional role and authority of the medieval scholar. In England, clergymen, academics and gentlemen met in the same colleges, while the interdependence between the established Church and University remained close; many brilliant ecclesiastical careers started as distinguished academic ones. This is a unique combination which we do not find in France, where universities hardly recovered from the sixteenth-century religious crisis. It firmly rooted the English system in its medieval past, while capitalising on the efficient integration of humanism at an early date. This structure favoured the emergence of a relatively homogeneous culture, shared by the clergy, the professionals and the gentry as well, with a quality of learning,[41] an ability to understand each other and a depth of understanding which often came as a surprise to Continental observers, with the obvious exception of the central period of the seventeenth century.

If we have undoubtedly located some of the key elements for a prehistory of 'the intellectuals', or for a history of intellectuals before the word, we still face the danger, in dealing with the Anglo-French couple, of deducing real differences between the two societies under the influence of two strikingly different sets of historiographical traditions, viewpoints and vocabularies. To establish that in the long run England and France had deep differences in the structures of political society and the cultural system of communication, the two determinant elements for the status and figure of the intellectual, would require a satisfactory comparative study of the two societies which simply does not exist.[42] Part of the difficulty in this comparison may be summarised here by the juxtaposition of two tricky words, the English 'gentleman' and the French 'intellectuel', which do not easily transfer from one language to another. The semantics of the word 'intellectual' in the French tradition implies both a posture of opposition to the dominant ideology (or at least isolation from it), and a degree of legitimacy in the public space which gives due weight to the appeal to a distinctive set of universal and philosophical values (including religious ones); these are thus effectively opposed to the values of members of the establishment or simply those in power. In England, this structure of opposition is not so obvious, or rather it is masked by the semantic connotations of the word 'gentleman', which implies a specific type of behaviour and sociability, an amateur status contrasted with the quasi-professional status of the French intellectual as author or journalist. It is possible, however, to detect the origins of this difference, which has struck all observers and at first sight appears to be a purely social phenomenon, in the restructuring of the public space and of the literary stage from the middle of the sixteenth century onwards, a restructuring which adapted to different political circumstances in France and in England.

Let us take one particular example, that of Sir Francis Bacon.[43] He may have been a key figure in English intellectual history, but he was a gentleman, not an intellectual. A member of the Cecil clan, son of Elizabeth I's Lord Keeper, a government pen in his youth, later Attorney General, Lord Keeper and Lord Chancellor, he was certainly a prominent member of the governing circles, even if his career ended in disgrace. A prolific writer, it must not be forgotten that much of his intellectual legacy was carefully reorganised and transformed by an amanuensis, William Rawley, who from 1626 to 1658 published posthumously and translated much of Bacon's work. Many of these texts had previously been circulated in manuscript and were known to a small but distinguished circle of friends and servants – most of them gentlemen, of course. Obviously, Bacon was an exceptional mind if not an exceptional man, but Pascal Brioist, in exploring 'scientific sociability' in the seventeenth century, illustrates nicely this problem of the status of the so-called 'amateur'.[44] Open political debate was left to pamphleteers, or religious dissenters, while men in important positions collected political papers or acquired copies of parliamentary speeches from specialised scribes.[45] Only on rare occasions, until the onset of political crisis in the reign of Charles I from 1629 onwards, did the writings and speeches of these cultivated (University and Inns of Court) gentlemen of standing surface in the public space as printed volumes. Few if any of their discourses were prepared for the College of Antiquaries, which met until its suppression in 1614.[46] The library of Sir Robert Cotton (in whose house the College had met) became a repository for official and unofficial political papers which was visited by historians and authors, but above all by gentlemen, before it was closed and its collection confiscated. Gentlemen met in taverns (such as the illustrious Mermaid[47]) or in private rooms, to discuss among other things (including science and religion) problems of social, moral and political interest. True, this structure of civilised conversation was partly due to the necessity of keeping, so to speak, the public private, in the face of growing hostility from the Stuart monarchy. But some of it remained in the restructuring of the public space which took place after the Glorious Revolution. If a structure of opposition existed in England in the public space, it was more in the religious field than in the literary or political fields proper.

One final remark to close this protracted survey: while always using the words 'France' and 'England', we have been moving from a period in which these terms applied only to limited or loose political constructions, to an era of nations (when 'English' would have to be replaced by 'British' in most cases) with national public spheres, a structure in which it becomes easier to observe cultural transfers (to use Michel Espagne and Michael Werner's phrase). But depiction of the medieval period inevitably reinforces the idea that all European countries have much in common, a cultural capital inherited from the first autonomous school system which slowly emerged in the twelfth century at the instigation of the Church and under its control, but with its own system of rules and intellectual references, many of which were of external origin (Greco-Roman antiquity, Jewish and Arabic science, Roman law). The primacy of Bible studies and Augustinian theology was mitigated by the introduction of Aristotelianism to give a new start to philosophy, and these elements remained the foundations of European culture, though humanism gave them new expression, until the 'Scientific Revolution' of the seventeenth century and the Enlightenment succeeded in offering radically new paradigms. None of these great cultural movements was 'nation-centred'; though humanism is usually described as 'Italian', for instance, there was no national state in Italy. However, there are national differences, and if these are cannot be related to the action of states, they do relate to the very different responses which widely different political societies offered to the growth of the modern state from the fourteenth century onwards. This makes it essential to remind ourselves that the public space and system of communication existing in different countries has a long history behind it, and is fashioned in a constant process of adaptation to the political and social realities of each period. The social structures of the countries under examination must therefore remain a primary object of investigation, without which cultural history would become unfounded and useless, and it is here that we may reap the profits of comparative history, especially in the case of the intellectuals, whose international relations exhibit what they owe to this common European culture, even while they are firmly rooted in the public space of their own particular country.

Notes

1 M. Bloch, 'Pour une histoire comparée des sociétés européennes' (1928), reprinted in *Mélanges historiques* (Paris: A. Colin, 1963), pp. 16–40, on which see W. H. Sewell, 'Marc Bloch and the Logic of Comparative History', *History and Theory*, 6 (1967), 208–11, and H. Atsma and A. Burguière (eds), *Marc Bloch aujourd'hui: histoire comparée et sciences sociales* (Paris: Editions de l'EHESS, 1996). See also H. Kaelble, *Der historische Vergleich: eine Einführung zum 19. und 20. Jahrhundert* (Frankfurt and New York:

Campus, 1999); M. Détienne, *Comparer l'incomparable* (Paris: Le Seuil, 2000), and a special issue of *Annales. Histoire, Sciences Sociales* on 'L'exercice de la comparaison', introduction by Lucette Valensi, 57:1 (2002). See also C. Charle, *Les Intellectuels en Europe* (2nd edition; Paris: Le Seuil, 2001) and *La Crise des sociétés impériales, Allemagne, France, Grande-Bretagne 1900–1940, essai d'histoire sociale comparée* (Paris: Le Seuil, 2001); W. Blockmans, J. L. Borges de Macedo and J.-P. Genet (eds), *The Heritage of the Pre-Industrial European State* (Lisbon: Arquivos Nacionais, 1996), and J.-P. Genet, 'Droits et pouvoirs à Rome et dans les débuts de l'état moderne européen: propositions pour une approche comparative', *Mélanges de l'Ecole Française de Rome, Moyen Age*, 113:2 (2001), 793–810, 2002 (on the typological characterisation of these two 'states').

2 Pierre Bourdieu points out that Durkheim explicitly identified sociology and comparative method (and one could add that this seems also to have been Max Weber's view). He usefully summarises the reasons for the historians' reserve in 'Sur les rapports entre la sociologie et l'histoire en Allemagne et en France', *Actes de la Recherche en Sciences Sociales*, 106–7 (1995), 119–20.

3 But see J. Le Goff, *L'Europe est-elle née au Moyen Age?* (Paris: Le Seuil, 2003).

4 M. Espagne, *Les Transferts culturels franco-allemands* (Paris: Presses Universitaires de France, 1999); M. Espagne and M. Werner (eds), *Transferts: les relations interculturelles dans l'espace franco-allemand* (Paris: Editions Recherche et Civilisation, 1988).

5 M. Espagne and M. Werner (eds), *Qu'est-ce qu'une littérature nationale? Approches pour une théorie interculturelle du champ littéraire* (Paris: Editions de la Maison des sciences de l'homme, 1994), and M. Espagne, *Le Creuset allemand, histoire interculturelle de la Saxe, XVIIIe–XIXe siècles* (Paris: Presses Universitaires de France, 2000).

6 M. Espagne, 'Sur les limites du comparatisme en histoire culturelle', *Genèses: Sciences Sociales et Histoire*, 17 (1994), 112–21, but see also M. Werner and B. Zimmermann, 'Penser l'histoire croisée: entre empirie et réflexivité', *Annales. Histoire, Sciences Sociales*, 57:1 (2003), 7–36.

7 See, for instance, my 'Histoire politique française, histoire politique anglaise', in F. Autrand, C. Gauvard and J.-M. Moeglin (eds), *Saint-Denis et la Royauté: Etudes offertes à Bernard Guenée* (Paris: Publications de la Sorbonne, 1999), pp. 621–36.

8 This is why the CNRS has created a research group 'France – Iles Britanniques', with the aim of promoting exchange and cooperation between British and French historians: see F. Lachaud, F.-J. Ruggiu and I. Lescent-Gilles (eds), *Histoires d'outre-Manche: tendances récentes de l'historiographie britannique* (Paris: Presses de l'Université Paris-Sorbonne, 2001), and P. Chassaigne and J.-P. Genet (eds), *Droit et société en France et en Grande-Bretagne (XIIe–XXe siècles): fonctions, usages et représentations* (Paris: Publications de la Sorbonne, 2003).

9 C. Charle, *Naissance des 'intellectuels' 1880–1900* (Paris: Editions de Minuit, 1990), shows that the term did not gain currency until the end of the nine-

teenth century. According to the *Oxford English Dictionary*, it can be found as early as 1652 in Edward Benlowes's *Theophilia* and it appears in Samuel Chandler's translation of Limborch's *Inquisition* in 1731, which speaks of 'heretike Intellectuals'.

10 J. Le Goff, *Les Intellectuels au Moyen Age* (Paris: Le Seuil, 1985; first published 1957).

11 J. Verger, *Les Gens de savoir en Europe à la fin du Moyen Age* (Paris: Presses Universitaires de France, 1997).

12 J. Le Goff, 'Les Intellectuels au Moyen Age', in J. Le Goff et B. Kopeczi, *Intellectuels français, intellectuels hongrois, XIIIe–XXe siècles* (Budapest and Paris: Akademiai Kiado, Editions du CNRS, 1985), pp. 11–39. The quotation from Aquinas (*Summa contra Gentiles*, book I, chapter 7) reads: '*Quamvis autem praedicta veritas fidei christianae humanae rationis excedat, haec tamen quae ratio naturaliter indita habet, huic veritati contraria non possunt.*'

13 O. Weijers, 'Terminologie des universités naissantes: étude sur le vocabulaire utilisé par l'institution nouvelle', in *Miscellanea Medievalia*, 12:1 (1980), 258–80, 279–80.

14 Charle, *Les Intellectuels en Europe*, p. 22.

15 Hence, whatever its limitations, the interest of the great German enterprise of the *Geschichtliche Grundbegriffe*: O. Brunner, W. Conze and R. Koselleck (eds), *Geschichtliche Grundbegriffe: historisches Lexikon zur politisch-soziologischen Sprache in Deutschland* (Stuttgart: Klett, 1972–92).

16 Charle, *Les Intellectuels en Europe*, p. 22.

17 On the evolution of the words *clericus* and *laicus*, see Michael Clanchy, *From Memory to Written Record: England 1066–1307* (Oxford: Blackwell, 1999), pp. 176–82.

18 J.-P. Genet, *La Mutation de l'éducation et de la culture médiévales* (Paris: Seli Arslan, 1999), 2 vols.

19 See R. J. Moore, *The Formation of a Persecuting Society: Power and Deviance in Western Europe, 950–1250* (Oxford: Blackwell, 1987). On the *Ecclesia*, see A. Guerreau, *L'Avenir d'un passé incertain: quelle histoire du Moyen Age au XXIe siècle?* (Paris: Le Seuil, 2001), pp. 28–31.

20 Especially *La Civilisation de l'Occident Médiéval* (Paris: Arthaud, 1964; new edition 1984) and *La Naissance du purgatoire* (Paris: Gallimard, 1981; new edition 1991). But see Moore, *The Formation*.

21 A. J. Minnis, *Medieval Theory of Authorship* (2nd edition, Aldershot: Wildwood House, 1988).

22 A. de Libéra, *Penser au Moyen Age* (Paris: Le Seuil, 1991).

23 Hence the renewed interest of historians and philosophers in the famous condemnations of 1277: see R. Hissette, *Enquête sur les 219 articles condamnés à Paris le 7 mars 1277* (Louvain and Paris: Publications universitaires, 1977); L. Bianchi, *Il Vescovo e i filosofi: la condanna parigina del 1277 e l'evoluzione dell'arisotelismo scolastico* (Bergamo: Lubrina, 1990); J. A. Aertsen *et al.*, *Nach der Verurteilung 1277: Philosophie und Theologie an der Universität von Paris im letzten Vierteil des 13 Jahrhunderts: Studien und*

Texte (Berlin: de Gruyter, 2001).
24 Clanchy, *From Memory to Written Record*, pp. 177–82.
25 A. J. Minnis and A. B. Scott (eds), *Medieval Literary Theory and Criticism c.1000–c.1375: The Commentary Tradition* (revised edition; Oxford: Clarendon Press, 1991), pp. 439–519.
26 G. Boccacio, *Esposizione sopra la Commedia di Dante*, ed. G. Padoan, in Boccaccio, *Opere* (Milano: Mondadori, 1994), vol. 6.
27 A. Grafton and L. Jardine, *From Humanism to the Humanities: Education and the Liberal Arts in Fifteenth Century Europe* (London: Duckworth, 1986).
28 J. Blanchard and J.-C. Muhlethaler, *Ecriture et pouvoir à l'aube des temps modernes* (Paris: Presses Universitaires de France, 2002), pp. 33–58.
29 A. Middleton, 'The Idea of Public Poetry in the Reign of Richard II', *Speculum*, 53 (1978), 94–114; and J. Burrow, *Ricardian Poetry: Chaucer, Gower, Langland and the 'Gawain' Poet* (London: Routledge & Kegan Paul, 1971).
30 J.-P. Genet, *La Genèse de l'état moderne: culture et société politique en Angleterre* (Paris: Presses Universitaires de France, 2003), pp. 151–3.
31 The first English example is the mid-fourteenth-century *Livre de Seyntz Medicines* by Henry de Grosmont, Duke of Lancaster: E. J. Arnould, *Le Livre de Seyntz Medicines: The Unpublished Devotional Treatise of Henry of Lancaster*, Anglo-Norman Texts, vol. 2 (Oxford: Oxford University Press, 1940).
32 J. Habermas, *The Structural Transformation of the Public Sphere: An Inquiry into a Category of Bourgeois Society* (Cambridge: Cambridge University Press, 1974).
33 R. H. Rouse and M. A. Rouse, *Manuscripts and their Makers: Commercial Book Producers in Medieval Paris 1200–1500*, 2 vols (London: H. Miller, 2000).
34 J. P. Boudet and H. Millet (eds), *Eustache Deschamp en son temps* (Paris: Publications de la Sorbonne, 1997).
35 See A. Viala, *Naissance de l'écrivain* (Paris: Minuit, 1985), and my own comments on the chronological discrepancies between France and England in *Histoire et Mésure* 2 (1987), 137–69.
36 C. Jouhaud, *Les Pouvoirs de la littérature* (Paris: Gallimard, 2000).
37 L. Stone, *The Causes of the English Revolution, 1529–1642* (London: Routledge & Kegan Paul, 1972).
38 E. Duffy, *The Stripping of the Altars* (New Haven: Yale University Press, 1992).
39 But see F. Cosandey and R. Descimon, *L'Absolutisme en France: histoire et historiographie* (Paris: Le Seuil, 2002), pp. 83–105.
40 M. Cottret, *Le Catholicisme entre Luther et Voltaire* (Paris: Presses Universitaires de France, 1996), and *Jansénisme et Lumières: pour un autre XVIIIe siècle* (Paris: Albin Michel, 1998). In this context, Racine appears as the man who refused to be an intellectual: see A. Viala, *Racine: la stratégie du caméléon* (Paris: Seghers, 1990).
41 L. Stone, 'The Educational Revolution in England, 1560–1640', *Past and*

Present, 28 (1964), 41–80.
42 An international group of scholars, mainly French and English, has undertaken a comparative study of French and English political societies in the fifteenth and early sixteenth century under the direction of Malcolm Vale, John Watts and myself.
43 L. Jardine and A. Stewart, *Hostage to Fortune: The Troubled Life of Francis Bacon 1561–1626* (London: Gollancz, 1998).
44 P. Brioist, *Les Cercles intellectuels à Londres, 1580–1680* (Florence: European Institute, 1993).
45 H. Love, *Scribal Publication in Seventeenth-Century England* (Oxford: Clarendon Press, 1993), pp. 9–20, on the flourishing trade in manuscript 'political separates' (some of Sir Robert Cotton's tracts are still extant in more than fifty copies); and A. Marotti, *Manuscript, Print, and the English Renaissance Lyric* (Ithaca: Cornell University Press, 1995), pp. 85–94, on the dissemination of political texts in poetic anthologies.
46 L. Van Norden, 'The Elizabethan College of Antiquaries', Ph.D., University of California, Los Angeles, 1946.
47 I. A. Shapiro, 'The Mermaid Club', *Modern Language Review*, 45 (1950), 6–17, and P. Brioist, 'Que de choses avons-nous vues et vécues à la Sirène', *Histoire et Civilisations*, 4 (1991), 89–132.

3

British exceptionalism reconsidered: Annan, Anderson and other accounts

STEFAN COLLINI

In Britain it has long been something of a cultural cliché to claim that intellectuals begin at Calais. Often, this is no more than a stock response to the term itself, assumed to designate a species essentially foreign (and therefore funny), but on occasion it can be worked up into the form of purportedly historical propositions about the absence of intellectuals in British history and culture (or, more deviously, the absence of 'real' intellectuals). For convenience, I shall refer to this whole cluster of claims and assumptions as 'the absence thesis', even though 'thesis' risks exaggerating the systematic and argued nature of the case. The claims, in their various forms, are too familiar to need elaboration here: they are a longstanding feature of English self-description, whether offered in a spirit of smug self-congratulation (most often from the right) or despairing self-dramatisation (more often from the left), and the unacknowledged slide between 'England' and 'Britain' is another characteristic feature of that self-description. I shall also take for granted here, though I would argue the point at length elsewhere, that these claims are not merely familiar; they are also unhistorical, unanalytical and untrue.

The search for the origins of these claims would take us back far beyond the point where the term 'intellectuals' itself first gained currency; it would take us, at the very least, back to questions about the perception and impact of the French Revolution in England and to the subsequent development in the nineteenth century of the Whig interpretation of Britain's peculiarly fortunate political history. In broad terms, that is, many of what were to become standard features of the absence thesis were already in place before the term 'intellectuals' itself became established and before, therefore, the thesis needed to be explicitly elaborated. However, although it would be true to say that the assumption that intellectuals were essentially a foreign species, unknown (or only very partially known) in England, was widespread in the first half of the twentieth century, one would be hard pressed to find any systematic exposition of this claim or any single *locus classicus*.

Moreover, the use of the term 'intellectuals' itself was so unstable during the first three decades of the century, sliding between several different senses, that it would have been hard to tie down an analytical case to the effect that the various human types referred to by some of these senses were entirely absent in Britain. And, in fact, I would suggest that if one were to view the topic from the vantage point of the late 1930s it would not have seemed obvious or even necessarily widely believed by that point that Britain was fundamentally deviant from a European pattern in respect of intellectuals. Indeed, given the widespread tendency during that decade, shared among the major European languages (including English), to use the term 'intellectuals' to refer principally to writers who took some public political stand, and given the centrality of the Spanish Civil War and the broader anti-fascist movement to politics across Europe, there was less and less reason to insist on a contrast in the matter of intellectuals between Britain and the rest of Europe.

The main argument of this chapter is that the now-familiar case for British exceptionalism in this matter received its decisive formulation only in the 1950s, and moreover that there are intimate and generally overlooked resemblances and continuities between that formulation and what has been perhaps the single most influential analysis of the allegedly distinctive position of intellectuals in Britain, namely that produced within the ambit of the *New Left Review* in the course of the 1960s. Most recent scholarship has tended, not always wittingly, to reproduce the outlines of the analysis broadly shared between these two accounts. And the two key elements in those analyses, I would argue, are, speaking schematically, the following: first, that the position of intellectuals is plotted on a chart which moves between the poles of 'alienation' and 'integration', with true intellectuals being assumed to be found only towards the 'alienated' end of the scale; and second, that the situation of intellectuals in Britain is measured against a supposed European norm which always turns out, on closer inspection, to be a selective picture of affairs in just one country, namely France. In the space available I cannot document all these assertions, so I shall simply concentrate on the two texts which have become constant reference points in this literature, Noel Annan's 'The intellectual aristocracy' and Perry Anderson's 'Components of the national culture'. A glance at the bibliographies of any of the literature on intellectuals in Britain which have appeared in the past thirty years will show that these two pieces have enjoyed an unrivalled primacy as sources.

Annan and the thesis of the 'intellectual aristocracy'

Annan's essay appeared, significantly, in a *Festschrift* for G. M. Trevelyan, one of the last, and most popular, representatives of the Whig interpretation of English history.[1] In this chapter, Annan appointed himself the Herald-Pursuivant of the intellectual aristocracy; the piece is a sustained exercise in collective genealogy, complete with interlocking family trees. By this means, Annan illustrated how the elite of a new professional-cum-intellectual class formed itself in the first half of the nineteenth century, and how its descendants came to play leading cultural, academic and administrative (though not, strictly, political) roles in the late nineteenth and early twentieth centuries. The metaphor of an 'aristocracy' was held to be enlightening because this elite practised 'persistent endogamy' well into the twentieth century, producing a complex web of family relationships among individuals in succeeding generations who had supposedly come to the fore through their personal talents and achievements. Wedgwoods, Darwins, Stephens, Keyneses, Arnolds, Butlers, Trevelyans – these were the names that recurred in this intellectual equivalent of *Debrett's*.

Annan drew an affectionate and entertaining group portrait of this kinship system, and his characterisation of an ideal-typical member of that high-minded, public-spirited, somewhat ascetic, largely Cambridge-educated caste in the mid- and late-nineteenth century is particularly felicitous. But Annan intended his genealogical charts to serve an explanatory as well as celebratory purpose. The demonstration of this elite's close familial links was intended to account for what was represented as being by this date a well-established truism, namely 'the paradox of an intelligentsia which appears to conform rather than rebel against the rest of society'.[2] (I shall return later to the question of the adequacy of this kind of thinly binary characterisation of the possibilities.) Annan's terminology did not suggest that 'intellectuals' or even an 'intelligentsia' (a term which appears to be used here, as so often, simply as the collective plural of 'intellectual') had not existed in Britain – quite the contrary. The Stephens and Trevelyans and Arnolds and company were proposed as constituting a significant number of Britain's intellectuals during this period, but their degree of 'social integration' was assumed to help explain their lack of 'dissidence' and 'alienation'. The implicit contrast, yet again, was with what 'real' intellectuals have been like elsewhere.

But even if one for the moment allows the terms of the supposed 'question' to pass unchallenged (as subsequent references to Annan's essay seem to have done), it is still worth probing why Annan's genealogical researches should be presumed to offer any kind of 'answer'. After all, what his evidence (itself highly selective and unsystematic, as he acknowledges) showed was that, in the course of the nineteenth century, a fairly extended network of families, which produced many of the leading intellectual figures of the time, had a tendency to intermarry. Whether they did so more than comparable groups or more than might have been expected on the basis of their social contacts, or more than intellectual elites of other countries or other periods, were not questions which Annan's examples allowed him to raise: the essay proposed no statistical or comparative analysis, merely the identification of a group of families whose lines of descent sometimes interlocked.

That this could in fact be used to support precisely the opposite conclusion to Annan's is suggested by the way in which the much more systematic and sophisticated researches on the degree of intermarriage among the French intellectual elite at the end of the nineteenth century, most notably by Christophe Charle, have been adduced as indicating the formation of a self-consciously separate intellectual stratum, and hence as establishing one of the essential conditions for the development of a corporate sense of 'intellectuals'.[3] It is worth remembering that, although Annan's essay is often cited as demonstrating British intellectuals' close integration into the upper or governing class, it actually suggests something rather different. Their endogamy, such as it was, precisely tended to *preclude* marriage into the really dominant elites of British society such as the aristocracy or the peaks of new money (the latter of which they robustly disdained). Indeed, Annan (rightly) emphasises their sense of distance from the style of life and the values of the landed and the seriously rich: 'the intellectual aristocracy never confused themselves with the real nobility and ruling class'. Nor was there much traffic in the other direction: as Annan notes, Bertrand Russell was 'the one aristocrat' who 'successfully transplanted himself to the rock-garden of the intelligentsia'.[4]

Indeed, the more one broods on the explanatory mechanism implied in Annan's account (and it is worth doing so, not just because his essay has been so influential, but because a similar form of 'explanation' has been assumed by so many other discussions of this issue), the more mysterious it comes to seem. Consider, for example, his first formulation of the argument. Members of these families were, he asserts at the outset, leaders of the new intelligentsia. Stability is not a quality usually associated with an intelligentsia, a term which, Russian in origin, suggests the shifting, shiftless members of revolutionary or literary cliques who have cut themselves adrift from the moorings of family. Yet the English intelligentsia, wedded to gradual reform of accepted institutions and able to move between the worlds of speculation and government, was stable. That it was so – that it was unexcitable, and to European minds unexciting – was in part due to the influence of these academic families.[5]

This passage is a revealing microcosm of a much larger world of assumption and assertion. To begin with, it has to be remarked that it is Annan who calls them an 'intelligentsia' in the first place. At a purely terminological level, therefore, he is responsible for setting up the 'paradox'. Moreover, it would be straining against any established usage of this term to include under it a large number of the individuals whom he mentions in this essay – colonial governors, society surgeons, senior judges, and even the occasional bishop. These were certainly members of a professional-cum-administrative-cum-academic elite, but the term 'intelligentsia' has never been used as an equivalent for that whole stratum of society. And, of course, he constantly omits – occasionally with acknowledgement, but more often silently – whole swathes of these families where only a few individuals in fact distinguished themselves in cultural and official activities. His introduction of the Wedgwood family is a striking example of this, since he has to admit that he is 'omitting the Master Potters among the Wedgwoods who carried on the craft'.[6] Nor, looking at the matter from the opposite end, as it were, do the names of most of those who might be thought to have made up an English intelligentsia in any given generation appear at all. His roll call is confined to those who happen to have common ancestors, descendants or affines. A quite other, and much more ambitious, enquiry would be needed to determine whether the figures he mentions composed a significant proportion of this larger group.

The 'paradox' is then further stiffened by his gloss on what he implies is the usual understanding of the term 'intelligentsia'. *Pace* Annan, it is far from obvious that individual members of an intelligentsia are assumed to be 'shiftless' or indeed that any grouping of them must be a 'clique'. Even more slippery is the implication about 'cutting themselves adrift from the moorings of family'. After all, even his shifty, cliquey members of (European) intelligentsias still *had* families: if 'cutting themselves adrift' means remaining out of touch or rebelling against parental expectations, then there was no shortage of such behaviour among the British families he mentions (Annan concedes in passing that among his cast 'some maintained while others rebelled against the ethos of their fathers').[7] If it means not marrying a partner drawn from the same class or network of families, there is nothing in Annan's essay to suggest that such behaviour was more or less common among professional-class British intellectuals during this period than among their Parisian or Muscovite or Viennese peers.

When, in the next sentence, he moves on to the kind of characteristic that might be argued to be more marked among the British exemplars – for example, being 'wedded to gradual reform of accepted institutions' – we have moved on to a matter of attitude and belief rather than genealogy. If one were looking for an explanation of the assumed greater prevalence of such an attitude among English intellectuals, one would surely have to start with the structure and ethos of the political culture as a whole, perhaps with the bald fact that institutions were in practice more reformable in nineteenth-century Britain than in, say, nineteenth-century Russia. But it is the introduction of the notion of 'stability' that really muddies the waters here. Annan's use of the term seems to blend a form of sociological fixity (members of the same group of families occupying the same place in the social structure across several generations) with a form of intellectual or political moderation (a tendency not to propose dramatic or violent change). The fact that in the last sentence of the quoted passage 'stable' seems to be equated with 'unexcitable' slides us further towards the latter meaning, especially when it is insinuated that (excitable) Europeans habitually make the superficial or predictable judgement that the English intelligentsia is therefore 'unexciting'. (It is remarkable, incidentally, how often in this literature one meets the pairing of 'unexcitable', meaning not prone to dramatic or wholesale responses, with 'unexciting', meaning intellectually uninteresting. This again suggests, from a different angle, how this topic has functioned as a kind of figure for or displacement of larger cultural attitudes.) In any event, the alleged fact that '*the* English intelligentsia', in the singular, was 'stable' is argued to be 'in part due to the influence of these academic families'. These families, this suggests, were thus only *part* of that 'intelligentsia', but they influenced the rest towards 'stability', and they are said to have done so, it seems, on no better ground than that they themselves had a tendency to marry their friends' sisters.

It is hard to know quite how to go about unpicking this tightly woven nest of assumptions, and it would perhaps be unrewarding to try to do so at any greater length. Presumably, a minor premise of the argument is that close social contact with friends and relatives who are personally involved in running many of the country's major institutions is likely to mean that one's criticisms will take a practical and piecemeal form. There is some plausibility to this, though it hardly seems to apply to such notable scions of the intellectual aristocracy as, say, Celia Pankhurst or Lytton Strachey or Aldous Huxley or dozens of others whose responses were – sometimes greatly to their credit, sometimes not – far from moderate or practical. Moreover, it is not clear how far the values of this high-thinking and plain-living stratum are supposed to be deviant from those of the larger society. For example, when touching on the Pease family, whose prominent members during this period were Quakers, Annan remarks that Edward Pease, Secretary of the Fabian Society, 'is an interesting example of the way in which the Society of Friends breeds that kind of nonconformity which is the life of an intelligentsia'.[8] In the context of the essay as a whole, this comes as a somewhat confusing claim. Does it imply that the intellectual aristocracy whose pedigree he is compiling has in general displayed such non-conformity, or is it rather that the Peases are exceptional or not really members of it? More pressingly still, what exactly does Edward Pease's 'nonconformity' consist in here? After all, joining the Fabian Society hardly seems a very telling way of signalling one's dissent from being 'wedded to gradual reform of accepted institutions'. Pease became the Society's secretary after an unsuccessful career as a stockbroker; are we to assume that his non-conformity lay in his abandoning that career or did it, rather, lie in his dalliance with Mammon in the first place? More broadly, one does not have to search far to find examples of well-connected professional-class intellectuals who were far from 'wedded to the gradual reform of accepted institutions', from John Ruskin and William Morris onwards. And of course the names of prominent English intellectual figures during this period who were *not* part of this kinship network is legion, stretching from, say, Herbert Spencer or John Morley through George Gissing or H. G. Wells to C. P. Snow or Richard Hoggart and beyond.

Undeniably, members of this intellectual elite did come to occupy many influential and prestigious positions, especially in government service and the ancient universities, and they were, at least during the mid- and late Victorian period, conscious of belonging to a kind of freemasonry. But the key to their sense of identity during that period was something less tangible than family connection as such: certainly, it presumed their membership of a gentlemanly class, economically prosperous and socially esteemed, but it crucially involved personal achievement in intellectual labour or public service. And the explanatory power of kinship is weakened still further when one recognises that none of these properties necessarily entailed a lack of radicalism or 'dissidence', as any number of examples from Bertrand Russell onwards could confirm. What is true is that most of the members of Annan's intellectual aristocracy displayed a considerable social confidence, a familiarity with other members of this elite, and an assumption of access to the wielders of power. A large number of other members of a putative 'English intelligentsia' during this period did not share these features, or did so to a much lesser extent. Substantial numbers of those who belonged to the comparable elites in other European countries exhibited some not dissimilar characteristics. But by now the part played by kinship, as opposed to larger questions of political culture and intellectual tradition, in explaining any alleged absence of 'dissidence' among English intellectuals has diminished near to vanishing point.

And perhaps in the end Annan was not displeased to have exhibited the fact of a certain kind of cultural continuity rather than to have identified a social structural explanation for it. Such explanations, after all, can have a reductive effect, making epiphenomenal what those involved understand to be essential, and Annan (who was to become Provost of King's College, Cambridge the following year) seemed far from sorry to find the attitudes he had characterised still in rude health: 'Here is an aristocracy, secure, established, and, like the rest of English society, accustomed to responsible and judicious utterance and sceptical of iconoclastic speculation'.[9] By this point, we really are among the clichés of the intellectual equivalent of the tourist industry. This is post-prandial England, rocking gently in the warm complacency of the mid-1950s, appreciatively sniffing the familiar bouquet of Whig history.

Anderson and the thesis of the 'missing intelligentsia'

It would be hard to think of an idiom which would make a sharper contrast than that to be found in the pages of the *New Left Review* in the 1960s. The character of the journal was largely set by a series of articles by Perry Anderson and Tom Nairn on the interpretation of the course of British history and its connection with 'the present crisis' ('crisis' was a greatly favoured word).[10] The governing assumptions of what was often referred to as 'the Anderson–Nairn thesis' or, simply, 'the *NLR* analysis', of the distinctiveness of the historical development of Britain, were most influentially expounded in Anderson's 1964 article 'Origins of the present crisis', which particularly insisted upon the absence of a 'proper' bourgeois revolution in British history and the consequent ease with which a kind of 'continuism' had muffled both challenges to the established order and any theoretically elaborated defence of that order.

Whatever the wider ramifications of this analysis, there can be no doubt that as far as the topic of intellectuals is concerned the key document was Anderson's celebrated essay 'The components of the national culture', first published in 1968. Its impact is not hard to understand: quite apart from the matter of its timing, the essay itself is a bravura performance, brilliantly suggestive and high-handedly schematic in almost equal measure. Any inclination one may now have to regard it indulgently as a youthful *jeu d'esprit* is countermanded not just by its continuing scholarly authority, but by Anderson's own reaffirmation of its claims in its most recently reprinted form.[11]

In reconsidering Anderson's essay here, it may be helpful to recall three general features of its argument that are not always properly acknowledged. First, and most important of all, we have to recognise that its only partly explicit starting point remained the assumption that the British case is 'aberrant' when measured against some (Marxist) historiographical norm. Second, for all its impressive range, its substance was strikingly academic: 'the culture' was conceived in terms of its constituent 'disciplines' and was explicitly confined to 'the human and social sciences'. Third, it is very noticeable now what a structuralist analysis it was. Anderson was charting 'the geography' of the disciplines, the 'ground-plan of their distribution': spatial metaphors played a large part in his argument, above all the notion of the 'absent centre'.[12]

Anderson's most celebrated explicit claim was that what was 'missing' in Britain was 'the discourse of totality' – that is, any attempt to theorise the society as a whole; on this view, the conspicuous absentees in British intellectual culture were Marxism and sociology. A (rather sketchy) historical explanation for this lack was given in terms of the way in which the 'bourgeoisie' had never overtly challenged the aristocratic hold on state and society and so had in turn never been 'forced' to produce an 'official justification of the Victorian social system' (I shall not pause to point out the limitations of this 'action and reaction' assumption, though it is widely shared in this literature). But embedded in this implicitly counterfactual argument was another about the 'failure' to develop of a 'dissident intelligentsia'. And the 'dissidence' is crucial, since Anderson seems at various points to allow that there was some form of intelligentsia (at least, if that term is not being used any more demandingly than as a collective plural of 'intellectuals'), as for example when he refers to 'the predominance of literary over visual values in the intelligentsia described by Annan' in the latter's 'intellectual aristocracy' essay.

Some later scholars who have explicitly addressed these issues within the terms set out by Anderson's essay have tended to conflate the 'absence of sociology' thesis with the 'absence of intellectuals' thesis, but that in fact was not the logic of Anderson's original argument. The nub of his actual claim is that no sociological theory developed in Britain because 'the dominant class and its intellectuals' were never really challenged and so never had to formulate a general theory in defence. The kind of challenge he has in mind is pretty clearly that from a 'revolutionary' working-class movement, which would have been furnished with a critical (essentially Marxist) theory of British society by *its* intellectuals. So, sociology is not being regarded as the product of 'dissident' intellectuals but of 'hegemonic' intellectuals (the presence of a Gramscian binary classification is repeatedly visible in the essay). Such hegemonic intellectuals, the essay repeatedly indicates, existed, but were allowed to be, as it were, indolent or uncreative, because not provoked into a 'defence' of their society. As far as sociological theory goes, their 'failure' is, as his examples reiterate, a failure to be Durkheim or Weber. The use of a counterfactual of this specificity in comparative historical analysis is always fraught with difficulties,[13] but we should at least be clear that the differences between, say, Durkheim and Hobhouse are here supposed to be ultimately explicable in terms of the degree of theoretical 'challenge' they respectively had to respond to.

The other claim for which Anderson's essay is well-known is his 'white emigration' thesis. He asserted that the great change that had happened by the middle of the twentieth century was that 'the phalanx of local intellectuals portrayed by Annan has been eclipsed. In this intensely provincial society, foreigners suddenly become omnipresent'.[14] It may be proper and charitable to treat this as a piece of symbolism or as a witty aperçu; as any kind of history, its methodological shortcomings are striking. It is described as 'white' emigration because its informing impulse was supposed to be counter-revolutionary: it was largely made up of intellectuals from Austria and Central Europe who were seeking to escape social upheavals by identifying with a famously stable society. The contrast is with a 'red' emigration, principally represented by German intellectuals, such as the members of the Frankfurt School, or others who remained committed to the *critical* analysis of their host societies (a familiar binary polarity of another kind lurks here). But Anderson does not distinguish between those who were refugees from persecution by the Right rather than upheaval from the Left (nor between Jews and non-Jews), nor does he distinguish the age at which they left their native countries – those who left as young children surely stood in a different relation to the culture of origin compared to those who had already experienced a political and intellectual life there. His account tended to exaggerate the determining power of the native culture, but only when it suited his case: for example, he alleged an 'elective affinity to English modes of thought and political outlook' in those formed by 'the parish-pump positivism of inter-bellum Vienna', an insinuation which may be convenient when discussing, say, Karl Popper, but would be rather less so if discussing, say, Eric Hobsbawm.

Again, one has to recognise that these European *émigrés* do not constitute the missing 'dissident intelligentsia', as casual references to Anderson's essay sometimes appear to assume: they are, rather, presented as the functional equivalents and successors to the traditional, 'hegemonic', intellectual aristocracy. But, tantalisingly, Anderson does not treat English culture as entirely incapable of producing a 'dissident intelligentsia'. In fact, he suggests that there were 'two moments in English cultural history' when it seemed that such a stratum might have 'emerged', the 1890s and the 1930s, but 'both were snapped off before they had time to develop'.

Again, the suggested historical explanation is almost parodically schematic. For example, the 1890s was 'when bohemianism as a significant phenomenon finally arrived in England – sixty years after its advent in Paris'. But the conjunction of such events as Beardsley's death and the outbreak of the Boer War 'dealt ... summarily with this revolt', and 'Mafeking submerged the memory of the nineties'. Even leaving aside the implicit teleology which can find in a few green carnations the first signs of the sprouting of an 'intelligentsia', it is hard not to be struck by the wilful holism which sees in the public reaction to the relief of Mafeking an event which is somehow on the same plane of cultural action as the publication of *The Yellow Book*. In any event, the outcome was again an absence: 'In 1900, the harmony between the hegemonic class and its intellectuals was virtually complete ... There was no separate intelligentsia.'[15] But here we need to probe a little more just what this intelligentsia was supposed to be dissident about or separate from.

'Dissident', as used here, presupposes the existence of a dominant consensus: it is not so easy to say who should be regarded as 'dissident' if one assumes instead that in any complex culture there will be a whole series of cross-cutting conflicts, disagreements, criticisms. In practice, it also assumes that the consensus will, ipso facto, be politically conservative and the 'dissidents' radical, though again this threatens to conflate forms and levels of difference: in Britain in the late 1940s, for example, it was, arguably, figures like Eliot and Oakeshott who saw themselves as opposing a dominant consensus, but they do not thereby become properly 'dissident' in Anderson's terms. It is not just a matter of political or intellectual convictions, however: not having too close a *social* connection with the governing classes also seems to be a minimum requirement. For example, Anderson returned to Annan's essay to observe that 'many of the intellectuals he discusses were based in Cambridge, then dominated by the grey and ponderous figure of Henry Sidgwick (brother-in-law, needless to say, of Prime Minister Balfour)'.

The sneer has a legitimate place in polemic, of course, but perhaps one is not being too priggishly resistant to its playful use by remarking that it is carrying a little too much explanatory weight here. After all, Sidgwick's almost exact contemporary, William Morris, was the son of one of the 250 wealthiest men in England (on Anderson's own much later reckoning),[16] but in his case no one is tempted to read off a lack of dissidence from social position. The well-connected and ever-judicious Sidgwick might seem an obvious candidate for the role of *bête grise*, and there was certainly little danger that his death in 1900 might be seen as the event which prematurely 'snapped off' the beginnings of a 'dissident intelligentsia' in the 1890s. But even so, his part in shaping the structural relation of intellectuals to British society may not be as simple as Anderson's side-swipe suggests. After all, in practice he was the chief moving spirit in setting up the British Academy, which was officially established in 1901, and, although that body has hardly been distinguished by its political or social dissidence, its establishment did mark, symbolically as much as actually, a significant step towards the assertion by an intellectual or scholarly stratum of a certain kind of autonomy for itself.[17] Since much recent French scholarship has tended to regard this as an essential precondition for the development of the self-conscious identity of 'the intellectuals' at the beginning of the twentieth century, Anderson's example here risks rebounding on him.

Throughout, Anderson used the phrase 'English intellectuals' very freely, and Annan's essay was his chief acknowledged source when speaking of the nineteenth and early twentieth centuries. (In passing, one has to remark how *marxisant* commentators in Britain have simply loved that essay, to which they have imputed an explanatory power in the intellectual sphere akin to that which is provided by a conspiracy theory in the political sphere.) But, as Anderson's analysis proceeded, quite what was supposed to be distinctive about the position, or absence, of intellectuals in Britain started to get blurred. For example, he fairly and generously acknowledged Keynes's stature, but in doing so also conceded that even the aberrant social formation of British society could produce 'genuine' intellectuals. Not only was Keynes's 'theoretical system validated practically', but he 'never hesitated to pronounce outside his subject ... He was an intellectual in a classical tradition.'

This is a revealing characterisation, since we seem for the moment to have left behind questions of dissidence and to be focusing instead on precisely what I have identified as the constitutive logic of the intellectual in the cultural sense, in Keynes's case the movement between the development of his 'theoretical system' and the activity of 'pronouncing outside his subject'.[18] Keynes earns further commendation for the fact that he 'never became a fanatical advocate' of his own society, and so he could be endorsed for remaining 'critical', the hallmark of the 'true' intellectual.[19] 'Fanatical' here is, of course, self-defeatingly slack: if not being a 'fanatical advocate' of their society is what constitutes being 'critical', then few English writers or scholars in the twentieth century could be excluded from the ranks of 'true' intellectuals. Nonetheless, Keynes's only failing at this point as a model English intellectual appeared to be that he was, as he famously observed we would all be in the long run, dead.

In 1968 no such disability attended Anderson's other example of a 'genuine' English intellectual, namely F. R. Leavis. Leavis partly earned Anderson's approval because he mounted his criticism of mass society with 'a violent zeal and fury' which 'defi[ed] every convention of the British intelligentsia'. Intellectual decorum was obviously as damning as social connection as far as constituting a true intelligentsia was concerned. But it was two other (alleged) characteristics that led Leavis to be singled out at this point. First, he 'is the only intellectual in this survey to have been significantly affected by Marxism'. And second, 'alone of the thinkers in this survey, he felt acutely aware that something had gone wrong in British culture'. Considered historically, these are extraordinary claims: it is only the circularity of the protective clause 'in this survey' that allows them to be put forward at all, and even then one might want to murmur Laski at the first clause and Tawney at the second. Casting the net more widely, their arbitrariness is at once apparent – to take just one aspect, the number of prominent social critics who, like Leavis, felt that industrialism and 'mass society' were what had 'gone wrong' in British culture was legion.

Still, in these few remarks, we see the germ of much subsequent discussion of Leavis and *Scrutiny* by such New Left-indebted scholars as Mulhern, Eagleton and Baldick, among whom the *Scrutiny* group even came to figure as an English equivalent of the Frankfurt School in its preoccupation with the deadening effects of mass culture; indeed, the major monographic study by Mulhern published in 1979 was to conclude that the Leavisites had constituted precisely the kind of 'radical, dissident intelligentsia' normally taken to be absent in Britain.[20] It is notable that at this point Leavis's lifelong connection with what in other contexts Anderson would stigmatise as one of the 'governing class's elite educational institutions' is not, unlike Sidgwick's, held against him (that connection was, of course, in part a self-consciously antagonistic one, but in practice Leavis well understood the importance of his Cambridge base to his career and his influence). Needless to add, Leavis fell far short of the ideal, above all because, hampered by his supposed 'empiricism', he was unable to develop a sophisticated *theoretical* critique of his own society. But he was at least 'oppositional': 'Leavis correctly sensed a cultural landscape of much mediocrity and conformity'.[21]

In some ways, Anderson's essay has to be seen as a cry of pain: its prose expresses a reaction, at times vengeful, at times despairing, frequently acerbic, to what many of his generation experienced as the stifling normality and coercive empiricism of the 1950s. On those grounds alone, it surely deserved its subsequent celebrity. But I would suggest that with the passage of time it has become clearer that Anderson's chief disability in dealing with this topic was that of being a theorist who overvalues the *historical role* of theories. His conception of 'a culture' is, in practice, framed too exclusively in terms of the Big Names, and the

Big Names are confined too exclusively to those who made some original or striking *conceptual* contribution. It is certainly a virtue of his essay that he is interested in the work of such Big Names across a wide range of disciplines and in their synchronic structural relations as well as their diachronic succession. But his is the makeshift intellectual history that always results from arranging a group of 'classic texts' in a satisfying pattern; the thick texture of intellectual life in any given period, as well as the sheer variety of figures, arguments and issues, are eliminated from the stark geometry of Anderson's 'structure of a culture'. Moreover, his emphasis falls too purely on the *content* of his chosen figures' ideas: we get little or nothing about such figures' roles and styles of performance, about their audiences and modes of address, about the debates they were involved in or the uses to which they were put, about the different levels of abstraction and sophistication at which a 'culture' operates, and so on. In this respect, the essay is premised on a curiously intellectualist mode of explanation. Despite his avowed commitment to sociological analysis, indeed Marxist analysis, Anderson's is in many ways still a Great Man theory of intellectual history.

Paradoxically, perhaps, given its materialist premises, the whole *NLR* frame of reference actually directed *more* attention to intellectuals than did other, ostensibly more 'idealist', styles of discourse. It is surely evident that Anderson himself has always been fascinated with the role of ideas in history, and we might even remark that E. P. Thompson's first major book was on Morris and his last on Blake. The question of how to *be* an intellectual in an unsympathetic cultural setting also exercised writers shaped by Marxist, and sometimes Leninist, theory. And we should recognise, too, that these writers shared a more general aspiration to replace the familiar, everyday language of social description with a more abstracted, estranging vocabulary: such defamiliarising and reclassifying is at the heart of the project of 'critique', and their use of 'intellectuals' was part of this purpose. In mid-twentieth-century England, to speak of 'novelists' or of 'dons' was to rest content with the familiar, concrete terms of everyday social description. The *marxisant* use of 'intellectuals', by contrast, achieved what might be called 'the theory effect', calling up a language of systematic social analysis that reveals the 'objective', functional role of the familiar occupations and activities.

As I have already remarked, the ostensibly comparative frame of reference of the *NLR* analysis actually encouraged a re-statement of the traditional story of British exceptionalism. And at the heart of that story was a contrast with France. Indeed, looking back on his and his *NLR* colleagues' essays of the 1960s more than two decades later, Anderson had to acknowledge that 'tacitly ... British history and society were analysed as exceptional against an unspoken background of what was taken as typical, derived from French experience'.[22] As I have already suggested, this was true not only for what constituted a proper bourgeois democratic revolution, but also for what constituted a properly separate and critical intellectual class. Following the impact of these essays on both Marxist and non-Marxist alike, the whole topic was, perhaps more than ever, defined in terms of a contrast with (an idealised conception of) the French case.[23] It may seem ungracious to say so in the setting of the present volume, but in my view the first step towards a properly historical account requires us to stop thinking of France as the norm and Britain as the exception and to start to see the nature and role of intellectuals in their respective societies as two among many different national patterns across which are to be found a range of overlapping and cross-cutting similarities and contrasts rather than the binary alternatives of either having 'real' intellectuals or being English.

Notes

1 N. Annan, 'The Intellectual Aristocracy', in J. H. Plumb (ed.), *Studies in Social History: A Tribute to G. M. Trevelyan* (London: Longman, 1955), pp. 243–87.
2 Annan, 'Intellectual aristocracy', p. 285.
3 See C. Charle, *Les Elites de la République 1880–1900* (Paris: Fayard, 1987), and *Naissance des 'intellectuels' 1880–1900* (Paris: Minuit, 1990).
4 Annan, 'Intellectual Aristocracy', pp. 248, 253, 281. Russell may have seemed a slightly awkward figure to accommodate to Annan's argument, since he comments: 'Non-conformity is not a middle-class monopoly and his adopted class owes much to his whig independence of mind' (p. 281).
5 Annan, 'Intellectual Aristocracy', p. 244.
6 Annan, 'Intellectual Aristocracy', p. 260.
7 Annan, 'Intellectual Aristocracy', p. 254.
8 Annan, 'Intellectual Aristocracy', p. 265.
9 Annan, 'Intellectual Aristocracy', p. 285. Fourty-four years later, Annan appeared less confident about these continuities. Shortly before his death, he included a highly edited version of this essay in his last book, *The Dons: Mentors, Eccentrics, and Geniuses* (London: HarperCollins, 1999), a version which omitted most of the historical characterisation, but which attempted, selectively, to bring the various family trees up to date (he does not acknowledge the alterations and describes himself, misleadingly, as simply 'reprinting' his original essay). In his new conclusion to the piece he reflects that aristocracies can disappear and that 'in the 1960s some of their children who might have been expected to excel abandoned the goal of a fellowship and with a sigh of relief dropped out …'. 'Whether the names of these families will continue to appear among the holders of fellowships and chairs

[an interesting narrowing of the range of achievement] in the twenty-first century remains an open question' (pp. 340–1).
10 For a list of the major contributions, see Anderson, *English Questions* (London: Verso, 1992), p. 121.
11 P. Anderson, 'Components of the National Culture', *New Left Review*, 50 (1968), 1–57, reprinted in his *English Questions* (London: Verso, 1992), pp. 48–104.
12 Anderson, *English Questions*, pp. 50, 51, 52.
13 Some of which I tried to address, partly with reference to Anderson's essay, in 'Sociology and Idealism in Britain 1880–1920', *Archives Européennes de Sociologie*, 19 (1978), 3–50; for a fuller analysis of the nature of such counterfactual analysis more generally, see G. Hawthorn, *Plausible Worlds: Possibility and Understanding in History and the Social Sciences* (Cambridge: Cambridge University Press, 1991).
14 Anderson, *English Questions*, p. 61.
15 Anderson, *English Questions*, pp. 53, 59, 84.
16 Anderson, *Arguments*, p. 163, citing W. D. Rubinstein, 'The Victorian Middle Classes: Wealth, Occupation, and Geography', *Economic History Review*, 30 (1977).
17 I have explored some of the complexities of Sidgwick's case, in relation to the question of intellectuals in Britain, in 'My Roles and Their Duties: Sidgwick as Philosopher, Professor, and Public Moralist', in R. Harrison (ed.), *Henry Sidgwick* (Oxford: Oxford University Press, 2001), pp. 9–49.
18 For a discussion that makes brief reference to Keynes in these terms, see my 'Eliot Among the Intellectuals', *Essays in Criticism*, 52 (2002), 101–25.
19 Anderson, *English Questions*, p. 80.
20 F. Mulhern, *The Moment of 'Scrutiny'* (London: New Left Books, 1979); see, for developments of this view, T. Eagleton, *Literary Theory: An Introduction* (Oxford: Blackwell, 1983), and C. Baldick, *The Social Mission of English Criticism 1848–1932* (Oxford: Oxford University Press, 1984).
21 Anderson, *English Questions*, pp. 99, 100, 102.
22 Anderson, *English Questions*, p. 6.
23 I have argued this in more general terms in '"Every Fruit-juice Drinker, Nudist, Sandal-wearer ...": Intellectuals as Other People', in H. Small (ed.), *The Public Intellectual* (Oxford: Blackwell, 2002), pp. 203–23.

Part II
An Anglo-French Republic of Letters?

4

The Royal Society and the Académie des sciences in the first half of the eighteenth century

Pascal Brioist

The Royal Society lacks two things that are highly necessary to men: rewards and rules. In Paris, membership of the Academy makes the certain fortune of a geometer or a chemist; in London, on the contrary, it costs to join the Royal Society. In England, anyone who says that he loves the arts and wishes to be a member can join the Society right away. In France, to be a member and pensioner of the Académie, it is not enough to be an amateur; one must be a scholar oneself, and strive for a place against competitors who are all the more formidable in that they are motivated by glory, by self-interest, by the challenge itself, and by that inflexibility of mind given by stubborn study of the numerical sciences.[1]

For the traveller Voltaire, a man of two cultures, comparison between the Royal Society and the Académie des sciences was imposed by very reason of the contrast between the two institutions. It was equally imposed by the fact that throughout the eighteenth century, despite periods of latent or open warfare between France and England (1702–13, 1742–63), the two countries constantly observed each other and borrowed fashions and discoveries, with the scholars of the Enlightenment sharing an ideology of Europe of the mind.

In fact, the destinies of the Royal Society and the Académie had been partly linked since their origins. The Royal Society had been founded in 1662 under the reign of Charles II, while in 1666 Colbert and Louis XIV decided to form the Académie des sciences. From the very start, the meeting of scholars, laymen, extensive correspondence and circulation of books bound the two institutions.

A sociological analysis of the first half of the eighteenth century would give Voltaire's description of these two scientific societies further precision. This period in which French science was shaped, despite some initial resistance, by the ideas of Newton and the adoption of a more refined instrumentation, was also that in which French forms of anatomy, entomology and probability theory were adopted in England. As relations between the Académie and the Royal Society seem to have had some connection with these phenomena, it may be pertinent to proceed to try and identify the means, institutional or otherwise, by which knowledge circulated between the two shores of the Channel. Such an analysis can lead to questioning the practices and the intellectual developments of exchange.

Structural comparison of the two institutions

The first notable difference between the Académie des sciences and the Royal Society bears on the number of members respectively affiliated. On the French side, the average annual membership was 153, divided between pensioners, associates and corresponding members. On the English side, there were 325 Fellows of the Royal Society (FRS), to which an average of 100 foreign Fellows should be added.

This is a proportion of almost one to three. In actual fact, on one side it was a prince, the King of France, who pensioned the greatest intellectuals of his time as a means of constructing his own glory and ensuring the expertise of knowledge in his kingdom; on the other there was a club of scientific amateurs, supplemented by few professionals, who recruited among their own ranks – with the King's approval – and operated by way of subscriptions that they paid.

The French and English societies proved to be diametrically opposed. Not only did the Royal Society accept men of letters as well as scientists, but it opened its doors to foreign correspondents. The broad lines of numerical development makes this still clearer, showing contrasts that express two different traditions. Whereas the Académie tended to remain beneath the limit of 150 (if with a certain variation: 138 members in 1699, 105 in 1720, 115 in 1730, and 125 from 1740 on), the Royal Society for its part experienced a continuous growth: from 131 Fellows in 1700, to 325 in 1750, and 531 by 1800. The limited membership of the Parisian body was enforced by control of the state that financed it, and by the availability of scholars, whereas the English dynamism derived from the enthusiasm for science among the British population as well as the need to increase contributions. The secretaries did their work so well that average income passed from £95 in 1700 to £978 in 1760.[2]

Comparison of the sociology of recruitment between the Royal Society and the Académie des sciences permits a further refinement of this analysis. Who were the experts that France, already well advanced in the process of bureaucratisation, dubbed with the title of academician? And who were the amateurs and virtuosi who rubbed shoulders in London's Royal Society?

It should be borne in mind that on one side of the Channel the King appointed academicians on the Académie's proposal (according to scientific criteria), while on the other side it was the Fellows of the Royal Society who admitted new members. This was not devoid of consequences.

Given the efforts of the French monarchy, which wanted its Académie to be at one and the same time a place for discussion, and for the accumulation and validation of scientific and technical knowledge, the academicians were selected essentially among the Third Estate of 'talents' (58 per cent in 1750), though the nobility and clergy were also represented (respectively 27 per cent and 15 per cent). The academicians were for the greater part medical doctors, professors or scientists. At the start of the eighteenth century doctors were by far the largest category (44 per cent), with professors making scarcely one third, and only 12 per cent being scientists by profession. In terms of education, a large number of these specialists had graduated from the University of Paris or that of Montpellier. By 1750, the balance had changed: doctors and professors each made up around 30 per cent , while scientists and military officers had gained slightly more representation, at 16 per cent and 9 per cent respectively (see Figure 4.1).[3]

The Royal Society of 1750 was no longer simply the club of gentlemen amateurs that it resembled in the seventeenth century, but for all that it still did not follow the French model. Indeed, the aristocracy and gentry still provided 40 per cent of the Fellows. Professors and clergy were each around 16 per cent , crown officials and military men some 10 per cent , the medical profession 25 per cent and lawyers 5 per cent. The Royal Society was above all else a society of notables, even if the course of time showed an increasing opening to professionals such as surgeons,

Figure 4.1 Professions of the members of the Académie des sciences in 1750

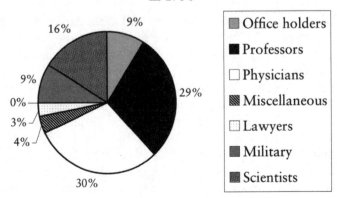

Table 4.1 Structure of the two institutions

Royal Society		Académie des sciences
Elected Presidents Isaac Newton (1704–27) Hans Sloane (1727–41) Martin Folkes (1741–)		*Nominated Presidents and Vice-Presidents* They change every year. One can pay special attention to the recurrent names of Bignon, Louvois, Gallois, Fontenelle, La Hire, Réaumur, Mairan, etc.
Secretaries 1 Richard Waller (1687–1709) John Harris (1709–10) Richard Waller (1710–14) Brook Taylor (1714–18) John Machin (1718–47)	*Secretaries 2* Hans Sloane (1693–1713) Edmond Halley (1713–21) James Jurin (1721–27) William Rutty (1727–28) Cromwell Mortimer (1728–30)	Secretaries Fontenelle (1666–1740) Dortous de Mairan (1740–43) Grandjean de Fouchy (1744–76) FRS N.B: Secretaries play a very important role, since they are also the publishers of the *Mémoires*
Treasurers The secretaries		*Treasurers* Couplet (1696–1717) Couplet de Tartreaux (1717–43) M. de Buffon (1744–88) FRS
Publishers of the Philosophical Transactions: Sloane (1695–1713) Halley (1714–19) Jurin (1720–27)		*Publishers of the* Mémoires: Fontenelle (1666–1740) Dortous de Mairan (1740–43) Grandjean de Fouchy (1744–76) FRS

apothecaries, instrument manufacturers and grammar-school teachers.[4] Furthermore, one of the most constant problems of the Society derived from the deficient talent of its members and the lack of commitment that many of them had to any scientific project.

It is hard to make exact comparisons, given that the sources (the biographical index of the Académie and the Chronological Index of the FRS) do not use the same categories, yet the distinction that Voltaire emphasised between expert scholars on the one hand, and notable amateurs on the other, comes through clearly enough. One should perhaps be equally aware of the almost equal importance of the medical profession in the two countries, which explains interests that are sometimes quite similar. The issue of hierarchy is a further way of approaching the problem.

A major characteristic of the Académie des sciences was its very marked hierarchical character, so well described in the regulations of 1699. There was indeed no equality among the members. As a society of scholars, the Académie was headed by twenty pensioners who each received 30,000 livres per year. In each of the fields of geometry, astronomy, mechanics, anatomy, chemistry and botany, three major names were retained. These names did indeed correspond to those remembered in the annals of science, in which no pensioner has remained anonymous. The associates – who, like the pensioners, lived in Paris – did not receive money, and were in theory 24 in number, joined by 12 honorary members, who were political figures rather than scholars. At the bottom of the hierarchy were the 50 or so free associates and corresponding members, who had the privilege of corresponding with the Académie and were allowed to attend its sessions. These corresponding members included foreigners, with at most 15 Englishmen in their ranks (6 per cent) between 1699 and 1750. The 50 other foreigners during the period were mainly Dutch, Italian German and Spanish or Portuguese.

In the Royal Society, on the other hand, the French academicians were far more numerous, with 95 of them being listed on the membership roll between the same dates. The dissymmetry here is particularly marked.

If we turn now to consider the operation of the two institutions, the picture grows less clear. Both societies were in fact coordinated by officials – presidents, secretaries and treasurers, and appointed in their ranks councils or committees to establish rules for regular meetings and maintain the privileged link with the monarchy. To understand the differences and similarities, it is useful to observe these institutional roles somewhat more closely, in which Table 4.1 will be of assistance.

The structures, then, appear similar as a whole, which is readily explainable if one recalls that both academies had common origins; but differences in their relationship to the monarchy explain the striking gaps between notions of the function of secretaries and presidents, for example. In the French case, in which the King financed the Académie, the officers were nominated to serve as cogs in a central administration, whereas in the English case, the officers were elected and their task was to advance the common work. The English King, from Charles II onwards, did nothing more than bring to the work of these gentlemen-scholars the support of his title. These divergences did not make for any obstacle to exchanges between the two bodies on either side of the Channel, but given the points made about their organisation what precisely were the forms of this exchange?

The forms of exchange

Three major modes of exchange can be distinguished: exchange by way of men; exchange by way of books; and exchange by correspondence.[5] The first channel of circulation of ideas between the English and French societies was clearly that constituted by travellers who could boast of having one foot in each of the institutions, and it is necessary therefore to examine the case of those *académiciens* who became Fellows of the Royal Society, and of Fellows who became foreign correspondents of the Académie des sciences. Between 1662 and 1800, Frenchmen made up some 5 per cent of members of the Royal Society, the total proportion of foreigners being 16 per cent.

The Royal Society was happy to accept foreigners in its ranks, with a dozen new members being received each year. These latter included travellers, members of the diplomatic corps (an embassy doctor, for example, Etienne François Geoffroy, a friend of Sir Hans Sloane), as well as religious exiles such as Jean Théophile Désaguliers and Abraham De Moivre, or even 'political' exiles such as Voltaire.

If, however, in the seventeenth century, membership of the Society had been little more than a formality for a gentleman or scholar visiting England, by the eighteenth century he would have to have given proof of his scientific credentials, and from 1730 be sponsored by three established Fellows. These would sign a certificate indicating his title, profession, name and qualifications. Buffon, for example, in 1739, before he even launched himself on his second career in natural history, obtained an attestation of his 'eminence in matter of knowledge and of mathematics'.

The selection criteria, however, were not always perfectly clear. Thus, when Diderot wished to rejoin the ranks of the London body in 1752, equipped with a letter of recommendation from such prestigious friends as Buffon, La Condamine, d'Alembert, Cassini de Thury, Jussieu, Needham, Warsley and Parsons, the vote went against him by a large margin. He was apprised that 'the Society [was] not yet acquainted with his merits'.[6] This was a very severe judgement on someone who was known as the editor of the great *Encyclopédie*. Other reasons for his exclusion undoubtedly came into play. Diderot had the reputation of an enemy of Church and State. Certainly, it was not because he was seen more as a literary man than as a scientist that Diderot was refused entry to the Royal Society, since both Voltaire and Montesquieu had been elected without difficulty in 1744, precisely on the basis of their reputation as Enlightenment men of letters. Diderot's atheism was not acceptable because orthodox Anglicans were deeply concerned about it.[7] In other words, Catholicism, deism (Voltaire's position) or even animism

The Royal Society and the Académie des sciences

was authorised in a Latitudinarian context, but unbelief remained scandalous (as much as Socinianism, Newton's hidden beliefs).

We need only consider the field of mathematics to show how selection, even if biased, was not too misguided, judging from the names of eleven Frenchmen honoured with the title of Fellow before 1750 for work in this field:

- Abraham De Moivre, elected 1697, recommended to Newton by the Earl of Devonshire and known to Thomas Halley, initially writing on the method of fluxions, investigated after 1708 the 'doctrine of chances' and hence the question of probabilities.
- Pierre Rémond de Montmor, elected 1715, great specialist in probability theory and combinatory analysis.
- Pierre Varignon, elected 1718, one of the first to have the intuition of the usefulness of integral calculus in mechanics.
- Pierre Louis Moreau de Maupertuis, elected 1728, champion in France of Newton's ideas on the shape of the earth, who measured this in Lapland.
- Joseph Privat de Molières, elected 1729, who defended Descartes against all comers. Privat de Molières, who taught at the Collège Royal, had been elected because he knew Newton's writings very well and had used its mathematical techniques to explore Descartes's and Malebranches's vortex theories.[8]
- Louis Bertrand Castel, elected 1730, Cartesian specialist in integral calculus.
- Alexis Louis Clairaut, elected 1737, mathematician working on curves of dual curvature, on integral calculus, and translator of Newton together with Mme du Châtelet.
- Georges Louis Leclerc, Comte de Buffon, elected 1739, discoverer of the binomial theorem and a talented probability theorist.
- Charles Marie De la Condamine, elected 1748, measurer of the earth in Peru.
- Jean Le Rond d'Alembert, elected 1748, founder of modern dynamics and the theory of limits, and renowned encyclopedist.
- Pierre Bouger, elected 1750, member of the expedition to Peru, an astronomer who invented photometry, as well as theorist of architecture and naval construction.

(We should also mention here Daniel Bernouilli, elected 1750, of Swiss nationality, but ten times winner of the prize of the Académie des sciences, and very influential intellectually in the Académie at this time.)

Acceptance of corresponding members of the Académie des sciences was governed by strict criteria, if only because the number of foreign correspondents authorised was very limited. The first 'Règlements pour les correspondants de par le Roy' were published only in 1753. Registers of the Académie's sessions bear the mark of royal preoccupations in this respect:

> His Majesty, being informed that in the regulations provided for the *académie Royale des Sciences*, there was nothing explaining the provision for correspondents who nevertheless contribute a good deal by their observations made in different parts of the World to the progress of the sciences, this being the object of the Académie, has judged that the more that distinctions accorded these up to now bring them close to the *académiciens*, the more it is necessary to regulate the form of their nomination and to make explicit what should be required of those who present themselves to obtain this title; and as a consequence His Majesty has resolved the present regulation that he decrees is to be exactly observed.

To say here that the Royal Society tended to rarefy its French recruitment would be an understatement. In fact, leaving aside the President of the Royal Society, who was considered a member of the Académie des sciences by right, the list of foreign correspondents of the Académie Royale from 1699 to 1748, as given in the periodical *La Connaissance des Temps*, contains only 51 individuals, of whom just 2 were English: M. Cheselden, surgeon of the London Royal Society, corresponding from 27 July 1729 with M. Morand; and M. Cromwell Mortimer, doctor of medicine, corresponding from 20 November 1734 with M. de Fouchy. Cheselden was a great anatomist and surgeon, who published in 1723 a work on the surgical removal of stones (vesical calculi), and it was his achievements in this field that made him known in Paris and in Europe for his discoveries in ophthalmology. Mortimer was also a doctor, friend of Sir Hans Sloane, thanks to whom he became an FRS. Both Cheselden and Mortimer occupied strategic positions in London society.

If we continue until 1754, we can add to these two names those of Abraham De Moivre, a Huguenot established in England since 1688. Moivre's case is particularly interesting in so far as this individual was equally at home in both French and English culture. In the late 1680s he obtained Newton's *Principia* and studied it in detail, becoming one of the first French specialists in Newton's thought; after his election to the Royal Society in 1697, at the suggestion of Comte Francis Robartes, he studied Montmor's texts on probabilities and spread this knowledge among his contemporaries in the *Philosophical Transactions*, then in a work title *Doctrine des Chances*. Given the interest in mathematical sciences in the mid-eighteenth century, he was an ideal correspondent.

The second mode of communication between the two societies was by way of books. This especially meant books that had not been translated.

The problem of language was now raised in a way that it had not been when Latin was still the common language of scholarship, as it had been in the seventeenth century. Translators were thus needed, and sometimes even commentators and popularisers. Emilie du Châtelet, the friend of Voltaire, and likewise Maupertuis and Clairaut, Fellows of the Royal Society, all played an important role in the French translation of Newton's *Principia*, which appeared in 1749. Père Côtes, translator of Newton's *Optics*, should also be mentioned here.[9] Translations appearing in the *Mémoires* of the Académie were often the work of clergymen, as with Ditton's work on tangential curves in 1705, or the works on the calculus of fluxions and on gravitation published in 1740 and 1745 thanks to the work of Père Pèzenas. Curiosity was fired by what was happening in England.

The *Philosophical Transactions* – the official periodical of the Royal Society – were regularly received in Paris, not just by the Académie but also by private individuals. Some issues were bound with a very useful French summary composed in 1739 by a certain M. de Brémont. Chancellor d'Aguesseau possessed a copy of that volume, which is today in the Bibliothèque du Muséum.[10] This circulation, however, was by no means one way; Huguenots such as Désaguliers and De Moivre, as well as Cambridge professors such as the Rev John Colson, all being involved, for instance, in the task of translating into English mathematical works such as those of Mariotte, Montmor or Clairaut.

The periodicals of the respective societies were undoubtedly a major place for the circulation of information between the two countries. The ideas of the neighbouring country were developed there in the local language. The difference between the *Philosophical Transactions* and the *Mémoires et Histoires* lay in that the English tended to translate more, but only articles from the *Mémoires*, whereas the French – and we should

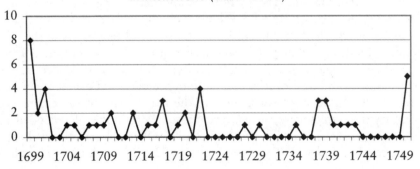

Figure 4.2 Articles published by French authors in the *Philosophical Transactions* (1699–1750)

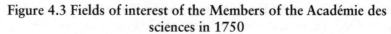

Figure 4.3 Fields of interest of the Members of the Académie des sciences in 1750

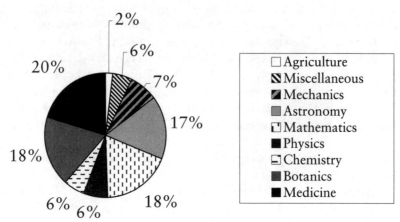

recall that the Académie was a society of experts – translated only rarely but discussed much more. They preferred to reserve their pages for the sacrosanct thought of the pensioners.

It is possible to follow French articles from 1700 to 1750 in the *Philosophical Transactions* (see Figure 4.2). The rhythm was fairly steady in the first quarter of the century, and in the second quarter it was only the years 1739–43 that showed a significant upturn. Curiously, neither the dips nor the gaps in the curve are explained by periods of war, science acting as if politics was foreign to it.

The list of subjects tackled (see Figure 4.3) provides an inventory of intellectual fashions, from anatomy at the start of the century to electricity in the middle years. The French were especially translated for their articles in medicine, anatomy and surgery (32 per cent of 51 articles), followed by around 10 per cent each for the categories of botany, physics, mathematics and technical subjects.

The bridge that the *Transactions* established between the Académie des sciences and the Royal Society followed, in fact, in the tracks of a more or less deliberately cultivated correspondence between the two bodies, read out publicly in Crane Court in London (where the Society stood). In the seventeenth century, when Oldenburg was secretary, a substantial and quasi-official correspondence was established, thanks to his goodwill and hard work, but by the early years of the eighteenth century the results were more uneven, since everything still depended on the goodwill of secretaries. Until 1713, under Hans Sloane, the exchange was rich, but under Halley, from 1713 to 1721, the work was so botched

Figure 4.4 Themes of the French articles in *Philosophical Transactions* from 1700 to 1750

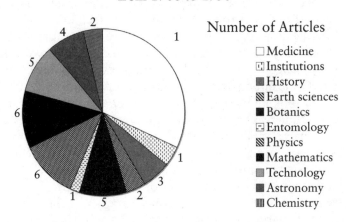

that it is hardly possible to keep track of the texts; James Jurin's filling of the post, from 1721 to 1727, proved an ephemeral renaissance, as he carefully built up a network of English correspondents living abroad which did not last. His contact in France was an oculist named Thomas Woodhouse, who practised in Paris and kept him informed of what was happening in the French capital.[11]

It is less easy to mark the English influence in the *Mémoires* of the Académie, and though this is sometimes explicit, as when M. De l'Isle discussed 'Observations on the variation of the needle with reference to M. Halley's map', it has in other cases to be divined implicitly, as in the efforts to measure the earth.

While the work of English scientists was well-known in the Paris Académie, the only forum in which these scholars were allowed to express themselves directly was in the Prizes for which they were authorised to compete (McLaurin received the prize for mathematical sciences in 1724 and again in 1740). In the same way, when English astronomic instruments were presented to the King, as in 1734, this was by a French philosopher, M. Godin. We may ask today what the results of these practices were, what exactly passed from France to England and from England to France in this period. What affinities between the two scholarly bodies took shape on either side of the Channel?

The attempt at an exhaustive exploration would certainly be in vain and, as the field has already been well covered, we must content ourselves here with simply recalling certain elements that may enable a different debate to be started.

The issues involved in exchange

In the first place, the Royal Society and the Académie des sciences were both conceived as places of verification of true fact and theory, and for the storing of knowledge in pursuit of utility, in the pure tradition of Bacon. The work of doctors and natural scientists of the two countries, as well as exchange between these, illustrates very well this kind of attitude, when they examined triple bladders or infants born without brains (Buissière), or took an interest in the effects of scurvy in Paris or plague in Marseille (Didier). The question of utility was not always posed in the same terms in France as in England, where entrepreneurs lobbied the Royal Society to promote their projects; in France, the Académie served the King to control manufacture and industrial progress.

The second issue in the circulation of texts and individuals between the Académie des sciences and the Royal Society was the diffusion and reception of Newton's work in France.[12] Newton had been made a foreign associate of the Académie as early as 1699, but the acceptance of his ideas was a slow process. His *Principia*, in fact, published in 1687, questioned such Cartesian principles as the doctrine of vortices, championed by the old guard (Fontenelle, Rohault, Régis, Saurin and Villemot). The Académie, disturbed by the new ideas, launched a study of tides (1701–14) in order to check the veracity of Newton's predictions. In 1713, Père Côtes translated the *Principia* into French, on the basis of a presentation edition that was in the hands of Jacques Cassini, its preface questioning the Cartesians. The debate took life. From 1718 to 1728, the Cassinis' measuring programme sought to decide the shape of the earth in favour of a Cartesian response if at all possible. The measures in question proved debatable, and Désaguliers criticised these severely in the *Philosophical Transactions*, suggesting that they could be amended by measurements made at the equator and the poles.

During this time, debate continued on all aspects of the thought of the English scientist – gravity, the pendulum, the precession of comets, chemistry and optics, with those *académiciens* who were also Fellows of the Royal Society making a particularly active contribution (Mairan, Privat de Molières). In 1728, Maupertuis, who was one of them, arrived in London and deepened his knowledge of Newton by his visits with Clarke, Désaguliers, Pemberton, McLaurin and De Moivre. In 1732, Maupertuis explained Newton's ideas in a *Discours sur les figures des astres*, and entered into correspondence with Voltaire, an enthusiastic populariser. In 1733, Maupertuis, Godin and De la Condamine proposed that the Académie should proceed to new measurements of the shape of the earth, and it was eventually agreed to launch expeditions to Peru and Lapland. Maupertuis and Clairaut themselves left for Sweden in 1734, together with Celsius, and here again the link with the Royal Society was important, as the secret weapon of the Newtonians against the Cassini clan was the precision instruments they had bought in London.

In the late 1730s, after these experiments had proved fruitful, evidence accumulated for the superiority of the Newtonian explanation of the world over that of Descartes. Yet, even if Descartes's champions sometimes grew critical of their master (Cassini de Thury accepted the elongation of the globe in 1740), Condorcet could subsequently write that 'when the *Eléments de la Philosophie de Newton* (translated by the Marquise du Châtelet) appeared, Cartesianism still had the upper hand, even in the Académie des sciences'. It was not easy to challenge the authority of tradition that the Académie accepted. Nonetheless, the Anglo-French link continued to play a major role in the development at work.

A final common point made possible a rapprochement between the Royal Society and the Académie des sciences. Both were obliged to take account of the fact that science had become an entertainment, and both depended on fashion. In France, the entertainment was first of all designed for the King, but was extended to the salons; in England, as Larry Stewart has magisterially demonstrated, the public was considerably wider and extended to the entire city in a space that included taverns, fairs, and even parks and bridges. (Here a figure such as Désaguliers, one of those Royal Society members of French origin, is central.)[13]

There was also a circulation of fashion between France and England. That for anatomical research, botany and entomology came from France in the early years of the century, while the fashion for electricity in the late 1730s, which we shall take as an example here, came from England. Static electricity and the experiments that could be done with it provided, in fact, the occasion for entertainments using an amusing branch of physics that were enjoyed by the public in the salons and taverns alike.[14] In England, it was once more Desaguliers, experimenter with the Royal Society, who had made electrical attraction into a sure source of income. In France, the fashion took hold slightly later, after 1740, but Abbé Nolet supplied it with letters of nobility by conducting his demonstrations in the Paris salons. The two-way exchange of information between the two countries on the results of electrical experiments shows the extent of the enthusiasm that the new science aroused. In 1750, this traffic flowed from France to England, when a letter concerning certain electrical phenomena from Abbé Nolet to the Duke of Richmond, FRS, was translated in the *Philosophical Transactions*. The Académie des sciences had to show to its sister institution that it had learned from the previous decades.

The first half of the eighteenth century thus appears as an important moment for interaction between the English and French scientific bodies.

During this period, the Académie des sciences acclimatised an English science that had become dominant at the end of the seventeenth century thanks to the dual paradigm of Bacon and Newton. The Anglophilia of a section of French society was fuelled by this movement, impelled by individual translators and by the circulation of texts that even the conditions of war seemed unable to prevent. The existence of a Huguenot community in England, to which Désauliers (for example) belonged, seems to have favoured contacts. But the mechanism of Franco-English intellectual exchange in this period did not operate simply as a diffusion of English science to France. While Newton's ideas, for example, were indeed 'verified' by the expeditions to Lapland and Peru, they also underwent a considerable development in the hands of certain French academicians. D'Alembert and Maupertuis, for example, sought to create a mechanics that was no longer graphic and vectorial, as that of the English master, but rather algebraic. This extended the generality of Newton's theory, for if Newton's mechanics were applicable only to solid objects, it became possible, thanks to the efforts of the French scientists, to work on the behaviour of fluids (fluid dynamics). Similar phenomena are observable, for example, in the field of research into electricity. The contrast between the Académie des sciences and the Royal Society that Voltaire emphasised thus finally proved fruitful.

Notes

1 Voltaire, 'On the Royal Society and other Academies', Letter 24 of *Letters Concerning the English Nation* (London: Peter Davies, 1926).
2 R. Sorrenson, 'Towards a History of the Royal Society in the Eighteenth Century', *Notes and Records of the Royal Society of London*, 50 (1996), 29–46, as well as R. K. Bluhm, 'Remarks on the Royal Society's Finances, 1700–1768', *Notes and Records of the Royal Society of London*, 13 (1958), 82–103.
3 On the sociology of the Académie des sciences, see also D. J. Sturdy, *Science and Social Status: The Members of the Académie des Sciences 1666–1750* (Woodbridge, Rochester: Boydell Press, 1995).
4 For a more detailed study of this development, see Michael Hunter, *Establishing the New Science: the Experience of the Early Royal Society* (Wolfeboro: Boydell Press, 1992); Sir Henry Lyons, *The Royal Society, 1660–1940* (Cambridge: Cambridge University Press, 1944), and R. Sorrenson, 'Towards a History of the Royal Society in the Eighteenth Century', 29–46.
5 It is not my concern here to analyse anthropologically the interactions between scholars, or to study the values or the behaviours of the Republic of Letters. On this subject, see D. Goodman, *The Republic of Letters, a Cultural History of the French Enlightenment* (Ithaca: Cornell University Press, 1994), and A. Goldgar, *Impolite Learning, Conduct and Community*

in the Republic of Letters, 1680–1750 (New Haven: Yale University Press, 1995).

6 G. Lamoine, 'L'Europe de l'Esprit ou la Royal Society de Londres', *Dix-Huitième Siècle*, 25 (1993), 153–98.

7 On Diderot's non-election to the Royal Society, see Marian Hobson's unpublished paper 'Pass the Parcel: the 1730s and 40s, Between Mathematics and Atheism, Between England and France', presented at the Franco-British colloquium 'French and British Intellectuals: Comparisons and Transfers', 2 March 2001, and D. Diderot, *Lettres sur les aveugles, Lettres sur les sourds et muets: à l'usage de ceux qui entendent et qui parlent*, ed. M. Hobson and S. Harvey (Paris: Garnier Flammarion, 2000).

8 See Joseph Privat de Molières's *Leçons de mathématiques à l'usage de ceux qui voient* (Paris: C.-L. Tiboust, 1725), and his *Leçons de physique* (Paris: Brocas, 1736).

9 Newton, *Optice*, trans. by Père Côtes, who published it first in Amsterdam in 1720, then in Paris in 1722: *Traité d'optique sur les réflexios, réfractions, inflexions et les couleurs de la lumière* (Amsterdam: P. Humbert, 1720 and Paris: Monalant, 1722).

10 Cf. *Table des mémoires imprimés dans les transactions philosophiques de la Société Royale de Londres 1665–1735, rangé par ordre chronologique, par ordre de matières et par noms d'auteurs par M. de Bremond, à Paris chez Piget, quai des Augustins*, work bearing the coat of arms of Henry François d'Aguesseau and including an epistle to Maurepas.

11 For the source here, see J. Jurin, *The Correspondence of James Jurin (1684–1750), Physician and Secretary to the Royal Society*, ed. Andrea Rusnock (Amsterdam and Atlanta: Rodopi, 1996). For a commentary on Jurin's network, see A. Rusnock, 'Correspondence Networks and the Royal Society, 1700–1750', *British Journal for the History of Science*, 32 (1999), 155–69.

12 P. Brunet, *L'Introduction des théories de Newton en France au XVIIIe siècle* (Genève: Slatkine, 1970); I. B. Cohen, 'Isaac Newton, Hans Sloane and the Académie Royale des Sciences', in I. B. Cohen and René Taton (eds), *Mélanges Alexandre Koyré*, vol. 1, *L'Aventure de la science* (Paris: Hermann, 1964); Rob Iliffe, 'Ce que Newton connut sans sortir de chez lui: la forme de la terre dans les années 1730', *Histoire et Mesure*, 8:3/4 (1993), 335–86.

13 L. Stewart, *The Rise of Public Science* (Cambridge: Cambridge University Press, 1992), and 'Other Centres of Calculation, or, Where the Royal Society Didn't Count: Commerce, Coffee-houses and Natural Philosophy in Early Modern London', *British Journal for the History of Science*, 32 (1999), 133–53.

14 J. L. Heilbron, *Electricity in the 17th and 18th Centuries: A Study of Early Modern Physics*, (Berkeley: University of California Press, 1979).

5

The English in Paris

Daniel Roche

In the perspective of a comparative study of English and French intellectuals that takes into account the social, cultural and intellectual dimensions, along with the various modalities of exchange, acculturation and transfer, it is important to emphasise the general conditions and means of a relationship whose results and objectives lie at the heart of the entire controversy concerning the functions of travel and travel writing. Already in the eighteenth century, the connection between these was an object of debate, with sentiments of Francophilia and Francophobia, Anglophilia and Anglophobia, symmetrically displaying the facilities and difficulties of very ancient relationships, and providing the opportunity to express either a rapprochement or a rejection – the interruption of a French air played in English style or an English song interpreted in French. This problem has been tackled by various historical traditions on both sides of the Channel, but perhaps in ways that bias a sociocultural approach and interpretation.

The history of the international relations between the two peoples, in its diplomatic, political and economic aspects, reveals – beyond wars, treaties and commercial struggles – a long alternation of crises and periods of accommodation. From the late seventeenth century to the Revolution, neither rivalry and conflict, nor a cooling of admiration, led to an absence of English visitors from France or French visitors from England. If the spectre of Charles I found a certain resonance for some commentators on French politics, the English had nothing equivalent yet in French tradition. As Paul Mantoux has shown, technological transfer and exchange were constant throughout this period: the Free Trade Treaty of 1786, however, was especially important, providing a more active model for three kinds of relationship.[1] Despite conflicts such as the Seven Years War (1755–63) and the American war (1778–83), there was never a breakdown in continuity, a definitive reduction in activity, while the outbreak of peace brought with it a renewed curiosity. After 1783, the push of Anglomania was strong, and corresponded to a Francophile upsurge on the English side. Of this steady relationship, however, we see only the superficial froth, without giving due weight to the variety of social levels, and to the various rhythms at which individuals in transit or actually established abroad participated differentially in cultural transfers.

The literary tradition of travel accounts tells a different story of Anglo-French mobility. On the English side, these accounts show the birth of a pre-tourism, developed since the Renaissance with the Grand Tour. French mobility, by comparison, was less systematically monitored. The education of an English *gentleman* required a visit to Paris, but the reverse was not so essential for the *gentilhomme*. Though France was not necessarily the centre of the English gentleman's apprenticeship, it remained a staging post to the continent as a whole. His French counterpart, by contrast, generally preferred to turn his steps to the south. Finally, this unequal exchange seems to have been brought into balance by the late eighteenth century.[2] Three questions must be raised, however, concerning the relations between the literary tradition of travel accounts between England and France, and actual Anglo-French mobility.

First of all, accounts of journeys and journeys actually made are too readily equated. Some descriptions were published, but many remained in archives. Second, though cultural exchange was constructed by travel, this was only one element in a wider complex, in which mobility was inspired by various motivations and subjected to different constraints, as well as authorising countless liberties. Finally, historians too hastily identify the results of travellers' observations conveyed in the formal structure of their accounts with the reality of exchanges and contacts. Acculturation between nations assumes complex configurations, and throughout modern times evidence of it has been debated. The discussion as to the 'utility of travel' shows its difficulties. We may add that the documentary and literary use of travel accounts does not always fulfil the triple comparison that is needed: analysis of a text that is both informative and deeply subjective, cultural as well as individual; analysis of a type of discourse with its conventions, objectives and modes of writing, its models and formulae, constants and breaks; finally, analysis of a network of practices articulated to the objectives of the account itself, as evidence of a social order of multiple communication and information. In this ensemble, the intellectual dimension is only one element, and cannot be divorced from other relationships – of family and kin, patron and client, society and the fashionable world – which are conflicting or harmonious depending on moral or material imperatives.[3]

Historians of ideas have used travel accounts to document philosophical exchanges in the tradition pioneered by Voltaire and Montesquieu,

Locke and the Scottish luminaries. They have neglected the intellectual economy of exchange and its costs, a study of the balance of 'Who gets what in return for what?' Three investigative threads should be held together: that of the social and material conditions of exchange compared with the results acquired, whose utility might vary in time and space; that of the imbrication of intellectual and material culture, and the fact that sensitivity towards things is as decisive as towards ideas, each transfer depending on constraining conditions that are accepted or criticised; and finally, that of the specific role of Paris in the Anglo-French relationship as in other exchanges.[4]

Paris, as capital of the absolute and administrative monarchy, and London, centre of the 'balanced' monarchy, presented themselves to both travellers and non-travellers as the theatre of a major rivalry: John Bull against the effeminate courtier, unserious and submissive. The spectacle was an attractive one, as it enjoyed an old reputation going back to Locke, and the tradition of Parisian *Guides de voyage* offered to all and sundry the keys for access to it and the justifications of its especially strong attraction.[5] Moreover, the rise of Parisian Anglomania profited from the stir it made in London and from relationships formed on either side of the Channel. A long-established publicity effect attracted people to the French capital,[6] which benefited from a striking literary tradition with Goldsmith, Sterne, Smollett and other travellers carrying on to Italy, as much as from the utilitarian and informative spirit illustrated by *Guides de voyage* such as that of Nugent or Dutens's *L'Itinéraire*, which went through six editions before 1789. If some works were published specifically for the English, they should be situated in the general movement and development of this genre. Between the two nations, therefore, there prevailed a spirit of comparison and fascination, of rejection and mistrust, in which one may be sure of English particularity in relation to Paris. Louis-Sébastien Mercier expresses this in chapter 61 of his *Tableau de Paris*: 'Paris reigns in Switzerland, Italy and Holland... but the country which serves as the best guarantee of French customs and has set its force and glory to resist it and oppose all its ideas is England.' We shall seek to explore this antagonism on two levels, by measuring the importance of the English in the French capital, their components and settlement, and by analysing the different sociabilities that organised this presence: travel, society and its rules.

The English of Paris

In seeking to investigate the size of a foreign population, other sources than travellers' accounts have to be found. This is simply a particular aspect of the general problem of floating populations in the study of urban demography. Paris at this time had no census of its foreign inhabitants – either actual or legally integrated Parisians – and offers scant resources for this before the Revolution, which established modern passports that can be used from then on. The revolutionary moment marked a major break in the definition of 'paper identities' (to use Gérard Noiriel's phrase) and in the need for a more precise identification of newcomers, affecting English among other foreigners. Police information had a dual origin, the surveillance of migrants staying in boarding-houses and hotels, and the surveillance of foreigners effected by agents of the *lieutenant de police*, and verified by the ministry of foreign affairs in *le travail du Vendredi*, at meetings attended by the interested authorities.[7] Both operations were inspired by the same desire, to assure the safety of Paris from dangerous professions or milieus productive of crime, but there was also the aim of keeping watch on dangerous religious or philosophical opinions – Protestants being a target of first importance, and intellectuals interesting the commissioners for both their ideas and their manners. Politics, the King, religion, God, and manners with their economic and moral implications, had top priority in police motivations as well as in those of the censorship authorities.

Information on the English population in France was collected in a number of different nets: diplomatic concerns, fiscal claims, distrust of political adventurers (the presence of supporters of the Stuarts on the Continent), the potential advantage that might be envisaged for the service or glory of the King, who could retain scholars, soldiers, entrepreneurs and inventors. Like all foreigners, the English were both courted and repulsed, importuned by the officials of a peasant kingdom that was self-sufficient, mercantilist, conformist and attached to ancient prerogatives, such as the *droit d'aubaine* which had precedence over natural right and treaties. They also benefited from the curiosity that people of the highest rank – members of the high administration, courtiers and aristocrats, reformers of the economy and finances on the model of Turgot, and members of cultivated circles and the salons – had about things English. Some of these sought to limit mobility, and others to accelerate it.

At the end of the seventeenth century, surveillance carried the day, and the tax on foreigners raised after 1697 served as an instrument to arbitrate an established presence: nine thousand foreigners paid the tax, i.e. those able to do so. Paris had at this time less than a thousand foreign inhabitants, some 11 per cent of whom were English, holding second place after nationals of the United Provinces and Flanders, but coming first in terms of wealth.[8] The stabilised English mobility revealed by the fiscal authority reflects the kingdom's growing relations with northern

Europe. The English in Paris at the dawn of the Enlightenment can be divided into two groups: a quarter belonged to the aristocracy, nobility, administration, clergy or army, while three-quarters were engaged in business, enterprise, trade, work, or salaried occupations. By the late eighteenth century, the intensification of Anglo-French relations and the acceleration of the Grand Tour following the Seven Years War changed the conditions of this relationship, and at the same time that of the surveillance that generated statistical effects and detailed reports.

Around 1745, on the eve of a conflict, the police counted 350 English out of 940 foreigners appearing in its reports (37 per cent). This is an underestimate, focusing on those above the middle range and showing a predominance of the aristocracy (46 per cent), with only a quarter involved in the economic activities predominant in 1697. The rest of the English living in the capital belonged to a motley collection of clerics (who were often tutors to young nobles), students (often of medicine), physicians and artists. Many were watched because they were suspected of Jacobite connections, as detailed by the report of the Marquis of Éguilles on the entourage of Charles Edward after 1746. Surveillance was triggered by a perception of political involvement, level of resources, networks of connivance and intrigue, and this biased the traits of the group observed.

English presence, British profiles

Forty years later, better sources enable a more precise picture to be drawn up for the 1770s and 1780s.[9] The archives on the surveillance of foreigners, despite their gaps and their confusion in defining an Englishman, a Briton, an English speaker, a Scot, an Irishman or an American (the latter category being used after 1780), now give firmer data as well as a clearer movement. Between 1774 and 1789, the policemen of Louis XV and Louis XVI counted 15,808 foreigners. English were the leading category with just over 3,500 representatives, followed by nationals of the Netherlands, the United Provinces and the Holy Roman Empire, who together came to around 6,000. The northern emphasis was stronger than at the beginning of the century, and the British played a major role. Even if we have to admit a possible underestimation, since not all travellers were registered and not all residents checked, some years also having been affected by diplomatic and military conflict, this annual total still falls considerably short of the estimates regularly made from the eighteenth century on by historians of the Grand Tour. Horace Walpole actually spoke of 40,000 English in France in 1784–86. Mrs Craddock, who visited Paris and crossed France in 1783, proposed a figure of 30,000

British, and on 29 August 1786 the *Daily Universal Register* spoke of 3,760 Londoners crossing the Channel in six weeks, which would mean a rate of some 32,000 per year. For want of any direct means to verify these statements (though one might try to find in England the passports supplied by the authorities), the surveillance of foreigners in France provides a minimal level, but the English were certainly less numerous than is often maintained.[10] The figure is supported by two other assessments, that of Baretti in his *Us et coutumes d'Italie* of 1788, who speaks of ten thousand English having made the Grand Tour between 1750 and 1760, masters and servants combined, in other words less than a thousand per year; while the dictionary of Ingamells, based on Italian archives and reports, cites a figure of over 8,000 English who had travelled to and stayed in the peninsula in the eighteenth century, which is clearly a very low estimate (see Table 5.1).[11]

Table 5.1 Movement of foreigners

	Total foreigners checked	*English at hotels*	*English in reports*
1772	3,626	—	—
1773	4,845	—	—
1774	4,352	120	66
1775	3,753	204	94
1781	2,486	277	60
1787	3,873	263	277
1788	4,374	676	283
1789	2,602	286	162
Total	29,911	1,826	942

The police reports confirm the above social orientations. Women are rare among the English travellers, but more numerous than in other foreign groups; young and old people are less strongly represented than are adults, but the police paid little attention to age, which is known in less than 10 per cent of cases. A few isolated travellers, 117 or 3 per cent of the total in 1774–89, with 7 per cent being women in married couples, show that there was a certain variety. In total, however, men made up some 90 per cent of all travellers. Professional situation and social characteristics are known for rather less than half of the total (Table 5.2), 1,741 cases remaining indeterminate, being often combined imprecisely with others. The English domination in the ranks of foreigners was most clearly distinguishable in Paris, where business travel was strongest (at least 55 per cent). Among the English, the majority were aristocrats, gentry or clergy of all levels, members of the liberal professions and scholars, with rather less than a third made up of active professions, bankers, traders, artisans and shopkeepers. English mobility was certainly already driven by an activity of leisure and culture, even if Paris visits do not allow a strict line to be drawn between different activities: in social terms the Thrals would be classed in the bourgeois business class, but they divided their activity between *otium* and *negotium*.

Table 5.2 Professions and social status of foreigners in Paris

	Foreigners			English		
	Total	%	ex. m	Total	%	ex. m
Clergy	232	1.4	2.02	16	0.4	0.8
Nobility	2,860	18.09	24.9	1,082	29.4	55.85
Artists and actors	192	1.2	1.6	14	0.4	0.75
Teachers, scientists and doctors	781	4.8	0.7	93	2.5	4.8
Merchants, bankers and traders	2,303	14.5	20.07	548	14.9	28.3
Liberal professions	60	0.3	0.5	27	0.7	1.4
Bourgeois status	325	2.05	2.8	—	—	—
Artisans and shopkeepers	3,743	23.6	32.6	101	2.75	5.2
Domestic servants	975	6.1	8.4	56	1.5	2.9
Miscellaneous, including women	4,337	27.5	—	1,741	47.35	—
Total	15,808	100	100	3,678	100	100

Note: ex. m = excluding miscellaneous

Travel for the nobility was a function of old-established connections, contact between ancient families – think, for example, of the La Rochefoucaulds and d'Argensons – educational initiative, and a specific taste for fairly protracted visits: 70 per cent stayed for three months from spring to summer, 10 per cent slightly longer, while 20 per cent of visits continued through the winter. Police reports were also interested in comings and goings that might mask spying activities, such as the journeys of Mr Forth in 1788 on which five reports were made. Forth was an Irishman, perhaps a gentleman, who behaved mysteriously and made contact early on with Lord Stormont, the British ambassador. He was probably part of the network of Lord Eden, who negotiated the 1786 treaty, and was in Paris in September and October 1789, when he was received by the duc d'Orléans, visited cafés, theatres and the National Assembly. Forth stayed at the 'Hôtel de Valois, but was not easily to be found', the police spy reported in April 1789. Colonel Arlympale, for his part, stayed from 23 May 1788 to 5 June 1789, followed the social season, and perhaps took part in the events of the time. The Duchess of Kingston was well-known to both the police and the social world: she had properties and lawsuits in England, a house in Rome, and interests in North Sea shipping. The movements of various individuals noted by the spies and inspectors could be followed step by step.

In this unstable society, intellectuals cut through all social levels. Clerics, tutors, writers, scholars and curates – Sterne, for example – rubbed shoulders with members of the royal family, enlightened lords, and a majority of representatives of the gentry, soldiers and diplomats. David Hume, who arrived in Paris in the entourage of Lord Hertford, the British ambassador, was simultaneously occupied both with his secretarial duties and as tutor to the young Lord Beauchamp, Lord Hertford's son. Doubtless for many, Paris was only a step towards the south of France, where a regular English tourist industry was beginning in Languedoc, centred on Toulouse, Montpellier and the Pyrénées, and on the Provençal coast. Further afield, Italy with its artistic treasures, sunshine and exoticism awaited dilettantes and simple tourists alike. The police surveillance emphasized the motivations for a Paris visit. 'It is good form in England, among both the nobility and those with wealth, to say in society that you have been in Paris and Italy,' so says the report on Lord Seeforth of 10 September 1774; 'he proposed to obtain this advantage for himself and this is the entire fruit he will keep from his travels'. The spies often wrote in moralising tone, and mentioned three major incentives: the quest for pleasure and a taste for girls – this was the case with Lord Berkeley, who was reported on 8 October 1773 as visiting gaming houses, shows, and brothels; intellectual and artistic study and curiosity, as with the example of Bohwn, or better known, Arthur Young, who did not warrant a police file, but stayed with the La Rochefoucaulds;[12] and finally politics, and less commonly business, in which diplomacy might be mixed with trade and speculation. Political reports as such are less common in the files of the 1760s than in those surviving from the 1740s, which are less numerous and less developed.

The Englishman's Paris

The English presence, regular from the seventeenth century, expanded with the general movement of arrivals and departures of foreigners of every origin. The English are found almost everywhere, but their concentration grew at the same time as the quantity and quality of travellers. The author of *Letters Concerning the Present State of England*, in 1772, notes that 'where there was one English traveller in the reigns of the first two Georges, there are now ten for the Grand Tour, and any citizen of fortune takes a general view of France, Italy and Germany on a summer journey.' In the 1740s, police reports indicate a settlement that was primarily on the Left Bank, with almost two-thirds of reported addresses being in either Saint-Germain, the Luxembourg, or the parish of Saint-André-des-Arts. The attraction there was that of the hotels, luxury shops and places of entertainment on the main streets around the foire Saint-Germain, the Comédie, and the cafés; this was the general choice for well-to-do foreigners,[13] of which the English formed part. The promenade, the schools of horsemanship, the opportunities to meet compatriots, all consolidated the habit of lodging in this district, in smart hotels or good-quality boarding-houses. Addresses on the Right Bank were less numerous.

By the 1770s, and still more so by 1787, the map had changed completely: the Right Bank now had the upper hand over the districts south of the Seine, with the exception of the faubourg Saint-Germain. Top of the list now were addresses in the quarters of Saint-Eustache, Palais-Royal, Montmartre, even the Louvre and Les Halles, where the newcomers joined in the characteristic social and national mix of the hotel clientele of the time.[14] The Paris of fashionable society and its distractions had shifted, with luxury trades and new shops situated on the streets of the northwestern quarters, the rue Saint-Honoré now being, par excellence, a road of renowned haberdashers and merchants of *Modes* and *Nouveautés*. The world of the salons was centred on Mme Geoffrin, the pole of Paris conversation, likewise on rue Saint-Honoré. Tourists from England were involved in this new orientation, where the Palais-Royal and the boulevards, with their theatres, social circles, trades, promenades, sociabilities and also surveillance, made up the new Paris of foreigners and Parisians alike.[15] Those English faithful to the Left Bank were also faithful to the renowned hotels of the rue Jacob: five establishments were particularly favoured, including the Hôtel d'York at 40 louis per apartment. In this establishment, 88 per cent of the reported clientele were English: the proportion at the Hôtel du Parc on rue du Colombier was 84 per cent, and 89 per cent chez Ballot on the same street, a total of eleven high-class establishments being located there. This whole world benefited from the vogue for the new quarter being built around the Théâtre and place de l'Odéon. The English were less concentrated in the hotels on the Right Bank, but still took part in their expansion: one establishment was noted on rue Saint-Honoré in 1781, growing to twenty-one by 1787; English formed 23 per cent of the clients of the Hôtel d'Angleterre, rue de Richelieu; but 80 per cent of those of the Hôtel de l'Université on the same street in 1788. Their tourism was a motive element, as it profited from the information accumulated and transmitted, through published accounts, letters and guides. Sometimes temporary rental formed the prelude to longer installation, as with Lord Eden who stayed first of all at an hotel, then rented a *maison à porte cochère* in the rue de la Chaussée-d'Antin. Some English attracted others, or were attracted to the same districts by their French connections or relatives. Montalembert, who had married an Englishwoman, thus received a 'Sir Ainslye'; the English nobility in Paris such as the Berwicks, Dillons, Fitz-Jameses and Drummonds welcomed their associates and sometimes lodged them. This general sociability was mentioned sometimes by the police, as well as by the authors of travel reports.

Journeys and social exchange

Out of the entire English population attracted temporarily to the French capital, only a fairly limited number were integrated into a relationship of exchange, let alone with the milieus of Paris intellectuals, philosophers, writers, scholars, academics, authors and art lovers. Among the travellers, depending on the year, between one third and two-thirds could make this claim, and, through the recommendations they had, or their established celebrity, could obtain access to those famous names who did not open their doors to all the world. It was a commonality of lifestyle, customs and interests that made this society receptive to such privileged visitors. To understand its practices it is necessary to change scale and analyse sources less formal than the police reports, sources that moreover have not yet been fully exploited. They are complemented by the travel accounts collected by Boucher de la Richarderie, Pinkerton, Michèle Sacquin, and by the Centre de recherches sur les aires culturelles.[16] A definitive study that would use all the information supplied by these various sources – published and manuscript in all their forms, travel accounts, real or fictional correspondence, memoirs, novels, French and British address books – remains to be written; it would show the whole network of English travellers and display its operation and organisation, as well as the choices made, the role of transmission and that of individuals such as Franklin. Here we shall have to focus on a group of major actors and on the relations established between them.

Over a hundred travellers left written records: ninety accounts actually published (in the strict sense) and twenty-two manuscripts. Some were already famous in the eighteenth century, such as those of Young, Moore,

Goldsmith, Sterne and Dr Maihows, and even sometimes translated into French. Others remained anonymous and unpublished. Of those authors who can be socially identified, some fifty belonged to the aristocracy or gentry, having their place in the ruling class, while the others belonged to the clergy or church hierarchy, together with scholars, professional intellectuals and artists. This picture is little changed by including correspondences published in the nineteenth century, for example those of Hume and of Horace Walpole (part of whose correspondence was known before 1800), or journals and memoirs, like those of Garrick or of Graville. The representatives of the great families – Grafton, Holland, Spencer, Walpole, Fox, the Bishop of Derry, and Lord Hervey of Bristol – rubbed shoulders with the world of squires and gentlemen, soldiers, politicians and clerics issuing from a common sociological matrix and disposing of similar symbolic and financial capital: Young, Taggart, Bentham, Peckham, Wilkes. Ambassadors and diplomatic personnel merit attention as they often remained for longer, and had contact in Paris with all kinds of informants: Lord Hertford, Hans Stanley and David Hume, for example, had connections early on with Helvétius and the duc de Nivernais, who had a doctorate in Law from Oxford and was posted to London in 1763. They introduced their friends, protégés and clients to those French associates that they knew and frequented. Stanley, via the duc de Nivernais, made the acquaintaince of Gibbon, Caylus, Duclos, d'Alembert, De La Bletterie, Foncemagne, Lacurne de Sainte-Palaye, i.e. the circles of the Académie française and the Inscriptions et Belles Lettres.

Letters and academic exchanges facilitated the establishment of relationships on the ground. At the Académie des sciences, Lalande played a similar role to Nivernais, sponsoring the visits of John Walsh, Thomas Pennant, Adam Walker, Squire Marshall and Dr Rigby. Buffon at the Muséum and Broussonet at the Société royale d'agriculture welcomed naturalists and agronomists. Lavoisier received the friends of Priestley. Recommended tutors and pupils could be introduced to figures from the worlds of letters, science and arts. Exchanges between English and French intellectuals must be understood as part of a large network of travelling practices including protection, recommendation, hospitality and correspondence, all linked to each other by a principle of reciprocity. Social and fashionable relationships, so central to the experience of English travellers in Paris, were governed by strict rules and meant that the utility of travels was not necessarily measured by the results obtained at the intellectual level. During a visit that was rarely very lengthy, Englishmen often found themselves first of all among themselves, and some were surprised at not being able to speak French. The examples of Adam Smith, David

Hume and Arthur Young, who had similar interests in moral philosophy, political economy and agronomy, illustrate this particularly clearly.

Adam Smith was in Paris between 1764 and 1766.[17] He had left his chair at Glasgow University to tutor the young Duke of Buccleuch, aged eighteen. On the way out to Toulouse, where he spent eighteen months, he stopped in Paris for only ten days. On return, however, he stayed from December 1765 to November 1766 – almost a whole year. It is Hume in his letters who tells us most about this visit, even though he had missed Smith, who arrived after his own departure. Hume largely prepared his friend's reception, and continued to look after him from a distance by his letters to his French correspondents. Adam Smith's interests were anchored in three favourite fields: opera, the salons and the economists. The tutor followed the general rule by visiting shows, and went regularly to the Opéra. He often visited the duchesse d'Enville and the La Rochefoucaulds, who served as an intermediary between the Société royale d'agriculture and the members of the *Secte*. He was found at Mlle de l'Espinasse's salon, and at those of D'Holbach and Helvétius. Eventually, his predilection for theoretical discussion led him to meet the Physiocrats and liberals; he met Turgot, Quesnay (who cured him of a bad case of fever) and Dupont de Nemours, who deemed him 'a judicious and simple man, but who is not yet of value'. This judgement shows that in Paris and fine society Adam Smith was not at ease. He spoke French poorly, he was not in complete agreement with the Physiocrats, he missed his English and Scottish friends and expressed his nostalgia in a letter of October 1766 to Andrew Meller, his publisher. Everything here depended on an ability to accept the host society's rules of fashion, which were far from indulgent.

It was this adaptability that had made for Hume's success.[18] He arrived in France preceded by an existing reputation; his work was already translated into French, he already had Paris correspondents, including Helvétius, Mme Dupré de Saint-Maur and Mme de Boufflers. He reached Paris in 1763, in the entourage of the ambassador Lord Hertford, whose son he was to tutor. He left the capital two years later, having served as *chargé d'affaires*. In this period Hume did not disappoint expectations. He was supported by eminent aristocrats, the duc d'Orléans, the duchesse de La Vallière, président Henault, close to the clique around the Queen; he dined at the duc de Praslin's and met La Pompadour; he was received by the Dauphin and his brothers, who honoured him with flattering and well-prepared compliments. Hume, for his part, was at home in the salons, whatever he might say of them in his *Life*, where he tries to pass himself off as simply a man of the study, declaring his repugnance 'to begin connexions with great men' and his distrust for polite society and the gaiety of the Paris *Sociétés* – a feature of his age and his character, showing his remove from the effects of fashion. He ascribes to fashion the excessive wordly success that he himself achieved: 'the more I resiled from their excessive civilities, the more I was loaded with them'. Hume was to be seen everywhere, at Mme Geoffrin's, at Mme Du Deffand's, at Julie de Lespinasse's and the home of the comtesse de Boufllers, whom he kept in touch with after his return to Britain. Hume's contact with the philosophers was immediate – D'Alembert, Duclos, Helvétius, Marmontel, Grimm, and of course Rousseau; he also saw a great deal of D'Holbach. Cochin and Carmontelle both painted his portrait. In short, he was a star, but crowned less by a genuine intellectual following, as was the case with Rousseau, than by his ability to play the role of open-air philosopher exhibited everywhere: at Versailles, in the *Sociétés*, and at Opéra performances between 'two pretty faces'. Lord Charlemont deemed this a ridiculous charade. Hume himself thought that his own diplomatic role and his social glory were part of a game of superficial civilities and that his hosts had little real interest in individuals and their ideas.

Arthur Young was perhaps more fortunate.[19] Between 1787 and 1789 he made extended visits to Paris, and above all he travelled through provincial France on horseback; Paris was the base from which he organised his agronomic tour. Success in his case was represented by a welcome that was both broad and select. His reputation as a gentleman agriculturalist opened doors to him, his address book was full of members of the Société royale d'agriculture: La Rochefoucauld, Lavoisier and Broussonnet all received him; he was made a corresponding member. But Young's particularity was to enjoy the sincere friendly protection of the La Rochefoucauld family, whose heirs together with their tutor Lazowski he had received at his home and taken round the English counties. The agronomist had been able to count on solid recommendations, and provide specialist information expected by a liberal and scholarly nobility, an intellectual milieu of economists and philosophers, leading scientists as well as amateurs, who gathered in the Académie des sciences, and could be met at the Jardin du Roi. Young did not make a division between fashionable sociability and intellectual exchange; supper parties were sometimes a better means of convincing his associates than were lectures. 'I welcome great talents, but on condition that they also have qualities that make us desirous to remain with them behind closed doors.' These were well-informed men, polished liberals, experimenting agriculturalists, and Young closely followed their speeches and writings; they all knew, as he did himself, how to cement positive relationships in which pleasure and seriousness were often combined.

French philosophers, English travellers

To understand this social and intellectual chemistry and its potential effect in terms of a successful and extended acculturation would require other studies, first among which would have to be that of the practice and teaching of languages, an analysis of publishing and the practice of translation in France and in Britain. The origin of travel and tourism took place in a perspective of general formation, the construction of social behaviour in which tradition and constraint, new curiosities and individual choices, all played a part. Thus Boswell's *Life of Samuel Johnson* (1791) and his own *Journal* emphasise along with other texts the importance of spleen, melancholy and health, which belonged both to the bitter experience of a journey to France and to the hope of cure it bore by offering a change of climate, a temporary transformation in social relations, and a metamorphosis by the extension of these. The economy of agreeability and pleasure cannot be separated from that of enriching intellectual development. The rules of etiquette for English travellers located them at the summit of civilisation, while the French, very often, were in their eyes no more than savages. France was in this respect worse than Scotland, except for the climate, and 'Nature has done much for France, but the French have not done very much for themselves', Johnson confided to Boswell in the 1770s. Paris as a city was not so interesting that one would want to remain there, and unless one only visited English people, it was sad to say that only French was spoken there. These remarks have the advantage of challenging a tradition of cultural transfer that is too readily accepted. To go further, we need more systematically to examine perceptions and compare the viewpoint of English travellers with that of their French hosts, in other words, to reflect on the rules, practices and results of an intellectual hospitality.

Diderot provides a case study for this. Here he is at D'Holbach's residence, at the centre of a salon, a coterie that attracts foreigners.[20] Two regulars, Helvétius and D'Holbach himself, have been in England, and their point of view is that if London is above all good for the English, Paris for its part is good for the whole world. The relationship is an unequal one. The encyclopedist philosopher never abandoned his interest in English literature and science, and what he owed to Chambers and Richardson is well-known. He was above all an adaptive translator. His perspective and knowledge drew on two regular sources of information, the ties formed with aristocrats and political figures in the course of their travels – the Earl of Suffolk, the Walpoles – and relationships of varying degree with many intellectuals, as found in his correspondence and in travellers' reports: Smith, Gibbon, Hume, Franklin, the American doctor

Rust, the painter Ramsay, the actor Garrick and the novelist Sterne. Charles Buracy, the musicologist, met Diderot in the salons, then at his home, on a more friendly basis, in 1770. With Wilkes, Diderot had a political correspondence that prolonged their relationship. This is a good example of a successful audience and reception, but in a limited circle that operated more by friendly interest than by recommendation.

It has both similarities and differences with the case of abbé Morellet, whose papers and *Mémoires* prove especially rich. This son of a Lyon merchant made his career in the shadow of the great men he met while studying at the Sorbonne, among them Turgot. He owed them positions and stipends, and was charged with missions and reports. For both him and them, it was necessary that he should be acquainted with all the founding fathers of 'English' political economy. The salons and the Académie française were his field of action, supplemented by more limited encounters with friends and passing connections. In 1772 the government sent him to London, where he returned again in 1783, this time in triumph and as a kind of ambassador of the Paris intellectuals. Between these two visits, he had turned his connections into profitable social capital. He drew these from the aristocratic and diplomatic circles that he frequented in Paris, at the house of Helvétius and the salon of D'Holbach: for example, David Hume, with whom Morellet corresponded after his return; Benjamin Franklin; Governor Morris; and Lord Richmond, the British ambassador in 1765, whom he saw again in London. Lord Shelburn, who negotiated the Versailles treaty, frequented the same coterie and entrusted his son to Morellet in 1784; then there was colonel Barré, a confidential agent of Lord Shelburn, and Lord Fitz-Maurier, who welcomed him on his visit. He had excellent relations with Sterne, who visited Paris in 1765 and described D'Holbach's salon as 'the café of Europe for political economy'; and with Adam Smith, who spoke with him about trade, public credit, and the 'great work he was cogitating' – which the abbé would later translate. He saw Garrick, who took Morellet's side in the heated discussions that he had with Diderot and Marmontel, and who led him to read *Othello* and *Richard III*, also taking him to Drury Lane. The attitudes of Morellet and Diderot were marked neither by total anglophilia or anglophobia. They were clear both in their admiration for England and in their criticism of its political system and corruption. Their distrust for the principles of the new political economy was combined with a genuine enthusiasm on some points in the debate,[21] which was waged between different networks: more intellectual, philosophical and political in Diderot's case; more official and aristocratic in that of Morellet. The exchanges were not always equal, there was a cost to pay in order to obtain this advantage, in the form of preliminary recommendations, entry guaranteed by regular habitués, or dispatch of works, and they led to relationships pursued beyond the meetings, attested by the visit of Morellet to London, or the correspondence of Diderot, who knew England only from reading and hearsay, which led for example to discussion with D'Holbach.

Already in the eighteenth century, the English propensity towards this movement had been emphasised on both sides of the Channel. Philip Thickeness confirmed in 1768 the view put forward by abbé Leblanc in 1742: the English travel more than any other European people. They had the freedom and resources to do so.[22] There was, moreover, something specific about the English in Paris compared with the other foreigners who arrived in the capital: they came regularly, and the abatement of conflict increased their numbers. They included many women, both as family members and sometimes independently. Of all the visitors, it was undoubtedly the English who were most attracted by Parisian social life, by the various curiosities offered, and by culture in general. Their presence rested on two types of exchange, governed by different situations. An important core was formed by a few dozen individuals, though with indeterminate and variable limits, who frequented the Parisian *monde* and Republic of Letters, with its salons, intellectual circles, political and literary coteries. This operated on the basis of a more or less equal exchange constructed from recommendations, correspondence and the dispatch of books, and often from extended friendships that the guests' visits confirmed. Larger in size, but equally variable with the political conjuncture and the seasons, was a group of a few hundred individuals, attracted both by business and by the taste for travel acquired from educational traditions, social customs and English liberties. Tourism and leisure played an ever more important role for this English population. The two milieus enjoyed neither the same resources nor the same resonance. The former hold first place in travel accounts (a hundred or more in the century) and in those reports on the surveillance of foreigners that were compiled for royal attention. They formed less than a quarter of the English population in Paris, if still more than the average for foreigners, who were observed and closely watched for their political, religious, moral and economic behaviour: some 12 per cent. The English predominance among the enumerated population was reinforced among those groups whose conduct was more closely examined. The others appear more as statistics and descriptive approximations. They form the backcloth to the theatre of the Grand Tours.

The two milieus enjoyed neither the same proximity nor possibilities. The fashionable and intellectual core were well-known, they sought out and got to know French people of similar quality and style of life.

They regularly gathered in a definite sociability, in which conversation and fashion decisively reigned: these were the preludes to an acculturation, and to deeper cultural transfers that established other modes of encounter and exchange. For French fashions, language and manners, they were the decisive agents. Louis-Sébastien Mercier well understood the mechanism that isolated these milieus, devoting a whole chapter to a question that concerned all foreigners, who all faced a similar problem: 'All these foreigners who have been told so much about Parisian society are astonished not to find any such thing: everyone lives here with their own particular customs and a great lack of concern about anyone else. It is difficult to enter certain houses, and no one is accustomed to receiving foreigners. They are forced back to their boarding-houses; and if you except the occasional dances and rare suppers, the houses are all closed or deserted. After the initial visits, no one bothers any more about the foreigner who wanders from house to house, and finally falls back on the Palais-Royal and its surroundings.'[23] Here we have, from the pen of the moral philosopher, the effect of numbers and the very success of a great capital, the foreigners being scattered between different societies that did not always bother to receive them. 'It is for him to court the Parisian,' but the reverse certainly will not happen. 'Parisian society almost resembles that of those savages who meet one another by chance and leave one another without ceremony, simply to relieve their boredom.'

The same observer notes a second effect: 'the foreigner in Paris maintains his particular character', and the English *habitus* is especially strong in this collection. Faced with a relaxed but chilly politeness, the Englishman maintains his independence, and instead of taverns and cabarets goes to restaurants and visits cafés where he finds the newspapers. He is put out when these no longer arrive, as noted by an observer for the *lieutenant de police* in January 1778: 'Since the 8th of this month, no English newspaper has been delivered ... The English in Paris feel a singular distress about the ban on their newspaper ...' The reasons for the prohibition were a function of the diplomatic tension, but what concerns us here is that this deprivation removed from the English 'a half of their existence; they do not know what to do, nor what is happening; even the cafés have been abandoned ...'[24] They can be seen on horseback, they no longer dress up, they stick to the same hotels on the Left Bank, and increasingly on the Right Bank, demanding punch, cold baths, roast beef, and impeccable service, as can be read in Sterne or Smollett. They are great carnivores, 'they taste our wines with appreciation and are delighted by our sunshine', which they proceed to seek out further south. In tracing these new characters, Louis-Sébastien Mercier emphasises what they have in common and what differentiates them, well understanding that his satire of the other demonstrates a difference in political behaviour, the existence of a form of independence and more widespread freedom in London, the particular and singular liberty reserved to circles who seek entertainment and worldly pleasure in Paris. An awareness of superiority on both sides comes into confrontation in mobility and the sociabilities that organise it. At the top level, it can arouse indifference, lower down a degree of antipathy that may vary, and that the American war was temporarily to reinforce, while strengthening in its turn the prejudices of the two nations.[25]

Half a century later, the consequence of a burgeoning tourism had not removed these difficulties, which have now to be taken into account in any study of cultural, material and intellectual relations, and sought out in a network of documents and texts that goes well beyond the straightforward travel accounts that are always cited. George Sand humorously provides a final perspective in support of our analysis. For her, the English knew better how to travel, and the French less so, than other people in Europe; if travel is not confused with general mobility, it remains an essential dimension of the awareness of identity and reciprocal acculturation of peoples who meet each other on the road or at an inn. Each nation bears with it the means of its representation, and thus its ability to understand the foreigner that it receives, just as the latter has to accept the differences noted in the behaviour of foreign visitors. With the nascent tourist industry, new stereotypes supplant the older characteristics or give them a new accent. This is what we are told by the hero of *Lettres d'un voyageur*:

> The islanders of Albion bring with them a peculiar fluid which I shall call the British fluid, in the midst of which they travel, as inaccessible to the surrounding atmosphere as a mouse in an insulating apparatus. It's not simply the thousand and one precautions they take ... It's because the outer air has no hold on them; it's because they walk, drink, sleep and eat in this fluid as under a twenty-foot-thick bell jar, through which they stare pityingly at wind-swept riders and walkers with snow-sodden boots ... The true goal of an Englishman's journey is 'to return home after having travelled round the world without having soiled his gloves or worn out his boots ... It's their wardrobes that travel, not themselves.[26]

Notes

1 P. Mantoux, *La Révolution industrielle au XVIIIe siècle: Essai sur les commencements de la grande industrie moderne en Angleterre* (Paris: Génin, 1959); F. Crouzet, *De la supériorité de l'Angleterre sur la France, l'économique et l'imaginaire XVIIe–XXe siècles* (Paris: Perrin, 1986); L. Hilaire-Perez, *L'Invention technique au siècle des Lumières*, (Paris: A. Michel, 2000).

2   A. Babeau, *Les Voyageurs en France depuis la Renaissance jusqu'à la Révolution*, (Genève: Slatkine Reprints, 1970), pp. 25–107, 198–251; J. Lough, *France on the Eve of Revolution: British Travellers' Observations, 1763–1788*, (London: Croom Helm, 1987); M. Saquin, 'Les voyageurs anglais en France et les voyageurs français en Angleterre de 1750 à 1789', unpublished thesis, Ecole des Chartes, 1977, 3 vols.
3   H. Walter, *Honni soit qui mal y pense, l'incroyable histoire d'amour entre le français et l'anglais*, (Paris: Robert Laffont, 2001); I. Buruma, *Voltaire's Coconuts, or Anglomania in Europe*, (London: Weidenfeld & Nicholson, 1999); D. Roche, *Humeurs vagabondes*, (Paris: Fayard, 2003).
4   D. Roche (ed.), *La Ville promise: Mobilité et accueil à Paris (1650–1850)*, (Paris: Fayard, 2000).
5   G. Chabaud, 'Aux origines du tourisme moderne, les grands tours de l'époque moderne', *Relations Internationales*, 102 (2000), 147–59; G. Chabaud and P. Monzani, 'Les Guides de Paris au XVIIe–XVIIIe siècle, image de la ville', unpublished Master's thesis, Université de Paris-I, 1979.
6   G. Ascoli, *La Grande-Bretagne devant l'opinion française, au XVIIe siècle*, (Paris: Librairie Universitaire J. Gamber, 1930), pp. 446–68.
7   Roche (ed.), *La Ville promise*, pp. 22–63, 221–88 (especially the chapters by Vincent Milliot and Jean-François Dubost).
8   J.-F. Dubost and P. Sahlins, *Et si on faisait payer les étrangers? Louis XIV, les immigrés et quelques autres*, (Paris: Flammarion, 1999), pp. 172–225.
9   Jean-François Dubost, in Roche, *La Ville promise*, pp. 240–9; *Mémoires de l'Abbé Morellet, sur le dix-huitième siècle et la Révolution*, (Paris: Librairie Française de Ladvocat, 1821, new edition Mercure de France, 1988), pp. 147–55.
10 See, however, R. Morieux, '"An inundation from our shores": Travelling Across the Channel Around the Peace of Amiens', in Mark Philp (ed.), *The Invasion of Britain: 1793–1815* (London: Ashgate, forthcoming).
11 J. Black, *The British Abroad: The Grand Tour in the Eighteenth Century*, (New York: Sutton, 1997); G. Ascoli, *La Grande-Bretagne*, pp. 257–73; C. Hibbert, *The Grand Tour*, (London: Thames Methuen, 1987); J. Ingamells, *A Dictionary of British and Irish Travellers in Italy, 1701–1800*, (New Haven and London: Yale University Press, 1997).
12 J. Birnbaum, 'Arthur Young en Europe, culture du voyage et cheminement des Lumières au XVIIIe siècle', unpublished Master's thesis, Université de Paris-I, 1997.
13 Roche (ed.), *La Ville promise*, pp. 108–59.
14 Roche (ed.), *La Ville promise*, pp. 282–8.
15 D. Roche, *La France des Lumières*, (Paris: Fayard, 1993), pp. 581–610; N. Coquery, 'Qu'est-ce que la remarquable économie? La boutique dans le paysage urbain à Paris d'après les Guides du XVIIIe siècle', in G. Chabaud (ed.), *Les Guides imprimés du XVIe au XXe siècle, villes, paysages, voyages*, (Paris: Belin, 2000), pp. 419–28.
16 Boucher de la Richarderie, *Bibliothèque universelle des voyages*, (Paris: Treuttel & Würtz, 1808) 6 vols; J. Pinkerton, *Catalogue of Books of Voyages*

and Travels, (London: T. Cadell & W. Davies, 1807); Saquin, 'Les voyageurs anglais', vol. 3, pp. 551–737; CRIDAF, *Répertoire des relations de voyage, mémoires et souvenirs de touristes et de résidents français en Grande-Bretagne et de touristes et résidents britanniques en France entre 1750 et 1980*, (Villetaneuse: Université Paris-Nord, 1988).

17 *The Collected Works of Dugald Stewart*, vol. 10: *Biographical Memoirs of Adam Smith, William Robertson, Thomas Reid: To Which is Prefixed a Memoir of Dugald Stewart, with Selections from his Correspondence* ed. by J. Veitch, ed. W. Hamilton (Edinburgh: Constable, 1858); J. Rae, *Life of Adam Smith*, (London & New York: Macmillan, 1895); I. Simpson Ross, *The Life of Adam Smith*, (Oxford: Clarendon Press, 1995); *Correspondence of A. Smith*, ed. E. Campbell Mossner and I. Simpson Ross, (Oxford: Clarendon Press, 1987). I have to thank Stéphane Van Damme, Nicolas Shapira and Antoine Lilti for their assistance with all the biographical documentation.

18 *The Letters of David Hume*, ed. J. Y. T. Greid, (Oxford: Clarendon Press, 1932); *The New Letters of David Hume*, ed. Raymond Klibanksi and Ernest C. Mossner, (Oxford: Clarendon Press, 1954); D. Hume, *My Own Life* (Dublin: Mermaid Turbulence, 1997), pp. 20–1.

19 A. Young, *Travels in France during the years 1787, 1788 and 1789*, (Cambridge: Cambridge University Press, 1929); Birnbaum, 'Arthur Young en Europe', bibliography and sources.

20 A. C. Kors, *D'Holbach's coterie and Enlightenment in Paris*, (Princeton: Princeton University Press, 1976); D. Diderot, *Correspondance*, ed. Georges Roth and Jean Varloot (Paris: Editions de Minuit, 1955–1970), 15 vols.

21 J.-C. Perrot, *Pour une histoire intellectuelle de l'économie politique, XVIIe–XVIIIe siècles*, (Paris: Editions de l'Ecole des Hautes Etudes en sciences sociales, 1992), and 'Nouveauté: l'économic politique et ses livres', in H.-J. Martin and R. Chartier (eds), *Histoire de l'édition française* (Paris: Promodis, 1983), vol. 2, *Le Livre triomphant, 1660–1830*, pp. 298–328; D. Goodman, *The Republic of Letters, a Cultural History of the French Enlightenment*, (Ithaca and London: Cornell University Press, 1994); A. M. Wilson, *Diderot, sa vie, son œuvre*, (Paris: Laffont, 1985), pp. 63–5, 355–7, 410–15 ; I. McIntyre, *Garrick*, (London: Allen Lane, Penguin, 1999).

22 C. Chastelhastel-Rousseau, 'Les Anglais sur la place Louis XV', *XVIIIe Siècle*, 32 (2000), 521–33.

23 L.-S. Mercier, *Tableau de Paris*, ed. J.-C. Bonnet (Paris: Mercure de France, 1994), vol. 2, pp. 1063–7.

24 Archives des Affaires étrangères, contrôle des étrangers, Report of 30 January 1778, vol. 290, ro. 69–71; this text was passed to me by Antoine Lilti, whom I sincerely thank.

25 L.-S. Mercier, *Parallèle de Paris et de Londres*, ed. Claude Bruneteau and Bernard Cottret (Paris: Didier, 1982), pp. 78–9.

26 G. Sand, *Lettres d'un voyageur* (1834) (Harmondsworth: Penguin, 1987), p. 258.

6

The French Republic of Letters and English culture, 1750–90

LAURENCE W. B. BROCKLISS

Calvet's web

It is a commonplace of the historiography of the French Enlightenment that the movement owed a great deal to contemporary British thought. Indeed, from the moment Voltaire published his *Lettres philosophiques* (or *Lettres sur les Anglais*) in 1733–74, France was supposedly overwhelmed with a passion for England and all things English, which only a few suspicious souls (notably Rousseau) were able to withstand. Hitherto, however, there has been little attempt to study the French *anglomanie* of the eighteenth century beyond the narrow and elevated confines of Parisian salon society.[1] While it may be true that the *philosophes* and their aristocratic friends were deeply enamoured of contemporary British science, philosophy and literature, it remains to be seen whether the more run-of-the-mill provincial members of the French Republic of Letters had the same enthusiasm. The purpose of this chapter is to explore the level of interest in British culture in the wider Republic. It does so by taking one particular and relatively unimportant group of provincial republicans about whom a lot of material survives and examining its openness to British science and letters from various angles. This group is comprised of an Avignon *érudit* – Esprit-Claude-François Calvet (1728–1810) – and his close intellectual friends.[2]

Esprit Calvet was a physician and professor of medicine with a particular interest in classical antiquities and natural history. On the eve of the French Revolution, he was one of the best-known antiquarians in the Midi and boasted a coin collection, judged second in its quality only to the King's. Thanks to the survival of his correspondence and papers, which he bequeathed to the city of Avignon and today are deposited in the municipal library he founded, it is possible to reconstruct his intellectual world in peculiar detail. In the course of Calvet's adult life, he seems to have corresponded with more than three hundred fellow republicans of letters, but only thirty-two were in persistent and regular contact.[3] Except for the four Parisians – and the Sicilian physician Micciari – all of the group lived in the Midi, chiefly in the Rhône valley. No different in their socio-professional background from republicans all over Europe, they were an amalgam of ex-army officers, *officiers,* clerics, lawyers and physicians. Only one – Passinges of Roanne – was a merchant (see Table 6.1).[4] None, not surprisingly, was a woman.

Although women played an important role in the Parisian republic of letters as salon hostesses, few were genuinely learned, and the provincial female republican was an extremely rare bird indeed. The French Republic of Letters in the eighteenth century, even more than in England, was decidedly gendered.[5]

Although half of the group published something, only three – the Paris aesthetician, the Comte de Caylus, the naturalist and eventual professor at the Musée Faujas de Saint-Fond, and the Nîmes antiquarian Jean-François Séguier – made any permanent impression on the Republic of Letters.[6] The majority, however highly thought of in their own day, rapidly vanished into obscurity. What bound them to Calvet for all or part of their life was a mutual enthusiasm for antiquities and/or natural history. While each member of the circle had his own personal correspondence network, many of its members were also close friends with one another.[7] Calvet's correspondence circle was therefore not a loose association but a tightly knit web. It was arguably just one of many similar webs which comprised the wider Republic of Letters in France, and as such can be taken as a figure for them all.

The web's knowledge of Britain and the English language

The first point to be made about the group's acquaintance with eighteenth-century English culture is that only five had actually visited Great Britain. Séguier had gone there as a relatively young man in 1736, while acting as secretary to the Italian *savant*, Francesco Scipione Maffei (1675–1755), whose acquaintance he had made when the latter passed through Nîmes on the start of his Grand Tour.[8] Caylus, too, seems to have visited London in the 1730s, but the other three crossed the Channel much later in the century. The Lyon naturalist, Claret de La Tourrette, inspector of books and director of the botanical garden attached to the new veterinary school in the city, visited Great Britain in 1766;[9] the following year, the country played host to the Parisian art and coin collector, Michelet D'Ennery;[10] while Faujas finally made the trip in 1784. Faujas's visit was the most extensive of them all, as he visited the whole of the country, not just London, and even explored the Hebrides.[11] In the course of their stay, the five seem to have got to know a number of leading figures in the English Republic of Letters and maintained at

Table 6.1 Calvet's web: biographical profile

Name	Dates	Chief Residence	Career	Publications	Visits GB and/or Italy
Achard, Cl. Fr.	1751–1809	Marseille	Medicine	Yes	No
Baudet, J. J. J (abbé)	Vivat 1800	Marseille	Teaching	No	No
Bedos, ?	Died c. 1770	Villeneuve-lès-Avignon	Army	No	No
Beraud, L. (S. J.)	1702–77	Lyon	Teaching	Yes	No
Bertholon, P. N. (abbé)	1742–1800	Béziers	Teaching	Yes	No
Calvière, Ch. Fr. (marquis de)	1693–1777	Vézénobres (near Alès)	Army	Yes	No
Caylus, A. C. P. (comte de)	1692–1765	Paris	Army	Yes	No
Contantin (abbé)	Died 1797	Aurel (Mt Ventoux)	Church	No	No
Courtois, J. Fr. B.	Died 1769	Beaucaire	Navy	No	No
D'Ennery, Michelet	1709–86	Paris	Finance (office)	No	Yes
Faujas de St Fond, B.	1741–1819	Montélimar	Law (office)	Yes	Yes
Gaillard, bailli (king of Malta)	Died 1780	Marseille	Military	No	No
Gaillard, Chrysostome (king of Malta)	Died 1797	Montélimar	Military	No	Yes
Gérouin (abbé)	Died 1760	Fourques (near Arles)	Church	No	No
La Tourrette, M. A. Claret de	1729–93	Lyon	Law (office)	Yes	Yes

Name	Dates	Chief Residence	Career	Publications	Visits GB and/or Italy
Micciari, J.	? – ?	Messina	Medicine	No	N/A
Molin, X. de	Died 1770	Arles	Army?	No	No
Niel, J. G.	1774–1853	St Paul Trois-Châteaux/Marseille	Medicine	Yes	No
Passinges ?	? – ?	Roanne	Commerce	No	No
Paul, Amand (S. J.)	1740–1809	Saint-Chamas	Translation	Yes	No
Paul, François	1731–74	Saint-Chamas	Medicine	Yes	No
Pellerin, J.	1684–1772	Paris	Administration		
Rivoire, A. (S. J.)	1709–90	Marseille/Ternay	Teaching	Yes	No
Roustan, J. B.	Died c. 1780	Nîmes	Medicine	No	No
Saint-Véran, J. D. (abbé)	1733–1812	Carpentras	Librarian	No	No
Saint-Vincens, J. Fr. P. de	1718–98	Aix-en-Provence	Law (office)	Yes	No
Sainte-Croix, G. E. J. Baron de	1746–1808	Mormoiron (Mt Ventoux)	Army	Yes	No
Sandricourt, Ch. Fr. S. de	1727–94	Agde	Church, bishop	No	No
Séguier, J. Fr.	1703–84	Nîmes	Law	Yes	Yes
Vaugelas, L. J. Lagier de (abbé)	1748–1800	Die	Church, canon	No	No
Vérone, M. J. B. Moreau de	1739–96	Buis, Vérone (Mt Ventoux), Grenoble	Law (office)	No	Yes
Vicq d'Azyr, F.	1748–94	Paris	Medicine	Yes	No

Sources: Calvet's extant correspondence and various biographical dictionaries, in particular the microfiche series, *Archives de biographie française*, series 1 and 2 (Munich, 1993–8): see Brockliss, *Calvet's Web*, pp. xvii and 413–15.

least a casual correspondence with several English *savants* thereafter. Séguier met the famous collector Sir Hans Sloane (1660–1753), counted him among his seventeen occasional London correspondents and sent him a copy of his *Bibliotheca botanica* from Verona in 1741.[12] La Tourrette, less fortunate, struck up a relationship with the notoriously unreliable naturalist Emanuel Mendes da Costa (1717–91),[13] who promised to send him mineral samples, but Faujas had better luck and cemented his correspondence with the President of the Royal Society, Sir Joseph Banks (1743–1820).[14]

The small number of the group who had been to Britain, however, may have reflected a lack of opportunity rather than a lack of interest. Significantly two out of the five were Parisians and a third, Faujas, had already moved there from Montélimar. It was much easier for Parisians to cross the Channel than people from the Midi, hundreds of kilometres to the south. Moreover, the majority of the group had a profession; their membership of the Republic of Letters was pursued in their leisure hours. Even if they were wealthy – and most (especially the clerics) were not – they had little chance to travel. Physicians, in particular, were rooted to their locality once they had begun to practise. Calvet himself was the son of an apothecary who had died while he was at college. His mother had enough money to allow him to spend two years in Paris (1750–52) after he had taken his medical degree at Avignon, but she refused him permission to next visit England as he requested.[15] Instead, he was hauled back to his home town to begin his career and he never left the area again. It was certainly not the antiquarian bent of most of Calvet's correspondents that explains their failure to visit Britain, since the seven who went in the opposite direction and travelled to Italy included the five who had crossed the Channel. Clearly, the average French republican of letters was not nearly so internationally mobile as one might expect in the age of the Grand Tour. Only the idle rich could really do as they pleased. One of the group, Moreau de Vérone, was the son of a judge at Buis-les-Baronnies in Dauphiné and had independent means. When his father ordered him to take up one of the new offices in the revamped Parlement of Grenoble in 1771, he objected vociferously, fearing it would put an end to his planned trip south of the Alps. In the event, he got leave of absence, as Calvet had suspected he would. Nonetheless, their mutual friend, Commander Gaillard, was overjoyed when the Maupeou *Parlements* were abolished in 1774 because Vérone was once more a free agent and could enjoy Italy in peace.[16]

A better indicator of the group's openness to British culture is the number who knew English. Here again this seems to have been true of surprisingly few. Although gaining a reading knowledge of English was now relatively easy, thanks to the ever-growing number of grammars and French–English or Latin–English dictionaries available in France, only a handful of Calvet's close correspondents seem to have taken the plunge. It can be assumed that the five who had visited Britain had a reasonable knowledge of the language, but even they cannot have used English very frequently. Séguier for one used French when he wrote to Sloane, while his vast library of 5,465 titles (or 6,951, if those with no place of publication are also counted) only contained 24 works in English.[17] Among the majority who never travelled to England, only the Jesuit Rivoire definitely had a good grounding in the tongue. Rivoire was an experimental philosopher and coin collector, based until the abolition of the Society in France at Marseille. His publications included a 1757 translation of Brook Taylor (1685–1731) on the principles of linear perspective (original 1719). Calvet himself had only the faintest smatterings of the language, although he did own a dictionary.[18] As a result, when the widowed Isabella Byron, the Countess of Carlisle (1721–95), who spent some years in Avignon in the 1770s and early 1780s, asked him to assist her in translating her brother, Admiral Byron's account of his shipwreck off Cape Horn, he could do little beyond correct her French.[19]

The web's acquaintance with English culture through translation

Admittedly, since anything of any significance published in English in philosophy, science, medicine and literature in the eighteenth century was soon translated into French, a knowledge of the language was hardly essential for those seeking to keep abreast of developments on the other side of the Channel. Ultimately, the best test of the group's acquaintance with contemporary British culture is to study its members' exposure to works by British authors in any language. The four surviving catalogues of their libraries, however, once more suggest that the majority had only a limited interest in eighteenth-century Britain. The Parisian collector D'Ennery left a small but select library of 460 volumes, chiefly works of history. Although he had been to England, as we saw, and was open to the ideas of the *philosophes* – he owned a first edition *Encyclopédie* and Jean-Jacques Rousseau's collected oeuvre – he had virtually no works by British authors beyond, somewhat oddly, a 1702 translation of the 1676 *Apology* for the Quakers by Robert Barclay (1648–90).[20] Calvet's own library was much bigger – 1,368 titles – and much better endowed with works by Britons – 55 (or 4 per cent of the total) – , but equally contained very little published after 1750 (see Tables 6.2 and 6.3).[21]

As was to be expected of a physician, he possessed a reasonable collection of British medical books (in Latin or French), including James's

Table 6.2 Books by British authors in Calvet's library

Category	All titles	British authors	British authors post-1750	All authors post-1750
Theology	93	3	1	21
Law	19	0	0	9
Science and Arts	356	32	8	134
Belles-lettres	354	5	0	69
History	254	9	3	51
Antiquities	233	6	1	49
Bibliography	59	0	0	27
TOTAL	1,368	55	13	360
(medicine)	(201)	(17)	(5)	(72)
(natural history)	(87)	(5)	(2)	(34)

Source: Bibliothèque Municipale Avignon MS 2346, fos. 277–368: Calvet's library catalogue.

Note: The five British works of natural history include two copies of *Géographie physique, ou essai sur l'histoire naturelle de la terre* (Paris: Briasson, 1735) by John Woodward (1665–1728).

Medical Dictionary (translated by Diderot). Apart from Robert Whytt (1714–66) on nervous diseases, though, he had nothing by the leading lights of the British profession in his own lifetime, such as Sir John Pringle (1707–82), John (1728–93) and William Hunter (1717–83), William Cullen (1710–90), or other professors of the Edinburgh medical school.[22] His holdings in British philosophy showed a similar bias towards an earlier period. He had the *De Cive* of Thomas Hobbes (1588–1679) and the *Essay on Human Understanding* of John Locke (1632–1704) in the 1729 Coste translation, but nothing by an eighteenth-century author.[23] Nor – despite the large number of books he owned on antiquities and history – did he demonstrate much enthusiasm for contemporary British historiography. He had William Robertson (1721–93) on America in a 1780 edition, and in the early years of the Revolution he purchased a copy of the *History of England* by David Hume (1711–76) in the translation of the Abbé Antoine-François Prévost (1697–1763).[24] But he significantly had no copy of *The Decline and Fall of the Roman Empire* of Edward Gibbon (1737–94), although this became gradually available in French translation from 1776. He had nothing at all in contemporary British literature, except the *Essay on Man* of Alexander Pope (1688–1744) (in a 1739 French translation).[25] Although he declared in later life that *Robinson Crusoe* was one of the few novels worth reading, he does

Table 6.3 Medical books with British authors owned by Calvet (by date of publication).

Author	Title	Place of publication	Date
Sir Kenelm Digby	Sur les guérisons par la poudre de sympathie	Paris	1666
Thomas Willis	Opera omnia	Cologne	1676
John Mayow	Opera omnia physico-medico	The Hague	1688
Richard Morton	Opera medica	Lyon	1697
Anonymous	Pharmacopoeia Collegii Regalis Londini	London	1699
Thomas Sydenham	Opera medica	Geneva	1723
John Freind	Emmenalogia	Paris	1727
Thomas Fuller	Pharmacopoeia extemporanea	London	1714 (1st edn 1703)
James Keill	L'Anatomie du corps de l'homme	Paris	1723
Archibale Pitcairne	Opera medica	Leiden	1737
? Turner	Traité des maladies de peau	Paris	1743
Robert James [trans. D. Diderot]	Dictionnaire universel de médecine	Paris	1746
Richard Mead	Opera	Paris	1751
James Keill	Tentamen medico-physica	Lucca	1756 (1st edn 1718)
Robert Whytt	Les vapeurs et les maladies nerveuses	Paris	1767
James Sims	Observations sur les maladies épidémiques	Avignon	1778
William Buchan	Médecine domestique	Paris	1785 (1st edn 1769)

Note: Calvet did not own Harvey's 1628 classic on the circulation of the blood.

not seem to have owned a copy.[26]

Even Séguier – despite his knowledge of England and English, his London correspondents, and his vast library – displayed little interest in the English culture of his day. He certainly bought books in London – his address book includes the names of London booksellers[27] – and he possessed 273 works published in England, but he seems to have primarily purchased editions of classical texts and works on experimental philosophy and antiquities, such as the 1709 study of light and electricity by Francis Hauksbee (d. 1713) and the *Inscriptiones antiquae, plerumque nondum ineditate, in Asia Minore et Graecia, praesertim Athenis collectae* published by the Magdalen Fellow and epigrapher, Richard Chandler (1738–1810) in 1774.[28] He had Côtes' 1729 translation of the *Opticks* of Isaac Newton (1642–1727) and a French version of the account of Newtonian philosophy by Henry Pemberton (1694–1771), but he had nothing in any language on British ethics or metaphysics – not even Locke's *Essay* – or by a British historian. He did own works by George Berkeley (1685–1753), but only the Bishop's theory of vision (in an Italian translation) and his promotion of the medical value of tar-water. Séguier equally had no work of English literature, from any century. He had two publications of Milton but they were both political pamphlets, including his response to the royalist *Eikon Basilike* (Greek).[29]

In fact only one of the four libraries contained a reasonable cross-section of works by eighteenth-century British authors: that owned by the Hellenist and historian, Baron de Sainte-Croix.[30] The Baron, who before the Revolution lived at Mormoiron on the southern slopes of Mont Ventoux, had been a captain in the French Grenadiers. He turned his attention to historical studies on his retirement in 1770 and was immediately rewarded for his efforts when his study of Alexander the Great was crowned by the Académie des Inscriptions in 1772. On his death in 1809 he left a library of 1,415 titles.[31] Although there is no evidence the Baron ever visited England or even had a deep reading knowledge of English, the library catalogue reveals he had a good acquaintance with modern English philosophy in French translations.[32] He had no Hume, but besides Locke's *Essay* and Locke on Christianity and on education, he had the neo-Platonist Ralph Cudworth (1617–88), the ethics of both Francis Hutcheson (1694–1776) and Adam Ferguson (1723–1816), and the latter's *History of Civil Society*.[33] He equally had a good collection of British historical works: Fergusson and Oliver Goldsmith (1730–74) on the Roman empire, Robertson's *History of Scotland* and *History of America*, and Gordon's *History of Ireland* – plus several important travelogues, including the *Voyages* of Captain James Cook (1728–79) in the translation of Jean-Baptiste-André Suard (1732–1817) and the account of a visit to China in the early 1790s by George, Lord Macartney (1737–1806).[34] Sainte-Croix even possessed some recent works of British literature, notably the *Night Thoughts* of Edward Young (1683–1765). In addition, he had important works by contemporary British antiquarians, including Chandler's *Inscriptiones* mentioned above.[35]

There is no reason to believe that the four libraries are not representative of the group's limited openness to contemporary British thought. A random study of the library catalogues left by other medical members of the French Republic of Letters suggests that even in Paris interest was largely restricted to British science and medicine pre-1750, and that British philosophy and literature was largely eschewed. The Paris physician Hyacinthe-Théodore Baron (1707–87), for instance, left a collection of 6,131 titles. Of the 839 classified as belles-lettres, only three were works of eighteenth-century British literature: *Robinson Crusoe, Gulliver's Travels* and Young's *Night Thoughts*, to which must be added Pope's *Essay on Man*, which was classed as philosophy.[36] His surgical colleague, Sauveur-François Morand (1697–1773), who could read English and bought books in the language, had only Pope's *Essay* and the *Tale of a Tub* by Jonathan Swift (1667–1745) among his literary titles (both in translation).[37] Séguier's friend, the Nîmois botanist-physician, Pierre Baux II (d. 1786) shared their narrow taste.[38] Although someone who had a large range of philosophy and subversive literature on his shelves – including the *De l'Esprit* of Claude-Adrien Helvétius (1715–71) – his holdings in English literature in French translation were equally limited to Swift and Pope.[39] In an age when supposedly the sentimental novels of Samuel Richardson (1689–1761), the pseudo-Gaelic lays of James Macpherson (1736–96), author of *Ossian*, and even Shakespeare, through the 1776–82 prose translations of Pierre Le Tourneur (1736–82), were gaining an audience in France, there is little sign that they were causing much of a stir among minor republicans of letters.

It is even possible that Sainte-Croix's commitment to British culture in the pre-Revolutionary era can be exaggerated. There is no doubt that, among Calvet's correspondents, the Baron was peculiarly fascinated by contemporary Britain. His *De l'estat et du sort des colonies des anciens peuples*, which appeared in 1779 in the middle of the War of American Independence, contained observations on the conduct of the British in America. Three years later, as the war in which France was fighting on the side of the Americans was drawing to a close, he published a two-volume *Histoire des progrès de la puissance navale de l'Angleterre*, where he warned the French government not to repeat the mistakes of the British in the 1763 Treaty of Paris and subject the defeated enemy to a humiliating peace.[40] It is clear, too, that the Baron had intellectual friends in England, whatever the standard of his English. When he heard that the Birmingham house of the Unitarian theologian and experimental philosopher Joseph Priestley (1733–1804) had been sacked by the mob in the summer of 1791, he was apparently unable to sleep for several nights because of the sufferings of his friend.[41] There again, it is impossible to know for certain what works by British authors he had in his library before 1789. The Baron's chateau and library were pillaged during the Terror. Many, perhaps most, of the works in the sales catalogue of 1809 could have been purchased after he moved permanently to Paris in the mid-1790s.[42]

Other forms of access to English culture

It is hard not to conclude, therefore, that if Calvet and most of his circle had a reasonable acquaintance with British science and philosophy of the seventeenth century, they had little detailed familiarity with their contemporary British culture. This is not to say, though, they had no knowledge of what was happening on the other side of the Channel, for they must have acquired a rudimentary understanding. In the first place, even the Provençals amongst them had access to a variety of journals and newspapers which would have kept them informed of British cultural and political developments. Calvet himself throughout his adult life subscribed to the monthly *Journal des Savants*, the chief French periodical for the arts and the sciences, and must have picked up some idea of contemporary British thought from its lengthy reviews.[43] He also must have frequently perused the twice-weekly *Courrier d'Avignon*, which was established in 1733 and was not just an advertising rag like other provincial *Affiches* but a proper newssheet with a printrun of 9,000 in the 1760s.[44] He even had indirect access to the Royal Society's *Philosophical Transactions*, which had been taken by one of his Jesuit friends in exile in the city from 1762, the experimental philosopher and astronomer Esprit Pézenas (1692–1776).[45]

Second, the circle continually played host to British visitors on the Grand Tour, who stopped off in Paris and the chief towns of the Rhône valley to see the sites and talk to recommended *gens de lettres* on their way to and from Italy.[46] Calvet's most prestigious visitor was Prince Augustus-Frederick of Hanover (1773–1843), the sixth son of George III, who passed through Avignon in April 1789. Always one to love a lord, the Avignon *érudit* claimed to have been charmed by the young man's modesty and seriousness, doubtless because he made suitably appreciative remarks about Calvet's collections.[47] How many or what other blue-blooded Britons the *Avignonnais* had encountered in earlier years is unrecorded, for Calvet referred to his visitors only occasionally in his correspondence and then seldom by name. Séguier, on the other hand, kept a careful record in the form of a visitors' book.[48]

The *Nîmois*, not surprisingly, had a large number of travellers turn up on his doorstep. The most famous republican of letters in a city renowned for its Roman amphitheatre and the owner of important natural history and antiquities collections, his was an obvious port of call for the tourist. In the last eleven years of his life, he received 1,536 visitors from France and the rest of Europe, 254 in 1777 alone. The largest number – two-thirds (a third from the Midi) came from France – but Britons formed the largest group of foreigners by far – 189.[49] Most of these were English gentlemen or gentlemen-clerics, often young men just out of university, who were travelling alone or with elder male companions. Several were well-to-do Catholics, such as Lord Clifford (probably the fifth Baron, Hugh [1756–93]), Charles Belayse (1750–1815), a doctor of the Sorbonne, and the Jesuit Charles Plowden (1743–1821), who passed through Nîmes on 8 November 1776.[50] Some of the most notable visitors, however, were en famille. Among the first to be recorded in the book were John, the first Earl Spencer (1734–83), his wife Georgiana (1737–1814) and two daughters, and their medical practitioner from Bath, who visited Séguier in 19 April 1773, en route to take the waters at Spa.[51] Occasionally the *savant* was even visited by unaccompanied English ladies. On 14 December 1777, for instance, he entertained Lady Phillipina Knight (1726–99), the widow of Admiral Sir Joseph Knight (d. 1775), and her nineteen-year-old daughter Cornelia (1757–1837), an oddly dressed, clever and strait-laced couple with limited means, on their way south to take up permanent residence in Italy.[52]

Although much of the conversation between Calvet's circle and their British visitors must have turned around the collections the latter had usually come to see, presumably the talk fell to some degree on British matters. The occasional laconic comment in Séguier's visitors' book would suggest that the *Nîmois* frequently used these casual contacts as conduits for his London correspondence. In 1776, for instance, he used two of his British visitors, Joseph Wilkinson of Hull and William Mitford of London, to carry seeds to John Stuart, Lord Bute (1713–92), who was a notable botanist as well as an erstwhile royal favourite and politician and had called on Séguier in 1768.[53] Séguier also from time to time picked up interesting titbits of information. On 24 June 1774 he learned from the Irish peer Lord Kingsborough (probably Robert, d. 1799) and his companion, one Tickell, that Josiah Wedgwood (1730–95) was successfully producing imitation Etruscan vases. Three years later he heard from a party led by a Mr Hurlock that Wedgwood was now counterfeiting engraved stones.[54] His most notable conversation, however, seems to have occurred on 12 May 1778, when he met one Thomas Greet. At this juncture Greet, the son of a London clergyman, was a young man of twenty-five or twenty-six, fresh out of University College, Oxford, with an apparent passion for epigraphy. One suspects that normally Séguier would have found such callow youths of little interest, but Greet was not a normal ex-undergraduate on the Grand Tour. The then Master of University College, Nathan Wetherell (1727–1808), was an intimate friend of Samuel Johnson (1709–84), and the learned doctor frequently dined in the College in the 1770s in the company of undergraduates. The young Greet was therefore able to regale his host with doubtless an eye-witness account of the famous author of the *Dictionary*.[55]

Some thoughts

Yet if Calvet and most of his circle had at best only a casual and superficial awareness of contemporary British science, philosophy and literature, their relative indifference must be placed in perspective. In general, the group was just as closed to other European cultures, and even to the work of the French *philosophes*.[56] This reflected the way in which its members structured their participation in the Republic of Letters. It is quite clear from their correspondence and the contents of their libraries that they took an interest in all the sciences and liberal arts. They were still Renaissance men, not narrow specialists. They only lay claim to expertise, however, in the disciplines in which they had a professional or scholarly interest. In other areas, they were content to have a general working knowledge of the subject's historical development prior to their own day. Calvet was exemplary in this regard. Besides medicine, natural history and antiquities/history, his library holdings were small and consisted of works largely published before his birth (see Table 6.2). In that he was not a free thinker, had no pretensions to be a philosopher (of any kind), and thought novels (with a few honourable exceptions) trivial, he clearly saw no point in wasting his limited resources on British philosophy and literature, even in translation. He did not spend his money on similar works by Frenchmen, Italians or Germans either.[57]

It might have been thought that as a physician, he would have shown more enthusiasm for contemporary British medicine, but Calvet was a medical practitioner whose allegiance lay with the iatromechanism of the first half of the eighteenth century, encapsulated by the Leiden professor Hermann Boerhaave (1668–1738). He was not interested in the vitalist medical philosophy that took hold of Europe (particularly at Edinburgh) in the second half of the century, nor, to any extent, in the new sciences of morbid anatomy and clinical pathology, and made no attempt to purchase any of the seminal works published by the Paris school in the last decade of his life.[58] Even in the areas in which Calvet took a special interest – Roman coins and antiquities, fossils and mineralogy – it is not surprising he purchased so little by British authors. This was an age of French cultural hegemony, and he and his friends automatically assumed that the most interesting work in their chosen fields was being done by Frenchmen. La Tourrette's judgement on the state of British science on his return from England in late 1766 confirmed that travel did not necessarily broaden the mind. In his opinion, the French pursued knowledge with greater vigour than their British colleagues, and even the great Sloane's collection could not hold a candle to the best in Paris. The English, he declared, were only ahead in agriculture, gardening and botany – pursuits for which Calvet had no enthusiasm.[59]

The group's particular indifference to British culture was also inspired by jealousy. Although there is no evidence that they saw Britain as the national enemy with whom France was involved in a struggle for world domination, they certainly resented its wealth and the ease with which British republicans of letters could travel around the Mediterranean hoovering up the best antiquities in a way they could not. Even the Midi was not safe from their clutches. The collection of one of Calvet's close correspondents, Xavier de Molin of Arles, which was eventually bought by the Provençal abbé Jacques-François-Paul-Aldonce de Sade (1705–78), would have fallen into the hands of John Manners, Marquis of Granby (1721–70), had the Marquis not died during the negotiations.[60] In response, the circle anticipated the modern European reaction to American cultural imperialism and took comfort in believing that the British were indiscriminate collectors[61] and poor scholars. There was no need then to purchase their works. When in 1788 the British antiquarian Thomas Pownall (1722–1805), had the temerity to publish a study on the antiquities of the Midi, Calvet and his friend, the Aix *parlementaire* Saint-Vincens, immediately denounced the work as shallow, even though they had only read an extract in translation in the *Journal des Savants*.[62]

Various factors thus explain why more run-of-the-mill members of the French Republic of Letters might not have shared the enthusiasm of Paris salon society for things British. It would be interesting to know whether a reciprocal lack of warmth towards French eighteenth-century science, philosophy and literature also characterised the broader membership of the British Republic of Letters, and whether the number of *savants* genuinely interested in each other's culture in either country was always small. Certainly, most Britons outside the Whig establishment were bitterly francophobic, and even those on the Grand Tour could be scathing about the intellectual and moral calibre of their French hosts, as the surgeon Tobias Smollett's travel diary reveals.[63] Arguably, genuine Anglo-French intellectual exchange in the last decades of the Ancien Régime was a commerce involving merely a small elite in London and Paris.[64]

It would be interesting, too, to know whether there was a greater openness to contemporary British and French culture among the foot soldiers of the Republic of Letters in other parts of Europe. To what extent did conventional allegiances affect levels of openness to foreign cultures? Calvet and his friends entertained Protestant visitors and disliked religious fanaticism, but with a few exceptions they were all Catholic believers.[65] Did this also affect their view of British science and scholarship? It is perhaps disingenuous to compare Calvet's attitude to British culture with that of the pious Swiss Protestant naturalist and physician Albrecht von Haller (1708–77). After all, Haller was a much more important international figure, he had visited London, knew English and held a chair at the Hanoverian University of Göttingen. Yet the difference in the level of their engagement with British culture is instructive. Of the Bernese's 1,200 correspondents, 40 were English, and 1, Sir John Pringle, was of particular importance. Haller, too, had a significant collection of modern British publications: 1,050 of his 13,000 books were published in England, 657 in the years 1751–77. Calvet, in contrast, had no British correspondents, even casual ones, and only owned 33 books printed in Great Britain (all in Latin).[66] The difference cannot just be coincidental. There is a tendency to think of the eighteenth-century European Republic of Letters as an international space, unaffected by linguistic, national and confessional differences.[67] This chapter would suggest this is too optimistic a viewpoint and that there is a need to identify and weigh more carefully than hitherto the non-disciplinary factors which shaped its citizens' allegiances.

Admittedly, historians writing about the Republic of Letters before 1700 have accepted that it was far more confessionally configured than its members might have liked to think. The late Hugh Trevor-Roper in particular was keen to emphasise that English intellectuals in the century 1550–1650 were part of a specifically Calvinist International not a cross-confessional Republic of Letters. If Frenchmen in the century after the Reformation took an interest in English literary and scientific culture, then they were frequently Huguenots, who shared the common Protestant obsession with Paracelsianism and the impending Millennium. Typical was the Montpellier-educated physician, Théodore Turquet de Mayerne, whose father had had to emigrate to Geneva during the Massacre of St Bartholomew and who would eventually be physician to Henri IV and James I and Charles I of England.[68] No one, however, has hitherto raised the possibility that the Republic of Letters remained confessionally divided, if only in part, during the Age of Enlightenment. It has been merely suggested that the abandonment of Latin as the European lingua franca in the eighteenth century did not necessarily make the transmission of ideas easier, especially in France, where English and German had not been traditionally taught as languages of civilisation.[69]

On the other hand, if the majority of French republicans of letters in the eighteenth century may have been much more intellectually introverted than we have imagined, it seems likely that their early nineteenth-century successors were far more cosmopolitan and much more Anglophile. At first sight this assertion might seem even more paradoxical. After all, in the period 1790–1830 French physical and medical science in particular were the envy of Europe. The ending of the long war with Britain in 1815 once more saw Britons crossing the Channel in droves, especially medical students seeking to sit at the feet of the great pathological anatomists of Paris. There is little evidence, however, that Frenchmen were scurrying in the opposite direction anxious to absorb London intellectual life.[70] Nevertheless, attitudes and interest were changing as a consequence of the prolonged hostilities. However much the period saw the Europe prestige of French science rise to new heights, it also witnessed the eventual emergence of a novel enthusiasm for English literary culture.

The conduit for this transformation were the *émigrés*. Whereas the tens of thousands of Huguenots who had left France for England after the Revocation of the Edict of Nantes in 1685 certainly helped the transmission of French culture in Britain, the very fact they went into permanent exile ensured they played only a limited role in introducing English intellectual life to their erstwhile countrymen. Rather, since they had friends and relations throughout the Protestant world, their presence in London only cemented more deeply the confessional nature of the Republic of Letters. The émigrés who fled to Britain during the 1790s, in contrast, were Catholics, who, provided they lived, eventually returned to their native land. Conservatives and liberals, priests, aristocrats, administrators and politicians, they represented a much wider cross-section of the French educated elite than their Huguenot predecessors. The interaction between the exiles and the host community was mutually beneficial. Old suspicions did not die, but the more liberal English Protestant, such as Prime Minister Pitt, began to look a little more kindly on Catholicism, while the French gained a lengthy first-hand acquaintance with Anglo-Saxon culture. Chateaubriand may have claimed to have starved in a London garret, but many exiles were reasonably well integrated with English intellectual society, especially those involved in exile journalism.[71] Even the exiled priests who were virtually interned lest they pollute the Protestant nation had some reason to remember their stay with gratitude: that bastion of the Anglican establishment, Oxford University Press, was happy to supply them with Catholic religious texts!

Above all, French émigrés brought back from their English experience the new Romantic aesthetic. Diderot's *Encyclopédie* had provided a measured critique of the dominant classical paradigm by emphasising the role of genius and imagination in artistic creation.[72] Despite this, the literature and drama of the Revolutionary decade and the Napoleonic era still remained largely indebted to the models of the reign of Louis XIV. In England, however, the same period saw both the theory and practice of the literary and visual arts undergoing revolutionary change, as a new value was attributed to the artist as 'seer' and new forms were invented for conveying the artists' subjective experience.[73] In consequence, even before the defeat of Napoleon, young innovatory writers were taking a new positive look at English literary culture *tout court*, especially Shakespeare, for so long an object of distaste in France. In the Restoration era, in the face of the continued conservatism of the Académie française, this admiration only grew, especially among ultraroyalists anxious to promote throne and altar. By the end of the 1820s the perception of the young literary lions was shared by the wider public. In 1822, when a troupe of English actors arrived in Paris to play Shakespeare in English, they were hissed off the stage; five years later, thanks in part to the intense debate roused by the publication of Stendhal's defence of the Bard in his *Racine et Shakespeare* of 1823 and 1825, they returned to public acclaim.[74] At the same time, English authors began to appear in the bestsellers' list. The first to do so was Calvet's favourite novelist, Defoe, whose *Robinson Crusoe*, an early eighteenth-century religious text recycled as a tale of Romantic heroism, sold in large numbers from the early 1820s onwards. But the real darling of the French reading public was Sir Walter Scott, whose historical novels of a lost age were particularly devoured in the decade 1826–35.[75]

Of course, the new Romantic aesthetic which rapidly took root in France after the Restoration and found its first home-grown expression in the highly popular *Méditations poétiques* of Lamartine (1820) was a German as much as an English creation. Indeed, the Protestant, Madame de Stael, daughter of Louis XVI's finance minister Necker, preferred to look across the Rhine for the signs of the cultural vigour that she believed was lacking in post-Revolutionary France when she took issue with French art and philosophy in her *De l'Allemagne* of 1813. But, although a bestseller and its contents judged suitably *shocking*, she never seems to have convinced her French readers that the artistic future lay in Berlin or Vienna. In part, this must be attributed to the fact that Stael did not discuss the achievements of the new generation of German poets, novelists and artists in her work, merely limiting herself to a description of the aesthetic of the Schlegel brothers. In part, and probably more importantly, it reflected the fact that Britain was the new world power, while Germany remained a geographical expression. Even the book itself had been initially published in London.[76]

That Britain was the victor in the second 'Hundred Years' War' also helps to explain why other aspects of contemporary British culture equally began to attract French attention after 1815. Many liberal opponents of the Restoration monarchy, such as Guizot, Professor of History at the Sorbonne, may have had little sympathy with the new Romantic aesthetic but they did find plenty to interest them in Scottish common-sense philosophy and the reform campaigns espoused by the Whigs and radicals in the *Edinburgh* and the *London and Westminster Review*. When the democrat Tocqueville visited England in 1835 his political soulmates were the Benthamite utilitarians.[77] The British also helped to promote their own cause by establishing an English-language book-review journal in the French capital in the 1820s, the *Paris Monthly Review of British and Continental Literature*. So pervasive was the belief that English culture stood for 'modernity' in the July Monarchy that Balzac in many of his novels of the 1830s and 1840s could accuse the British of poisoning French society with their money-grubbing bourgeois values. Defeat in 1815, then, was the catalyst for a re-evaluation of British culture after more than a century of French cultural hegemony. The same reaction would occur in 1871 in response to the defeat by Prussia, when German science, until then largely neglected, would suddenly become an object of obsessive concern.

This is not to say that, had Calvet been born a generation later, he would have found British contemporary culture much more exciting and filled his library with the works of English poets and novelists, albeit in translation. Given his general lack of interest in modern European culture, this is highly unlikely. It very possible, though, that his youngest permanent correspondent eventually succumbed to the charms of English literature. This was the physician Jean-Gabriel Niel (1774–1853), a scion of the Avignon printing dynasty who corresponded with Calvet between 1796 and 1805 while resident at Saint-Paul-Trois-Châteaux and Marseilles. We know very little about his life, except that in retirement he moved to Dinan in Brittany, where his patients included Chateaubriand and his sister Lucille and that romantic scourge of the Church establishment, the abbé Lammenais.

Notes

1 J. Grieder, *Anglomania in France, 1740–1789: Fact, Fiction and Political Discourse* (Geneva: Droz, 1985).
2 For a detailed account of this group and its interests, see L. W. B. Brockliss, *Calvet's Web: Enlightenment and the Republic of Letters in Eighteenth-Century France* (Oxford: Oxford University Press, 2002). This work only mentions the group's absorption of contemporary British culture in passing.
3 The profile of the thirty-two is fully explored in Brockliss, *Calvet's Web*, chapter 2, section 2.
4 See the information in D. Roche, *Le Siècle des lumières en province: Académies et académiciens provinciaux, 1680–1789* (Paris: Mouton, 1978; 2nd edition: Paris: Editions de l'Ecole des Hautes Etudes en sciences sociales,

1989) 2 vols, vol. 1, chapter 4. This remains the only scholarly overview of the French Republic of Letters in the provinces.

5 On the Parisian *salonnière*, see D. Goodman, *The Republic of Letters: A Cultural History of the French Enlightenment* (Ithaca: Cornell University Press, 1994), and A. Lilti, 'La femme du monde est-elle une intellectuelle? Les salons parisiens au XVIIIe siècle', in N. Racine and M. Trebitsch (eds), *Intellectuelles: du genre en histoire des intellectuels* (Bruxelles: Editions Complexe, 2004). For a good account of one of the few provincial *savants* of the period, see B. Byrd, 'Intellectual Liaisons: Women and the Republic of Letters: The Case of Marie Masson Le Golft', Ph.D. dissertation, University of Oxford, 2005.

6 Caylus was the author of *Recueil d'antiquités égyptiennes, étrusques, grecques et romaines*, (Paris: Desaint and Saillant, 1752–67), 7 vols, which was intended to re-educate French taste away from the Rococo. See M. Fumaroli, 'La République des Lettres VI: un gentilhomme universel: Anne-Claude de Thubières, comte de Caylus (1694–1765)', *Annuaire du Collège de France*, 93 (1992–3), 563–81. Faujas was an important geologist and vulcanologist: the only study of his life remains in L. Freycinet, *Essai sur la vie, les opinions et les ouvrages de Barthélemy Faujas de Saint-Fond* (Valence: J. Montal, 1820). Séguier is famous as the *savant* who cracked the inscription on the Maison Carrée at Nîmes by studying the surviving rivet holes. For his life and work, see E. Mosele (ed.), *Un Accademico dei Lumi fra due citta: Verona e Nîmes: scritta in onoré di Jean-François Séguier nel secondo centenario della morte* (Bologna: Comune di Bologna, 1987).

7 Of the group of thirty-two, only Séguier's correspondence circle can be properly reconstructed, because his is the only correspondence to have survived. He had roughly the same number of correspondents at Calvet but only twenty-six regular contacts (eight in his case outside France). Judgement based on the information in *Catalogue général des bibliothèques publiques de France: départements*, vols 7 and 8, under 'Nîmes', MSS 103, 309–10, 415–16, 498 (inventory of Séguier's correspondence). For an introduction to its contents, see D. Roche, 'Correspondance et voyage au XVIIIe siècle: le réseau de sociabilité d'un académicien provincial', in D. Roche, *Les Républicains des lettres: gens de culture et lumière au XVIIIe siècle* (Paris: Fayard, 1988), chapter 11.

8 Bibliothèque Municipale Nîmes MS 129, Séguier, 'Notes de voyage en France, en Angleterre et en Hollande'. For Maffei, see *Nuovi studi Maffeiani: atti del convegno Scipione Maffei e il museo Maffeiano* (Verona: Comune di Verona, 1985). For an account of his travels with Séguier, see G. P. Marchi, 'Il viaggio di Maffei e Séguier attraverso l'Europa', in E. Mosele (ed.), *Un Accademico dei Lumi*, pp. 51–9.

9 Bibliothèque Municipale Avignon MS 2358, fo. 226: La Tourrette to Calvet, 7 December 1766.

10 Bibliothèque Municipale Avignon MS 2367, fos 9–10: D'Ennery to Calvet, 10 January 1768.

11 Barthélemy Faujas de Saint-Fond, *Voyage en Angleterre, en Ecosse et aux*

Hébrides, où l'on trouve la description détaillée de la grotte de Fingal, à l'île de Staffa (Paris: Jansen, 1797), 2 vols.

12 Roche, 'Correspondance', p. 270; British Library Additional MSS 4056, fo. 293; 4057, fo. 54; 4069, fos. 58, 83: Séguier to Sloane, letters 1741–2.

13 G. Rousseau and D. Haycok, 'The Jew of Crane Court: Emanuel Mendes da Costa (1717–91), Natural History and Excess', *History of Science*, 38 (2000), 127–70. Da Costa was eventually expelled from the Royal Society for fraud.

14 *The Banks Letters: A Calendar of the Manuscript Correspondence of Sir Joseph Banks*, ed. W. R. Dawson (London: British Museum, 1958), pp. 321–3 (twenty-four letters).

15 Bibliothèque Municipale Avignon MS 2349, fo. 394r: Calvet's autobiography. For his life and family, see Brockliss, *Calvet's Web*, chapter 1, section 1.

16 Bibliothèque Municipale Avignon MS 4447, fos 125–6: Calvet to Vérone, 15 September 1772; MS 2365, fos 142–3, 148–9: Vérone to Calvet, n.d. and 7 August [1772]; MS 2355, nos 64. 66: Gaillard to Calvet, 31 December 1774, 18 January 1775.

17 E. Mosele, *Un Accademico francese del Settecento e la sua biblioteca (Jean-François Séguier 1703–84* (Verona: Libreria universitaria editrice, 1981), p. 87. Based on a study of Bibliothèque Municipale Nîmes MS 285, 'Catalogue des livres de Jean-François Séguier en 1760 et années suivantes'.

18 *A Large Dictionary, the English before the Latin, the Latin before the English*, in folio (London: Rawlins, 1677): Bibliothèque Municipale Avignon, MS 2346, fos 313v–14r: no. 529 in Calvet's library catalogue: see also, note 20 below.

19 Bibliothèque Municipale Avignon, MS 2349, fo. 400: Calvet's autobiography. The English original was published in 1768. Lady Carlisle was the poet Byron's great-aunt.

20 *Catalogue des livres du cabinet de feu M. D'Ennery* (Paris: n.p., 1786), nos 9, 59, 106. Although this is a sales catalogue and therefore not necessarily a complete list of D'Ennery's books (ephemera and scandalous works were usually not recorded), there is no reason to believe it underestimates his holdings of British authors.

21 Bibliothèque Municipale Avignon MS 2346, fos 277–368. The catalogue was completed by Calvet in the autumn of 1791 and organised conventionally into books on theology, jurisprudence, sciences and arts, belles-lettres and history. The books were numbered 1 to 1,382 and a further 154 purchases added later. For a full account of the library's contents and purchase, see Brockliss, *Calvet's Web*, chapter 6, sections 1 and 2.

22 James, no. 263 (Paris, 1746); Whytt, no. 365 (French translation, 1767).

23 Hobbes, no. 86 (Amsterdam, 1769); Locke, no. 152.

24 Robertson, no. 1085 (French translation, 1780); Hume, fo. 347v (unnumbered entry; Amsterdam, 1765). Calvet had been offered a Hume by another one of his close correspondents, Amand Paul, in 1774, which had been belonged to the library of his dead brother, but he had declined: Bibliothèque Municipale Avignon MS 2352, fo. 153: Paul to Calvet, 20 December 1774.

25 Bibliothèque Municipale Avignon MS 2346, library catalogue, no. 682 (French translation: Lausanne, 1738).
26 Bibliothèque Municipale Carpentras MS 1722, fo. 96: Calvet to Saint-Véran, 16 July 1805.
27 For example, John Whiston of Fleet Street: Bibliothèque Municipale Nîmes MS 284(i), fo. 3: Séguier's address book.
28 Bibliothèque Municipale Nîmes MS 285, pp. 72, 144. Séguier's catalogue is set out in alphabetical order, which is unusual for the period.
29 Bibliothèque Municipale Nîmes MS 285, pp. 30–1, 218.
30 M. Larroutis, 'Le Baron de Sainte-Croix: Un Comtadin injustement oublié (1746–1809)', *Mémoires de l'Académie de Vaucluse*, 7th series, 3 (1982), 211–23.
31 *Catalogue des livres de la bibliothèque de feu M. Guilhem de Clermont Lodève de Sainte-Croix* (Paris: n.p., 1809). This is prefaced by Silvestre de Sacy, 'Notice historique sur sa vie et ses oeuvres'.
32 The Baron did own an English and Italian grammar (1798) and Thomas Nugent's *French–English Pocket Dictionary*: ibid., nos 441 and 442.
33 *Ibid.*; no. 171: Locke, *Le Christianisme raisonnable* (1731); 174: Cudworth, *Systema intellectualis* (1773); 282: Ferguson, *Ethics* (1775); 284: Hutcheson, *Ethics* (1770); 291: Locke, *Education* (1759); 294: Ferguson, *Civil Society* (1783); 312: Locke, *Essay* (1700).
34 *Ibid.*; no. 870: Cook (1778); 924: Macartney (1805); 1120: Goldsmith (1801); 1121: Ferguson (1784); 139: Robertson, *Scotland* (1785); 1195: Gordon (1808); 1239: Robertson, *America* (1778).
35 Ibid., nos 672: Young (1765); 1293: Chandler (1774).
36 *Catalogue de la bibliothèque de feu M. Baron* (Paris: n.p., 1788), nos 615 (Pope), 4841 (Young), 5041 (*Robinson Crusoe*); 5042 (*Gulliver's Travels*). Baron had Locke's *Essay* (no. 614), the philosophical works of Hume in an Amsterdam edition of 1759 (no. 416) and the *Fable of the Bees* by Bernard Mandeville (1670?–1733) (French edition 1750) but no other work of eighteenth-century British philosophy or history.
37 *Catalogue des livres de la bibliothèque de feu M. Morand* (Paris: n.p., 1774), nos 1946 and 1997. He had no contemporary British philosophy or history, except the *Cyclopaedeia* of Ephraim Chambers (1680–1740) in English (no. 130). He did have the *Book of Common Prayer* (no. 94).
38 Bibliothèque Municipale Nîmes MSS 449–50. The second MS is a catalogue of Baux's library c. 1736–7, when, presumably, he inherited it from his father. The first MS lists his purchases from 1736 to 1772.
39 Bibliothèque Municipale Nîmes MS 449, p. 146 (*De l'esprit*); MS 450, under 'poètes': Pope's *Rape of the Lock* (1728) and *Essay on Man* (1737); under 'romans': *Gulliver's Travels* (1727); under 'satires': *Tale of a Tub* (1732). The last was obtained in 1736 through the good offices of Baux's Montpellier friend and later professor of medicine: François Boissier de Sauvages (1706–67): Bibliothèque Municipale Nîmes MS 414, no. 62: Sauvages to Baux, 3 February 1736. After 1737, Baux bought a few works of British science and William Wollaston (1660–1724) on natural religion in a 1726

French translation (p. 23), but nothing else by British philosophers, historians or theologians; he even seems to have sold his (father's?) copy of Locke's *Essay* (pp. 9–10).

40 De Sacy, 'Notice', pp. xiv, xvii–xix.
41 Bibliothèque Municipale Avignon, MS 4447, fo. 177: Calvet to Vérone, 5 July [1792]; MS 2367, fo. 183: Saint-Vincens to Calvet, 29 June 1792.
42 De Sacy, 'Notice', pp. vii, xxiii.
43 Bibliothèque Municipale Avignon, MSS 5621–2: Calvet's account book 1776–1810; MS 2346, 'library catalogue', no. 1334. Calvet had a complete set of the *Journal des Savants* and definitely subscribed annually from 1776. There is no study to date of the amount of space the *Journal* gave to reviewing works by Britons.
44 R. Moulinas, *L'Imprimerie, la librairie et la presse à Avignon au XVIIIe siècle* (Grenoble: Presses universitaires de Grenoble, 1974), part 2. From 1775, the newspaper was printed by Calvet's friend Jean-Joseph Niel (1739–94).
45 Séguier borrowed copies on several occasions, e.g. Bibliothèque Municipale Nîmes MS 140, fos 49–50: Calvet to Séguier, 5 July 1765. Pézenas had also been based at Marseille. Perhaps members of the Society had a better knowledge of English than other republicans of letters in the Midi.
46 J. Black, *The British Abroad: The Grand Tour in the Eighteenth Century* (Stroud: Sutton, 1992).
47 Bibliothèque Municipale Avignon MS 2348, fos. 397–8: Calvet's account of their meeting in a short piece entitled on the 'Avantages des collections de curiosités'(!).
48 Bibliothèque Municipale Nîmes MS 284, no. 2: visitor's book (in Séguier's hand) 1773–83.
49 Roche, 'Correspondance et voyage', pp. 272–8, especially table p. 277. By my own calculations, Séguier had only 153 visitors from the British Isles and the colonies. He had only two British visitors in 1781 and in 1782 at the height of the War of American Independence.
50 Bibliothèque Municipale Nîmes MS 284 part, fo. 9. Information on their travels in J. Ingamells (ed.), *A Dictionary of British and Irish Travellers in Italy 1701–1800* (London and Newhaven: Yale University Press, 1997), pp. 74, 218–19, 776.
51 Bibliothèque Municipale Nîmes MS 284 (2), fo. 2: Ingamells, *Dictionary*, pp. 882–4; Amanda Foreman, *Georgiana, Duchess of Devonshire* (London: HarperCollins, 1998), p. 14. Georgiana (1757–1806) was one of the daughters.
52 Bibliothèque Municipale Nîmes MS 284 (2), fo. 13; Ingamells, *Dictionary*, pp. 581–3.
53 Bibliothèque Municipale Nîmes MS 284 (2), fo. 9, under 3 October and 30 November I know nothing of either individual. Bute must have asked Séguier to send him some specimens. For their original encounter, see British Library Additional Manuscripts 22935, fo. 290: Séguier to Antoine Gouan (1733–1821; a Montpellier professor), 27 November 1768.
54 Bibliothèque Municipale Nîmes MS 284 (2), fos 4, 10. Hurlock was travelling

on the continent with his daughter, who in 1777 married the future MP Edmund Bunney (1749–1833), a visitor to Séguier a few months later (fo. 11); Ingamells, *Dictionary*, p. 249. Wedgwood opened his factory, christened Etruria, in 1769.

55 Bibliothèque Municipale Nîmes MS 284 (2)., fo. 15. I owe the information on Greet and Johnson's connections with University College to Robin Darwall-Smith, who is at present writing a history of the College.

56 Only La Tourrette corresponded with Voltaire and Rousseau, although Séguier had met Voltaire early in his life, while in Paris with Maffei in the 1730s: see Brockliss, *Calvet's Web*, pp. 392–6.

57 The structure of his library is discussed in Brockliss, *Calvet's Web*, chapter 6, section 1.

58 Brockliss, *Calvet's Web*, chapter 3, section 2, esp. Table 3.3 (p. 154). For the achievements of the new Paris school of medicine founded in 1794, see E. Ackerknecht, *Medicine at the Paris Hospital* (Baltimore: Johns Hopkins University Press, 1967).

59 See note 8. Sloane's collection was bequeathed to the nation on his death, so La Tourrette must have seen it in the new British Museum, opened in 1759.

60 Bibliothèque Municipale Avignon MS 2355, nos10, 15: Commander Gaillard to Calvet, n.d. and 23 November 1770; MS 4447, fo. 107: Calvet to Vérone, 30 June 1771.

61 For example, Bibliothèque Municipale Avignon, MS 2355, nos 16, 20: Gaillard to Calvet, 1 January and 29 October 1771.

62 Bibliothèque Municipale Avignon MS 2346, fos 302–8: Calvet to Saint-Vincens, 24 August 1788; MS 2367, fos 166–7: Saint-Vincens to Calvet, 29 August 1788.

63 T. Smollet, *Travels through France and Italy*, ed. O. Sitwell (London: L. Lehmann, 1949), passim. For Francophobia, see especially R. D. E. Eagles, 'Francophilia and Francophobia in English Society, 1748–1783', Ph.D. dissertation, University of Oxford, 1996.

64 As Pascal Brioist has shown in chapter 4, above, there was genuine exchange between the Royal Society and the Académie des sciences in the eighteenth century, however different their organisation. On the other hand, as Daniel Roche points out in chapter 5, most British visitors to Paris in the years before the Revolution kept themselves to themselves and had limited contact with the local culture.

65 Of Calvet's close correspondents, only Caylus was a free-thinker. See Brockliss, *Calvet's Web*, pp. 51–8, 106, 392–3.

66 Information based on a communication from Dr Hubert Steinke of the Bern Haller project. Details at: www.ana.unibe.ch/MHIUB/Haller: list of correspondents and library. The most important collections of Haller's letters are being published, for example, *John Pringle's Correspondence with Albrecht von Haller*, ed. Otto Sontag (Basel: Schwabe, 1999). For the place of publication of Calvet's books, see Brockliss, *Calvet's Web*, pp. 285–7.

67 This is very much the picture painted for an earlier period in A. Goldgar, *Impolite Learning: Conduct and Community in the Republic of Letters*,

1680–1750 (London, New Haven: Yale University Press, 1995).
68 Trevor-Roper's fullest account of the Calvinist international will appear in his forthcoming posthumous biography of Mayerne.
69 R. A. Houston, *Literacy in Early Modern Europe. Culture and Education 1500–1800* (Harlow: Longman, 1988), p. 232; L. W. B. Brockliss, *French Higher Education in Seventeenth and Eighteenth Century France: A Cultural History* (Oxford: Oxford University Press, 1987), pp. 120–1.
70 The literature on French science in the post-Revolutionary era is huge, but for a valuable introduction see J. and N. Dhombres, *Naissance d'un pouvoir: sciences et savants en France 1793–1824* (Paris: Editions Payot, 1989). For Parisian medicine and British medical students, see in particular R. Maulitz, *Morbid Appearances: The Anatomy of Pathology in the Early Nineteenth Century* (Cambridge: Cambridge University Press, 1987), and 'Channel Crossing: The Lure of French Pathology for English Medical Students', *Bulletin of the History of Medicine*, 55 (1981).
71 S. Burrows, *French Exile Journalism and European Politics 1792–1814* (The Boydell Press: Bury St Edmunds, 2000).
72 O. Bleskie, 'An Emotional Enlightenment: Epistemological Innovation and Artistic Paradigm Shift in Diderot's *Encyclopédie*', Ph.D. dissertation, University of Oxford, in progress.
73 C. Thacker, *The Wildness Pleases: The Origins of Romanticism* (Beckenham: Croom Helm, 1983); M. H. Abrams, *The Mirror and the Lamp: Romantic Theory and the Critical Tradition* (Oxford: Oxford University Press, 1971); R. Porter and M. Teich (eds.), *Romanticism in National Context* (Cambridge: Cambridge University Press, 1988), chapters 2 and 5. In England's case the new aesthetic was most famously expressed in Wordsworth's and Coleridge's 1798 *Lyrical Ballads*.
74 Stendhal, *Racine et Shakespeare: études sur le romanticisme* (Paris: Garnier-Flammarion, 1970), introduction by Roger Fayolle. Stendhal, a Bonapartiste not an ultra, argued that literary forms and subject matter were a reflection of the cultures which produced them. Racine belonged to the world of Louis XIV. Shakespeare was a good model for his own day because the 1820s had much in common with England in the 1590s.
75 M. Lyons, *Le Triomphe du livre: une histoire sociologique de la lecture dans la France du XIXe siècle* (Paris: Promodis, 1987), chapter 5.
76 Madame de Stael, *De l'Allemagne* (Paris: Garnier-Flammarion, 1968), 2 vols, especially part 2, 'La littérature et les arts'. Earlier she had used Italy as a cultural counterweight to France in *Corinne* (1807).
77 A. Jardin, *Tocqueville: A Biography* (New York: Farrar, Strauss, 1988), pp. 230–8.

Part III
Cultural transfers

7

Reading revolution: towards a history of the Volney vogue in England

ALEXANDER COOK

This chapter traces the reception of a French book in England. More broadly, it examines a process in which aspects of French revolutionary political thought and language were appropriated for use in English reform campaigns during the first half of the nineteenth century. The book is entitled *Les Ruines, ou Méditation sur les révolutions des empires*. First published in 1791, it was dedicated to the revolutionary National Assembly of France, of which its author was a member. The author, Constantin Volney (1757–1820), was a political theorist, historian and travel writer. Now a largely forgotten figure, in his day Volney was one of the most notorious writers in Europe. He was unquestionably the most popular revolutionary author in the Anglophone world, and he remained one of the most widely read French writers in Britain through the first half of the nineteenth century.

For fifty years following the revolution, *Les Ruines* served as a key text in British campaigns for political and religious reform. Eleven books were published specifically to refute Volney during this period in England. Numerous pamphlets and articles were written on the subject of his supposedly destructive influence. The consequence, for historians, is an unusually detailed record of the process by which a French philosopher was received and *used* across the Channel. In this chapter I want to discuss why *Les Ruines* was so successful in England in comparison with other literature of the French Revolution and to examine how the book functioned within the field of English radical politics. As a case study it offers a fascinating perspective on the complex history of intellectual opposition and exchange between the two countries. It also highlights the importance of understanding changing contexts of consumption and utilisation if we wish to study what reception theorists like to call the 'effective history' of literature – its productive potential in the social world.

Les Ruines: form and content

Les Ruines seems a curious book to modern readers. It blends large passages of straight political and moral philosophy with a poetic style, a first person narrator and a fictional structure that includes dream sequences, genies and revelations. The narrative is set in 1784. The narrator is a traveller in the Orient, as Volney had been at the time. While wandering in the desert, he stumbles across the ruins of the ancient city of Palmyra. This spectacle of decay inspires a prolonged meditation on the rise and decline of civilisations, the art of government, the ethics of social life and the prospects of progress. The narrator falls asleep before the city. In his dreams he receives a revelation from a spirit guide, a 'genie' who emerges from the ruins to explain the dynamics of human history and to offer a vision of a better future. The mood of the text varies radically from an initial sense of tragic pathos at the cycles of empires and the frustration of human ambition, through a phase of anger at human folly and corruption, to a final vision of hope that the errors and failures of the past might finally be overcome through the gradual enlightenment of the species.

Within this structural framework, we can trace several philosophical propositions that seem to have been important for early readers. First, Volney set out a theory of history in which the rise and decline of states was related to the justice of their internal organisation. The ruin of ancient civilisations was related not to divine decree or to the corrosive hand of time, but to the failure of legislators and peoples to understand their true interests and the means to pursue them within the logic of social life. The claim was that, in the long term, a society is only as strong as the number of individuals with a personal interest in maintaining it. The lesson for legislators was that injustice is an act of imprudence.

For Volney, it was an immutable fact of human psychology that individuals are ultimately driven by the desire to procure personal advantage. At the most basic level, this was the desire to procure pleasure and avoid pain. Morally speaking, this was a neutral fact. The pursuit of self-interest was not inherently positive or negative, because it was not a question of choice. It could be socially useful or destructive depending upon how it was managed. The key, for legislators, was to align public and private interest through a combination of social reorganisation and education. Only then could the fatal conflicts that had undermined the vitality and strength of all civilisations be overcome.

Les Ruines depicts the history of social conflict as the perpetual battle of two classes – the 'classes oisives', parasites who wish to live off the labour of others, and the 'peuple', consisting of those who contribute by their labour to the national prosperity.¹ Volney claimed that 'tous les vices, tous les désordres politiques se réduisent là: des hommes qui ne *font rien*, et qui *dévorent* la substance des autres'.² The origin of this conflict was unenlightened *amour-propre* – an imprudent desire to accumulate luxuries and leisure at the expense of others, stimulated in the ignorant by the first hints of material prosperity. Thus '*Cupidité*, fille et compagne de *l'Ignorance*, est devenue la *cause* de *tous les maux* qui ont désolé la terre'.³ The short-term consequence was that the strong united to dominate the weak, who were kept in subjection by their disunity and naivety. The long-term consequence had been an endless series of societies degenerating towards instability and ruin.

Only in the modern age did the opportunity arise to break the cycle of history. The prerequisite for this achievement was the enlightenment of the People concerning its true strength and interests, and the enlightenment of legislators concerning the principles of good government. With the progress of science and, crucially, the invention of the printing press, this development was finally conceivable. By providing a means of communicating 'en un même instant une même ideée à des millions d'hommes', printing rendered obsolete all attempts to suppress the Republic of Letters or to halt the global march of mind. There had developed a 'masse progressive d'instruction'. Enlightenment of the species would lead by an ineluctable logic to its moral elevation: 'à force d'expérience, il s'éclairera; à force d'erreurs, il se redressera; il deviendra sage et bon, *parce qu'il est de son intérêt de l'être'*. In the end, all would recognise that 'le bonheur individuel est lié au bonheur de la société'.⁴

The main obstacle to the perfectibility of society was the division of humanity into mutually hostile religious camps – each committed to its own prejudices and unwilling to tolerate free debate. This hindered both the international development of philosophy and the security of any free state.⁵ For this reason, almost half the book is devoted to an analysis of the genesis and history of religion, designed to reveal the common origins of religious belief while undermining the truth claims of *all* organised cults. Volney suggested that all religions had their genesis in the worship of the 'physical forces of nature'. The proof of this could be seen half-buried in their mythological systems. These were allegories of natural processes filtered through a symbolic language derived, in large part, from the astrological astronomy of ancient Egypt. The numerous stories of death and resurrection related to the natural cycles of the seasons and, in particular, to the passage of the sun through the heavens. In Christianity, for example, the story of Jesus was merely one variant of an ancient myth that referred originally to the 'birth' of the sun at the winter solstice, and to its death and resurrection at the spring equinox.

The secret of this natural code had been lost in the mists of time – the allegorical had been taken for the literal, and modern religion had degenerated into a cynical exercise in social control.[6]

The key to creating a stable and prosperous society, in Volney's view, was to develop a political and moral science that would provide a renovated system of ethics as a substitute for conventional religious morality. This system would overcome the social divisions engendered by religious prejudice. It would also provide a more solid basis for morality than any system based on vain appeals to self-sacrifice in the interests of the higher good – whether religious or secular. To be successful, the new system would need to overcome the historical opposition between private and public interest. For Volney (this is the most ambitious and controversial part of his philosophy) reason could teach people that the path to virtue was also the path to happiness.

The text culminates in a vision of the French Revolution, presented as a future event, in which it serves as a sign for the peoples of the world to rise up against their oppressors and declare themselves free. A general assembly of peoples is summoned to determine the path to the future. It is here that religious hostility manifests itself most forcefully, and it is in this forum that the demonstration of the history and failures of positive religion is given. *Les Ruines* concludes with an appeal from the peoples of the world to the legislators of the regenerated French nation: 'enseignez-nous, après tant de religions d'illusions et d'erreurs, la religion de l'évidence et de la vérité!' This code, was to be based on 'l'examen des attributs physiques et constitutifs de l'homme, des mouvemens et des affections, qui le régissent dans l'état *individuel* et *social*'. The result, for man, would be a knowledge of 'les lois sur lesquelles la Nature elle-même a fondé son bonheur'.[7]

In 1793, Volney published a small additional tract entitled the *Loi Naturelle: ou catéchisme du citoyen français*. This tract was an attempt to set out systematically the ethical system derived from 'natural laws' described above. It claimed to show how all the virtues, both private and social, could be rationally justified to individuals as the behaviour recommended by an enlightened knowledge of private interest. Moderation of physical appetite was dictated by the desire to preserve the body. Sociable behaviour was dictated by the psychological and physical benefits derived from communal life. The text culminated in the motto

> Conserve-toi;
> Instruis-toi;
> Modère-toi;
> Vis pour tes semblables, afin qu'ils vivent pour toi.[8]

By the end of the 1790s, the *Loi naturelle* had been appended to *Les Ruines*, in both France and England – appearing as the fulfilment of the promise of the final chapter of the main work. Its title was altered to read *Loi naturelle, ou principes physiques de la morale déduits de l'organisation de l'homme et de l'univers*.[9]

The most distinctive feature of the text, perhaps, was not the contents of its philosophy but the form in which it was presented. Volney's approach to psychology and ethics could be traced to a long French tradition, associated particularly with Helvétius, but also with the Baron d'Holbach and many of his associates.[10] Volney's anti-clerical polemic was hardly novel, and a great number of his mythographic theories were derived from prior scholarship.[11] Yet *Les Ruines* offered its readers a series of political, ethical and religious doctrines presented with the artfulness of an Oriental tale or a Gothic novel. As the literary critic Sainte-Beuve presented it in 1853, Volney had written, 'dans le genre sec, un livre fastueux, quelque chose comme du Raynal plus jeune, en turban et au clair de lune'.[12]

Another striking feature of *Les Ruines* is that, despite Volney's hostility to revealed religion, much of the book develops along para-religious lines. The text is saturated in biblical language, and it seems clear that Volney deliberately adapted religious metaphors to his story as part of a rhetorical strategy. The vision at its centre is presented as a secular revelation, and it is possible to read the entire text as a meditation on the theological problem of the origin of evil – an attempt to explain the sources of human misery. For Volney, however, the fall came not with the growth of a desire for knowledge, but with the growth of desire unchecked by knowledge.[13]

In their attempts to describe the book, a number of historians have suggested it can be seen as a fusion between Enlightenment and Romantic cultural modes.[14] It is easy to see the appeal of that description. While much of the content can be considered an adaptation of elements of *philosophe* thought to a revolutionary problematic, the fictional framework has many features that we posthumously tend to associate with Romanticism. With its solitary wanderer, Gothic ruin motif and Orientalist chic, *Les Ruines* anticipated a wide body of subsequent literature – from Byron's early narrative poems to the travel accounts of Chateaubriand.[15] With its Manichaean depiction of social division and its dream of an international golden age, *Les Ruines* also captured something of the melodramatic sensibility and millenarian energy stimulated by the Revolution – both of which are often claimed to be significant elements in the early matrix of Romanticism.[16]

Yet the attempt to position Volney relative to a binary system divided between 'Enlightenment' and 'Romanticism' may be to miss the point. It certainly runs the risk of presenting *Les Ruines* as a more eccentric book than it was. The very notion of an opposition between reason and sentiment, or philosophy and poetry, is in many ways a nineteenth-century development, and one interesting feature of Volney's work is the way it refuses those dichotomies. We should not forget, either, that Oriental settings and 'Orientalist' styles were far from new in the late eighteenth century. The rise of the Oriental tale in eighteenth-century Europe has been well documented, as has the fact that it could serve the purpose of philosophical parable as easily as that of salacious fantasy.[17] The systematic use of ruins as a stimulus to meditation also had a strong pedigree – from the architectural fashion for follies, to the art of Piranesi and Hubert Robert – and the theme of decline and fall was one of the staples of eighteenth-century political thought.[18] Moreover, the fictional structure in which a naive but worthy young man receives his political education from a semi-divine guide, had an obvious predecessor in the relationship between Mentor and his pupil in Fénelon's *Télémaque* – the most popular book in eighteenth-century France after the bible.[19] In all these ways, Volney's book tapped into a pre-existing literary vogue as much as it foreshadowed a new one.

However its character is defined, contemporary debates attest that the religious and literary resonance of *Les Ruines* were crucial to its popularity. For this reason, the *poetics* of the work are as important as its politics if we wish to understand the nature of its original appeal and its perceived political utility. If that is our goal, we also need to think about the way the text made the transition from French to English culture, and the creative re-reading and misreadings to which it was subjected in the process.

A French text in an English context

Les Ruines was translated and published in London within a year of its first appearance.[20] Within ten years, it had run through multiple editions in Britain and America and there were three competing translations.[21] Excerpts and summaries were reproduced in numerous pamphlets and penny-subscription journals for distribution to a mass public. By the end of the 1790s the book had become a canonical text in an emergent corpus of literature combining political and religious criticism with appeals for mass action in pursuit of social reform. Its influence on English radical culture during this period was second only to the writings of Tom Paine.[22] This popularity continued well into the 1830s. Waves of publication and promotion rose and fell with the general level of political agitation. There was a burst of initial enthusiasm during the mid-1790s, when *Les Ruines* was widely reviewed and quoted in the radical press. During these years it was distributed through interlinked networks of 'corresponding societies' and 'infidel societies' that sprang up in London and the provinces. After the suppression of the radical movement during the later 1790s, publication rates declined significantly until the end of the Napoleonic Wars. Thereafter, they rose again. By 1820, a single bookseller was claimed to have sold 10,000 copies of *The Ruines*.[23] The publication rate did not substantially decline until the end of the 1830s, and it continued at a more measured pace until towards the end of the century.[24]

A catalogue of figures and groups who made use of Volney's work during this period would list a substantial proportion of English ultra-radical activists. To name only the most prominent, we can find regular favourable reference to Volney amongst the London Corresponding Society, the Johnson circle and the followers of the agrarian socialist Thomas Spence during the 1790s. In the postwar era, Volney was embraced by Richard Carlile and his Zetetic movement, T. J. Wooler, John Wade, Thomas Davison, James Watson and Robert Taylor. We could take this influence right through to Chartist groups associated with both Feargus O'Connor and George Julian Harney during the 1830s and 1840s. Indeed, by the middle of the century *Les Ruines* was as much a part of the cultural heritage of English radicalism as any domestic production.

There has been growing awareness of Volney's importance in British cultural history for some years now. Amongst historians of English 'radical' politics, the sheer density of references to Volney in the sources has slowly begun to make an impact.[25] Students of English literature have also shown increasing awareness of Volney's significance in their field. From William Blake, to the Shelleys, Lord Byron, Thomas Moore and Thomas Love Peacock, scholars have found numerous connections between English writers and the themes and philosophy of the French 'infidel' author.[26] Although the seriousness of these authors' engagement with Volney varied from Shelley, who could almost be termed a disciple in his youth, to the more ephemeral stylistic and thematic borrowings of Byron and Moore, the cumulative picture increasingly suggests an extraordinarily rich and diverse cultural legacy. Indeed, so extensive is the Volney vogue in Britain now considered to be that the literary historian Marilyn Butler has gone so far as to dub Volney 'the Foucault of his day'.[27]

Despite this growing awareness of Volney's importance in Britain there has never been a study focused on the reception of his writing. There has been no attempt to trace the real extent of his readership, or to explain the diverse ideological and cultural milieus in which he seems to have been embraced. Moreover, the extensive pro- and anti-Volneyan literature has never been examined.

A major factor discouraging focused study of Volney's role in English history has been the disciplinary division between intellectual historians, historians of political culture and literary scholars. While members of each group have found Volney important within their area of specialisation, few have felt comfortable enough straying beyond their territory to examine the whole field. Literary historians usually discuss Volney as a source for a particular brand of poetics in which the ruin motif stands as a warning against the decline and fall of corrupt civilisations, or the Orient is appropriated as a symbol of a decadent West.[28] Scholars of religion and irreligion in the early nineteenth century list Volney, together with Charles Dupuis, Richard Paine Knight and William Drummond, as the source for allegorical readings of religion based upon astral and solar worship.[29] Scholars of radical political culture cite Volney as a conduit for an ill-defined 'Jacobin' influence on various groups of English activists. Yet no British scholars have seriously attempted to explain how contemporaries read Volney, or what the possible links between these various themes might be.

To explain the extensive dissemination of Volney's writings in Britain, we need to consider the role of his texts, his ideas and his literary strategies both as *tools* in domestic British political struggles and as *resources* for domestic literary production.[30] To do this seriously, it is important to know what aspects of Volney's work contemporary readers regarded as important, and how they adapted his themes to their own situations. There are many occasions when these questions are unanswerable for historians. Yet the richness of the historical record regarding Volney permits at least a partial understanding of this process.

The proliferating references to Volney as a major conduit for the influence of French revolutionary thought in England have thrown up some interesting questions. In particular, when we compare the interpretation of Volney in the two countries, it is striking that the political characterisation of the author was markedly different. In post-revolutionary France Volney was, and indeed remains, usually associated with a moderate, 'bourgeois' and proto-liberal strand of revolutionary thought.[31] In England, in contrast, Volney was frequently identified by contemporaries with an extreme, populist, quasi-Jacobin position.[32] In part this distinction no doubt derives from a difference in the spectrum of available political positions in the two countries. In France, the experience of revolution quickly fractured many allegiances within the Third Estate. Issues that were of minor concern in 1789 (with regard to the practical application of popular sovereignty or the property question, for example) quickly became the source of major divisions in revolutionary ranks and led to a corresponding reclassification of political theorists. In England, in the absence of a revolution, the 'popular front' of late eighteenth-century radicalism survived for longer. Its emphasis on the issue of representation and its tendency to direct grievances at the abuse of political power continued as primary characteristics of plebeian politics into the 1840s at least. Another factor is that in England, at a distance from the revolution, the personal biography of an author – his social connections, his political alliances, his positions on critical issues such as the royal veto, the constitution of 1793 or the Brumaire coup – were less immediately present to the minds of readers. In this context (or this relative absence of context), Volney's generalised parable of liberation through enlightenment, a depiction that is more concerned with the process of liberation than with the shape of post-revolutionary society, may have been open to more free-ranging interpretations.

There is some evidence to suggest there were sociological differences in Volney's audience in the two countries. I do not have space in this chapter to explore Volney's French readership in detail, but the journals that most frequently made favourable reference to Volney in France during the revolutionary decade tended to be moderate republican instruments such as the *Journal de Paris*, the *Moniteur* and *La Décade*.[33] In later years, this discussion was most frequently conducted in liberal organs such as the *Minerve Française*.[34] In England, in contrast, we find comparatively little sustained attention to Volney within the 'respectable' reformist press – in the *Edinburgh Review*, for example, or the *Westminster Review*.[35] Where we do find repeated references is at the 'popular' end of the political market – or, to be more precise (since 'popular' does not necessarily mean more widely read in this context), amongst journals aimed largely at those excluded from the political nation: artisans, labourers and dissenters in religion.[36]

Many critics in England felt that the book's destructiveness was intimately related to the character of its readership. Critics frequently lamented the circulation of his writings amongst the 'ignorant', the 'young', the 'impressionable', or the 'lower orders'. By the turn of the century, Volney was being listed as a key influence in the free-thinking 'infidel societies' which had supposedly reached plague proportions in London during the preceding decade – societies that, according to an exposé published in 1800, signalled 'the first period in which the doctrines of Infidelity have been extensively circulated amongst the lower orders'.[37] The fusion of political and religious criticism within these societies was deemed particularly dangerous, and the author lamented that 'the idea of a Deist and a good democrat seemed to have been universally compounded'.[38] Twenty years later, a satire against Volney's followers sneered at a faith that 'anticipated, under British journeymen and mechanicks, the triumphs of a project, which lamentably failed under French statesmen and philosophers'.[39]

Xenophobia is another recurrent feature of this literature. The same author declared Volney to be 'one of the most shallow and impudent of empiricks, that ever figured in a nation, as little famed for their depth as their diffidence'.[40] The Reverend Thomas Broughton emphasised the alien nature of the whole 'school of political naturalists', declaring Tom Paine and his followers to have been 'mere illiterate pupils of the French', while the latter had been infiltrating English culture with their tracts 'published and sold in twopenny numbers, to undermine Christianity and the British constitution'. Volney, he declared, was 'the champion of the class'.[41]

We can find hostility to Volney *within* the radical community as well. A significant number of reformers, perhaps even a majority, developed a real ambivalence about the French Revolution and about the applicability of French philosophy to the British situation. Associated with figures like Cobbett, Cartwright and Burdett in the early nineteenth century, or with Henry Hunt after the wars, this group retained an ongoing hostility to foreign influence on the culture of British politics, and it remained relatively suspicious of the 'French' discourse of natural law. Its adherents preferred to place their faith in notions of the 'free Englishman', of protestant particularity, and of an inheritance of constitutional liberty that must be reclaimed.[42] Cobbett, for example, launched an open attack on Volney while the two men were in America in the late 1790s. His attack was based in large part on appealing to an instinctive antipathy towards the French, 'a merciless horde of infidels and cannibals' who had 'done more toward the destruction of Europe by their political emissaries, preaching their vile doctrine of infidelity ... than by the combined strength of their armies'.[43]

While the very Frenchness of the text was clearly an obstacle for some readers, there were others for whom it may have added a certain frisson. Particularly after the patriotic frenzy of the war years had passed, there are signs of an increasing relish in parading knowledge of French texts in English radical circles. Activists grown impatient with the appeal to patriotism as a strategy to silence political dissent revelled in the opportunity to demonstrate their cosmopolitan sympathies and education. In addition to Volney, we find much use of D'Holbach's *Système de la nature* during this period, as well as texts by other French philosophers such as Helvétius, Diderot and Raynal.[44] The prominence of these figures, in the iconography of cosmopolitan radicalism is testified in the numerous records of radical toasts from this era.⁴⁵ An increasing number of radical journals used the word 'republican' in their title, and the cap of liberty also gathered strength as a symbol of radical commitment.⁴⁶ Throughout this period, the middle-class wing of the English reform movement revealed a distinct ambivalence about mass political action. In many cases, the more philosophically ambitious reformers, such as the Benthamites and the Owenites, felt the same and revealed a palpable distaste for more plebeian organisations. The sense of disaffection this provoked amongst the latter no doubt contributed to the seemingly widespread preference for French literature, or for the Paineite texts of the previous generation.⁴⁷ As both Blaise Wilfert and Pascale Casanova highlight in their contributions to this volume (see chapters 9 and 11), using literary importation to provide an alternative fund of intellectual capital has often been a favoured strategy amongst groups wishing to express dissent from the established terms of national debate.

Beyond the generalised allure of forbidden foreign literature, however, Volney's book offered a perspective on French politics that gave it a genuine international significance. The vast bulk of political writing produced in France during the revolutionary period was very obviously addressed to a French audience, and dealt with the pressing issues of the day in Paris. Amongst French literary productions of the era, perhaps only Condorcet's *Esquisse d'un tableau historique des progrès de l'esprit humain* and the writings of Anarcharsis Cloots on a *république universelle* showed the same degree of ecumenical concern in presenting the revolutionary juncture as an opportunity for a general liberation of humanity. Yet both lacked the literary resources of Volney's text, its rhetorical force, and its heady blend of religious and political critique. Although both these men were known in England, and selectively admired for their revolutionary commitments, neither reached a genuine popular audience in the Anglophone world.⁴⁸

A common accusation amongst critics was that *Les Ruines* was a deliberate attempt to dupe the young, ignorant and vulnerable through a sinister abuse of literary artifice. The Reverend William Hails complained:

> It is calculated to seduce the young and inexperienced. To them it is particularly dangerous, because it is written in the manner best adapted to their habits of thinking – it is a work of the imagination: a romance rather than a sober and patient investigation ... decked out in all the flowery magnificence of oriental poetic imagery.⁴⁹

Another anxious cleric suggested that 'a visionary being does not offer a fair and simple view of the subject' and accused Volney of 'catching the imagination by a fabulous imagery'.⁵⁰

The claim that Volney's writing had insinuated itself into public consciousness through its poetic resonance was largely endorsed by Volney enthusiasts. In an article devoted to the strategies of infidel propaganda, Richard Carlile claimed that 'Volney's *Ruins*, as a metaphorical work, is certainly useful; it made the first impressions on my mind; and I believe it has led thousands beside myself to search after truth.'[51] He would later declare it was a work that had 'made more deists and atheists than all the other anti-Christian writings that have been circulated in this country'.[52] With its sonorous language and biblical imagery, *Les Ruines* was perfect for reading in public meetings. In the 1830s, Carlile's business partner Robert Taylor (known popularly as 'the devil's chaplain') used it frequently to open proceedings at his infidel sermons at Blackfriar's rotunda – sermons which, at their peak, attracted thousands of people every night.[53]

There can be no doubt that the combined assault on the spiritual and temporal powers was a major aspect of Volney's appeal across Europe in an era when the dissociation of the two powers was much less explicit than today. It may have had an added appeal in England due to the prominent role that religious dissent, and particularly rationalist Socinianism, had played in the formation of demands for political reform in England during the eighteenth century. By rejecting the historical account of Jesus contained in the New Testament, and seemingly undermining the prospect of an afterlife, Volney's depiction of natural religion moved well past the bounds of the Socinian brand of Christianity, yet there was widespread contemporary belief that the two were competing for the same market. Volney's first publisher in Britain, Joseph Johnson, was the official bookseller for the Unitarian Society. The Unitarian Minister Joseph Priestley was one of Volney's most committed opponents during the 1790s, yet he openly admitted that there were many instances of the transition to 'French principles' from the Socinian community.[54] It is certainly clear that the social groups in which Volney made the greatest impact (skilled artisans, small businessmen and proprietors, workers in the printing trades) were those that had traditionally been the stronghold of 'rational dissent'.[55] This community was used to reading unconventional theological literature, and to encountering a fusion of theology with politics – the commitment to freedom of religious opinion was also deeply entrenched. As dissenting communities that had originally welcomed the French Revolution tended gradually to distance themselves from its more extreme manifestations, it is not surprising that there should have been some leakage into more radical forms of religious free thought from dissatisfied members.[56]

Volney's book also circulated beyond the limits of infidel circles to a wide variety of subgroups within the radical community.[57] Indeed, if contemporary evidence is anything to go by, the most moving and effective passage of *The Ruins* for English audiences had nothing to do with its critique of religion. Rather, it was the prophecy that once 'The People', enlightened as to its true strength and interests, stood up against its oppressors and declared itself independent, the forces of a despotic regime would collapse before it. From the first publication of *The Ruins* in English in 1792, it was this segment (the fifteenth chapter, called 'The New Age') more than any other that was reproduced in radical journals and circulated in pamphlet form. It even appeared under the independent heading 'A Revolution in England'.[58] It was still being read at radicals' ceremonial dinners as late as 1838.[59]

The reason for the particular appeal of this chapter has been a subject of some curiosity to historians. Edward P. Thompson, anxious to explain the seeming incongruity of the popularity of a French bourgeois philosopher amongst English plebeian radicals, attributed it to 'a curious effect of translation' that made Volney's views appear 'more radical in English than in French'. His claim was that in English 'the notion of the parasitic aristocratic estate or order comes through as the more generalized "class" of the wealthy and idle' and that this matched 'the sociology of post-war radicalism'.[60] A comparative analysis of the two texts provides little evidence to support any direct endorsement of Thompson's claim in the sense of a modification of the literal meaning of the words in the two languages – Volney himself never reduced his analysis to the terms of the French estate system.[61] If we extend the notion of translation to a more metaphorical level, however, Thompson may have had a point. Bracketing out the question of Volney's intentions, his formulation of 'The People' versus the *'classes privilégiées'* or the *'classes oisives'* was certainly capable of an easy adaptation to the language of nineteenth century popular reform. Both in Britain and France, a language that distinguished virtuous 'industriels' from parasitic 'oisifs' (or the 'productive' from the 'parasitic' classes) was embraced across a broad political spectrum. The difference between groups, in many cases, lay not in the choice of words but in the nuances of definition.[62] In this situation, the Volneyan parable clearly offered a vision of the future that was capacious enough to support a wide variety of political typologies.

An important aspect of Volney's depiction of liberation for English audiences was his emphasis on the process of enlightenment as a means to procure reform. The culture of 'improvement' that saturated radical politics during this period, and the related movement for moral 'self-government', chimed perfectly with the Volneyan theory that education was the key to moral renovation. As the editorial introduction to an early edition of *The Ruins* put it:

> The period is arrived when men should be taught, by the conviction of their own senses, that the radical source of their melioration and moral improvement is to be looked for in their organization, in the direction and interest of their passions.[63]

In a world of autodidacts who cherished their hard-won education as the key means to procuring social advancement and political reform – the vision of a people that learns to effectively resist oppression through self-enlightenment offered hope.[64]

When we attempt to explain the particular reasons for Volney's success in England, some consideration must no doubt be given to fortuitous factors. Volney was translated and put into circulation in England at a time when enthusiasm for the French Revolution was comparatively strong in reformist and dissenting circles and before the mechanisms of state suppression had been activated. Once that situation changed, the opportunities for translation and publication of new revolutionary literature declined. By that time, however, *The Ruins* was already an available text in the vernacular. Selling illicit literature has always been an opportunistic activity and republishing a pre-existing English text is easier than translating a new one. By the time radical publishing properly recommenced after the wars, Volney's book was already considered a classic text in the *English* radical canon. Just as with Paine, to refer to it conjured a whole series of heroic associations.

It is also clear from any examination of early English responses to *The Ruins* that different aspects of the book could appeal to different groups. If its infidel content was attractive to free-thinkers, others found inspiration in its powerful rhetoric of class struggle. Some readers admired its ambition to ground politics and morality in the study of human nature. Others embraced its utopian parable linking enlightenment, moral renovation and political reform. In painting this picture, *Les Ruines* offered a reading of revolution in the modern world that implied that reading itself was a key means of effecting social change. It enticed readers of all social backgrounds to join in the collective quest for knowledge and it implicitly presented itself as a key text for those commencing the journey.

The political diversity among Volney's admirers, between countries and even within them, suggests that *Les Ruines* exemplified a crucial characteristic of the French Revolution as a whole: its capacity to generate a terminology powerful enough to colonise the discursive field of reformist politics. The historical ambiguities inherent in concepts like 'Justice', 'Liberty', 'Progress' or 'the People' were key factors in that process. Yet *Les Ruines* was also particular within the field of revolutionary literature, both in its insistence on the global implications of events in France and in its systematic appropriation of the devices of melodrama and mythology to make its case. As a tool for propaganda, this made it extraordinarily effective and ideal for further adaptation – whether by journalists, who dismembered and relabelled the text for pamphlet consumption; by poets, who stole its metaphors and reworked its themes; or by infidel preachers, who popularised the work for mass audiences with the aid of props and other theatrical devices.

There is a resilient tendency amongst English historians, particularly those sympathetic to English radical culture, to emphasise the indigenous elements of the 'radical tradition' in their country. To some extent, this tendency has been an extended polemical response to an accusation that can be traced back to Burke and to the period examined in this essay – a claim that the radical ideology of the 1790s was a fragile import from foreign soil.[65] While the local roots of English radicalism were indubitably strong, with origins stretching back to the commonwealth debates of the 1640s and beyond, the tendency to highlight these strands at the expense of more cosmopolitan influences runs the risk of making the movement seem more insular and provincial than it really was. It also obscures the intellectual diversity and eclecticism that were key features of this culture. The Volney vogue in England is just one example of the important intellectual links between France and Britain in the nineteenth century. If the anxiety it raised highlights the ambivalence that has often accompanied those connections, the fertility of the exchange shows their creative potential.

Notes

1 C.-F. Volney, Œuvres, ed. A. Deneys and H. Deneys (Paris: Fayard, 1989), vol. 1, p. 254. The 'peuple' consisted of labourers, artisans, merchants and 'toutes les professions utiles à la societé'. Its enemy consisted largely of priests, courtiers and a rentier nobility, but it extended to include all the 'agents civils, militaires ou religieux du gouvernement'.
2 See Volney's accompanying footnote, in which he claims that this opposition 'est l'analyse de toute société'; Œuvres, p. 391.
3 Volney, Œuvres, vol. 1, p. 203.
4 Volney, Œuvres, vol. 1, pp. 243–4.
5 Volney, Œuvres, vol. 1, chapter 14, pp. 247–51.
6 Volney, Œuvres, vol. 1, chapters 21–3 of Les Ruines.
7 Volney, Œuvres, vol. 1, p. 378.
8 Volney, Œuvres, vol. 1, p. 499.
9 The public had no doubt been prepared for this action by the fact that the original edition of Les Ruines ended with the declaration 'fin de la première partie'.

10 Volney spent time at D'Holbach's salon during the early 1780s, and subsequently with the circle associated with Helvétius's widow at Auteuil. It is clear that both authors were key influences in his philosophical development, although politically Volney moved beyond them during the revolutionary period.

11 Aspects of Volney's theories on ancient nature worship and astrological allegory could be found prefigured in a number of books in D'Holbach's library, particularly *La Fable du Christ dévoilée* (undated, probably 1760s), attributed to Sylvain Marechal; and *La Verité, ou Les Mystères du christainisme approfondis et reconnus physiquement vrais* (1771), attributed to Bébescourt. Volney was particularly influenced by the theories of Charles Dupuis, who set out a similar case in his subsequent *L'Origine de tous les cultes, ou Religion universelle*, (Paris, 1795). For more information on this tradition, see M. H. Cotoni, *L'Exégèse du Nouveau Testament dans la philosophie française* (Oxford: Voltaire Foundation, 1984), especially pp. 381–7.

12 C.A. Sainte-Beuve, *Causeries du lundi*, (Paris: Garnier Frères, 14 February 1853), vol. 7, p. 410.

13 The resemblance between this aspect of Volney's work and the theory of the fall of man was noticed by contemporary critics, e.g. P. Roberts, *Christianity Vindicated in a Series of Letters Addressed to Mr Volney*, (London, 1800), p. 12.

14 For example, J. Domenech, 'Volney, voyageur, moraliste: l'interaction entre discours des lumières et récit de voyage', in S. Linon-Chipon *et al.* (eds), *Miroirs de Textes: récits de voyage et intertextualité* (Nice: Publications de la faculté des lettres, arts et sciences humaines, 1998), p. 251; or A. Viatte, *Les Sources occultes du romantisme: illuminisme, théosophie, 1770–1820* (Paris: Bibliothèque de la revue de littérature comparée, 1928), vol. 1, p. 85.

15 In many cases the line of influence was pretty direct – even in instances where the politics were radically different, as with Chateaubriand. On the relationship between Volney and Chateaubriand, see Jean Gaulmier's essay 'Chateaubriand et Volney', in J. Gaulmier (ed.), *Autour du romantisme: de Volney à J. P. Sartre* (Paris: Ophrys, 1977).

16 On the French Revolution and 'the melodramatic imagination' in European culture, see P. Brooks, *The Melodramatic Imagination: Balzac, Henry James and the Mode of Excess* (New Haven: Yale University Press, 1976), p. 19.

17 The rise of the Oriental tale in Europe was stimulated especially by Antoine Galland's translation of a collection of Arabian folk stories as the *Mille et une nuits* in 1704. From then the vogue only grew, attracting writers of the stature of Voltaire, Diderot and Samuel Johnson, as well as a host of less well-known figures.

18 Through his drawings, Giovanni Battista Piranesi was perhaps the key figure in a process that would eventually make a personal witness of the ruins of Rome an essential part of the philosophical education of any young man of breeding. The decline and fall theme can obviously be found in Gibbon, but also in the work of Mably, Raynal or Adam Ferguson, to name but a few.

19 On the popularity of *Télémaque*, see Patrick Riley's introduction to Fenelon's

Telemachus, Son of Ulysses (Cambridge: Cambridge University Press, 1994), p. xvi.
20 The translator was James Marshal, a friend of the political philosopher William Godwin. The publisher was Joseph Johnson, a revolutionary sympathiser, and printer for the Socinian dissenting community who published a high proportion of the literature sympathetic to the French Revolution in England during the 1790s – including Paine's *Rights of Man* and *Age of Reason*.
21 Both Joseph Johnson, and H. D. Symonds were on their third London editions by 1801, together with two by Seale and another one in Dublin by Stockdale. There had also been at least two American editions by 1802. The three translations were: the first by Marshal (published by Johnson); the second done anonymously and published in Philadelphia; a third done by Joel Barlow (and Thomas Jefferson), sponsored by the author and published in Paris.
22 This was certainly the view of many contemporaries, e.g. William Reid's *Rise and Dissolution of the Infidel Societies of the Metropolis* (London: Hatchard, 1800), p. 6
23 The bookseller was Thomas Tegg, one of the major distributors of radical literature in London. See *Republican*, 15 December 1820, p. 562.
24 In England the text went through at least eight editions between 1819 and 1835, not counting reprints or the many excerpts and serialisations. It was still being produced in the 1880s and 1890s by the Freethought Publishing Company run by Charles Bradlaugh and Annie Besant.
25 Since E. P. Thompson drew attention to Volney's influence on plebeian radicalism in his paradigmatic study of *The Making of the English Working Class* in 1963 (reprint London: Penguin, 1980), pp. 107–8, 815, a number of more specialist studies have cited Volney as an ideological source or a literary model for various groups. Volney's central importance for Richard Carlile and his 'Zetetic' movement for useful knowledge during the 1820s has long been known – e.g. J. Weiner, *Radicalism and Freethought in Nineteenth-Century Britain: The Life of Richard Carlile* (Connecticut: Greenwood Press, 1983), especially pp. 63–4 – but the Frenchman has also been suggested as the probable source for William Benbow's 1832 proposal for a general strike – I. Prothero, 'William Benbow and the Concept of the "General Strike"', *Past and Present*, 63 (May 1974), 164 – and as a major source of inspiration for the important early socialist thinker Thomas Spence – I. McCalman, *Radical Underworld: Prophets, Revolutionaries and Pornographers in London* (Cambridge: Cambridge University Press, 1988) pp. 24, 244.
26 This process began in the 1890s, when Lawrence Kellner highlighted the intimate connections between *Les Ruines* and Shelley's first major poem, *Queen Mab* (1814). Recently, however, critics have found evidence of Volney's influence amongst a wide selection of poets and novelists writing from the 1790s until the 1830s and beyond. The single greatest influence in highlighting Volney's impact on English Romantic literature has been Marilyn Butler. She has set out various points of contact with all of these

authors in articles, including: 'Telling it Like a Story: The French Revolution as Narrative' in *Studies in Romanticism*, 28 (1989), 345–65; 'Byron and the Empire in the East', in A. Rutherford (ed.), *Byron: Augustan and Romantic* (London: Macmillan, 1990), pp. 63–81; and 'John Bull's Other Kingdom: Byron's Intellectual Comedy', *Studies in Romanticism*, 31 (1992), 281–94. Other authors to explore Volney's influence include J. Mee, *Dangerous Enthusiasm: William Blake and the Culture of Radicalism* (Oxford: Clarendon Press, 1992), pp. 4–5, 13, 120–1, and S. Deane, *The French Revolution and Enlightenment in England* (Massachusetts: Harvard University Press, 1988), pp. 98–9.

27 Butler, 'Byron and the Empire in the East', p. 71.
28 This is, together with the impulse to infidelity, the primary nature of Marilyn Butler's interest in the articles cited above.
29 See, for example, J. Godwin, *The Theosophical Enlightenment* (Albany: State University of New York Press, 1994), pp. 27–48.
30 As Pascale Casanova highlights in chapter 11, it is important for any students of reception to recognise the *active* process by which any intellectual product is reconstructed in the process of transposition into a particular cultural milieu. It is for precisely this reason that the comparative study of reception has the potential to offer important insights into prevailing conditions of discursive exchange and inter-group struggle within specified cultural fields.
31 This characterisation runs through the historiography focused on France, from Sainte-Beuve, who regarded Volney as a 'homme de 1789' to be distinguished from the 'homme de 1793', through more modern interpretations such as that of J. Gaulmier, *L'Idéologue Volney: Contribution à l'histoire de l'Orientalisme en France* (Beirut: Imprimerie catholique, 1951), or, more recently, R. Barney, 'Les pamphlets de Volney', in J. Roussel (ed.), *L'Héritage des Lumières: Volney et les Idéologues* (Angers: Presses de l'université, 1987), pp. 23–4), or the Canadian Martin Staum, 'Volney et l'idée d'une science morale à l'Institut', in Roussel (ed.), *L'Héritage des Lumières*, pp. 136–8.
32 Amongst critics, of course, the title 'Jacobin' was often a polemical strategy for marking all revolutionary thought with the stigma of the Terror, but even admirers of Volney during this period tend to show a much less precise conception of his biography or position in the French political spectrum than is apparent in the French literature.
33 We find discussion of Volney in all of these journals during the 1790s, as well as contributions by him. The *Moniteur* was a moderate paper owned by Pankoucke. It became the official paper of the Napoleonic regime from 1800. The *Journal de Paris* was another moderate paper, with Garat then Condorcet involved early in the Revolution and under Roederer's direction from 1795. It also became pro-Bonaparte. *La Décade* was the journal run by the Idéologues, and edited in large part by Jean-Baptiste Say.
34 See, for example, the favourable reviews in *Minerve Française*, 2, (1818), 353–61, 7 (1819), 394–401, and 6 (1820), 358–61.
35 I have examined both of these journals, the *Edinburgh Review* from its

introduction in 1802 to 1808, and during the height of the Volney renaissance from 1820 to 1825. The *Westminster Review* I have checked from its inception in 1824 until 1829. Neither journal has any mention of Volney. The *Westminster Review*, in particular, had quite extensive discussion of French politics and of the Revolution, but its admiration tended largely to be reserved for figures like Necker and Mounier.

36 Examples from the 1790s include Daniel Isaac Eaton's *Politics for the People* (1795) and Thomas Spence's *Pennyworth of Pig's Meat*, 1 (1793). Examples from the era of the unstamped press after the Napoleonic Wars include Carlile's *Republican* (e.g. 18 February and 18 April 1820) and *Moralist*; T. J. Wooler's *Black Dwarf* (26 August and 7 October 1818, 10 February 1819, 11 October 1820); and Davison's *Medusa* (10 and 24 April 1820); see also Doherty's *Poor Man's Advocate*, 26 March 1832; and Harney's *London Democrat* 13 April 1839.

37 W. Reid, *Rise and Decline*, p. iii.

38 Reid, *Rise and Decline*, p. 8.

39 'A Reformer', *Fragments of a Civick Feast: Being a Key to M. Volney's 'Ruins'* (London, 1819), p. 5.

40 'A Reformer', p. 2.

41 Thomas Broughton, *The Age of Christian Reason: Being a Refutation of the Theological and Political Principles of Thomas Paine, M. Volney and the Whole Class of Political Naturalists* (London: Rivington, 1820), p. 24.

42 For a recent study of this culture, see P. Spence, *The Birth of Romantic Radicalism* (Hampshire: Scholar Press, 1996), chapters 1 and 2.

43 *Porcupine Gazette*, 22 June 1798. See G. Chinard, *Volney et l'Amérique: d'après sa correspondance avec Jefferson* (Paris: Presses Universitaires de France, 1923), p. 98. This outburst was made during Cobbett's most Francophobic phase, before he had really ascended to his eminence in the radical movement, but Cobbett always retained his little-England approach to radicalism.

44 Entire editions of D'Holbach's *Système de la nature* were issued in London in 1795, then in 1834 and 1839 (the latter two by Richard Carlile), but there were many other examples of pamphlet synopses and commentaries, such as the *True Meaning of the System of Nature*, published in Edinburgh in 1799. Helvétius's work was of substantial importance in England, not least through its influence on Bentham. His two major works were translated into English not long after their first appearance in France (*De l'esprit* was first released in English in 1759, and *De l'homme* in 1777), both were re-released by James Cundee in 1810. The abbé Guillaume-Thomas Raynal's *Histoire philosophique et politique des établissements et du commerce des Européens dans les deux Indes* was one of the bestsellers of the eighteenth century across Europe. In England it had gone through more than ten English printings before the Revolution, starting in 1776, and they continued into the nineteenth century. None of these works, however, equalled the level of circulation of Volney's text in the period from the end of the Napoleonic Wars until the decline of Chartism.

45 This is best typified by Carlile's Zetetic movement (see, for example, the toast to 'Helvétius, Voltaire, Mirabaud [Holbach], Condorcet, Volney, Elihu Palmer, Shelley, and all others whose writings may have contributed to the advancment of Civil and Religious Liberty' in *Republican*, 26 March 1824). We can find similar trends amongst the Spenceans, and later amongst Chartist groups (see, for example, the toast to the memory of 'Volney, Voltaire, Bronterre, Mirabaud, Robespierre, Condorcet and Diderot' in the *Northern Star*, 17 November 1838).

46 Examples are Carlile's *Republican* of the 1820s and Lorymer's *Republican* of the 1830s. On the proliferation of the word 'republican' in the unstamped press, see J. Dinwiddy, *Radicalism and Reform in Britain, 1780–1850*, (London: Hambledon Press, 1992), pp. 215–16; on the use of the cap of liberty as a symbol in radical circles, see J. Epstein, 'Understanding The Cap of Liberty: Symbolic Practice and Social Conflict in Early Nineteenth-Century England', *Past and Present*, 122 (1989), 75–118.

47 In this context, Volney was perhaps particularly useful as a compact, cheap, accessible introduction to the materialist strand of French revolutionary thought. As the editorial introduction to an English edition of *The Ruins* put it, 'nothing, in general, is of more real utility than a good elementary treatise'. See H. D. Symond's publication of *The Ruins* (London, 1801), pp. ii–iii.

48 Cloots's writings were never translated into English, so he existed largely as a name in British radical circles, marked by his presence in toasts. Condorcet's *Esquisse* was published in translation by Joseph Johnson in 1795, but it never received a second edition. Malthus's *Essay on the Principle of Population* (1798) stands out as the only significant response to it in England and even this was directed more substantially at the work of William Godwin.

49 W. A. Hails, *Remarks on Volney's Ruins of Empires,* (London, 1825), p. 2.

50 P. Roberts, *Christianity Vindicated*, pp. 2–3.

51 *Republican*, 18 February 1820, p. 148.

52 *Republican*, 15 December 1820, p. 562.

53 For a detailed account of Taylor's infidel services, see I. McCalman, 'Popular Irreligion in Early Victorian England', in R. W. Davis and R. J. Helmstadter (eds), *Religion and Irreligion in Victorian Society: Essays in Honour of R. K. Webb* (London: Routledge, 1992), pp. 51–67. The efficacy of the text's literary structure in conveying its political message was no doubt what attracted the ambitious and idealistic young Percy Shelley to Volney when he wrote *Queen Mab*, with its visions of 'Palmyra's ruined palaces' and its promise of redemption for an oppressed humanity. Volney's writings on the origins of religion proved congenial to a large number of authors in the early nineteenth century. His influence can be traced on a generation of mythographers, from the MP and diplomat William Drummond, author of the infamous free-thinking tract *Oedipus Judaicus* (1811) to the Norwich shoemaker Samson Arnold Mackey, who published *The Mythological Astronomy of the Ancients Demonstrated* in 1822. Mackey even quoted Volney on the title page of his book.

54 J. Priestley, *Observations on the Increase of Infidelity,* (London, 1793), p. 141.

Priestley returned again to the subject of Volney in his *Letters Addressed to the Philosophers and Politicians of France* (Philadelphia, 1795) and his *Letters to Mr Volney* (Philadelphia, 1797).

55 On the sociology of dissent, see, for example, Thompson, *Making*, pp. 29–58.
56 A version of this argument linking 'extreme radicalism' and free thought is presented in E. Royle and J. Walvin, *English Radicals and Reformers, 1760–1848* (Brighton: Harvester Press, 1982), p. 184. See also E. Royle, *Radical Politics 1790–1900: Religion and Unbelief* (London: Longman, 1971), preliminary chapters.
57 Thomas Spence, who publicised Volney extensively during the 1790s, was a millenarian Christian. Thomas Wooler was an open critic of infidel religious opinions, yet he nonetheless made frequent use of Volney in his influential journal *Black Dwarf* during the postwar era.
58 See, e.g., D. Isaac Eaton's *Politics for the People*, 1795; Thomas Spence, *Pig's Meat*, 1 (1793); T. J. Wooler's *Black Dwarf*, 10 February 1819; Richard Carlile, *Republican*, 18 April 1823; and James Watson's *Brief Sketch of the Life of C. F. Volney* (London, 1830). 'A Revolution in England' was Volney's fifteenth chapter published anonymously in London in 1830.
59 *Northern Star*, 17 November, 1838, p. 5. This was an anniversary of the birthday of Henry Hunt; cited in J. Epstein, *Radical Expression: Political Language, Ritual and Symbol in England, 1790–1850* (Oxford: Oxford University Press, 1994), p. 149.
60 Thompson, *Making*, 1980, p. 108.
61 I have performed a detailed analysis which suggests that the rendering of '*classe*' as 'class' and '*état*' as 'estate' is pretty literal, as are the descriptions of the trades of the component members. Jean Dierickx has performed the same comparison and come to the same conclusions, see 'Réflexions sur la traduction anglaise des "Ruines" et son influence', *Etudes sur le XVIIIe siècle*, 7 (1980), 201–7. Moreover, if we read Volney's pre-revolutionary pamphlets, we can find a clear distinction between parasitic bourgeois rentiers and those who live by their labour, which belies Thompson's implicit suggestion that Volney's analysis was originally a straightforward description of the estate system. See Volney's *Lettres des Bourgeois aux gens de la campagne* (Angers, 1789), reproduced in *Volney: Oeuvres*, vol 1, p. 131.
62 On the English tradition of this language, see G. Stedman Jones, 'The Language of Chartism', in his *Languages of Class* (Cambridge: Cambridge University Press, 1983), pp. 131, 168–9; for a related conceptualisation amongst the French Saint-Simonians or indeed amongst followers of Blanqui, see M.-F. Piguet, *Classe: histoire du mot et genèse du concept des physiocrates aux historiens de la Restauration* (Lyon: Presses Universitaires de Lyon, 1996), especially pp. 111–40.
63 H. D. Symond's, editorial introduction to *The Ruins* (London: Symonds, 1801), p. v.
64 The emphasis on self-education as the key aspect of radical political strategy was important for many groups – but nowhere was it stronger than amongst

Carlile's Zetetic movement (the term itself was derived from the Greek verb 'to seek'). It is no accident that it is here, more than amongst any other English groups, that Volney's appeal was most strongly felt. For an excellent analysis of the Zetetic culture, see J. Epstein, 'Reason's Republic: Richard Carlile, Zetetic Culture, and Infidel Stylistics', in his *Radical Expression*, pp. 100–46.

65 The impulse to emphasise the indigenous elements of radicalism remains very strong to this day in Britain. Recent examples include J. R. Dinwiddy, *Radicalism and Reform* (London: Hambledon, 1992), e.g. pp. 214–15, 227–8, and Spence, *Birth of Romantic Radicalism*, chapter 2. For earlier examples, see Royle and Walvin, *English Radicals and Reformers,* p. 47, and even H. T. Dickinson's *British Radicalism and the French Revolution* (Oxford: Blackwell, 1985), pp. 1–6.

8

Mid-nineteenth century 'moral sciences' between Paris and Cambridge

DAVID PALFREY

'I liked the name moral sciences. No-one knew what it meant but it sounded very impressive.'[1]

From Condorcet to Sidgwick?

The French economist Léon Walras, asking in 1879 who practised 'l'enseignement des sciences morales et politiques' in England, was told by William Stanley Jevons that the greater part of the philosophical teaching was done at Oxford and Cambridge. At Cambridge, ethics and mental and logical philosophy flourished under the chief authority of Henry Sidgwick.[2] Sidgwick tutored in moral sciences, defined institutionally at Cambridge as a 'tripos', or written honours examination.[3]

This Cambridge 'moral sciences tripos' (MST) was externally positioned alongside a growing number of other Cambridge examinations: mathematics, classics, natural sciences, law, history and so on.[4] It was internally composed of five subjects: logic, mental science, political economy, moral philosophy and the history of philosophy.[5] Tuition was dominated by followers of J. S. Mill: philosophical empiricists, political liberals and religious agnostics.[6] Cambridge Millians were conservative in comparison to their London contemporaries: philosophically, they emphasised the autonomy of ethics from physiology; politically, many became 'academic Unionists' over Home Rule; theologically, they hankered after a substitute for lost Christian certainties.[7] Yet they established a formal, broadly ahistorical, self-consciously secularising and internationalist programme for 'moral sciences'. In Sidgwick's phrase, this was philosophy 'from the point of view of the universe' – from which 'the good of any one individual is of no more importance ... than the good of any other'.[8] Especially characteristic was a juxtaposition of mathematical logic and probability to political economy.[9]

Sidgwick's MST can be viewed as a distant heir to Condorcet's *sciences morales*, given institutional expression when the 1795 Thermidorian

Convention, largely following Condorcet's proposals, established a Class of Moral and Political Sciences as the Second Class of the new National Institute.[10] The Second Class was externally positioned alongside two others: mathematical and physical sciences, and literature and fine arts.[11] Internally, it was composed of six sections: analysis of sensations and ideas; ethics; social science and legislation; political economy; history; and geography. Membership was dominated – if not numerically, then in public perception – by *Idéologues* trying to preserve revolutionary liberties while maintaining post-revolutionary stability.

Ian Hacking – invoking Daunou and Condorcet's vision of moral science as the 'sweet despotism of reason' – explicitly claims this Paris–Cambridge filiation:

> In the course of effecting its mid-nineteenth-century reforms, Cambridge University introduced a faculty of moral sciences to embrace economics, politics, psychology, metaphysics and ethics. This classification in a single faculty was borrowed from the French, who had in turn invented the idea of moral science by idealizing their two English heroes [Newton and Locke].[12]

In Hacking's implicit model of conceptual transfer, institutional organisations of knowledge take the best part of a century to drift across the channel. Yet the model seems, to say the least, historically underspecified.[13] If we take institutions seriously, we encounter a serious problem in conceptually relating 'sciences morales et politiques' within the late eighteenth-century Paris Institut to 'moral sciences' within Sidgwick's late nineteenth-century Cambridge: prima facie, the two institutions were so different. These differences reflected contrasting institutional contexts.

Contrasting institutional contexts

Perhaps most obviously, Condorcet's Institut and Sidgwick's Cambridge operated in a dramatically constrasting *political* context. Before 1789, twenty-two French universities prepared students in the four faculties in a similar way to German universities; richly endowed ecclesiastical *collèges* also taught arts. The Revolution's uncompromising destruction of these ancien régime structures put 'public instruction' at the heart of politics – announced as a 'fundamental provision' by the first Revolutionary constitution, and returned to in a series of committees, conventions and councils throughout the 1790s.[14] Educational institutions were to stand in direct relation to political authority, in conditions charged by extreme political uncertainty. Condorcet's proposals for an *Institut* – like those of Daunou and Talleyrand – were part of attempts to build and preserve a new republican nation-state. The claim to public authority of such *savants* proved sufficiently troublesome for Napoleon to suppress the Second Class in 1803, redistributing members into more traditional classes. By contrast, the late nineteenth-century Cambridge MST played for far less dramatic stakes. Cambridge University was cosily embedded in a stable national political constitution, in which landowning Oxbridge colleges maintained financial and political independence from the state.[15] The hesitant political status of late nineteenth-century English 'public moralists' was a faint echo of the *longue durée* tradition of French *savants* claiming direct public political authority.[16]

Second, they operated in a contrasting *religious* context. In France, the abolition of church property left early nineteenth-century Catholics vainly clamouring to regain lost educational influence, paradoxically resorting to the political vocabulary of 'liberty'.[17] By contrast, Cambridge colleges successfully maintained their 'liberty' as allegiance to an unrepresentative establishment church. The Cambridge geologist Adam Sedgwick had to correct a French visitor in 1853: a fellow of a Cambridge college was not an '*élève*' but 'a Protestant monk, a *frère*, and nothing more'.[18] Formal religious exclusion was abolished for graduates in 1854, and college fellows in 1871. Yet clergymen and chapels still dominated Cambridge, and the university continued preparing a significant proportion of its students for clerical life.

Third, *sciences morales* and moral sciences operated in contrasting *social* and *pedagogical* contexts. The Institut was not a teaching institution, but a research academy designed to transmit enlightenment through publication and political influence. Yet it was envisaged as the pinnacle of a comprehensive new national state education system. By 1795 there was a new central secondary school system, its modern curriculum emphasising sciences, French, modern languages and history. Unfortunately, wartime lack of funds made ambitious educational plans impossible to implement.[19] Napoleon's 1802 reorganisation replaced central schools with lycées, instituting a new Baccalauréat examination with a more classical curriculum. But there were still no universities equivalent to those in Germany or Britain. Napoleon's 1808 *Université impériale*, a public corporation of educational administrators and teachers, offered no post-lycée non-specialist study.[20]

The revolutionary abolition of ancien régime universities in fact catalysed a succession of new European institutional forms for higher learning: Humboltian research universities in Germany, and Restoration 'state universities' in Austria, Spain, Belgium and Holland.[21] By comparison, English universities changed at a glacial rate. England's state schooling lagged behind her continental rivals, and English universities interacted with an exclusionary jumble of private schools. The expense of residential

Oxbridge education, and a matriculation requirement of classical languages, ensured ongoing class exclusion at English universities, to an extent unmatched by their continental counterparts. Despite late nineteenth-century reform efforts, Cambridge colleges still subordinated research to tuition, providing a narrow social elite with non-vocational education.[22] Whewell had developed the ideal of 'liberal education' in self-consciously conservative opposition to French mathematics and Franco-Scottish modes of professorial instruction.[23] Education, in constrast to mere instruction, involved the inculcation of gentlemanly moral discipline through an essentially religious practice of mortification of the will. Whewell hoped that geometry and classics, submitted to as traditions, would not unbalance young minds with unearned velocities of thought or the distracting allure of 'useful knowledge'.[24] While Sidgwick struggled to expand the parameters of 'liberal education', he never dislodged the ideal itself.[25]

Fourth, Condorcet's Institut and Sidgwick's Cambridge operated in contrasting *geographical* contexts. Paris was a great cosmopolitan capital city, while Cambridge was a quiet, university-dominated town in sparsely populated fenland. Nationally, this contrast was reversed: agrarian France contrasted with the aggressively urbanising 'workshop of the world'. The national claims of Cambridge and Paris were thus geographically vulnerable in opposing ways. The vulnerability of attempts to export Parisian knowledge arose from a rural periphery's resistance to instruction. By contrast, Cambridge's national claim was threatened by the new urban dynamisms. As Rothblatt has argued, early nineteenth-century English universities relocated the eighteenth-century ideal of 'liberal education', an education of the 'whole person', 'from polis to garden'.[26] This geographical removal of knowledge from the city inspired nineteenth-century Cambridge self-conceptions and ideals of knowledge. Cambridge poetry celebrated detached 'scholè'.[27] Practical efforts to insulate Cambridge students from metropolitan hybridities mirrored Coleridge's philosophical insulation of 'persons' from mere 'things', a distinction grounding Cambridge ethics from Coleridge and Whewell through Sidgwick to G. E. Moore. Yet urban modes of administration threatened the social terms of Oxbridge influence: mid-century English critics saw Paris as illustrating the advantages of metropolitan education.[28] Oxbridge also faced increasing competition from the new metropolitan universities within England. Despite Sidgwick's sympathy with these new initiatives, his centre of gravity remained Cambridge rather than London. In particular, Sidgwick's hierarchical model of philosophy's relation to other sciences – philosophy was the validating 'crown' of science, rather than equal citizen in the republic of science, or proleptic 'germ' of future progress – characterised Cambridge in opposition to London: detached reflection cutting experimental urban knowledges down to size.[29]

Moral sciences contested

So the conceptual relation between *sciences morales* and moral sciences cannot be understood without registering contrasting institutional contexts – and these contrasting contexts clearly include 'national' contexts. Yet cultural constrasts, as Michel Espagne has emphasised, cannot stay at the purely comparative level. Cultural history needs to be relational, precisely because cultural agents themselves idealised, internalised and normatively deployed such contrasts and comparisons.[30] Both the fluidity and the constraining effect of such deployments are demonstrated in the contributions of Julien Vincent and Christophe Charle (see chapters 10 and 12).

In a similar way, two English discourses of 'moral sciences' are clearly distinguishable from the 1820s. The sustained opposition between these discourses depended, I argue, upon the implicit deployment of national sterotypes. University College London – England's first metropolitan university – self-consciously looked beyond both Anglican religion and 'English' university ideals. The UCL 1826 prospectus positioned 'moral sciences' alongside seven other proposed groupings: history, mental science, political economy, language, mathematics, physics and medical science. Four moral sciences courses were announced: 'Moral and Political Philosophy', 'Jurisprudence, including International Law', 'English law, with (perhaps) separate Lectures on the Constitution' and 'Roman Law'.[31] Two paragraphs emphasised an absolute distinction between 'Ethics and Jurisprudence'. Most provocatively, UCL announced the moral sciences as a secular object of study.

By contrast, Coleridge's 1825 *Aids to Reflection* insisted that true 'principles of Moral Science' implied a Platonic Christian theology, contemplating human action 'in its originating spiritual source, without reference to Space or Time or Sensible Existence' and aiming at 'communion with the Spirit of God'.[32] Remarkably, Coleridge claimed Platonism as a specifically English philosophical heritage. Combatting utilitarianism and revolutionary perfectionism, Coleridgean moral science interpreted history to yield the Christian 'Mystery' of original sin, which only a 'permanent Learned Class' could make an 'AXIOM of Faith in all Classes'.[33] At Cambridge, the conservative churchman H. J. Rose preached on this passage;[34] after Coleridge had amplified his sociology of the 'clerisy' in *Church and State*, Rose established King's College in London as the Anglican response to UCL.

Whereas UCL saw King's College as irredeemably 'English', King's College saw UCL as irredeemably 'French'. The idealisation involved in these representations is suggested by the remarkable influence of Auguste Comte on J. J. Park, King's College's first professor of English law. Yet contestation over the concept of 'moral sciences' continued to structure itself by means of implicit national stereotypes. Early nineteenth-century statistical societies, established on both sides of the Channel, rarely talked directly of 'moral sciences'.[35] Yet English statistical societies were responsive to the example of their international counterparts, and to the potential of comparative statistics. Like UCL, they pushed the Anglican universities into opposition. The British Association's 1833 Cambridge meeting, attended by Adolphe Quételet, briefly promised an alliance between statistics and Cambridge knowledges.[36] Quételet helped members of a loose 'Cambridge network', including Whewell, organise a new statistical section for the Association. Whewell hoped to chasten deductive Ricardian political economy with inductive statistics.[37] But Whewell soon privately complained that 'the statistical Section ought never to have been admitted'.[38] As BAAS President in 1841, he publicly dressed it down: provincial statisticians, refusing proper theoretical subordination to clerical philosophers or government legislators, were prey to political agitators. In turn, statisticians attacked the exclusive English universities, calling for government intervention as in France. The young Joseph Kay, appointed to a Cambridge 'travelling bachelorship', outraged college heads by publishing comparative statistics on European education and highlighting English deficiencies.[39] Kay cheekily dedicated his book to Whewell; Whewell rushed to disassociate himself.[40]

At stake were not just ideals of social enquiry, but ideals of political 'reform' in response to the French Revolution.[41] A religious language of interiority, in fact characteristic of the pan-European counter-revolution, sustained Whewell's insistence upon 'internal reform' – his reactionary attempt to save the English university as an exclusionary corporation by asserting its inviolable, and essentially 'English', autonomy. By contrast, statisticians wanted 'external reform' – an essentially secular attempt to transform the corporation by explicit legislation, thereby incorporating the hitherto incorporated.

These secular, progressive reform aspirations were given an especially important Francophilic gloss by John Stuart Mill's (1843) *System of Logic*. This articulated a clearly secular notion of 'sciences morales', integrated through probabilistic logic.[42] Book VI, taking its epigraph from Condorcet, dealt with 'the logic of the moral sciences', 'those which relate to man himself': these were, or at any rate included, 'the sciences of Ethics and Politics'.[43] Behind Mill's attempt to capture the vocabulary

Table 8.1 The internal structural composition of moral sciences / *sciences morales* as an academic field

Institut, seconde classe: Sciences morales et politiques (Paris 1795–1803)	*Académie des sciences morales et politiques* (Paris 1832–)	Cambridge University moral sciences tripos (Cambridge 1848–60)	Cambridge University moral sciences tripos (Cambridge 1867–)
Analysis of sensations and ideas			Logic
			Mental science
Ethics	Moral philosophy	Moral philosophy	Moral philosophy
Social science and legislation	Legislation	General jurisprudence	
	Public law and case law	English law	
Political economy	Political economy	Political economy	Political economy
History	History	Modern history	
Geography			
			History of philosophy

of 'moral sciences' was frustration at English non-conformist parochialism.[44] But Mill also aimed at English universities – whose curricula neglected these 'moral sciences' – and specifically at Whewell, by now Mill's most prominent English philosophical adversary.

I have argued that Coleridge and Whewell often presented their conservative agendas as a protection of English institutions, and specifically the universities, from destructive exposure to French heresies (atheistic mathematics, Comtean sociology and so on). Yet the fault lines between progressive, secular social enquiry and more conservative Christian modes were also, of course, visible in French intellectual debates and institutions. In particular, they were visible in Guizot's (1832) Académie des sciences morales et politiques (hereafter ASMP). Established in conscious imitation of Condorcet's Second Class, it was nevertheless characterised by a demonstrable shift in philosophical and political orientation.

Table 8.1 shows how differences between the Second Class and the *ASMP* were reflected in their internal structural composition. Sophie-Anne Leterrier's detailed study has charted the progression, and argued that the *ASMP* was structured by tension between a conservative, religious 'academic orthodoxy' (prominent amongst its historians and moral philosophers) and more secular, progressive social investigation (prominent amongst its lawyers and economists).[45]

In what follows I try to situate Leterrier's analysis within a larger pattern of Anglo-French interaction over the content of 'moral sciences'. Table 8.1's chiastic structure summarises the interpretative strategy of this paper as a whole. First, the table shows the shift in content from the Institut's Second Class to the *ASMP*. I illustrate this shift using the educational writings of Condorcet and Guizot, paying particular attention to their polarised analysis of 'the English example'. Second, the table suggests a remarkable congruence between Guizot's Académie and the Cambridge MST as established by Whewell in 1848. I argue that precisely the tension which Leterrier has identified in the *ASMP* also existed in Whewell's MST.

Finally, the table shows the extent to which the MST under Sidgwick in turn differed from the MST under Whewell. Hacking is correct to see a filiation from late eighteenth-century *'sciences morales'* to late nineteenth-century 'moral sciences'. Yet the filiation is indirect, and inexplicable without attention to intervening institutional forms of the earlier nineteenth century. At every step, the debate drew conceptual and institutional distinctions which depended upon the normative deployment of national stereotypes.

From Condorcet to Guizot: *'instruction publique'* and the English example

Whewell and Sidgwick debated pedagogy using the vocabulary of 'liberal education'; Condorcet and Guizot did so using that of *'instruction publique'*.[46] In Condorcet's 1791 *Cinq Mémoires sur l'instruction publique*, the basis of his 1792 report to the Legislative Assembly, Condorcet identified a threefold social obligation to provide universal public instruction.[47] Public instruction for the people – reading, counting and basic property law – would eliminate popular dependency on a learned class, making equality actual rather than merely formal; it would also reduce inequality arising from social distinctions of taste and morality, and extend general enlightenment. Public instruction for the professions would ensure equal access, and make professions safer, more useful and more progressive. Finally, public instruction would help perfect humanity, by giving opportunity to natural genius, improving culture for successive generations, and preparing society for change.

Condorcet was also heir to the Scottish Enlightenment. Educational flexibility was needed to preserve publicity in the face of modernity's *division of labour*. Different levels of elementary instruction must reflect differences in available time for study. Otherwise, as Adam Smith had warned, mechanical occupational specialisation threatened popular stupidity.[48] Restricting political knowledge to a political class characterised by 'vanity and ambition' also undermined 'public opinion': instruction must create a new, 'disinterested' class. Public functions – professions aimed at society as a whole – must never become the preserve of private institutions, as had happened with English law.[49]

Condorcet contrasted modern 'instruction' to ancient 'education'. First, 'education' assumed a common social trajectory, precluded by modernity's division of labour (and only possible for the ancients by restriction to slave owners). Second, modernity needed to respect religious liberty, separating public power (governing actions) from religious authority (governing conscience).[50] Secular public instruction must never authorise the teaching of religious or political 'opinion' as truth. To ensure this, the state must fix the 'object and extent' of instruction, rather than leaving it to such exclusive and 'self-perpetuating teaching bodies' as English universities:

> Whether these bodies are monastic orders, semi-monastic congregations, universities, or simple corporations, the danger remains the same. The instruction they give will always be intended not to advance the progress of knowledge but to increase their power.[51]

On the other hand, the state should not fix exclusive doctrine – especially in the radically uncertain moral and political sciences. Even the political constitution should be taught as fact, rather than justified or worshipped. Again, 'the example of England' was a cautionary lesson:

> In that country a superstitious respect for the constitution (or for certain laws to which it has become the custom to attribute national prosperity) and a servile cult of a few maxims consecrated by the interest of the rich and powerful classes are incorporated into the educational system. They are maintained in the interests of all those who aspire to wealth or power, and they have become a sort of political religion which renders almost impossible any progress toward the improvement of the constitution and the laws.[52]

Whereas Condorcet's progressive liberal theory of public instruction was crucially illustrated by English educational deficiencies, an important element of Guizot's conservative liberalism – the emphasis on institutional variety – first appeared as a lament for precisely such ancien régime educational structures. Guizot's first publication, his *Essai sur l'histoire et l'état actuel de l'instruction publique en France* (1816), began by acknowledging the state's responsibility to provide education.[53]

Yet Guizot, against Condorcet, refused to limit government activity to instruction: '*Education*, in general, is not less important than *instruction*, and perhaps the government must even exert, in this connection, a more direct action and more exact surveillance.'[54] Guizot's distinction between ancient and modern turned on neither the division of labour, nor freedom of religious conscience, but institutional hybridity:

> With the ancients, and especially with the Greeks, instruction was free; the state did not take a hand in giving it or ruling it ... but education proper was national, and governed by the state itself ... With the moderns, the course of things has become more complicated ... It is by a conjunction of sovereign authority, church authority, municipal authorities and private activity that the universities, gymnasiums, colleges and all the public educational establishments survived and still survive in most European states.[55]

Only in the absence of such mixed institutional forms was the choice forced 'between absolute liberty and the authority of the state, between private activity and the care of public wisdom'.[56] Guizot's 1816 *Essai* made no explicit reference to England, but his later writings – especially after his 1848 exile – turned to the 'example of England' with unfailing respect. His history of the English revolution and biography of Peel idealised a providential English balance between liberty and order, society and government.[57] Explaining himself for the *Quarterly Review*, he claimed the English educational non-system to be superior wherever 'liberty' existed as a social precondition.[58] He pilloried Condorcet's drive to mitigate dependency as a 'puerile' sacrifice of 'philosophical ambition' for 'revolutionary excitement': 'chimaeras hovered over ruins' in the name of a 'tyrannical notion of equality'.[59]

Yet France needed practical initiatives of public instruction, and the French state needed to recapture the allegiance of intellectuals. 1820s restoration liberals repeatedly tried to revive some society of moral and political sciences. Guizot's ministry eventually established an Académie des sciences morales et politiques in 1832.[60] Guizot wanted the *ASMP* to buttress state authority by intellectually containing the political and religious tensions of French society. To present it as having institutional continuity with the second Class, Guizot invited 'as the nucleus of the new academy, the twelve members still living of the old class of moral and political sciences'. Yet he skilfully forced 'the sensualistic school of the eighteenth century' to co-exist with 'spiritual philosophy and the sentiment of religion'.[61]

Initially, this generational gulf within the *ASMP* structured its ideological tension. Yet ideological differences were increasingly structured by the *ASMP*'s internal composition. There were now five sections: moral philosophy, legislation, public law and case law, political economy and statistics; and general and philosophical history.[62] And, while moral philosophy and philosophical history (exemplified by Cousin and Guizot) tended to appeal to 'pouvoir spirituel', the *ASMP*'s economic and legislative sections characteristically operated with more materialist categories of thought.

Like the Institut, the ASMP had pan-European aspirations; unlike the Institut, the ASMP looked to England.[63] No Britons had been elected non-resident members of the Second Class. Yet four out of nine 'foreign associates' elected to the 1832–48 *ASMP* were British: Brougham, Malthus, Hallam and McCulloch. Others were elected as correspondents: James Mill, Pritchard, Chalmers, Austin, Lingard, Hamilton, Senior, and Babbage 1832–48; Whately, Macaulay, Tooke, Whewell, Grote and John Stuart Mill 1848–60.

This was a relatively broad incorporation of British thought. Cambridge was far more selective in its reception of the *ASMP*. The holdings of Trinity College library, including works by about half of the 1832–48 academicians, exemplify this selectivity.[64] Thiers had five titles to his name; Mignet and Rémusat each had four; André Dupin, Charles Dupin, Tocqueville and Franck had three; and Destutt de Tracy, Laborde, Charles Comte and Jouffroy had two apiece. The library also held volumes by Daunou, Naudet, Feuillet, Broglie, Blanqui, Passy, Beaumont de la Bonninière, Giraud and Duchatel. But a quartet of academicians stood out: Guizot (with 27 titles), Michelet (with 19 titles), Cousin (18 titles) and Barthélémy Saint-Hilare (14 titles). This was a conservative reception of the *ASMP*, focused around the works of history and spiritualist philosophy grouped together by Leterrier as the 'academic orthodoxy'. Notably absent, for example, was any text by the prolific (and well-translated) physiological materialist Broussais. And notably underrepresented were economic and legal works, corresponding to the *ASMP*'s secular pole, attempting to grapple with or statistically investigate social problems.

The 1848 Cambridge tripos: between theology and law

The *Athenaeum* indirectly attributed the introduction of the Cambridge MST to continental political events: 'the revolutionary movements of the last eight months [had] hastened by half a century, or at all events by an entire generation, that Reform in our University which has long been the almost undenied opprobrium of our country.'[65] Cambridge certainly only adopted the MST (and its partner, the natural sciences tripos) extremely reluctantly. Curricular reform was an absent-minded, reactive attempt to pre-empt the threat of government interference in university governance.

Pre-existing Cambridge chairs were hastily grouped together to form a new examination.

Where Russell and Prince Albert had hoped for 'historical sciences', a Cambridge committee decided upon 'moral sciences'. The new label may have been little more than an opportunist bid by Whewell – by now moral philosophy professor and domineering master of Trinity College – to gain personal control. Whereas Condorcet's Institut had insisted on equality of status between all subjects and members, Whewell established himself as clearly dominant in the Cambridge MST – helped by the fact that his fellow professors were either aged and infirm (Pryme, Amos, Stephen) or extremely young (Maine).

Yet, as I have argued, the phrase already had some resonance. Within the English context, Cambridge 'moral sciences' challenged Mill's annexation of the phrase, recapitulating the 1820s debate between Coleridge and UCL. And Guizot's *ASMP* now provided a further model. Just as morals and history were the 'academic orthodoxy' of the *ASMP*, so Whewell tried to make moral philosophy the 'orthodoxy' of the MST. His morals aimed to reclaim secular jurisprudence for the Anglican establishment, as his philosophy of science aimed to reclaim natural science for the church.[66] This was an aggressively conservative religious and political project. Whewell had reacted against 1820s secular radicalism, viewing 1832 as unprincipled capitulation to popular protest, and striving for a new Christian moral philosophy. He secured his chair, formally one of 'moral theology and casuistical divinity', with sermons promising an anti-Lockean natural theology of 'conscience'.[67] He aimed to sustain the established church's national influence from the university, by re-presenting morality as the political and pedagogical heart of Anglicanism.

Whewell also wanted to encompass jurisprudence within morals. Inspired by imperial Rome's *jus naturale*, Whewell drew international law and then political theory into his synthesis: in order to stretch from Anglican moral psychology to law and politics, *The Elements of Morality, Including Polity* (1845) glossed over moral epistemology, tensions between common and civil law, and issues of legal reform.[68] Although an influential textbook, reviewers criticised its authoritarian conservatism: Whewell subordinated morality to both existing law and established religion.[69] Tellingly, the only surviving student response to Whewell's lectures is a protest against his defence of capital punishment.[70]

As in the French *ASMP*, history located itself close to moral philosophy within the MST. Although the Cambridge Modern History chair was a government appointment, it was not, as in France, tied to state-sponsored historical publication.[71] When J. M. Kemble suggested uniting the chair with a stalled government project to edit Saxon charters, he received a frosty response.[72] Cambridge professors were left free to determine their own curriculum, and a minor local tradition of commentary on France emerged. Cambridge saw the first English academic lectures on the French Revolution, delivered by William Smyth from 1826.[73] Smyth welcomed the revolution as a young man, vacillated over the justifiability of war with Napoleon, and after 1815 was influenced by de Staël and Burke to reconsider the revolution itself. 'I preach moderation ... I see nothing for this country and never did but an Aristocracy with popular feelings, everything else seems to me to lead to Servility ... and Republicanism.'[74] Citing Malthus against perfectibility, reacting against political utilitarianism and the 'democratic doctrine' of the Reform Act, Smyth's lectures mixed 'old whiggery' with occasional political romanticism. Burke's *Reflections* had dramatised the revolution as tragedy through appeal to his own memory of the young Marie-Antoinette, and a 'natural' rush of chivalric sentiment at her fate.[75] Smyth's popular Cambridge lectures recreated such a moment of personal emotion as professorial display.[76]

Outside the universities, historians like Henry Hallam combined conservative whiggery with sharp anti-clericism. But Smyth's Cambridge successor, teaching history within the MST, was the evangelical colonial administrator James Stephen. Stephen's earlier essays on church history had engineered rapprochement between the *Edinburgh Review* and evangelicalism.[77] His Cambridge lectures – against Whewell's advice, and to the chagrin of the Prussian diplomat-historian Bunsen – continued to treat French history.[78] But Stephen wanted to give them a theological spin: his lectures on Church and State in France – prepared in a few hurried months consulting Paris archives – were to illustrate 'the great scheme of Providence' in history.[79]

Whewell, reluctantly accepting Stephen's chosen topic, turned to Guizot to ask which 'works of history used in Paris colleges ... might be used at Cambridge'.[80] Stephen's first lecture course, delivered in 1850, expounded French history from Roman Gaul onwards. The Albigensian crusades forced Stephen into explicit defence of providential historiography: a twenty-five-page digression criticised Comte, and his English advocates Mill and Grote, for appealing to laws of society without any law-giver.[81]

Stephen originally intended completing his lectures with 'a review of the Causes of the Decline and Fall of the French Monarchy at the Revolution of 1789'. Here his courage failed him. Only elements of Stephen's response to the revolution survive. First, he suggested that 1789 was powerless to disrupt *longue durée* national 'character'. Stephen's final lecture, 'The growth of the French and the English monarchies compared', defended Sharon Turner's romantic narrative histories against Guizot's criticisms, attributing English liberty to Germanic racial inheritance.[82] Second, to protect this inheritance, Stephen – like Whewell – appealed to a moral pedagogy of 'hard' or 'deep' reading. His fear of 'desultory' reading was sharpened by fears of the revolutionary moral and political effect upon 'character' of new publishing technologies. Bad reading habits, Stephen warned a Young Men's Christian Association audience, attended and were even partly responsible for the Revolution.[83]

For Stephen, even the Cambridge MST – a product of the general 'revolutionary spirit' of the age – was 'of very doubtful utility', encouraging examinees to substitute 'shabby plausibility' for 'sound knowledge'.[84] Stephen found it hard to structure his historical material for either student examination or direct furtherance of Whewell's moral project. Yet the providential inflection he gave to social enquiry, his opposition to secular French historiography, his fears of university reform, and his anti-revolutionary pedagogy, all identify him with Whewell.

Whewell and Stephen represent one pole of the Cambridge MST – mirroring the 'academic orthodoxy' forming one pole of Guizot's Académie. At the opposing pole were three secular moral sciences refusing truck with Whewell's clerical morality: political economy, English law and general jurisprudence.

George Pryme, political economy professor, lectured Cambridge on political economy from 1818 to 1863. Though acknowledging Dugald Stewart as his primary influence, Pryme's introductory lecture followed J. B. Say in characterising political economy. First, political economy (dealing with the 'natural state of man') was contrasted to political philosophy (dealing with the 'moral state of man'); second, as a science of 'general facts', it was contrasted to statistics, the science of 'particular facts'.[85] Seeing political economy as independent of political philosophy, and as generalising rather than inductive, put Pryme in straightforward opposition to Whewell.[86] Pryme's insistence upon the political neutrality of political economy – indeed, like that of Say – may have been tactical: he was an enlightenment radical-whig lawyer-MP, encouraging Cambridge town corporation to politically assert itself and turning away from Trinity clerical life to secular metropolitan political activity. His lay evangelicalism was radical where Stephen's was conservative: he resisted dissenters' restrictions at Cambridge, and tried to bring on a government commission into the university. He was a member of the political economy club, a free trade internationalist happy to identify himself with Ricardian economics. Philosophically, he was a Lockean scornful of Whewell's intuitionist morality. As early as 1831, Whewell was unsuccessfully plotting to 'get rid of Pryme' as professor: Whewell's own anti-Ricardian economic efforts aimed to undermine Pryme's certainties.[87]

Andrew Amos, English law professor, was equally disenchanted with the state of Cambridge, privately supporting a government commission to force change.[88] As a young barrister, Amos used French law to highlight the confusions and inequity of English law of fixtures.[89] As UCL English law professor from 1828 to 1833, Amos encouraged medical jurisprudence, hitherto a Franco-Scottish specialism; he also invited James Humphreys, whose call for radical reform of English real property law was informed by continental codes, to lecture UCL students.[90] In the 1830s Brougham appointed Amos a criminal law commissioner: over two decades this commission used continental codifications, including the *Code Civil*, to construct a projected code of English criminal law.[91] And, as Cambridge professor from 1849, Amos's examination questions provocatively situated English law in comparative context. After one pointed comparison of the *Code Napoléon*'s property distinctions with those of English law, Amos asked, 'What rules are exclusively applicable to real and personal property respectively; and how far are they warranted by the nature of objects, or are they attributable solely to obsolete circumstances of society?'[92]

Codification's political failure – in the face of what Amos despairingly labelled English 'codiphobia' – kept English law as remote as ever from French law. And the limited terms of Amos's Cambridge chair inevitably inhibited Amos from paying sustained attention to French law within the MST. Amos had poor health, his chair had little Cambridge status, and he found it hard to interest an aristocratic audience in law. He increasingly retreated to unsystematic legal antiquarianism, using literary allusion to seduce Cambridge students into the particularities of English legal history. While evading Whewell's control, Amos never directly challenged Whewell.

Henry Maine, civil law professor, taught 'general jurisprudence' for the MST. Civil law was a pan-European jurisprudential lingua franca, crucially informing Napoleon's *Code Civil* and the German codification dispute. Maine, aged 27 when appointed, had only taken up Roman law three years earlier: though evolving the comparative and anthropological interests for which he was later famous, he could not yet afford to be too adventurous in his teaching. Given his chair's meagre salary, he was also forced to combine it with London journalism. Maine's secular conservatism distinguished him from both Whewell and Amos. Self-consciously cosmopolitan ('It is always difficult to know what requires to be proved in England'), an early publication, written soon after leaving Cambridge for London, praised codification: 'the conversion of Written into well Written law ... indicates one of the highest and worthiest objects of human endeavour.'[93] What impeded the project – here came a sniff at Amos – was only its feasibility in a country so ill-educated in civilian jurisprudence.[94] Maine also rejected Whewell's subordination of the variable 'fact' of law to the invariant 'idea' of religious moral duty: morality was only one way by which law developed. *Ancient Law* (1861) saw legal theory and practice in continual (often ironic) slippage. Fictions, equity and legislation were mechanisms of legal change with no built-in teleology. Indeed, *Ancient Law* cheekily subordinated theology to jurisprudence, crediting Western Christianity's metaphysical structure to Roman's law's influence.[95] The lawyer trumped the cleric.

This tension between theology and law ran through the 1848–60 MST. Whewell tried to hold law in subordinate attachment to theology at a time when clerical and legal networks increasingly detached from one another in English public life. The tension was reflected in the social destination of MST students: 52 per cent chose the church and 40 per cent law as their profession. Such a polarisation between the Church and the law was not a feature of parental occupation: it was generated by a Cambridge education, and specifically by the 1851–60 MST.

Conclusion: between Condorcet and Sidgwick

This has been an exercise in relational conceptual history: the concept in question was clearly given different institutional form at different times and places. To control this diversity, I have made individual authors metonymic representatives of institutions. I have spoken of Condorcet's Second Class, Guizot's *ASMP*, Whewell's MST and Sidgwick's MST. Such simplification obviously runs the risk of neglecting other agency – and so I have attempted to recover the internal tensions of the MST under Whewell in a degree of detail which bears comparison to Leterrier's work on the *ASMP*.

I began with Sidgwick. Cambridge moral sciences under Sidgwick were essentially philosophy, and Cambridge philosophy thereafter increasingly celebrated for its 'analytic' idiom. By contrast, as we have seen, the 1848–60 MST included no psychology, metaphysics or history of philosophy. Modern history, common law and general jurisprudence (predominantly Roman law) took their place beside moral philosophy and political economy. These 'moral sciences' were ethically and historically structured social sciences – rather than formal or ahistorical philosophy. They were not internationalist: political economy and general jurisprudence were in tension with more nationally inflected modes of enquiry: common law, modern history and moral philosophy. And the relevant religious context was crucially not yet agnosticism but enforced Anglicanism.

Between Condorcet and Sidgwick there was a complex moment of conceptual interaction between French *'sciences morales et politiques'* and English moral sciences'. Since 'moral sciences' were essentially contested, contrasting national contexts were constructed and deployed as political positions within national debate. In turn, these political positions were then redeployed across national boundaries.

Striking similarities mark the conservatism of Guizot and Whewell. Both celebrated English constitutional history as a uniquely successful compromise between 'order' and 'liberty'. Both adopted a political position where – in English terms – conservative Whiggery met Toryism. Both characterised the relations between individual and State as reciprocal relations of duty. Both emphasised the State's duty to educate, not merely instruct. Both intended such education – the deliberate formation of character – to form a social class to stabilise the political order. Both were crucially informed by a religious view of the world – though Guizot was cautious in openly expressing the political bearing of his religious conviction, while Whewell was more obviously and objectionably partisan.

There were also striking similarities between Guizot's 1832 *ASMP* and Whewell's 1848–60 Cambridge MST. Each awkwardly constructed their domain as stretching from ethical and religious philosophy to economy and legislation. One pole represented conservative Christian 'academic orthodoxy'; the other, progressive secular social enquiry. At Cambridge, the centre could not hold. First law, then history, claimed independence from the MST in the 1860s. By contrast, 'moral and political sciences' remained a recognisable grouping of studies within the French Institut. Indeed, at the very end of his life, Sidgwick helped establish London's British Academy – chartered to promote 'study of the moral and political sciences, including history, philosophy, law, politics and economics, archaeology and philology' – in imitation of the Parisian model.[96] But that is another story.

Notes

1. Michael Frayn, *Guardian* interview, 14 August 1999.
2. Walras to Jevons, 17 February 1879; Jevons to Walras, 21 February 1879. L. Walras, *Correspondence of Leon Walras and Related Papers*, ed. W. Jaffé (Amsterdam: North-Holland Publishing Company, 1965), pp. 596–7, 599–600.
3. What follows draws upon D. S. Palfrey, 'The Moral Sciences Tripos at Cambridge University, 1848–1860', Ph.D. dissertation, University of Cambridge, 2003.
4. Cambridge examinations varied markedly in status: older triposes (pre-eminently mathematics) attracted more students, and ranked examinees more exactly.
5. See Table 8.1. Despite contributing equally to examination results, tripos

components differed in status. Alfred Marshall struggled for two decades to free political economy from subordination to moral philosophy within the MST. He established a new economics and politics tripos in 1902, after Sidgwick's death.
6 As Sidgwick recalled, 'from about 1860–65 or thereabouts [Mill] ruled England in the region of thought as very few men ever did'. Quoted in S. Collini, *Public Moralists* (Oxford: Clarendon Press, 1991), p. 178.
7 J. B. Schneewind, 'Sidgwick and the Cambridge Moralists', *Monist*, 58 (1974), 371–404; and *Sidgwick's Ethics and Victorian Moral Philosophy* (Oxford: Clarendon, 1977); C. Harvie, *Lights of Liberalism* (London: Allen Lane, 1976); F. M. Turner, *Between Science and Religion* (New Haven: Yale University Press, 1974).
8 H. Sidgwick, *Methods of Ethics* (6th edition, 1907; London: Macmillan & Co.), p. 382. Cf. B. Williams, 'The Point of View of the Universe: Sidgwick and the Ambitions of Ethics', in *Making Sense of Humanity and Other Essays*, (Cambridge: Cambridge University Press, 1995).
9 S. J. Cook, 'The place of Reforming Cambridge in Alfred Marshall's Construction of an Economic Organon: 1861–1890', Ph.D. dissertation, University of Cambridge, 2001.
10 S.-A. Leterrier, *L'Institution des sciences morales* (Paris: L'Harmattan, 1995); M. Staum, 'The Class of Moral and Political Sciences, 1795–1803', *French Historical Studies*, 11 (1980), 371–97, and *Minerva's Message* (London: McGill-Queen's University Press, 1997). For Condorcet's earlier attempts to discover laws of the 'moral sciences' by applying Laplacian probability, see K. M. Baker, *Condorcet* (Chicago: Chicago University Press, 1975).
11 Equality of status of the *Institut*'s three classes was elaborately safeguarded: this was especially necessary since the Second Class, unlike the other two, could claim no ancien régime heritage. Leterrier, *L'Institution des sciences morales*, chapter 1.
12 I. Hacking, *The Taming of Chance* (Cambridge: Cambridge University Press, 1990), pp. 37–8.
13 Indeed, on Hacking's own terms, it also seems a *philosophical* underspecification of the concept's translation. Though Hacking describes his work as 'not history' but 'philosophical analysis', this is for him investigating concepts as 'words in their sites ... sentences *and* institutions'; Hacking, *The Taming of Chance*, p. 7. Emphasis added.
14 R. R. Palmer, *The Improvement of Humanity* (Princeton, NJ: Princeton University Press, 1985), chapter 3, 'Politicization'.
15 Although I will not further consider this question here, the MST was arguably more directly engaged in state-building at Britain's imperial periphery.
16 Collini, *Public Moralists*, p. 178. 'It is an old practice, in France, for Government to consult the *savants* upon great occasions; and the practice has been held as wondrous wise. In England, we do not so much bow to their opinions; and this custom is held to be a still greater proof of wisdom', R. Chevenix, 'State of Science in England and France', *Edinburgh Review*, 34 (1820), 383–422.

17 F. Guizot, 'On the State of Religion in France', *Quarterly Review*, 83 (1848), 199–277.
18 A. F. Hort, *Life and Letters* (London: Macmillan, 1896), vol. 1, p. 257.
19 B. Stone, *Reinterpreting the French Revolution* (Cambridge: Cambridge University Press, 2002), pp. 188–9.
20 F. Ringer, *Education and Society in Modern Europe* (Bloomington and London: Indiana University Press, 1979), pp. 115, 146–7.
21 L. W. R. Brockliss, 'The European University in the Age of Revolution, 1789–1850', in M. G. Brock and M. C. Curthoys (eds), *The History of the University of Oxford.*, vol. 6. *Nineteenth Century Oxford, Part I* (Oxford: Clarendon Press, 1997), p. 125. F. Ringer, 'Patterns of access to the modern European university', in *Toward a Social History of Knowledge: Collected Essays* (Oxford: Berghahn Books, 2000).
22 Most Cambridge students attempted no competitive honours degree, only a so-called 'poll' degree.
23 W. Whewell, *Thoughts on the Study of Mathematics as a Part of a Liberal Education* (Cambridge: J. & J. J. Deighton, 1835), *On the Principles of English University Education* (London: J. W. Parker, 1837), *Of a Liberal Education in General* (London: J. W. Parker, 1845, 1850), 2 vols.
24 S. Schaffer, 'The History and Geography of the Intellectual World: Whewell's Politics of Language', in M. Fisch and S. Schaffer (eds), *William Whewell: A Composite Portrait* (Oxford: Clarendon, 1991); J. Wilkes, '"A Mist of Prejudice": The Reluctant Acceptance of Modern History at Cambridge, 1845–1873', in J. Smith and C. Stray (eds), *Teaching and Learning in Nineteenth-Century Cambridge* (Woodbridge: Boydell Press, 2001).
25 H. Sidgwick, 'Liberal Education', *Macmillan's Magazine*, (1867); 'The Theory of Classical Education', in F. W. Farrar (ed.), *Essays on a Liberal Education* (London: Macmillan, 1867).
26 S. Rothblatt, 'The Limbs of Osiris: Liberal Education in the English-speaking World', in S. Rothblatt and B. Wittrock (eds), *The European and American University since 1800: Historical and Sociological Essays* (Cambridge: Cambridge University Press, 1993), p. 39.
27 In Henry Maine's 1843 prize poem *Plato*, Socrates led his pupil outside the city to philosophise in bucolic seclusion. George Pryme's 1812 valedictory *Ode to Trinity College* dramatised the tension between urban activity and rural seclusion in terms less sympathetic to the university. In fact, both Maine and Pryme juggled Cambridge chairs with metropolitan activity. H. J. S. Maine, *Plato: A Poem*, ed. J. W. Clark (Cambridge: privately printed, 1894); G. Pryme, *Ode to Trinity College, Cambridge* (London: J. McCreery, 1812).
28 J. Forster, 'Encouragement of Literature by the State', *Examiner*, 5 January 1850, p. 2.
29 Sidgwick, 'Is Philosophy the Germ or Crown of Science?', unpublished essay. Trinity College Library, Cambridge (hereafter TCC), Add.Ms.c.96/2.
30 M. Espagne, 'Sur les limites du comparatisme en histoire culturelle', *Genèses: Sciences Sociales et Histoire*, 17 (1994), 112–21.

31 Confusing ethics ('the science of reasonable being, apart from the consideration of the injunctions of law') with jurisprudence ('the science of rights and of crimes', presupposing 'the authority of government, and ... limited in its direct operation to the outward actions of men') had 'contributed to disturb the theory of Ethics, and to corrupt the practice of legislation.' N. Harte and J. North, *The World of UCL, 1828–1990* (revised edition; London: UCL, 1991), pp. 17–19.
32 S. T. Coleridge, *Aids to Reflection*, ed. J. Beer (London: Routledge, 1993), pp. 293–4.
33 S. T. Coleridge, *Aids to Reflection*, p. 273 n. 33, 295–7.
34 H. J. Rose, *The Commission and Consequent Duties of the Clergy* (London: C. & J. Rivington and J. & J. J. Deighton, 1828).
35 As Hacking notes, Guerry spoke of 'moral analysis' and Quételet of 'moral statistics'.
36 L. Goldman, 'The Origin of British "Social Science": Political Economy, Natural Science and Statistics 1830–1835', *Historical Journal*, 26:3 (1983), 587–616; L. A. J. Quételet, *Notes extraites d'un voyage en Angleterre* (Brussels, 1835).
37 J. P. Henderson, 'The Place of Economics in the Hierarchy of the Sciences: Section F from Whewell to Edgeworth', in P. Mirowski (ed.), *Natural Images in Economic Thought: 'Markets Read in Tooth and Claw'* (Cambridge: Cambridge University Press, 1994); J. Morrell and A. Thackray, *Gentlemen of Science* (Oxford: Clarendon, 1981); R. Yeo, *Defining Science* (Cambridge: Cambridge University Press, 1993).
38 Morrell and Thackray, *Gentlemen of Science*, p. 294.
39 J. Kay, *The Education of the Poor in England and Europe* (London: J. Hatchard and Son, 1846). Joseph Kay to Whewell, 14 March 1846, 4 April 1846. TCC, Add.Ms.a.207/144–5.
40 Whewell to Adam Sedgwick (draft letter), 4 April 1846. TCC, O.15.45/183.
41 Another source for contested notions of 'reform' was the Protestant Reformation: 'reformation', 'reform' and 'revolution' were not consistently distinguished at the time; D. Beales, 'The idea of reform in British politics, 1829–1850', *Proceedings of the British Academy*, 100 (1999), 159–74.
42 J. S. Mill, *A System of Logic, Ratiocinative and Inductive* (London, 1843), 2 vols.
43 James Stephen, recommending Mill's book to Macvey Napier, remarked that 'No man is fit to encounter him who is not thoroughly conversant with the moral science which he handles'. Stephen to Napier, 14 May 1845, in C. E. Stephen, *Life of Stephen* (London: printed for private circulation only, 1906), p. 89. Mill's terminology, when translated into German, famously prompted the coinage *Geisteswissenschaften*.
44 Robert Blakey's *History of Moral Science* (London: James Duncan, 1833), stubbornly uncomprehending of foreign authors, irritated Mill into denouncing the state of English philosophy, and defending (in an early use of the phrase) 'continental philosophy'. That year, Mill projected a (never-written) essay on the 'ambiguities of moral science'; J. S. Mill, 'Blakey's History of Moral Science', *Monthly Repository*, 7 (1833), 661–9.

45 Leterrier, *L'Institution des sciences morales*.
46 The phrase emerged amongst mid-eighteenth-century physiocrats and theorists of 'legal despotism'. P.-P. Mercier de la Rivière, *L'Ordre naturel et essentiel des sociétés politiques* (London & Paris, 1767), 2 vols; F. Quesnay and P. S. Du Pont de Nemours, *Physiocratie* (Leyden: Merlin, 1767). Dupont popularised *'instruction publique'* in *Ephémérides*; significantly, as *Ephémérides* editor, Dupont retitled it *Bibliothéque raisonnée des Sciences Morales et Politiques*.
47 J.-A.-N. D. Caritat marquis de Condorcet, *Ecrits sur l'instruction publique*, ed. C. Coutel and C. Kintzler (Paris: Edilig, 1989), 2 vols. The first memorandum is translated in K. M. Baker (ed.), *Condorcet: Selected Writings* (Indianapolis: Bobbs-Merrill, 1976). It is available in French and English at Julian Bourg's Condorcet website: http://ishi.lib.berkeley.edu/~hist280/research/condorcet/pages (accessed November 2003).
48 A. Smith, *Wealth of Nations*, ed. R. H. Campbell, A. S. Skinner and W. B. Todd (Oxford: Clarendon Press, 1976), 2 vols, V.i.f.50.
49 'When the making of laws, the administration and judicial functions become private occupations reserved for those who have prepared for them through specialised study, it can no longer be said that real liberty exists. There necessarily forms in such a nation a kind of aristocracy, not of talent and knowledge, but of occupations. Thus it is that in England the profession of law has succeeded in concentrating all its real power among its members'; Baker (ed.), *Condorcet: Selected Writings*, p. 119.
50 This passage informed Constant's famous distinction between ancient and modern liberty. B. Constant, *Political Writings*, trans. B. Fontana (Cambridge: Cambridge University Press, 1988), p. 103.
51 Baker (ed.), *Condorcet: Selected Writings*, p. 128.
52 Baker (ed.), *Condorcet: Selected Writings*, p. 133.
53 F. Guizot, *Essai sur l'histoire et sur l'état actuel de l'instruction publique en France* (Paris: Maradan, 1816), p. 1.
54 Guizot, *Essai*, p. 4.
55 Guizot, *Essai*, pp. 126–7.
56 Guizot, *Essai*, pp. 127–8.
57 See the contributions of Philippe Raynaud and Alan Kahan to M. Valensise (ed.), *François Guizot et la culture politique de son temps: colloque de la Fondation Guizot-Val* (Paris: Gallimard, 1991).
58 F. Guizot, 'Public instruction in France under M. Guizot', *Quarterly Review*, 84 (1848), 238–64.
59 F. Guizot, *Memoirs*, ed. R. Bentley (London, 1860), 4 vols, vol. 3, pp. 24–6.
60 Staum, *Minerva's Message*, pp. 226–8.
61 Royer-Collard's refusal to join illustrated *doctrinaire* ambivalence. Conversely, Daunou initially refused to countenance Cousin's election. Guizot, *Memoirs*, vol. 3, pp. 141–2.
62 'Analysis of sensations and ideas' and geography were abolished; 'social science and legislation' was partitioned into 'public law and case law' and 'legislation'.

63 S.-A. Leterrier, 'Un réseau de pensée européen: l'Académie des sciences morales et politiques sous la Monarchie de Juillet', *Revue d'Histoire du XIXe Siècle* (1991).
64 I have counted all items in Trinity's present-day holdings published before 1866 (the year of Whewell's death). This may overestimate mid-nineteenth-century holdings.
65 *Athenaeum*, November 1848.
66 For Whewell's philosophy of science, see M. Fisch and S. Schaffer (eds), *William Whewell: A Composite Portrait* (Oxford: Clarendon, 1991); Yeo, *Defining Science*.
67 W. Whewell, *On the Foundations of Morals* (Cambridge, 1838).
68 W. Whewell, *The Elements of Morality, Including Polity* (London: J. W. Parker, 1845), 2 vols.
69 S. A. Dunham, 'Whewell's *Elements of Morality, including Polity*, *Athenaeum*, 925 (1845), 709–11; J. Martineau, *The Elements of Morality, Including Polity*, *Prospective Review*, 1:4 (1845), 577–610; J. S. Mill, 'Whewell's Lectures on the History of Moral Philosophy in England', *Westminster Review*, (October 1852), 349–85.
70 Members of the moral philosophy class to Whewell, undated. TCC, R.6.13/30.
71 F. Gilbert, 'The Professionalization of History in the Nineteenth Century', in J. Higham, L. Krieger and F. Gilbert (eds), *History*, (Englewood Cliffs: Prentice-Hall, 1965).
72 Kemble to Lord Aberdeen, 19 February 1844, 8 October 1844. James Graham to Aberdeen, 14 October 1844. London, British Library, Aberdeen Papers, Add.43242, fos 187–8; Add.43190, fos 127–30.
73 H. Ben-Israel, *English Historians on the French Revolution* (Cambridge: Cambridge University Press, 1968), pp. 72, 77, 81–4.
74 Smyth to Roscoe, 22 April 1827. Ben-Israel, *English Historians*, pp. 27, 78, 84.
75 D. Bromwich, 'Edmund Burke, Reflections on the French Revolution in France', in D. Wu (ed.), *A Companion to Romanticism*, (Oxford: Blackwell Publishers, 1998), pp. 116, 118.
76 R. A. Willmott, 'Arnold and Smyth on modern history', *Fraser's Magazine*, 26 (1842), 631–45.
77 J. Stephen, *Essays in Ecclesiastical Biography* (London: Longmans, 1849).
78 P. Slee, *Learning and a Liberal Education* (Manchester: Manchester University Press, 1986), p. 36; F. B. Bunsen, *A Memoir of Baron Bunsen* (London: Longmans & Co., 1868), 2 vols, vol. 2, pp. 228–9.
79 Stephen to Isaac Taylor, 1850; Cambridge University Library, Cambridge, Add.7888/II/118.
80 Guizot recommended Poisson's *History of Rome*, Ruelle's *History of the Middle Ages* and Rayon's *Abridged History of Modern Times;* Guizot to Whewell, 3 December 1848. TCC, Add.Ms.a.205/59.
81 J. Stephen, *Lectures* (2nd edition, London & Cambridge, 1852), vol. 1, pp. 234–58. The third (1857) edition reorganised this material as an introductory

historiographical lecture: 'On certain (so-called) Philosophies of History.'
82 Stephen, *Lectures*, pp. 485–95. Kingsley, Stephen's Cambridge successor, developed this grand narrative of competing racial inheritances within a providentialist historiography. C. Kingsley, *The Roman and the Teuton* (Cambridge & London: Macmillan, 1864).
83 J. Stephen, *On Desultory and Systematic Reading* (London, 1853). For a context in which to situate Stephen's worries, see C. A. Hesse, *Publishing and Cultural Politics in Revolutionary Paris, 1789–1810* (Berkeley and Oxford: California University Press, 1991).
84 Stephen, *Lectures*, vol. 1, pp. vii–ix.
85 G. Pryme, *An Introduction to a Course of Lectures on the Principles of Political Economy* (Cambridge, 1823); see also J.-B. Say, *Traité d'économie politique* (Paris: De Chapelet, 1803), 2 vols.
86 Here it is necessary to correct James Henderson, who groups Whewell and Pryme together as Cambridge 'reformers'. J. P. Henderson, '"Just Notions of Political Economy"; George Pryme, the first Professor of Political Economy at Cambridge', *Research in the History of Economic Thought and Methodology*, 2 (1984).
87 Whewell to Richard Jones, 9 May 1831. TCC, Add.Ms.c.51/105.
88 Amos to Forster, 11 November 1850. London, National Art Library, Forster Collection, F.48.b.3/33.
89 A. Amos and J. Ferard, *A Treatise on the Law of Fixtures* (London: J. Butterworth and Son, 1827). Amos turned to P. Lepage and A. B. Desgodets, *Lois des bâtimens: ou, Le Nouveau Desgodets, traitant, suivant les codes Napoléon et de procédure* (Paris: Garnéry, 1808).
90 J. Humphreys, *Observations on the Actual State of the English Law of Real Property with Outlines for a Systematic Reform* (London, 1826).
91 J. Hostettler, *The Politics of Criminal Law Reform in the Nineteenth Century* (Chichester: Barry Rose, 1992); M. Lobban, 'How Benthamic was the Criminal Law Commission?', *Law and History Review*, 18:2 (2000), 427–32.
92 1856 English Law examination, question 5.
93 H. J. S. Maine, 'Roman Law and Legal Education', in *Cambridge Essays, Contributed by Members of the University, 1856* (London: 1856), p. 19.
94 'When it does not seem yet conceded that we can produce a good statute, it appears premature to ask for a Code'; Maine, 'Roman Law', p. 19.
95 H. J. S. Maine, *Ancient Law* (London: Murray, 1861), pp. 335–9.
96 http://www.britac.ac.uk/misc/charter.html (accessed November 2003).

Part IV
The internationalisation of intellectual life

9

Literary import into France and Britain around 1900: a comparative study

BLAISE WILFERT

A fundamental dimension of both British and French intellectual life around 1900, especially for men of letters, was their involvement, as specialists in the articulation of scholarly and artistic discourse, in the nationalisation of societies, a process that underwent a remarkable acceleration and deepening from 1880 onward, and in the production of a national identity in literature which served as one of the foundations for this nationalisation. A good way of approaching this movement in an empirical fashion is to compare in each country the forms assumed by literary import, i.e. everything that bears on the work of making known, directly or otherwise, foreign literary production in the national space, with all that this can arouse in the way of debate and transformation of literary life. The introduction of Zola and Ibsen into Great Britain, or Tolstoy and Nietzsche into France, among many other examples for the period 1885–1895, aroused major controversies, mobilising in each country intellectual and artistic authorities, as well as significant sections of the legal, political and moral authorities.

These complex and multiform controversies are privileged observation posts for understanding and comparing the operation of two intellectual fields that historiography traditionally presents as fundamentally different. Yet, with the exception of certain rare pioneering works, the violent confrontations that took place on both sides of the Channel in these 'fin-de-siècle' years, around foreign literature and its import, have been the subject of very few systematic investigations, outside of studies of its reception that have traditionally been the province of comparative literature; in particular, there has been no synthetic study of their combined effects, not just on national literary life, but also on intellectual life as a whole and its articulation with the political processes under way, especially that of the nationalisation of European societies.[1]

In France, literary import in the late nineteenth and early twentieth centuries challenged a number of established cultural legitimacies; it presented a key issue at stake for literary life, powerfully contributed to the redistribution of legitimacies in the literary field, and to the reformulation of central political discourses, with the period of the Dreyfus Affair and its wake forming the crystallising moment. The import of foreign work then lent itself to strategies whose issue went beyond the works themselves, strategies that questioned the status of the writer, his position in the space of power, and the limits and norms of the national cultural space. The establishment of the 'nationalism' of Maurice Barrès, Charles Maurras and Léon Daudet found its first sustenance at this point, even before the convulsions of the Dreyfus Affair, and the lines of force of intellectual life that were established at this point remained largely fixed for the next thirty years.

But the logical horizon of such an analysis cannot be confined to the national space, especially in the French case. French writers still exported more works than those which they got to know from abroad, a case almost unique in Europe, since only British writers found themselves in the same position as net exporters. More interesting still, the French and English literary markets were each reciprocally the leading customer and supplier of the other, a situation already long established, but which was reinforced at different levels by the parallel development of the realist novel and, from 1860 onwards, by the simultaneous assertion of artistic groups and attitudes with a provocative and dissident tendency, all bent on subverting the established canons. In this regard, the various forms of internationalism that moored French to British literary life are the spur to a dense and precise work of interacting analysis, based both on systematic comparison and the history of transfers, with a view to displaying the social and intellectual dynamics at work in the recent history of what could be called, for the moment just in jest but perhaps more seriously in the future, 'Englance or Frangland'.

If the situation that faced writers in both countries around 1900 authorises a comparison of this kind, it is because their essential dynamics were similar. The transformation in the role of the State in education and culture, the reassertion of academic dignity, the liberalisation of public expression, the rise of a culture escaping that of the well-read, the increase in the number of both literary producers and readers, seen as a danger[2] – all these developments weighed on the intellectual life in a comparable manner. The same held true for literary geopolitics: these were two 'imperial literary societies'[3] with a prestigious past, a growing production, a metropolis with a strong radiation,[4] a developed system of publishing and distribution and, not least, a world export of literary works. In his *Atlas of the European Novel*, Franco Moretti has shown how the first half of the nineteenth century had been dominated by the production of novels from Great Britain and France, a situation of condominium in which all that each of the two countries really knew of foreign literature was that of its counterpart across the Channel.[5] This division of literary 'power' echoed in 1900 the outward spread of the two empires, no matter how the forms of this hegemony might differ.

At first sight, the English and French intellectual fields seem to present at this point an analogous polarity, counterposing the disciples of foreign literature (aesthetic decadents, symbolists, 'Zola-ists', all challenging the national isolation and provincialism – and the frontier guards – of academic institutions and morality leagues standing watch over the national spirit) to the new-style 'nationalists', whether these were followers of Barrès or Maurras, anti-decadents, imperialists or simply champions of 'national efficiency' in the field of art. The recent *Oxford Guide to Literature in English Translation*,[6] for example, suggests that the terms of debate on English literature were fixed precisely in the 1890s: translation from other contemporary cultures was held to present, from the nationalist perspective, a risk to the divine morality of the English nation, while aestheticism combined both literary import and countervalues. The role of watchdogs of the classical tradition, complacently assumed in France by the Maurrasians and other 'nationalists', invites at first sight an analogous representation of the French debate, opposing smugglers and defenders of the frontiers.

Synthetic and undeniably heuristic, however, this model does not take full account of the process of literary import around 1900 and all its consequences. Thus, in 1919, Edmund Gosse was presented with a bust by a phalanx of luminaries, including Rudyard Kipling, Arthur Pinero, Lord Curzon, Campbell-Bannerman and both Anglican archbishops.[7] As adviser to the prime minister, an influential member of the Newbolt commission, national cultural representative during the Great War, spokesman for the heights of British letters, Gosse appeared an archetype of the national writer, the actor and product of a complete literary nationalization. Yet he had himself been a persistent importer of foreign literature. His first work in 1872 had been a presentation of Ibsen, then unknown; in 1877, he set up as champion of French poetry from Villon to Banville, and from 1888 to 1893 that of Ibsen and Mallarmé, defending at the same time also Zola and Vizetelly, before becoming in the 1900s the introducer of Gide. Gosse's importance, the broad scope of his activity and his particular status as Franco-English intermediary, make his case a telling one for questioning a number of received explanations, and looking into tracks that have up to now been little noted, if at all. His career presents an imbrication of two ideal-type figures that have traditionally been opposed in the historiography, the national writer and the 'cosmopolitan' man of letters. It is tempting to bring this atypical model across the Channel – Gosse himself did not refrain from doing so, which adds still more to his interest for us – to embark on comparison and an analysis of transfers through the prism of literary import.

Confronting the literary foreigner: two narcissistic and protectionist nations

Though the global extent of the import phenomenon, measured in terms of the flow of translations, is certainly important, especially for understanding the reactions it arouses, it is also particularly problematic. It is tempting to try and give an overall figure in terms of number of titles and copies, so as to ascertain, for example, if foreign works actually presented any competition to indigenous ones. This is an enquiry that Franco Moretti undertook for the first half of the nineteenth century. But the results are flawed by significant methodological bias.

I have presented in detail elsewhere the concerns that should accompany the use of available bibliometric sources and, above all, any results derived in the context of an evaluation of literary transfers. For France, the *Catalogue général de la librairie française* and the *Bibliographie de la France* enable us to establish that foreign works translated, which reached a low point in the 1870s at around 3 per cent of national production, experienced a resurgence between 1885 and 1895, attaining a maximum of 5 to 6 per cent of the total number of books published in France at the very moment at which polemic on the import of foreign literature was reaching an apogee. As we can see, this high point was still very modest, not being surpassed until the late 1920s, and cannot in itself explain the reactions provoked by the presence of foreign literature. The French literary field, largely self-sufficient, was also singularly sensitive, protectionist and narcissistic on the whole.

If these figures are to be reliable and precise, they require painstaking, exhaustive and large-scale work. It has not been possible at this point to conclude the research needed to reach equivalent results for translation in Great Britain. Moreover, there are several problems concerning the sources. The *English Catalogue of Books* does not give any entry by genre (novel, poetry, theatre...) comparable to its French equivalents, which makes it impossible to undertake an overall count for a given period. The *Publisher's Circular*, for its part, only supplies figures for translation from 1911 onwards (even then, the figures disappear again some years later), at which time the level of translations stood at about 5 per cent of national production (190 titles out of some 3,850). Christopher Campos, basing himself on unknown sources, estimated the translation of French works as about 3.5 per cent of fiction and poetry titles between 1900 and 1913, these making up more than half of the total translations at this time.[8] On top of these imprecise figures, we should add the difficulty posed by the circulation of works translated into English by American publishers, which circulated freely on the British market unless they fell foul of the censor.

Other sources and markers have been used for the French case, to give a more precise picture of literary import, especially general cultural reviews and more specialist literary reviews, which from time to time presented translations of foreign works, longer or shorter, as a function of their resources, and sought through criticism, literary history, and cultural information in a broader sense, to make known certain aspects of foreign literatures. In the case of the major established reviews close to the Académie française or the academic sphere, such as the *Revue de Paris* or the *Revue des Deux Mondes*, the publication of novels in translation made a genuine breakthrough in the second half of the 1880s, from which date it could regularly occupy a quarter or even a third of the editorial space, whereas the avant-garde literary reviews from the *Revue wagnérienne* to the *Nouvelle Revue Française*, often founded during the period 1885 to 1895 and appealing to foreign artistic reference points, gave such translations a key place in their critical or information columns, unable as they were to bear the cost of major translations themselves. In this way, the modest presence of foreign literature in the total statistics was transformed into a high visibility among the political and cultural elites, who formed the pool of readers for these periodicals.

Here again, the systematic large-scale counting applied to French periodicals has only been sketched for the British ones. The lesser place given to literature, and especially to the direct publication of fictional texts, in magazines and reviews such as *Nineteenth Century*, *Fortnightly Review*, *Contemporary Review* and *National Review*, to take different kinds of cultural publication with a medium-scale circulation, and the lesser accessibility of avant-garde literary magazines with a limited circulation such as the *Savoy Magazine* and the *English Review*, has so far made any exhaustive count impossible. It is true nonetheless that the 1890s were, for almost all the periodicals consulted, a moment of breakthrough for literary discourse, principally critical discourse in the British case, and a large part of this was around questions bearing on foreign literatures, from Zola to D'Annunzio by way of Ibsen, Racine or Maeterlinck. In a general sense, as far as both its presence in reviews and in the counts carried out using large-scale bibliometric tools, the difference in literary import between Britain and France does not appear at all decisive.

Contrary, therefore, to what was sometimes said at the time, and what cultural historiography has sometimes repeated,[9] it is in no way certain that Britain in the late nineteenth century was still more closed to foreign literature than was France. Some indications even enable us to think the opposite. The introduction of Ibsen in England dates from 1872, with an article by Gosse in the *Spectator*, and 1880, when the first production of *A Pillar of the Community* was given at the Gaiety Theatre, in a translation by William Archer. *A Doll's House*, translated in 1888, sold 14,000 copies in five years, exceptional for a dramatic work, while in France it sold only 89 copies in its first year of publication, half of these being sold abroad.[10] By 1913, all Gerhart Hauptmann's stage works were available in English, while Heinemann had brought out a thirteen–volume edition of Bjørnson; there had been several complete editions of Alexandre Dumas, including one in sixty volumes. Maupassant had been fully translated in 1914; Daudet, Tolstoy, Anatole France, Balzac, Voltaire, Flaubert, Hugo, Mallarmé, Marcel Prévost and Sudermann had been translated either in full or large part, whereas Tennyson, Thackeray, George Eliot, Meredith and Hardy had appeared in French at best very partially, while Swinburne, Pater and Henry James were totally unknown. Only Charles Dickens, Walter Scott and Oscar Wilde were fortunate in this regard, followed by H. G. Wells and Rudyard Kipling. The British provincialism that was so often attacked by English writers of the time is thus quite relative, and it is only in the import of Russian novels and Nietzsche that an English 'delay' is observable, even this being almost completely made up by 1914, with the translations from Russian by Constance Garnett and the work of A. O. Orage for Nietzsche.

These overall observations enable us to establish, at least for the end of the century, that France and Britain, which, as literary markets, had had little outward opening, were once again starting to open up under the pressure of generations of authors from afar, such as the Russians, Scandinavians, Poles, Italians and Spanish, who had become capable, especially by imitation, of supplying in their turn literary products receivable at the 'centre' of European literature. A distinct flow of works that were marginal in commercial terms but decisive intellectually was rapidly growing, especially in Britain. The symbolic and material survival of many poets and esoteric authors in Europe and its Atlantic margins often depended on their ability to link up with their counterparts abroad.

The key factor making for this overall similarity is that both French and British literary fields experienced between 1890 and 1910 more or less the same waves of import. On top of their mutual exchange, which was already very copious, the two countries saw the inflow of Scandinavian authors, the wave of Russian novelists followed by Chekhov, the distribution, far more limited, yet decisive in intellectual terms, of

Nietzsche's work, the 'Latin Renaissance' with D'Annunzio, Fogazzaro, Deledda and Serao. In both cases, Europe's literary margins were very well defined: the literatures of Central Europe were more or less absent, even the rich new Viennese literature, with the exception in France of the fashion for Sienckiewicz between 1898 and 1905; Hispanic literature was little represented, while the rest of the world had no more than an anecdotal presence.[11]

In several respects, the critical reception of foreign literature took a similar form in both countries. The 1880s were marked by national psychodramas, hinged on the introduction of foreign texts. The flamboyant rise of Henry Vizetelly culminated in his lost trials and imprisonment. Opposition to the naturalist novel was expressed by many critics, Robert Buchanan leading the charge backed by the neo-conservatism of William H. Mallock and George Saintsbury.[12] The National Vigilance Association and others of its kind managed to mobilise the Parliament, where the moral rot that had already ravaged France and now threatened Britain was denounced in strong terms. Censorship aroused the disgust and commitment of several writers in defence of Zola's work: the status of literary activity, public morality, and the country's religious soul were all threatened by the import of the French novelist. The same process followed the introduction of Nietzsche in France, the actors here being above all writers, and of Scandinavian theatre: the destabilisation desired by the young anarchists and anti-Wagnerians who imported Nietzsche – Georges Palante, Daniel Halévy, Pierre Lasserre, George Sorel – was countered by defensive action by academic Kantians and moderate ideologists of the Republic, from Emile Boutroux to Alfred Fouillée. The debate penetrated the political arena on several occasions, in the guise of an avatar of the Franco-German opposition. The theatre of Ibsen and Bjørnson aroused a flood of criticism in Parisian newspapers,[13] mobilising the most eminent publicists such as Jules Lemaître, Francisque Sarcey and Henry Fouquier, just as in Great Britain, as well as a large section of young symbolist writers, and it seemed to many observers that the issue at stake was the nature of French theatre and the future of the national spirit, beyond the question of the qualities of a good play and the role of criticism. Such leading figures in political life as Jean Jaurès and Georges Clemenceau intervened at times in the debate, making a connection with party struggles.

The example of Ibsen enables a close comparison of these debates.[14] Like Sarcey in the *Figaro*, Clement Scott of the *Daily Telegraph* raged against the Scandinavian playwright, amid a journalistic output that counted five hundred articles on *A Doll's House* in 1890 alone, while young dramatists mobilised in Ibsen's defence, along with a number of acute critics including Shaw, Lang and Archer, and the entire theatrical institution, along with the censorship and high society, embarked on a debate that questioned the rules of correct behaviour on the stage and the representation of femininity. The difference from the French reception of Ibsen was, however, significant: once the first phase of confrontation was over, Ibsen was accepted and became a classic of the theatre of manners in the West End, whereas in Paris critical opposition to Ibsen had contributed to the failure of the Théâtre Antoine and the Théâtre de l'Œuvre, virtually stopping the staging of Ibsen for twenty years. Conservative opposition to Ibsen in London took the form of puritanical objection to a content that was overly daring and demoralising to the social order, as a continuation of debate on the status of women, sexual liberation and eugenics, while the conflict in France turned around a question of national aesthetics, Scandinavian theatre being rejected en bloc as foreign to the French soul which was Latin, clear and classical.[15] As Bjørnsterne Bjørnson put it in 1900, France had behaved as the 'China of Europe', wrapped up in its backward isolation and hostile to the invasion of the 'barbarians'.[16]

In both countries, the logic of the great debates around foreign literature was thus similar in the 1890s, apart from certain details: the imports were accompanied by an enormous critical output,[17] fuelling polemics that served as crucibles for the definition of good and bad literature, for redefining positions in the intellectual field, and reasserting the importance of literature in national life. The literary and ideological reorientations that intervened in the mid-1890s were, to a large degree, a result of these conflicts over the foreign references that both aestheticism and symbolism resorted to at this time. A closer focus on the actors involved in this import will enable us to explain why it was able, at this point, to challenge the rules of intellectual life in both countries.

The barbarians' harbingers: literary import between the proletarianisation of letters and aesthetic subversion

The essential fact is that the translation and active promotion of literature from abroad allowed the entry into the literary world of social categories that were a priori poorly suited to taking such a place. These importers, in both France and Great Britain, included large numbers of young men and women endowed with a medium level of social and cultural capital, young writers of foreign or provincial origin with no distinct specialism, often attached to radical and marginalising political activity of a socialist or anarchist kind, a high proportion of women, most often from the established bourgeoisie, who in their translation activity hid both behind male names and those of the male writers they translated: as examples falling under various of these categories we may mention Theodor de Wyzewa, a symbolist who had rallied to the *Revue des deux mondes* from a horror of poverty; Albert Savine, the anarchist from Languedoc who promoted Catalan literature; the Alsatian Henri Albert, a critic of German-language literature in the *Mercure de France*; the 'wives and mothers of ...' who included Eleanor Marx, translator of Flaubert; Constance Garnett, translator of Tolstoy; Mme Jean Dornis or Arvède Barine; journalists and critics beating on the academic door such as George Saintsbury, who had failed to become a Fellow at Merton College, but succeeded in returning to his alma mater as a specialist in 'vulgar' literature thanks to his numerous articles in London magazines. In general, import was an activity of literary beginners.

At the bottom of the ladder stood the translators, for the most part the wretched of the literary field, 'failures' or eternal beginners, whether indigenous or foreign, who found it impossible to get published in their own right and whose trace is retained only in the mention of their name on the title page – dozens of title pages, in some cases. The many women who hid behind male pseudonyms, at a time when female authors were still rare and badly viewed, especially in France, counted among the most dominated of these hack writers. The 'translation workshops' for Russian fiction managed by Halpérine Kaminsky, the long series of translations by Albert Savine, exploited by Pierre Victor Stock to pay off his debts,[18] those of Constance Garnett, hailed by the public but very badly paid by William Heinemann[19] – she did remarkable translations of the major works of Tolstoy and Dostoyevsky, but never obtained any share in the royalties – provide some examples of this 'literary proletariat' who found in translation a way of access to literary life, often experienced as provisional, as a prelude to more 'serious' activity, but who in most cases found it extremely hard to 'escape' from this.

There were then the polygraphs and critics, often regular contributors with a column on foreign literature, who sometimes did succeed in this way in winning sufficient recognition before going on to write on more prestigious national subjects, such as Saintsbury, Gosse, E. M. de Vogüé or André Bellessort. Editors of foreign literature series made their appearance at this time, such as Edmund Gosse or Henry Davray, even if the actual content of their work was still poorly defined, only becoming more consistent in the inter-war years. It was still a little-formalised activity, poorly paid and experienced as a *pensum* more than an intellectual project, as can be seen by the example of Charles du Bos. Magazine publishers and the leaders of subversive groups did not flinch from organising regular import campaigns, reserving for themselves the noble tasks of criticism and debate, such as Rémy de Gourmont, T. S. Eliot or Ezra Pound at the start of their career, or Charles Morice at the beginnings of the *Mercure de France*; these operations of accumulating symbolic capital enabled him to link his obscure name with that of an author recognised abroad. This hierarchy in the import process, which ranged side by side recognised specialists, importers of a particular literature who transformed their long-term investment into a synthesis of literary history, and university professors of foreign literature whose profession was on the way to institutionalisation, was at the same time mostly a *cursus honorum*: Rémy de Gourmont had started with bread-and-butter translation work in 1880, Saintsbury steadily laid siege to the domain of English literature, while Henry Davray had begun at *Mercure de France* as a simple reporter before becoming a regular consul of English letters in France. But this elevation was highly selective, most translators and importers remaining in the shade, while true recognition meant admission into the circle of those – *académiciens*, academics or editors of magazines – who were authorised to speak on the national literature.

The connection between literary import and an entry position bore also on publishers. Walter Scott, William Heinemann and Henry Vizetelly, the English publishers who were in the forefront of literary import, were newcomers to publishing, both Heinemann and Walter Scott having an industrial background, and Heinemann even being a recent immigrant.[20] Heinemann started publishing Bjørnson and Maupassant in 1890 and Ibsen the following year; he published eight titles by D'Annunzio, translated by Arthur Symons, and in 1901 started a series of French novels. In a few years he managed to build up a publishing house that was commercially successful and intellectually respected, making judicious use of foreign literature. In France, the editions of *Mercure de France*, the *Revue Blanche*, the Stock publishing house which took over the titles of Albert Savine, followed by Rieder in the 1920s, based their reputation to a great extent on literary import. These publishers took part in the movement, especially in France, where the fashion for Russian novels was supported by the scholarly houses of Perrin and Plon, but they often adopted the discoveries of small publishers and distributed these with all their resources, thus drawing a greater profit.

The rising tide of literary import was thus one of the consequences of the social opening of intellectual life in the late nineteenth century. According to Christophe Charle, the accelerated growth in the number of writers and journalists was the most common feature in the development of elites in France and Great Britain: the number of 'authors' and 'editors' of periodicals in Britain rose from 6,300 in 1881 to 13,000 in 1911, and in France from 4,200 in 1876 to 9,200 in 1906.[21] This is one of the aspects which censors hostile to the introduction of foreign literature were able to oppose, making a grimacing face at the 'degradation' of letters by a superfluity of authors and the supposed dissolution of critical judgement. Representation of the status of translator, and reflection on translation, are good indications. There was very little reflection on translation in France at this time, when the status of translator seems to have been at its lowest – Valéry Larbaud's *Sous l'invocation de Saint Jérôme*,[22] which now serves as a memorial on the translator's profession, is an isolated and belated case. In Britain, translation seems to have been a little less devalued, in so far as it was applied to classic texts: Matthew Arnold, Gilbert Murray, William Morris and even W. E. Gladstone attest to this as a possible source of prestige in a literary life. In both countries, however, the social position of importers ruled out any professionalisation and any consistent theorisation of translation.

In the Taylorian Lectures given in Oxford in 1931, thus at the end of an already long career, Hilaire Belloc proposed a general reflection on the meaning of translation and the status of translator, summing up quite well the reaction of the intellectual field towards the new social face of importation.[23] Belloc put forward as an essential principle that the translator should be above all a specialist in his mother tongue, holding mastery of the language translated a secondary matter. A translation had to be nationalising, and was only acceptable when the task of the language specialist was to maintain the purity of the national idiom.[24] Any form of 'estrangement' was proscribed. Above all, Belloc was equivocal about the steady increase in the number of translations over the last three decades: they were increasingly bad. This degradation was explained by the appetite for profit of a broad intellectual proletariat, as well as the passive reception of foreign literature, which Belloc blamed on the popular press, an attitude which in his view could only provoke a return of isolationism. To avoid such reaction, which he considered would be damaging – 'at the end is the death of our culture. For no province of Europe can stand alone'[25] – the importance of translation had to be recognised, and translators properly rewarded, giving them half the royalties and half the glory. Nothing in British legislation secured the rights of a translator over his work until 1912, at which point translators were recognised as co-authors, though they still had no claim to a royalty unless this was acceptable to the publisher.[26] In France, a translator's rights were protected by law, in the wake of a more precise legislation on author's rights in general, but the prestigious authors of this time, a rare number, were quickly forgotten despite this: the anger of Louis Fabulet, when Kipling was feted at the Sorbonne in 1921 without him (the most determined importer of the English novelist) being invited or even mentioned, attests to this implicit disdain.[27] In France as in Britain, the apparent explosion in the number of translators and their participation in the waves of foreign literature thus appeared to many, even to an assiduous importer such as Belloc, the most unpleasant form of industrialisation of the literary profession.

This attitude was supported by the symbolic role that the most poorly endowed importers of foreign literature assigned to this import in their personal trajectory. It was often an initiative aiming at aesthetic subversion. The introduction of foreign texts offered advantages to those who embarked on the struggle from a peripheral or secondary position: the effort that they made placed them temporarily in a monopoly position; they made themselves spokesmen of a reputation established elsewhere, which spared them a long effort of accumulation of personal or collective prestige. When E.-M. de Vogüé presented the great Russian novelists in the *Revue des Deux Mondes*, his purpose, as well as contributing to a Franco-Russian rapprochement, was to restrain the domination of the novel by the naturalist school, and reassert the existence of an 'idealist' novel.[28] It took several years until his analyses could be challenged, for want of competence. That the work hailed from a foreign rival could double its subversive power: taking up the cause of Wagner in France between 1885 and 1895 coupled the effect of aesthetic scandal with a particularly provocative political charge. The French reference constantly mobilised between 1870 and 1920 by English-speaking poets of limited circulation – aesthetes, decadents and modernists – attests to the same concern for subversion of the main stream in English literature, derived essentially from romanticism, but in a form that they judged bastardised, being consecrated officially with Tennyson and Austin, poet laureates in the reigns of Victoria and Edward VII. French poetry, and sometimes novels as well, presented a model of formal research and esoteric challenge, but it was also always associated with the scent of scandal, a miraculous combination that referred both to the *Yellow Books* and to Baudelaire's *Fleurs du mal*, a poetic model for Swinburne. In the 1880s, this posture served writers who were Irish, Scottish or Welsh by birth, as well as some native English, as a war machine against the conventional grandiloquence of late romanticism and the moral concern of Victorian letters, and it served again, in the persons of Rimbaud, Laforgue and Gourmont, for the Anglo-Americans T. S. Eliot, F. M. Ford and Ezra Pound.

In the majority of cases, being an important part of a more or less organised campaign of subversion of established norms, often undertaken by the workhorses of literary life, literary import was thus, for its opponents, one of the most disturbing aspects of the crisis of cultural regulation that affected both France and Britain around 1900. In the face of the popular press, the birth of best-sellers, the explosion in the number of authors and the provocative avant-garde, the instances of production of cultural value adopted attitudes of resistance that were sometimes quite hysterical. In both countries, but especially in France, foreign works particularly acted as abscesses on which attention was fixated: the Russian novel, Zola and Ibsen embodied par excellence the uncontrollable, throwing all existing references into crisis. The intrusion of the literary foreigner concentrated, for its detractors and the majority of established authorities, a visible form of literary 'democracy': the proliferation of texts, the commodification of letters, the confusion of standards of judgement, the depreciation of the figure of the writer, at the very moment at which the professions were managing to organise themselves by controlling their conditions of practice in order to have their social and national role recognised.

The ambivalences of 'cosmopolitanism': literary import and nationalism

It was at the moment when conflicts over the importability of foreign literatures culminated that a large part of the symbolist generation abandoned its internationalism and rallied to a neo-conservatism that continued into Action française.[29] In the same years, the establishment of the 'regatta' around William Henley, a reader of the Parnassians and admirer of French literature who became the theorist of an anti-decadent literature harking back to the great epochs of the English past, then the Oscar Wilde trial, which had strong anti-French connotations, marked a significant 'national' inflection of literary life, of which Kipling became the flag-carrier.

In both Britain and France, the 1900s were thus 'national'. Nevertheless literary import did not decline: the structures of distribution, specialised series, magazines, collections of literary history, now well established, continued to supply both markets, still more readily given the pool of translators that the precariousness of literary movements and the fashion of the previous decade for foreign literature had aroused. From a commercial standpoint, the supply continued, but import now essentially ceased to be part of an overtly internationalist or cosmopolitan strategy. In both countries, intellectual debate was occupied by a general effort to (re-)establish a literary dogma responding to the crises that the profession of letters had experienced, and to the requirements of national mobilisation. In England there was Georgian poetry, the Tudor aesthetic, the campaigns of the English Association for the teaching of

English as a national cement, and the intense production of literary history organised around the Elizabethan Golden Age.[30] In France there existed the decline of symbolism in the face of an 'eminently French' neo-classicism, from the *Nouvelle Revue Française* to *Action française*, the debate against the 'new' Sorbonne, the restoration of ancient languages and the triumph of the reference to the seventeenth century. In both countries, a (re)nationalisation of intellectual life was under way, founding itself on the crisis opened up by the inflow of 'foreign' legitimacies and the opportunities that had been offered them. Definition against the foreigner was at the heart of the transformation of writers into 'national intellectuals',[31] and the supposed cosmopolitanism that had been the fashion of the previous decade now seemed to be overshadowed by narcissistic and protectionist preoccupations.

From a retrospective point of view, what was most disturbing about this 'cosmopolitanism' is that a fair number of leading importers of the 1890s found a place among the defenders of the national ideal in the following decade. A well-known example is that of E. M. de Vogüé, who, from the mid-1890s, became, in the Académie française, a promoter of French latinity, then an active supporter of neo-classicism. Edmund Gosse's case is very similar: a former champion of Ibsen and French poetry, he had been involved with all the 'dirty tricks' of importation, but the *History of English Literature* that he produced from 1898 on was full of a national literary mythology, according to which the history of English literature amounted to a war of independence against French influence. President of the English Association, he counted among the leading cultural ambassadors of Great Britain. More generally, the presidents of the English Association between 1904 and 1921 included three other recognised and renowned importers besides Gosse: George Saintsbury, Sidney Lee and H. Herford. For France, the ambivalence of the founders of Germanistic or comparative literature, at the same time active importers and theorists of an irreconcilable opposition between the French and the German mind, became clearly apparent when they rallied to war propaganda, but they had been involved in the hardening of cultural identities long before 1914.[32]

How can we explain this ambiguity, which clouds the generally accepted distinction between cosmopolitans and nationalists, smugglers and frontier guards? A first explanation can account for the most flagrant of turns, such as that of Maurice Barrès, the European of 1892 turned protectionist, of William Henley or Richard le Galienne: the effect of legal or informal censorship on the literary field in the mid-1890s was very painful in both countries for the symbolist/decadent writers who had established their networks and resources within a multinational or even anti-national system, and essentially made it their business to distance literature from social demands and language from its national role. On the contrary, the rallying to nationalism could appear as a solution when the conditions for a genuine independence of the writer were not fulfilled. The neo-classical injunction with its xenophobic dimension, and its neo-romantic variant in the English case, amounted to accepting anew this national status of language, that of the elites and above all of the state. Those in the best position to impose themselves as national authors were able to reconvert, like Shaw who, as the head of the New Drama, could permit himself, in his preface to *Major Barbara*, to reject any influence of Ibsen, Schopenhauer or Nietzsche on his theatre, and claim this was rooted in an old national tradition, that of the modest Belfort Bax.[33] This possibility of reconversion could also be seized by figures who in retrospect seem more modest, but who counted for much in the intellectual life of their time, such as the internationalist symbolists Camille Mauclair and Théodor de Wyzewa, who in gradual stages became nationalist importers. Import remained an essential resource for survival, in the form of criticism in magazines and reviews, but this was now steered in the direction of a defence of frontiers and a theory of national identities grasped in their literary contrasts. Even a radical anti-nationalist such as Rémy de Gourmont succumbed to these sirens at the end of his life, when it seemed to him that cosmopolitan symbolism had given way to neo-classical nationalism.

The fragility of the social positions of the importers is thus part of the explanation for the reversibility of attitudes towards foreign literatures.[34] But we can risk going further, and bring to light a fundamental ambiguity in this import activity. With both de Vogüé and Archer, who each used a scarce resource that was available to them by personal accident – family in Norway, a diplomatic position in Russia – the import of eminent authors was justified by a discontent with national literary life and a desire to 'get level' with the foreigner or rediscover a national tradition. The campaigns in favour of Ibsen thus served also as an active advocacy of a national theatre that would at last perform the English repertoire. The champions of the Scandinavians argued from the need to catch up with the main literary heroes of Europe and take part at last in modernity. Archer, and with him Shaw, might thus appear, in a certain sense, premature activists of 'national efficiency' applied to the literary world,[35] reproaching the English theatre for not being sufficiently national and competitive. In this case, the importer in actual fact acted as a nationaliser, the foreign source serving both as conceptual antithesis and as actual model, enabling the birth of a national art that would supplant the French 'well-made' play.

Moreover, the literary importers, by the contacts that they had with other Europeans, became in their turn the intermediary of these foreigners in their own countries. Edmund Gosse rapidly established himself as a specialist on England in France, while Henry Davray, known especially as the translator of H. G. Wells, became the unofficial representative of France in Britain, meeting one another for example in the associative and parapolitical structures of the Anglo-French Society. Condemned to a mediocre level in their role as importers, especially in France, these authors were thus able to invent careers for themselves in which they served as cultural interface, specialists in a country whenever they addressed the public in the other, not without a certain imposture. Many importers are to be found among the diplomats of the time – de Vogüé, for instance, or Jules Jusserand, a historian of English literature and French ambassador to the United States, whose work was praised by English literary historians. This tendency for international literary relations to select specialists who were reversible for their own country and for the other, later found its apogee in war propaganda.

These examples of 'returned' internationalists, of a literary interface, of cultural diplomats or nationalising importers, give literary import a different image from the classic couple of open, generous and abused cosmopolitan versus protectionist, academic and blinkered nationalist. Valéry Larbaud and Charles Maurras were only marginal cases. Literary import and the construction of national identity were closely linked around 1900 in both Britain and France. Discourse on other countries formed an essential site of legitimacy for discourse on one's own, and all the more essential in that issues were at stake there for literary life, the regulation of value, the relationship with the public and the state, and the status of the man of letters. It is certain that an essential part of literary import was to undertake a kind of 'empirical literary ethnology' in which literature was the manifestation, par excellence, of the spirit of a nation.[36] From this point of view, many importers took part in the effort of cultural legitimation of the imperial nation-states, giving these the appearance of eternal consistency. They thus acquired the informal status of theorists of the national and national intellectuals, at the same time as they elaborated, through their international contacts, a regulated space of competition between literatures.

This picture, however, needs to be qualified to some degree by indicating two significant differences between France and Great Britain in the 1900s. In Britain, the ebb of decadence did not prevent the re-establishment of a modernist pole distinct from Georgian poetry or the Edwardian novel, appealing like its forerunners to foreign example, especially French, as a basis for its desire for the new and its formal demands. T. S. Eliot,

Ford Madox Ford, Ezra Pound, T. E. Hulme, O. A. Orage and James Joyce himself reformulated an avant-garde project from the legacy of symbolism, taking J. Laforgue, R. de Gourmont, L. Tailhade and T. Corbière as their guides in experimentation. Embodied in the *English Review*, *Blast*, the *Egoist* and the *New Age*, this modernism nourished by American émigrés had no equivalent in France: the *Nouvelle Revue Française* sought to be French above all, leaving only a small part for foreign reference, with the exception of Dostoyevsky and the English adventure novel; poetic modernism around Apollinaire seemed to be obscured by the neo-classicism of the *NRF* and *Action Française*, and was scarcely interested at all in foreign literature. The rallying of Apollinaire to the Maurrasian national tradition during the Great War was nothing surprising in this respect.[37]

The second difference, operating in the same direction, lay in the different treatment of national literary identity in the voluminous literary histories that flourished at this time on both sides of the Channel. The part played in editing these in England by major figures of importation such as Gosse or Saintsbury forced their integration into a university system that was reticent towards them, and is partly explained by the fact that the English identity that was developed in these was a hybrid one, the product of Saxon, Latin, French, Italian and German sources, thus anchored in a tradition of importation that was constitutive of the national habitus. This is why the Newbolt report, drafted partly by the same authors, could maintain in 1921 that the capacity to assimilate human diversity was the 'native experience of men of our race and culture'.[38] This definition, very much in the spirit of free trade and liberal imperialism, was in singular contrast to the contemporary French representation, 'indigenist' and protectionist, of Ferdinand Brunetière, René Doumic, Petit de Julleville or even Gustave Lanson: French literature for them had become what it was when it was freed from Italian tutelage and became 'classical' in the time of Louis XIV. Though structurally similar in each country, the place of literary import in the nationalisation of literary life in Britain and France thus presents significant differences of accent, and – as opposed to what is often said, and was said already at the time – French literary life was the more closed to foreign example.

Conclusion

Symptom and harbinger of the crisis of intellectual identities in 1900 Europe, the promotion and reception of foreign literatures played a direct part, in both France and England, in the process of intellectual nationalisation. It reveals the different modalities in which French and English writers were able to find a partial solution to their difficulties by elaborating the role of guardian intellectual of national identity, specialist in the literary spirit of different peoples and constructor of closed identities. The national writer, almost a state figure, presented a solution of effective refashioning for a 'trade' in crisis, capable of offering the advantages of professionalisation without its inconveniences. The elaboration of this position based itself on intense mobilisations, on large-scale polemics that by their very existence contributed to accrediting the idea that literature, a reflection of the national soul, was an essential interest at stake in national life, and this owes much to the importers of foreign literature themselves, in their role as constructors and manipulators of national frontiers before being cosmopolitan 'smugglers' across these.

There has been a frequent tendency to exaggerate the differences dividing intellectual life in France and England. The mechanisms of literary import, its actors, the literatures imported, the reactions of institutionalised criticism and the scope of debates aroused in the entire public space, including that of politics, were essentially comparable in both cases. If initial differences did exist, these had a tendency to diminish, as the overall movement of convergence of European societies, the product of a generalised competition between rival powers, did not spare literary life. Differences of stress may be laid, but these are inscribed within a parallel and even common process, with the construction of national identity in European states, especially in France and England, appearing as a dialogic process. If comparativism has great virtues, it has also to my mind a possible fault, i.e. the need to produce difference in order to justify its particular discourse. We have seen how, in a certain sense, the birth of a comparative literature around 1900 responded to a widespread social or political demand for the cultural differentiation of national states; the reflexivity facilitated by a historicisation of discourses on national identity should enable us to avoid precisely this problem with the comparativist posture, the immediate justification for which is the presupposition of difference. It can thus also give itself the task of maintaining that, on the essential level, intellectual life in both France and Great Britain around 1900 was quite close in many respects, even if one of its dominant motives, at the time, was precisely to show how the two countries were essentially different.

Notes

1 See, however, B. Wilfert, 'Paris, la France et le reste: importations littéraires et nationalisme culturel en France, 1885–1930', unpublished doctoral thesis, Université Paris-I Panthéon-Sorbonne, 2003.

2 The bibliography is compendious. We can simply quote here *Les Intellectuels en Europe au XIXème siècle* by Christophe Charle (2nd edition, Paris: Le Seuil, 2001; first edition 1996) and Stefan Collini, *Public Moralists* (Oxford: Oxford University Press, 1991).
3 The concept developed by Christophe Charle to denote the organisation of the three main belligerents in the Great War should be indicated here, these each being shaped 'by the sacralisation of the nation and the deployment in its service of all material, social and cultural forces'; *La Crise des sociétés impériales* (Paris: Le Seuil, 2001), pp. 16–17.
4 The fin de siècle saw the British capital rediscover a metropolitan role, from the standpoint of both empire and political and cultural life. See in particular P. Cain and A. Hopkins, *British Imperialism* (London: Routledge, 1993), vol. 1; T. W. Heyck, *The Transformations of Intellectual Life in Victorian England* (London: Croom Helm, 1982); and José Harris, *Private Lives: Public Spirit: A Social History of Britain, 1870–1914* (London: Penguin, 1994).
5 F. Moretti, *Atlas du roman européen* (Paris: Le Seuil, 2000), in particular chapter 3.
6 *The Oxford Guide to Literature in English Translation*, ed. Peter France (Oxford: Oxford University Press, 2000), p. 73.
7 On Edmund Gosse, see A. Thwaite, *Edmund Gosse: A Literary Landscape* (London: Secker and Warburg, 1984).
8 Christopher Campos, *The View of France from Arnold to Bloomsbury* (Oxford: Oxford University Press, 1965), Appendix, pp. 245ff.
9 This is, for example, the perspective of S. Hynes, *The Edwardian Turn of Mind* (London: Pimlico, 1968), chapter 9, 'The Human Character Changes', as well as that of the *Oxford Guide to Literature in English Translation* cited in note 6.
10 See, on this subject, K. Shepherd Barr, *Ibsen and Early Modernist Theatre, 1890–1900* (Westport, CN and London: Greenwood Press, 1997), and J. Robichez, *Le Symbolisme au théâtre. Lugné-Poe et le théâtre de l'œuvre* (Paris: L'Arche, 1957).
11 For example, Rabindranath Tagore, whose Nobel prize was awarded above all for his efforts in promoting the British Empire in its most benign aspect.
12 On this point see, in particular, John Lucas, 'Conservatism and Revolution', in J. Lucas (ed.), *Literature and Politics in the Nineteenth Century* (London: Methuen, 1971).
13 See A. Dikka Reque, *Trois Auteurs dramatiques scandinaves devant la critique française, 1889–1901* (Paris: Champion, 1930) and J. Robichez, *Le Symbolisme au théâtre*.
14 For a fuller presentation of this key case for the present question, see chapter 11 of this volume.
15 It was symptomatic that Ibsen was received as a critical realist in Britain, and as a nebulous symbolist in France.
16 *Revue Hebdomadaire*, 2 March 1901, p. 99: 'There are two distinct races on our old Continent: the cosmopolis of the United States of Europe on the one hand, and on the other, isolated from the rest by a Chinese wall, France.'

17 Besides articles in the press, several works of synthesis appeared on imported authors and the different national literary histories, such as the Heinemann collection and its French counterpart from Armand Colin.
18 Albert Savine alone contributed forty-four of the seventy-two titles of *Cosmopolite* available in 1919. For the bulk of this work he used students and foreigners who have left no trace.
19 On Constance Garnett and William Heinemann, see J. Saint John, *William Heinemann: A Century of Publishing, 1890–1990* (London: Heinemann, 1990), and R. Garnett, *Constance Garnett: A Heroic Life* (London: Sinclair-Stevenson, 1991).
20 Saint John, *William Heinemann* and Garnett, *Constance Garnett*.
21 C. Charle, *La Crise des sociétés impériales*, p. 146, and *Les Intellectuels en Europe au XIXème siècle*, p. 151.
22 Valéry Larbaud, *Sous l'invocation de Saint Jérôme* (Paris: Gallimard, 1946). This was a collection of articles mostly written in the 1920s and 1930s.
23 Hilaire Belloc, *On Translation* (Oxford: Clarendon Press, 1931).
24 On translation as domestication and naturalisation of the foreigner, see in particular Lawrence Venuti, *Translator's Invisibility* (London: Routledge, 1995).
25 Belloc, *On Translation*, p. 44. These were the final words of this lecture.
26 On this point, and more generally on the legal conditions for translators, see L. Venuti, *The Scandals of Translation: Towards an Ethics of Difference* (London: Routledge, 1998).
27 See Y. Guérin, *Une Œuvre anglo-indienne et ses visages français* (Paris: Publications de la Sorbonne, Didier, 1971), pp. 50–8.
28 See, on this point, M. Cadot (ed.), *Eugène-Melchior de Vogüé, le héraut du roman russe* (Paris: Institut d'études slaves, Presses de la Sorbonne, 1989), C. Charle, *Paris fin-de-siècle: culture et politique* (Paris: Le Seuil, 1998), chapter 6, 'Champ littéraire français et importations étrangères: la naissance du nationalisme littéraire', and B. Wilfert, 'Paris, la France et le reste', part 1, chapter 2.
29 On this point, see B. Wilfert, 'Paris, la France et le reste', part 3.
30 See M. Jey and B. Wilfert, 'Deux constructions d'un classicisme national par l'université: XVIIe siècle classique et siècle d'Elisabeth, France-Angleterre, 1890–1914', in *Quelques 'Dix-septième siècles': fabrications, usages et réemplois, Cahiers du Centre de recherches historiques*, April 2002 (Paris: EHESS, 2002).
31 Brian Doyle, *English and Englishness* (London: Routledge, 1989), p. 63.
32 See M. Espagne, *Les Transferts culturels franco-allemands* (Paris: PUF, 2000), and P. Gruson, 'A propos de la carrière universitaire de Victor Basch', in F. Basch *et al.* (eds), *Victor Basch, un intellectuel cosmopolite* (Paris: Berg International, 2000).
33 J.-C. Amalric, *George Bernard Shaw, du réformateur victorien au prophète edwardien* (Paris: Didier, 1979), pp. 203–4.
34 On the other hand, the tenacity of Valéry Larbaud, despite his modest success and the incomprehension of his friends on the *Nouvelle Revue Française*,

owed much to the financial security that enabled him to keep his distance from certain classicising and national demands.

35 I am drawing here on the analyses of political and social debate in the 1890s by G. R. Searle, *The Quest for National Efficiency: A Study in British Politics and Political Thought, 1899–1914* (Oxford: Blackwell, 1981), though these do not specifically bear on literature.
36 The word here is from M. Espagne, *Le Paradigme de l'étranger: les chaires de littérature étrangère en France au XIXe siècle* (Paris: Le Cerf, 1993), p. 134.
37 See A. Boschetti, *La Poésie partout: Apollinaire, homme-époque* (Paris: Le Seuil, 2001).
38 See, on this point, Jey and Wilfert, 'Deux constructions d'un classicisme national par l'Université'.

10

The commerce of ideas: protectionism versus free trade in the international circulation of economic ideas in Britain and France around 1900[1]

JULIEN VINCENT

> It has become a necessity for the modern scientist to be as cosmopolitan in their knowledge as those of the last generation, at least in France and England, were narrow and insular.[2]

> The German Manchester School is French.[3]

There are two widespread though unverified assumptions about the respective contributions of Britain and France to the development of economic science after 1870. The first is that, after a long era during which political economy remained a largely Franco-British conversation, Germany and the United States came to occupy a central place in the international Republic of Economic Letters. British and French economists, as if tired of their long-running dialogue, became less interested in each other as the Germans and the Americans introduced exciting new subjects into the conversation. The flow of economic ideas between France and Britain, so it is generally believed, dried up as a consequence.[4] The second assumption relates to the so-called 'decline' of French economic thought, which is deemed to have lost its appeal and influence around the time of the creation of university chairs of political economy in the law faculties by the Republicans in 1878.[5] As Alfred de Foville wrote in the *Quarterly Journal of Economics* in 1889, 'we must admit that Political Economy in France has lost, during the past ten years, much of the ground which it had gained in earlier years'; while Henry Higgs noted in the same journal that 'there has been a marked drifting of English economists from the influence of French writers'.[6] The main reason of this decline, we are told, is that years of sterile political (rather than scholarly) confrontation, between university professors and those whom Joseph Schumpeter called the 'Paris Group' of laissez-faire individualists, left the French school spiritless.[7] Whereas the former were generally influenced by the German economic historians Roscher and Schmoller, the latter were still fascinated by a largely idealised 'Manchester School' whose days had now long passed.

I want to challenge these two related assumptions by suggesting that the language of nationality and internationality in economics – without which, incidentally, these assumptions could not have been formulated – was in fact a largely normative language of scientificity. If we start from a more contextualised understanding both of economic science and of nationality, we shall find that the flow of economic ideas between Britain and France did not really dry up, but was rather redirected to channels of intellectual exchange not usually taken seriously by historians of economic thought. By referring to a 'British' or a 'French' school, we underestimate the extent to which these expressions conceal the fact that these so-called national schools were in reality battlefields on which rival definitions of economics were contested. If we start from this more dynamic and conflict-ridden view of national traditions of thought, we shall find that the international circulation of ideas was more complex than it seems. In order to support this argument, I shall focus on a quantitative study of reviews of foreign books in four economic journals in Britain and France. My selection of journals, putting the largely forgotten *Economic Review* on an equal footing with the celebrated *Economic Journal*, and the declining *Journal des Economistes* with the rising *Revue d'Economie Politique*, is meant to provide a more historicised view of the field of economics than is usually allowed. In the remainder of this chapter I shall attempt to account for the main discovery of this quantitative study of book reviews, i.e. the surprising interest of *Economic Review* contributors in French, rather than German or Italian, economic literature.

Political economy and the inevitability of nationality

Historians of economic thought have been more interested in why the adjective 'political' was dropped from the expression 'political economy' in the late decades of the nineteenth century than in why the adjective 'English' appeared in the expression 'English political economy' at about the same time. The years of *Methodenstreit* ('conflict of methods') in political economy, however, were also those when the 'dismal science' became increasingly characterised as 'English', while debates over the scope and method of the science were also to a large extent political discussions of national character.[8] The so-called 'internationalisation' of economic science during the 1880s and 1890s coincided with a wave of economic protectionism in Europe and America and with what may equally be described as a 'nationalisation' of economic thinking. The language of cosmopolitanism, in economics and other fields, cannot be understood unless put in the context of an equally influential language of nationality.[9] Although economists were generally committed to the view that there ought to be no national boundaries in the Republic of Economic Letters, they were captivated by the language of nationality. They pondered over the role of national character in economic theory and practice. They lovingly documented the history of each national school. They were intensely concerned about issues of priority, as the following anecdote suggests.

Jevons, a firm believer in the internationalism, and indeed cosmopolitanism, of science, had no time for generalisations about national peculiarities. He proved this in a provocative study of Cantillon published in 1881 in the *Contemporary Review*. Displaying laborious research and a keen sense of humour, he demonstrated that Cantillon was 'born from an Irish family of the County Kerry, bred we know not where, carrying on business in Paris, but clearly murdered in Albemarle Street' in London, printed his Treatise 'in Paris in the guise of a French translation, purporting to be published by Fletcher Gyles over against Gray's Inn in Holborn', a Treatise which had remained 'entirely mis-interpreted in England, while in France it [had] been explicitly acknowledged to be the source of the leading ideas of the great French school'.[10] Jevons was trying to deconstruct the idea of the 'nationality' of scientific knowledge to a point where it became a meaningless and almost absurd enquiry, but this was not enough to affect the general interest in the topic. Far from being confined to a sort of economic antiquarianism, questions of nationality permeated almost every area of economics, and played a conspicuous role in the re-establishment of its authority with the public. It may therefore be asked why, after Jevons's demonstration of the absurdity of such an enquiry, and given the rise of confidence in the combined cosmopolitanism and scientificity of the discipline after the marginal utility principle was discovered simultaneously in Austria, France and England in the 1870s, the view did not prevail that economic theory, by virtue of its abstract and scientific character, could not and should not have any nationality at all. The most obvious answer to this question is that the language of nationality was so constructed as to operate as a discourse of scientificity as well. This was done in a variety of ways.

A first common interpretation of the 'nationality of political economy' may be traced to Montesquieu's national 'character', to Madame de Staël's national 'literature', and to what had become in the nineteenth century, according to Michel Espagne, an 'empirical literary ethnology'.[11] It followed the traditional idea of national 'styles of thought', with the abstruse and philosophical German, the literary and political French, and the factual and practical English. The problem with this view of nationality, as was often noted at the time, was that it was too obviously incompatible with the issue at stake in the Anglo-German *Methodenstreit*, in which the English Ricardian economists stood for an abstract and deductive approach, and the German economists for an historical and inductive one.[12] A common rhetorical manoeuvre, in order to reconcile epistemology with the existence of rival national schools, was to emphasise the unity of economic science. Sketching the history of the inductive and historical versus the deductive and abstract methods in economics in his authoritative treatise on *The Scope and Method of Political Economy*, John Neville Keynes drew heavily on the language of nationality. These two methods, according to Keynes, had taken the form of rival national traditions in the nineteenth century, with the English school (Ricardo, Mill) on the one hand and the German school (List, Schmoller) on the other hand. Increased internationalisation, he argued, raised the hope that these national traditions would be brought together again into a unified, cosmopolitan science. This kind of theoretical narrative may indeed have been too abstract and deductive to be appreciated by many sober and factual English minds, but there were other ways to reconcile classical political economy with 'Englishness'. Walter Bagehot and Alfred Marshall traced Ricardo's genius for abstraction to his Jewishness, while arguing at the same time that his abstraction was in fact of a very practical character, therefore eminently English.[13] As for J. S. Nicholson, he turned the German historicists' weapons against them and suggested that historicising the history of English economic thought should lead one to escape from German historicist simplifications. As he put in his chapter on 'British economists' in the *Cambridge Modern History* in 1907:

> The appeal to the actual literature of Political Economy during this period [Smith, Malthus, Ricardo] proves not only that the British economists, from the time of Adam Smith, made popular certain fundamental ideas on the benefits of freedom of competition, or more generally of the system of natural liberty, but also that they showed the necessity of testing ideas by experience. Hence their influence on practical legislation and policy was always real and considerable: the so-called abstract ideas were themselves modified by circumstances of the times in which they were propounded.[14]

The language of the nationality of political economy, however, was not always tied to the traditional idea of 'character'. Indeed it was often embodied in the metaphor of a scientific 'race' between nations. Luigi Cossa's *Introduction to the Study of Political Economy*, a general survey of the discipline originally published in Italian and translated into several languages during the 1880s and 1890s, provides an example of this latter version of the language of the nationality of science. Characteristically, the author used his *Introduction* to discuss the different *national* schools of what he claimed was becoming an increasingly *international* discipline. According to Cossa, political economy was primarily a cosmopolitan science, like chemistry or physics, but its progress came about through national scientific communities. His views are encapsulated in the following quotation, in which he explains the intellectual primacy of England. Cossa here derives his understanding of progress from biological notions whereby the whole cannot be reduced to a mere sum of its constituent parts, while advancement is achieved through both cooperation *and* competition between the national schools. With this interpretation it becomes possible to identify different national styles of economic thought, to compare them and draw up a hierarchy between them:

> For many years now England has gone on maintaining her primacy as of yore, though there is from time to time an attempt, especially on the part of Germany, to challenge it. For twenty years past Germany has been gradually taking up the attitude of a lofty-minded renovator of the science, nor have German historical and statistical researches already made failed to enrich the field of economics ... This, added to a gift for abstruse reasoning and a trained practical sense, augurs well for the important investigations now in German hands. France, on the contrary, the sometime rival of England, is falling behind a little so far as theoretic work is concerned, and for this she has the exclusiveness of her predominant school of economics to blame. In Austria, Italy, and Holland, as well as Russia and the United States, where the movement is more recent, use is being made of English and German ideas, – of the latter with some caution in view of certain defects in the present tendency in German economics, – and marked progress is the order of the day. Scandinavia, meanwhile, and the lesser Latin and Slav States, as well as Hungary, are distanced in the race.[15]

As we can see in this passage, the metaphor of harmonious competition between national schools is by no means in contradiction to the more traditional idea of 'character'. Indeed, whereas the language of character is used to neutralise the cosmopolitan connotation of the scientific 'race', the emphasis on scientific co-operation/competition gives a modern flavour to the traditional idea of character. Having thus reworked and modernised the old interpretation of the nationality of political economy, Cossa could conclude that 'fifteen years [after] ... sceptics predicted the ruin, total and immediate, of English economics', it had 'not only [maintained] but [had] actually [enhanced its] time-honoured ascendancy in Economics at large'.[16]

The logic of the international commerce of ideas

In the long passage by Cossa reproduced above, we can recognise both of the modern assumptions against which the present chapter is written. This fact deserves some consideration. Although they were fond of talking about 'national' schools, distinguished economists such as Cossa or Keynes probably never believed that their own crude generalisations could ever be considered accurate representations of reality. When they talked of 'English ideas', Cossa and Keynes meant those ideas generally considered sound and orthodox in Britain. To a certain degree, however, economic orthodoxy in Britain meant economic orthodoxy in the rest of the world. Just as 'England' was often a misnomer for 'Britain', 'English', when applied to political economy, was often used as synonymous for 'orthodox', even though it was common knowledge that there was a heterodox school even in England. These simplifications can become a very serious obstacle to a proper historicisation of economic thought, if we take this language of nationality at face value and assume that whatever was considered heterodox in Britain was not British. These prevailing representations of nationality can be all the more damaging to the study of the circulation of ideas given that orthodox and heterodox economists, in so far as they were interested in what was written abroad, were interested in different things. That, after all, is part of what it means to be heterodox. From this it follows that an inadequate definition of what is 'British' or 'English' leads inevitably to a distorted view of intellectual exchange between Britain and other countries. This means that, as historians, we cannot hope to make any progress towards understanding the circulation of ideas from one country to another between 1890 and 1914 unless we become alert to the performativity and normativity of the language of the nationality of ideas. Discourses on the supposed characteristics of each 'national' school, and the fact that 'foreign' books might or might not be reviewed, translated, prefaced, or included in 'international' series, were two sides of the same coin. To put it differently, the normative language of nationality versus cosmopolitanism was part of a broader set of attitudes, of intellectual 'protectionism' or intellectual 'free trade'.

This is essentially the view held in Pierre Bourdieu's essay on 'the social conditions of the international circulation of ideas', an attempt to link the international circulation of ideas to the peculiarities of the national fields between which these ideas circulate. Since its publication in 1990 historians and sociologists, mainly in France, have attempted to apply his hypotheses to several intellectual fields. Although many different periods of history have brought their own revolutions in international intellectual exchange, recent studies suggest that the years 1870–1914, which were also paradoxically years of unprecedented nationalism in Europe, marked the beginning of a new process of internationalisation in intellectual life.[17] Of course, internationalisation was in many ways as old as political economy itself. It was the result of incremental change, dating from as far back as the very invention of a specifically economic vocabulary can be traced, first circulating in French and in English, and soon being translated into other languages. But it reached a crucial phase after 1870, due to the combination of such factors as a growing interest in comparing the dissimilar economic performance of industrial countries, the introduction of new communication technologies, and the specialisation and professionalisation of knowledge. The fact that Menger in Austria, Jevons in England and Walras in France and Switzerland had not been aware of each others' work when they 'discovered' the marginal principle in the early 1870s is certainly telling of the major changes that occurred in this respect during the following decade, when such lack of awareness of foreign scholarship became unthinkable.

One important aspect of this internationalisation is the emergence of an increasingly professionalised industry of translating, prefacing, reviewing and debate of foreign books. This new industry had far-reaching consequences on economists. Whereas British and French economists had a reputation for being too 'narrow and insular' to take notice of foreign sources, as the first epigraph to this essay suggests, the new impetus given to translations in the late nineteenth century fostered new attitudes. Economic writers were now expected to discuss foreign literature at length. These new attitudes were in no way specific to political economy but seemed to reflect a series of changes in intellectual life in the late nineteenth century, as both Casanova and Wilfert suggest (see chapters 9 and 11). Sometimes foreign writers were discussed as authorities with a view to demonstrating the 'objectivity' or 'universalism' of a given opinion. On other occasions, in contrast, these writers were dismissed as prejudiced and too narrowly 'national'. But there is another way in which the field of political economy can be compared with the literary field as described by Casanova and Wilfert. Just as the circulation of works by Ibsen and others in Britain and France must be put in the context of literary debates about 'realism' in the 1890s, so the circulation of economic ideas was facilitated by the demise of 'classical political economy' and the revival of epistemological debates over the nature and scope of the discipline after 1870.[18] There was an acute consciousness, in the late decades of the nineteenth century, of these intellectual exchanges with other countries. Internationalisation was perceived to be a new phenomenon. The general assumption was that political economy had consequently become more complex and that the interplay of intellectual influences was increasingly difficult to trace. As Edwin Cannan put it in the 1903 edition of his *History of the Theories of Production and Distribution*,

> In the origin and development of the doctrines dealt with in the present work, France certainly played a great and often underrated part, but the historian could safely neglect the rest of the world. During the last half century not only Germany, and at a later date Austria and other European countries, but also America, have entered the lists, and have so profoundly modified English economics that the world of the historian has become much wider and complicated.[19]

The idea of an intellectual condominium of France and Britain in the eighteenth century is a historiographic cliché which is rightly challenged by Laurence Brockliss in this volume (chapter 6), but it was widely shared by economists of the period. Cannan's extraordinary ignorance of German, Spanish, Russian or Italian economists of the past – in spite of Adolphe Blanqui's classic overview of this literature in the last chapters of his *History of Political Economy* in 1837 – illustrates not only how an English economist of the 1890s could still be blind to other possible approaches to the subject, before 1848, than those of the English and French masters, but also how vividly the new internationalisation of economics was perceived during that decade.[20] In Cannan's view, this internationalisation was linked to the progress of economic science. Other economic writers may have had a different interpretation of the actual scope, meaning and consequences of the trade of ideas between countries. But the important fact is that they all used the same language of 'free trade' versus 'protectionism' in the international commerce of economic ideas. The historical economist William Cunningham, in an essay entitled 'Why had Roscher so Little Influence in England?', claimed that the English orthodox school had deliberately cultivated a climate of intellectual protectionism and general indifference to the 'real ideas' of the German historical school.[21] His defence of the historical method was couched in the language of intellectual 'free trade'. Another 'heterodox' economist, the American publicist Henry George, reversed Cunningham's argument by advocating more intellectual protectionism. He condemned the transfer of foreign words and concepts into the domestic marketplace of ideas:

> What has succeeded is usually denominated the Austrian School .... The inquirer is usually referred to the incomprehensible works of Professor Alfred Marshall, of Cambridge, England ... or to a lot of German works written by men he never heard of, and whose names he cannot even pronounce. This pseudo-science gets its name from a foreign language,

and uses for its terms words adapted from the German – words which have no place and no meaning in an English work. It is, indeed, admirably calculated to serve the purpose of those powerful interests dominant in the colleges under our organisation, that must fear a simple and understandable political economy, and who vaguely wish to have the poor boys who are subjected to it by their professors rendered incapable of thought on economic subjects.[22]

As these examples suggest, the *language* of 'intellectual protectionism' versus 'intellectual free trade' was in large part a normative language in which economists could articulate their political or 'scientific' views. In exactly the same way, the different possible *attitudes* towards foreign writers, 'protectionist' or 'cosmopolitan', reflected different views on the nature of political economy. Historians of 'economic analysis' have been particularly interested in reconstructing the 'logic' of the circulation of economic ideas from this latter perspective. Such a logic seems particularly clear in the case of the mathematical economists of the 1870s. As T. W. Hutchison pointed out in 1955, W. S. Jevons's attack on 'the obnoxious influence of authority', at the end of his *Theory of Political Economy*, was followed by a list of works, many of them French or German, which endorsed the mathematical method he himself advocated. Although Hutchison centred his study on the case of Jevons's reception of Cournot, Dupuit, Walras, Gossen and Von Thünen, other examples suggest that there is some truth in the principle that also guides Casanova's and Wilfert's chapters in this volume; namely, that the 'importation' of foreign ideas can generally be linked to a challenge of established intellectual legitimacies within the national arena.

Two examples in particular show how theoretical debates were linked to strategies of importation of foreign ideas. The first example, which relates to the history of the theory of value, brings us back to the passage from Henry George. The late nineteenth-century rise of interest in the Austrian school, about which George complained with such bitterness in 1897, can effectively be traced to Scottish concerns over the classical theory of value. William Smart and James Bonar, the two main propagators of Austrian ideas in Britain and the United States, both studied philosophy in Glasgow in the 1870s with the Hegelian philosopher Edward Caird. Caird, who had grown dissatisfied with classical political economy, was one of many scholars who, in the 1870s, questioned the classical theory of value. Smart and Bonar, neither of them mathematicians, began to study the Austrian theory of value under his guidance. Smart wrote a small book on Austrian economics and translated or supervised translations of Böhm-Bawerk and Von Wieser, while Bonar published what soon became regarded as seminal articles on the Austrian theory of value, both for the *Quarterly Journal of Economics* and for Palgrave's *Dictionary of Political Economy*.²³ The history of the wages fund theory, our second example, seems to follow a comparable sequence of events. The theory was discarded during the 1870s, but before a new orthodoxy of the remuneration of the factors of production arose there was a gap of several years, during which the only impregnable position seemed to be agnosticism. As Sidgwick put it in 1879, in reference to the theory, 'I think there is a growing tendency in the organs of cultivated opinion to treat it as exploded.' However, as Sidgwick aptly noted, nothing had yet replaced it.²⁴ What is interesting for our purpose, however, is to note that this theoretical crisis can again be linked to an increased international circulation of ideas. As James Thompson has shown, the demise of the wages fund theory facilitated and was facilitated by the spread of Lujo Brentano's work on the history of the English guilds and inspired a new generation of historical economists who used his work to reconsider the role of trade unions in determining wages.²⁵ These two examples, incidentally, seem to qualify Hutchison's contention that the spread of mathematical methods and the 'increasingly professional intellectual status and standards of the pioneers of marginal analysis' were the two *main* factors in the internationalisation of economics.²⁶

All the same, it is not the object of this chapter to collect examples on each and every aspect of economic theory. However interesting the idea of a 'logic' of the international circulation of ideas may be, it remains unclear whether the previous examples can be used as confirmation that the main flow of economic ideas to Britain at the time came from the German-speaking world. To maintain this thesis, one would have to start from the circular assumption that by 'economic ideas' we mean those ideas discussed in journals dedicated to the pursuit of economic theory as understood by Alfred Marshall and other university professors associated with the *Economic Journal*, in countries such as Britain, Austria, Germany and the United States. This approach, which can be found in various historical surveys of economic thought in the 1890s and 1900s, means that British heterodox economists such as those writing in the *Economic Review*, not to mention French economists, can be 'safely neglected'. To exclude the heterodox *Economic Review* from such surveys, however, is problematic. The editors of this periodical, a publication of the Oxford Branch of the Christian Social Union, were careful not to call it a 'Journal of Social Reform', as Marshall had suggested they should.²⁷ As the editors explained in the first issue of the *Economic Review* 'it is impossible ... to draw a sharp line between the spheres of the Economic Moralist and of the scientific Economist'.²⁸ Those intellectuals who, in Britain as well as in France in the 1890s, approached economic questions from the point of view of 'social reform' or *économie sociale*, rather than from the point of view of 'science' as understood by Marshall or Edgeworth, may well have relied on a deficient definition of economics. It was, however, their definition, and their aim was explicitly to have an impact on *economic science* rather than on the science of social reform only. The *Economic Review* was conceived as a contribution to economic knowledge, even if – to use John Neville Keynes's distinction in *The Scope and Method of Political Economy* – this knowledge was of an 'ethical' rather than of a 'scientific' character. If we start from this more fully historicised view of economic thought, we shall find material to qualify prevailing accounts of the international circulation of economic ideas during the decades before 1914.

The statistics of the international commerce of ideas

While intellectual historians may examine the way in which particular ideas or sets of ideas are 'transferred' from one cultural sphere to another, it is more difficult for them to assess the balance of ideas between countries. If we want to have a more than an impressionistic idea of the international flow of ideas, it is important to couple intellectual history with a quantitative approach. This is what is attempted here through a quantitative study of reviews of foreign books. In order to avoid the pitfalls of circular reasoning, however, such a quantitative study must be based on a careful selection of sources. While a comparison between Britain and France is perhaps less usual than between Britain, Germany and the United States, the 'great' nations of economic thought after 1870, the inclusion of journals such as the *Economic Review*, the *Revue d'Economie Politique* and the *Journal des Economistes* presents a story of post-1870 economic thought which is clearly unfamiliar to historians of neo-classical theory and economic analysis.

The most striking fact emerging from this quantitative comparison is that the *Economic Review* covered twice as many books in French as books in German. This result suggests that the impact on British thinkers of what was described by Cossa as the 'dogmatic' French school, with its coterie of laissez-faire propagandists on the one hand, and its Republican school of lawyers and cooperators on the other hand, has been overlooked. Table 10.1 shows the language of the books reviewed in the four principal publications dedicated to political economy in Britain and in France between 1890 and 1910. It gives us a rough idea of the aggregate flow of ideas towards Britain and France.[29]

Whereas the number of reviews of foreign books in English or German in the French journals is more or less matched by the number

Table 10.1 National origins of the books reviewed in French and English economic reviews

Books reviewed	Economic Journal + Economic Review (%)[a]	REP + JdE (%)[b]
English (UK, US, Canada, etc.)	67.3	8.1
German (Germany, Austria, etc.)	14.2	10
French (France, Belgium, etc.)	13	68.3
Italian	4.7	8.6
Other	0.8	5
Total	100 (1,761 books)	100 (1,428 books)

[a] 1,761 books were reviewed in the *Economic Journal* (1,199) or the *Economic Review* (939) between 1891 and 1910: 1,186 in English, 250 in German, 229 in French, and 82 in Italian and 15 in other languages. Among these 1,761 books, 382 were reviewed in both journals, 817 were reviewed in the *Economic Journal* only, and 562 were reviewed in the *Economic Review* only.

[b] Sample of 1,428 books taken from an ongoing database project in 1888–1890, 1892, 1894–1899, 1903–1910.

of reviews of books in Italian or in other languages (mainly Spanish), in the British journal by contrast the emphasis is on German and French. Apart from these differences, however, these figures suggest a similar pattern in both the British and the French 'balance of intellectual trade': more than two-thirds of the books selected for review were written in the native language of the reviewers. This fact reflects the comparable position of the two countries in the international commerce of economic ideas. First, Britain and France, like Germany, belonged to the few intellectually 'self-sufficient' nations whose economic debates were on the whole conducted by national economists, and within a national tradition of thought. Second, the circulation of economic ideas between Britain and North America on the one hand, and between France, Belgium and Switzerland on the other hand, was facilitated by a common language. Germany, whose intellectual influence was felt throughout Central and Eastern Europe, was in a similar position to that of Britain and France. It would be misleading, however, to go so far as to speak of a complete intellectual self-sufficiency; just outside this inner circle, which may be compared to an intellectual *Zollverein*, there was a second circle of preferred intellectual trading partners, namely Britain, France and Germany. Finally, a third circle was made up of comparatively 'small countries' of economic thought, such as Sweden, Spain, the Netherlands or Japan, easily outdistanced in the race.

These figures enable us to qualify two general assumptions about intellectual exchanges in political economy at that time. The first is that intellectual life after 1870 experienced a major 'Germanisation' – what has famously been described by Claude Digeon as a 'German crisis of French thought', and is generally assumed to have been the case in Britain, as well.[30] Although the intellectual influence of German thought is undeniable, it has been somewhat misrepresented. It is an undeniable fact that the military defeat of France in 1870, together with the patriotic urge to understand the reasons for the superiority of Germany in the one case, and the increasing competition and threat of Germany to the British economy in the other, are two contexts without which it is impossible to understand the influence of German social and economic thought in Britain and France before 1914. However, it is perhaps more accurate to distinguish between content and form, i.e. between the facilitating political and cultural factors which tended to give great prominence to German questions, and the underlying revolution in the conditions of intellectual exchange at an international level. The influence of German thought should thus be placed in the context of an increased circulation of economic ideas, and understood as one feature in a more general internationalisation of intellectual life; it cannot be understood simply in terms of pre-1914 French and British fears about Germany.

Secondly, while it is often assumed that the main foreign sources of inspiration in British social and economic thought after 1890 were German or American, Table 10.1 suggests that French sources were very significant indeed. Does this mean that French economists also had an impact on British economic thought? In order to answer this question we must turn to Table 10.2, which focuses on British sources only, and on the 'second circle' in the international trade of ideas – that concerned with reviews of foreign books written in a foreign language.

British attitudes to intellectual free trade: a comparison of the *Economic Review* and the *Economic Journal*

French writers may have been of little interest to the 'scientific' economists influenced by Marshall and Edgeworth and writing for the *Economic Journal*. But the *Economic Review*, their direct rival at Oxford, reviewed more books in French than in German. Whereas German and American 'influences' were strong indeed, the figures show that the reviewing policy of the *Economic Review*, contrary to that of the *Economic Journal*, privileged books in French. Indeed there were two systems of international circulation of economic ideas, rather than one. While the first system was focused on economic science and the study of economic uniformities,

Table 10.2 Distribution of the national origins of books reviewed in the *Economic Journal* and the *Economic Review*

	Economic Journal		Economic Review[a]	
English	803	67%	706	75%
French	129	10.8%	133	14.3%
German	190	15.8%	72	7.7%
Italian	68	5.7%	22	2.3%
Other	9	0.7%	6	0.7%
Total	1,199		939	

[a] Among the 562 books reviewed by the *Economic Review*, but not by the *Economic Journal*, there were 383 in English, 100 in French, 60 in German, 14 in Italian, and 5 in another language.

and linked the *Economic Journal* to German sources, the other system stressed books related to social reform, 'ethical economics' or what the French called *économie sociale*, and linked the *Economic Review* to French sources.

The different reviewing policies between the *Economic Review* and the *Economic Journal* reflect rival and complementary positions within the field of economics.[31] Each position was characterised by its own particular viewpoint on the scope, method, boundaries and applications of the discipline, and by its own selection of 'relevant' books within the available literature – indeed a policy of reviewing is always a policy of not reviewing as well. With these rival positions were associated distinct, if sometimes overlapping, networks of economic writers and reviewers, whose linguistic skills, academic or non-academic responsibilities, and social attitudes, differed in the same way. Finally, as both consequence and cause of the previous remarks, it seems that each journal had different, if partly overlapping, readerships. Whereas the readers of the *Economic Journal*, during the first years of its existence, were more or less the members of the British Economic Association, a large portion of whom were recruited from business, political and academic circles, the readers of the *Economic Review* were mainly social reformers, including a large proportion of women, clergymen and Oxford dons.[32]

These differences of readership seem to have had far-reaching consequences on each journal, and help explain the differences in reviewing policies noted above. Books reviewed by the *Economic Review* did not simply include economic textbooks, historical studies or empirical surveys, but also, in equal proportion, works in ethics, political philosophy, political science, theoretical and historical sociology, law, practical manuals for cooperators and social reformers, as well as a great many essays dealing with general problems of the time and written by politicians, moralists, or amateur social scientists. A large proportion of the space allocated to reviews was devoted to such essays or surveys on a particular issue, which made technical questions accessible to the unspecialised reader while providing him or her with material for thought. As far as foreign essays of this kind are concerned, *Economic Review*-ers seem to have had a particular taste for the French books, which, unlike the German, they tended to cite in the original language. French essay writers, moreover, had a reputation for clarity and were often praised for this quality in the reviews. Whether true or not, this view was largely shared among English reviewers at the time, who liked to contrast the scholarship and obscurity of German writers with the elegance and clarity, though sometimes lack of thoroughness, of the French. As R. R. Marett, a sociologist of religion and reviewer of many French and German books on the subject, suggests: 'A French writer may usually be trusted to be clear; and, when he is thorough as well, he is indeed hard to beat'.[33]

John M. Ludlow, the 'historic' Christian Socialist, had been brought up in France. The co-operator H. W. Wolff wrote two tourist guides of the (French-speaking) Vosges. Both were very productive reviewers, but the fact that these and many other prominent members of the Christian Social Union and *Economic Review* contributors had personal links with France was not the only reason for their interest in French intellectual life.[34] British Christian Socialists had absorbed the ideas of Buchez and Lamennais in 1848, and were alive to the more recent developments of French Catholic economics.[35] In the 1900s, the 'Modernist' theology of French liberal Catholics was discussed by many members of the Christian Social Union, including sympathisers such as A. L. Lilley, and critics such as W. R. Inge.[36] Given this convergence of factors, it is not surprising that readers of the *Economic Review* should have been expected to be reasonably interested in contemporary French thought.

A possibly more important reason for the large number of French books reviewed in the *Economic Review*, however, is the emergence in France, during the 1890s and 1900s, of a very active school of social reform, comparable in many ways to the British and American 'Progressive' movement. This *nébuleuse réformatrice* ('reforming nebula'), to use Christian Topalov's phrase, was organised by a number of loosely related institutions such as the Musée social, various book series such as Reinwald's *Bibliothèque d'histoire et de sociologie* and Alfred Bonnet's *Bibliothèque internationale d'économie politique*, the '*solidaristes*' and cooperators associated with the '*économie sociale*' of Charles Gide, the

Société Saint-Vincent-de-Paul, Le Sillon, and other societies associated with 'social Catholicism'. The *Economic Review*'s notice of a translation of Charles Gide's *Political Economy* lists some of the reasons for the closeness between the Christian Social Union and French social reformers. This textbook, the reviewer says, combines an examination of the general aspects of economic reasoning, but also of applied economics, as for instance poor relief and housing: 'It is a book for the library of the club, the Co-operative Society, and the Tutorial Class; a model of method in arrangement, and free from academic technicality'.[37]

If British social reformers had many good reasons to read Charles Gide, there was no shortage of such interesting progressive economists in other countries than France. A third reason for the comparatively large number of French books discussed in the *Economic Review* was, paradoxically, the existence in France of what could be perceived as an old-fashioned 'Manchester school' which had more or less disappeared in England, the 'liberal' school of laissez-faire and individualist economists associated with the *Journal des Economistes* and the Librairie Guillaumin. The fact that a significant number of such books were reviewed in the *Economic Review* can be found surprising, but it is precisely because so many of the publications of French 'liberals' displayed such ideal-typical individualism that they were reviewed here. It was what social reformers, in England and elsewhere, felt to be the rather extreme character of the polarisation of the French economics field which aroused the interest of the editors of the *Economic Review*. While the French '*économie sociale*' echoed the concerns of the Christian Social Union, the 'liberal' French school provided *Economic Review* writers with many opportunities to contrast their ethical and 'socialist' approach with the individualism of an economic school once dominant in Britain. The survival of a strong school of laissez-faire political economy particularly impressed *Economic Review* contributors and was a central concern to them, as revealed by the following passage from a review by John Carter, in which he stressed that there were 'still economists abroad, like those represented by the *Journal des Economistes* and the *Giornale degli Economisti*, who frankly accept the principle of laissez faire, laissez passer in all its simplicity'.

The point, however, was not simply to focus on an easy target. The ideology and optimism embodied by the French school still existed in Britain. The group of economic thinkers associated with the Liberty and Property Defence League and with the ideas of Herbert Spencer, of which Thomas Mackay was a leading figure, may with certain qualifications be compared to the old Manchester individualist school. But, in sharp contrast to the French Guillaumin school, they were now considered 'heterodox' by professional economists.[38] Indeed it had become almost difficult, by the 1890s, to find an academic authority in Britain to support the views held in 1863 by Henry Fawcett in his *Manual of Political Economy*. It is not surprising, in this context, that many commentators in search of English individualist ideas should have followed the example of W. E. H. Lecky, who, in support of his attack on socialism in *Democracy and Liberty*, in 1896, decided to rely on Paul Leroy-Beaulieu and Yves Guyot.[39] While English economics were no longer 'individualist' in the old sense, the members of the Christian Social Union felt nonetheless that they were confronted daily, in their parish, club or city council, with old-fashioned individualists and laissez-faire ideologists who, the Christian Social Union members claimed, were undisturbed by the objections raised against the now obsolete 'dismal science'. This was particularly the case within the Church of England. As Edward Norman has pointed out, 'the adoption of collectivist solutions by Church leaders took place at a time [the end of the Victorian period] when the ideals of laissez-faire had just acquired an orthodoxy among the parochial clergy'.[40] This view is certainly confirmed by an examination of the correspondence of L. R. Phelps, fellow of Oriel College, Oxford, and editor of the *Economic Review* between 1891 and 1897, and of the papers of John Carter, editor of the *Economic Review* between 1891 and 1914 and bursar of Pusey House, Oxford. In Carter's collection of newspaper cuttings from the *Church Times*, the *Guardian* and other journals, in particular, we find several articles and letters from correspondents still subscribing to the views of the old economic school. These views, although no longer held in more enlightened circles of economists, were still common in the provincial industrial class, and still had a reputation of 'Englishness' about them. One of the questions in which the *Economic Review* was most interested was indeed why the English had been committed to individualism and laissez-faire so early and for so long.[41] The complacency with which the *Economic Review* dwelt on the question of French economists' individualism is reminiscent of Luigi Cossa's statement that the so-called Manchester school never really existed, but was a German invention. In fact, the French school was much more akin to the German idea of the English: 'the German Manchester School is French'.[42]

Notes

1 I am grateful to Vincent Bourdeau for his help while compiling the data on which this chapter is based. David Fernbach has revised my English.
2 E. R. A. Seligman, *Political Science Quarterly*, 1:4 (1886), 704.
3 L. Cossa, *Introduction to the Study of Political Economy* (London: Macmillan, 1893), p. 369.

4 T. W. Hutchison, 'International Flow of Economic Ideas: Insularity and Cosmopolitanism in Economic Ideas, 1870–1914', *American Economic Review*, 45 (1955), 1–16.
5 L. Levan-Lemesle, *Le Juste et le riche: L'enseignement de l'économie politique 1815–1950* (Paris: Comité pour l'histoire économique et financière de la France, 2004).
6 A. de Foville, 'The Economic Movement in France', *Quarterly Journal of Economics*, 4 (1889), 222; H. Higgs, 'Frédéric Le Play', *Quarterly Journal of Economics*, 4 (1889), 408.
7 J. Schumpeter, *History of Economic Analysis* (London: Routledge, 1997).
8 See, for example, Alfred Marshall's first historical chapter in the 1890–1907 editions of his *Principles of Economics* (London: Macmillan).
9 T. W. Hutchison, 'International Flow of Economic Ideas'.
10 W. S. Jevons, 'Richard Cantillon and the Nationality of Political Economy', *Contemporary Review*, 1 (1881), 61–80.
11 See M. Espagne, *Le Paradigme de l'étranger: les chaires de littérature étrangère en France au XIXe siècle* (Paris: Le Cerf, 1993). For a fuller discussion of the relations between 'national character' and social sciences that shows the way, in which the late nineteenth-century discussion was shaped by earlier debates see R. Romani, *National Character and Public Spirit in Britain and France 1750–1914* (Cambridge: Cambridge University Press, 2002).
12 J. S. Nicholson, 'A Plea for Orthodox Political Economy', *National Review*, 6 (1885), 553–63.
13 W. Bagehot, *Economic Studies* (2nd edition, London: Longmans, 1888), pp. 62–3; Alfred Marshall, *Principles of Economics* (London: Macmillan, 1890), p. 60.
14 Lord Acton (ed.), *Cambridge Modern History* (Cambridge: Cambridge University Press), vol. 10 (1907), p. 784.
15 Cossa, *Introduction*, p. 323.
16 Cossa, *Introduction*, p. 365.
17 P. Bourdieu, 'Les conditions sociales de la circulation internationale des idées', *Acts de la Recherche en Sciences Sociales*, 145 (2002), 3–8; C. Charle, *Les intellectuels en Europe au dix-neuvième siècle: essai d'histoire comparée* (Paris: Le Seuil, 1996; 2nd edition: 2001); P. Casanova, *La République mondiale des lettres* (Paris: Le Seuil, 1999; American edition: Cambridge, MA: Harvard University Press, 2004); B. Wilfert, 'Paris, la France, et le reste … Importations littéraires et nationalisme culturel en France, 1885–1930', unpublished doctoral dissertation, University of Paris-I Panthéon-Sorbonne, 2003. On translation and the international circulation of ideas, see the various contributions to *Actes de la Recherche en Sciences Sociales*, 144 and 145 (2002).
18 T. W. Hutchison already noted that, before 1870, 'there had been hardly a trickle, much less a flow, of economic ideas into Britain from elsewhere' and linked the subsequent 'international flow of ideas' to mathematisation and professionalisation in his 'International Flow of Economic Ideas', pp. 3–6. Hutchison gave many interesting examples but took the point of view of a

'retrospective' historian of economic science as conceived around 1955.
19 E. Cannan, *History of the Theories of Production and Distribution in English Political Economy from 1776 to 1848* (London: P. S. King, 1917), p. 395.
20 J.-A. Blanqui, *History of Political Economy in Europe* (New York: Putnam's Sons, 1880).
21 W. Cunningham, 'Why Had Roscher so Little Influence in England?', *Annals of the American Academy of Political and Social Science*, 5 (1894), 317–34.
22 H. George, *The Science of Political Economy* (London: Gay & Bird, 1897), p. 208, quoted by William Smart, himself a translator of Austrian economists, in *Taxation of Land Values and the Single Tax* (Glasgow: MacLehose, 1900), p. 500.
23 See, for example, J. Bonar, 'The Austrian Economists and their Views on Value', *Quarterly Journal of Economics*, 3 (1888), 1–31, and 'The Positive Theory of Capital', *Quarterly Journal of Economics*, 3 (1888), 336–51.
24 Henry Sidgwick, 'The Wages Fund Theory', *Fortnightly Review*, 25 (1879), 401 and 411.
25 J. Thompson, ' "A Nearly Related People": German Views of the British Labour Market, 1870–1900', in D. Winch and P. K. O'Brien (eds), *The Political Economy of British Historical Experience* (Oxford: Oxford University Press, 2002), pp. 93–115.
26 T. W. Hutchison, 'International Flow of Economc Ideas', pp. 5–6.
27 A. Kadish, *The Oxford Economists in the Late Nineteenth Century* (Oxford: Clarendon Press, 1982), p. 187.
28 *Economic Review*, 1 (1891), 2.
29 In the following tables, I have included both longer reviews and the shorter, anonymous ones sometimes included under the heading 'short notices'.
30 C. Digeon, *La Crise allemande de la pensée française* (Paris: Presses Universitaires de France, 1959).
31 P. Bourdieu, *The Rules of Art: Genesis and Structure of the Literary Field* (Cambridge: Polity Press, 1996), pp. 177–284.
32 On the members of the British Economic Association, see A. W. and Sonia E. Coats, 'The Changing Social Composition of the Royal Economic Society 1890–1960 and the Professionalization of British Economics', in A. W. Coats, *The Sociology and Professionalization of Economics: British and American Economic Essays* (London: Routledge, 1993), vol. 2.
33 *Economic Review*, 13 (1903), 488.
34 H. W. Wolff, *The Country of the Vosges*, (London: Longmans, 1891), and *The Watering Places of the Vosges* (London: Longmans, 1891).
35 See, for example, T. C. Fry, the headmaster of Berkhampstead School, on Count de Mun and the 'Société catholique d'économie politique et sociale' in *Economic Review*, 1 (1891), 270.
36 See, for example, A. L. Lilley, *Modernism. A Record and Review* (London: Pitman, 1908).
37 *Economic Review*, 24 (1914), 468.
38 M. W. Taylor, *Men Versus the State; Herbert Spencer and Late Victorian Individualism* (Oxford: Clarendon Press, 1992).

39 W. E. H. Lecky, *Democracy and Liberty* (London: Longmans, 1896), vol. 2, pp. 322–3 and A. L. Lilley, 'Lecky's Political Pessimism', *The Commonwealth*, 1:6 (1896).
40 E. R. Norman, *Church and Society in England, 1770–1970, A Historical Study* (Oxford: Clarendon Press, 1976), p. 123.
41 This is reflected in the later work of R. H. Tawney, one of the youngest contributors to the *Economic Review* before 1914; see *Religion and the Rise of Capitalism* (London: John Murray, 1926).
42 Cossa, *Introduction*, p. 369.

11

The Ibsen battle: a comparative analysis of the introduction of Henrik Ibsen in France, England and Ireland

Pascale Casanova

Any attempt to compare and retrace, even in the most succinct fashion, the story of the introduction of Henrik Ibsen in England, France and Ireland is in my view a way of grasping the reality of the mechanisms of international circulation of literary texts. The object here is not to present what is generally called a 'reception study'. In fact, a simple comparative table of the different interpretations that have been made of the work of the Norwegian dramatist contributes, right from the start, to 'denaturalising' these, while juxtaposition of the different reappropriations of his plays as they were diffused across Europe leads to re-historicising the readings that have been made of them. The fact that Ibsen could be interpreted in almost opposite terms in England and France – the crudest realism on the one hand, and the most ethereal symbolism on the other – should spur us to question the historicity of interpretative categories.[1]

One of the postulates of literary comparison, even if its traditions differ from one country to another, is that an identity or kinship can be established between literary objects that are far removed in time and space (on the basis of a kind of principled dehistoricising of literary objects), or between different national productions and traditions. In all such cases, nations and national spaces are viewed as distinct ensembles, closed in on themselves, entities that are irreducible to one another yet produce, on the basis of an autarchic specificity, literary objects that are more or less comparable. Stefan Collini, for example, has been able to show that in Great Britain, at least, definition of so-called national literature rests on a tautology: 'Only authors who display these supposed qualities are recognized as authentically English, a category whose definition rests on examples drawn from texts written by these very same authors.'[2] These national 'monads' are accordingly viewed as strictly equal and lacking any effective connection, i.e. any real interaction of some of them on others. The question is to compare, 'other things being equal', objects that have been declared to be separate and scarcely belonging to the same universe.

It is precisely against this national essentialism, and basing myself on the case of Ibsen, that I propose here in a more general way to try and construct a different type of literary comparison. The particular history of Henrik Ibsen's recognition in Europe can in fact facilitate the testing of a method of analysis that takes into account the effect of the structures of each national field (as sub-space of the international literary field) and is inseparably interested in both reception and production. The object is thus to propose a kind of relational or structural comparison. As against the assumptions made by a dehistoricised and thematic comparativism, I will attempt to use comparison in order to disclose the structures acting in different fields; to see how the same work, producing different effects (by being interpreted in different or even divergent terms in the three countries studied here), makes possible a systematic investigation of the structures, i.e. the un-thought, the aesthetic and literary evidence in the three spaces, their resemblances as well as their irreducible differences. This will lead to showing how it is impossible to describe the import of a play from one country to another, its acclimatisation, recognition, translations and productions, without taking into account, on the one hand, the structure of relations of force governing the entire space of world literature, and, on the other, the struggles specific to each national space, in which the imported text is deployed as a new weapon to permit the appearance of a new position.

On this working hypothesis, neither the notion of 'reception' nor that of 'influence' – key ideas of traditional literary history, implying a static and fatalist conception of literary circulation – come into play: in that implicit model, countries are seen as just passively exposed to a kind of immaterial 'radiation'. This particularly presupposes the existence of two literary worlds, one influencing, one influenced, both synchronic and equal, in this way obscuring the fact that objective relations are involved. In the perspective I propose here, however, the question is no longer to 'compare', but rather to describe a relationship of domination which, through the resistances it provokes (which may take the paradoxical form of borrowings and imitations), elicits specific forms and contents. In other words, given the power and structuring character of this relationship of domination in the international literary space, even that which is incomparable, dissimilar, and apparently with no common measure, has still to be understood in relational terms. The majority of literary phenomena (manifestos, schools, critical movements, formal inventions, aesthetic demands...) produced in the dominated spaces – and all literary spaces have been dominated at one moment or another in their history – are constituted *against* a domination, *against* an aesthetic movement imposed from without. And the dominant foreigner may serve either as opponent or as ally vis-à-vis the national conservatism.

By bringing these three national spaces into consideration, I also seek to show that, even if they differ structurally and historically, they are also linked (in literature, theatre and aesthetics) by specific relations of force. These are not three literary worlds that are closed and impermeable. On the contrary, the members of the 'international club' of Ibsen's discoverers – formed by Antoine, Lugné-Poe, Shaw and Joyce – were all mutually acquainted: Lugné-Poe was invited to London for his symbolist productions of Ibsen; Shaw travelled to Paris to see productions of the Norwegian dramatist there; Joyce read Shaw's *Quintessence of Ibsenism*, and so on. Moreover, they each occupied analogous positions in their respective fields, and practised the same action of 'undermining' existing theatrical conventions. As well as these interactions among the agents involved, the three spaces were connected by objective relations that were both specific and political: in the 1890s, France dominated European literature; Ireland was a colony of England; London was a literary rival of Paris, etc. And it is only in these relations of domination and/or dependence that the paths of circulation and adoption of texts can be truly grasped. Ibsen serves here as a kind of 'revealer' of the structure of relations of force.

My aim, in other words, is not to measure in objective terms the success or failure of the 'reception' of a foreign writer through a quantitative study of reviews in the press, sales in bookshops and representations on stage. Rather, I attempt to describe the material, intellectual and aesthetic conditions of the importation of Henrik Ibsen's work in each of these three literary spaces, i.e. the characteristics of each intermediary in relation to the balance of literary forces within each importing country This is why, in order to reach a global account (both of the specific action of Ibsen's theatre on the formation of theatrical fields in Europe at the end of the nineteenth century and of the effect of domination imposed on certain spaces by other spaces), I propose here to sketch out a comparative study both of the three dramatic spaces and of the trajectories and positions of the four importers.[3] Each of these, in fact, made a particular use of the work he introduced; each deployed Ibsenian innovations as specific instruments or weapons in order to carry out revolutions in his national world. To put it another way, my object is to investigate the actual uses of Ibsen's work in the theatrical worlds of London, Paris and Dublin, and thus in a more general way the use of a foreign culture in national literary and theatrical combats.

Comparisons

If there were major differences between each of the national spaces that gradually 'digested' Ibsen's novelty, there were also similarities that explain why these introducers were fascinated by Ibsen rather than any other particular innovator. In each case, the avant-garde took the form of a foreigner introduced by a marginal figure outside the rules of the game, who used this import to denounce the academicism of existing conventions and fundamentally overthrow the existing rules of the game.

Lugné-Poe and Antoine on the one hand, George Bernard Shaw on the other, and subsequently James Joyce, made their respective appearance in worlds that were monolithic (one could almost say 'monochrome'), and where scarcely any divergent or discordant voice could be heard. By brandishing and gradually imposing the 'Norwegian master', they established a position that had not previously existed. One might say, taking up Christophe Charle's analysis apropos the French field after the irruption of Antoine's productions,[4] that they provoked the appearance of a second pole in their respective theatrical worlds, i.e. of a genuine field in the sense that Pierre Bourdieu gave this term.

All three of them (in Paris, Antoine and Lugné-Poe were in some sense, despite all their differences, a single body with two heads) were 'young' artists on the rise, by which I refer to literary rather than biological age. In 1890, Lugné-Poe was 21 and Bernard Shaw 36, while Joyce published his first text on Ibsen in 1900, at the age of 18. These three all saw Ibsen as a hero and model who enabled them to break free of conservative theatrical and moral codes. They were young pretenders to the title of recognised director, dramatist or writer. And, in all cases, their use of Ibsen as a 'revolutionary' manifesto had positive effects. In their capacity as introducers, the shift they begun in the 1890s was successful. It was in a production by Lugné-Poe that the Comédie-Française gave *Hedda Gabler* in 1925, in some sense, the culmination of the cycle of canonisation; Bernard Shaw received the Nobel Prize the same year; while *Ulysses*, the book that Joyce considered his own *Peer Gynt*,[5] escaped Anglo-American censorship by being published by Sylvia Beach in Paris in 1922, and in French translation in 1929.

To finesse these structural and chronological rapprochements, however, it must be emphasised that in all three spaces into which the Norwegian writer was imported this was done in the name of 'realism'.[6] This apparent unanimity actually hid profound differences, since it was by no means the same kind of realism that was involved in each case. Even if this became in Europe at the time a kind of unifying slogan that focused these literary and especially theatrical revolts, the term had a specific usage in each national space. It would be illusory, moreover, to believe that the same changes were carried out in the name of the same conceptions. The variations in the use of the term 'realism' involved two aspects: the state of the literary field (at the moment in question, but being always the product of a long and specific history) and the disposition of the particular mediator. Shaw and Joyce, for example, despite having much in common (especially their Irish nationality), had neither the same concerns, the same adversaries, nor the same political and aesthetic background.

We have finally to take into consideration the fact that, in the theatrical field of the late nineteenth century, there was also a strong French domination, exercised at both poles of theatrical spaces. In France in the 1890s, the theatrical world was dominated by the triad of Augier, the younger Dumas, and Sardou, as well as the influence of Scribe (dead already in 1861); in other words, by comedies of manners and vaudevilles.[7] Not only did this model dominate the whole of French theatrical production, but also a large part of European theatre. One of the first translators of Ibsen into English, and one of his most ardent champions, William Archer, had himself tried to write plays in the late 1880s, which according to Bernard Shaw, whom he hard tried to associate with his initiative, was 'on the technical lines of the "well made" constructed plays of Scribe and the French school'.[8] In other words, even the dominated fraction of the English theatrical field, opposed to the dominant theatre of the day, still based itself on the dominant French model. And, for the young Ibsen himself, at the moment of his conversion to 'modernism', i.e. when he abandoned the Norwegian neo-romantic aesthetic of the 1860s, Scribe was the model par excellence for contemporary prose drama.[9] It was a surprising paradox, then, that Ibsen went on to overthrow, and relegate completely to the past, the Scribean aesthetic of the 'well-constructed' play.

In the same way, at the other pole – that of the avant-garde theatre – new European companies were established explicitly after Antoine's model, sometimes even using a similar name (the Independent Theatre in London clearly owed much to the Paris Théâtre-libre, as did the Freie Bühne in Berlin),[10] but inspired above all by the forms and contents of the break effected by Antoine.

Ibsen in Paris: a single body with two heads

In the decade of the 1880s, the French theatrical landscape was in some sense immobilised, being completely devoted to the commercial stage. The domination of the Augier/Dumas/Sardou triad was institutionalised to the point that Emile Perrin, administrator of the Comédie-Française, could say: 'I don't need any new authors; one year Dumas, the next Sardou, the third year Augier is quite enough.'[11]

Into this situation of tacit agreement between all parties there burst an amateur actor working for the Paris gas company, André Antoine, who disrupted the whole system of aesthetic foundations, rhetorical and moral conventions, by establishing the 'Théâtre-libre' in 1887. Antoine's project amounted to importing the aesthetic and political revolution of the naturalist novel into the theatre. He staged plays by Zola, Becque and the Goncourts; above all, he imposed (in agreement with Zola) a whole series of technical innovations against the dominant bourgeois theatre, questioning the very foundations of theatrical representation of the time.

Against the pompous declarations, neo-tragic hieraticism, mechanical entries and exits, Antoine trained a company made up of amateur actors, demanding from his players a natural style as close as possible to genuine conversation, promoting the effect of reality in his backdrops (the famous theory of the 'fourth wall'), imposing darkness in the house (the Wagnerian principle), and privileging the selection of genuine props, as opposed to objects merely depicted on the scenery.[12] The aim for both him and Zola was to introduce into theatrical representation a social category completely absent from the bourgeois theatre except in the form of servants, i.e. the popular classes. To give a 'realist' representation of the people or the popular classes was one of the greatest innovations that Antoine and Zola introduced at the Théâtre-libre.[13]

Unfortunately, the naturalist movement took longer to achieve in the theatre, where it proved more difficult than in the novel.[14] The French naturalist writers, Zola above all, did not meet the expectations of the theatre directors. Zola's career as a playwright was a series of disappointments, which helps to explain why Antoine turned so rapidly towards authors from northern Europe.

He first staged Ibsen's *Ghosts* in 1890, having discovered the play in Brussels in 1888 in a German production.[15] It immediately provoked a major polemic: French critics denigrated the 'Scandinavian mists', and above all what Sarcey remarkably described as 'the intentional brutalities of realist drama'.[16] Indeed, this 'family drama in three acts', as its subtitle has it, was no aseptic piece in the style of the younger Dumas. Quite the contrary, as Antoine himself maintained, it was 'highly subversive' and did indeed break brutally with 'ordinary' theatre. In no way did it lead to a denouement that respected the appearances of bourgeois morality. Everything was set up to lead to catastrophe, which was all the more unsupportable according to the French dramatic canon of the time, in that the play actually ended with a question. It was a new kind of tragedy that had erupted on to the French stage: equally different from both classical French tragedy and from the ancient Greek, often staged in the 1880s; a tragedy that Maeterlinck would call 'everyday'.

At all events, Ibsen was steadily established as one of the dramatists of the modern age, and became in Paris a kind of support for naturalism in the theatre, for want of authors or genuine innovation locally. In a certain sense, this harnessing of Ibsen to the naturalist battle against literary and theatrical de-realisation was not totally contrary to the conditions in which his work originally appeared in Norway. Ibsen had been a disciple of Georg Brandes, the celebrated Danish critic who, after a long stay in Paris, had exported French naturalism to all the Scandinavian countries, thus provoking the emergence of a broad aesthetic-political movement, the *Genemmbrot* or 'modern breakthrough'.[17] His famous slogan, to 'raise problems for discussion', overthrew all literary production in Scandinavia; in this way Brandes sought to promote a literature that, on the model of French naturalism, would be the expression of social, political and aesthetic issues, and effect a critique of the values of idealism imposed by the German tradition. Those choosing to claim the supremacy of Paris sought in this way to struggle against the German cultural ascendancy that had dominated these countries without a break throughout the nineteenth century, transforming them indeed into mere aesthetic provinces of Germany. For Ibsen, however, at the time of his conversion to 'modernism', the question was to struggle against not only German neo-romanticism and de-realisation, but also and above the national or nationalist Norwegian romanticism to which he had himself previously adhered.[18]

In Paris, Lugné-Poe arose suddenly in 1891, the very year of Antoine's production of *The Wild Duck*. He was himself an actor in Antoine's company, before joining up with Paul Fort and his Théâtre d'Art, proponents of symbolism and thus opponents of the naturalists. Lugné-Poe acted in Maeterlinck's *The Intruder* and *The Blind*. Very soon, in 1892, he staged *The Lady from the Sea* in a symbolist style, then went on to found the Théâtre de l'Œuvre the following year. To secure his position as innovator and declare his aesthetic positions, he set out to metamorphose Ibsen into a symbolist author.[19]

The symbolist theatre may be described as an opposition to naturalism, each of its aesthetic and technical innovations responding term by term to Antoine's choices for the stage: the declamatory tone, going as far as psalmody; hieratic poses; few and solemn movements; the removal of action behind a transparent curtain; suggestive and sometimes allegorical decor, as opposed to Ibsen's very detailed indications which Antoine respected to the letter, a dark stage, etc.[20] Against the natural style that Antoine had demanded of his players, Lugné-Poe adopted a solemn and monotonous performance that erected the slowness of diction – which contributed to de-realising the text – into a theatrical manifesto. In one of his productions, the heroine of *The Woman of the Sea* was played by an actress with a background in Maeterlinck, who was transformed into 'a strange creature with long veils, a white phantom'.[21]

The critical success of this first production sealed the annexation of Ibsen by the French symbolists. The 'missionary of symbolism' then sought to convert Europe to his aesthetic conceptions, and organised foreign tours.[22] In the summer of 1894, Lugné-Poe travelled to Sweden, Denmark and Norway; he hoped to introduce Maeterlinck and the symbolist theatre to the Scandinavian public but, above all, to obtain support to justify his interpretation of Ibsen. But well before the arrival of his company, celebrated in Norway as 'an event in the national dramatic movement',[23] his new interpretation of Ibsen had been criticised on all sides. True, this criticism generally accepted the French 'naturalisation' of Ibsen, so as not to damage his exceptional standing in Paris, but it explicitly condemned the symbolist interpretation of Lugné-Poe: 'It is not only in France that a too strong inclination has developed to find symbols in the most human characters of Norwegian dramas ... But it is France that holds the palm for these fantastic interpretations.'[24]

Lugné-Poe then organised an English tour in 1895. At the invitation of Jack T. Grein, he presented Maeterlinck and Ibsen in a small London theatre. The reviews were savage;[25] but William Archer and G. B. Shaw, the English introducers of Ibsen who sought support and legitimacy from the Paris Ibsenites, defended the productions of the Théâtre de l'Œuvre. They admitted a certain poor quality, 'the shabby appointments and ridiculous incidents',[26] but stressed, in Shaw's words, 'the true atmosphere of this most enthralling of all Ibsen's works rising like an enchanted mist for the first time on English stage'.[27] Lugné-Poe abandoned his symbolist productions after 1897, thus demonstrating that his new staging had been simply an effect of position and opposition.[28]

We thus see that the introduction of Ibsen in France was more or less a double one. His work was annexed twice over to problematics that were foreign to him: on the one hand, to serve the naturalist school, and to show that naturalism in the theatre was a fertile way forward; and, on the other hand, to illustrate the theories of symbolist theatre. These two rival interpretations, however, helped Ibsen to be rapidly recognised and adopted. In 1894, only four years after Antoine's first production, the Théâtre du Vaudeville successfully staged *A Doll's House*, with Réjane in the role of Nora. In 1898, with the Dreyfus Affair in full swing, Lugné-

Poe gave a gala performance of *Enemy of the People* at the Œuvre: he changed the lines, and the audience cried out 'Vive Zola'. Ibsen was played for the first time at the Comédie-Française in 1921, and the process of adoption culminated in 1925 with the dual recognition of both playwright and director: *Hedda Gabler* was given 'au Français', in a production taken directly from that of Lugné-Poe; with this, Ibsen entered definitively into the repertoire of the Comédie-Française.

Ibsen in London: the appearance of 'social realism'

The London theatrical landscape of this time was quite similar to that in France: closure, repetition, immobility, and the domination of the commercial stage. The popular audience was served on the one hand by melodramas, music halls and variety theatres, while for the middle classes there were the vaudevilles of Pinero and Johns, operettas, and Shakespeare plays presented in spectacular productions.[29]

Here again, Ibsen and his importers were to change radically the theatrical world. Ibsen was already known here well before the 1890s, and had been championed, appreciated and commented on long before the first French productions. Edmund Gosse, the eminent literary critic and historian, published his first study on Ibsen in 1879.[30] The same year, the British Scandinavian Society published Ibsen's *Selected Pieces*, and several translators offered further extracts from his work.[31] William Archer was the key figure in this phase of discovery, following translations of individual texts with a five-volume edition of Ibsen's plays in 1890–91.[32] It was Archer who introduced Ibsen's work to Shaw,[33] and he also replied to enthusiastic letters from the young James Joyce.

Starting from the 1890s, a group of marginal figures, opposed to both the political and aesthetic status quo, sought to promote the Norwegian dramatist's work, seeing it as the banner of a possible renewal of the English theatre. Besides William Archer and George Bernard Shaw, at that time a young music and theatre critic, they also included the director Jack Thomas Grein. It was Grein who founded the Independent Theatre Society in 1891, on the explicit model of Antoine's Théâtre-libre. The same year, Shaw published *The Quintessence of Ibsenism*, and Grein staged first *Ghosts*, then *Hedda Gabler*, arousing great scandal. In 1892, Grein directed *The Master Builder*, applauded by the audience but savaged by the critics. Three years later, in March 1895,[34] he invited Lugné-Poe to perform *Rosmersholm* and *The Master Builder* in London.

One might well speak of a 'battle' over Ibsen, in both London and Paris, and Shaw's extraordinary polemical articles show what stakes were at issue. The absence of social criticism in a frozen theatrical world, and the repetition of academic forms and genres, led him to write, for example, in October 1889:

> This year there was a revival of hope because Mr Pinero,[35] in a play produced at the Garrick Theatre, walked cautiously up to a social problem, touched it, and ran away. Shortly afterwards a much greater sensation was created by a Norwegian play, Ibsen's *Doll's House*, in which the dramatist handled the same problem, and showed, not how it ought to be solved, but how it is about to be solved.[36]

The Ibsen battle was a genuine replay of the Wagner battle. This is certainly not the place to relate the story of the introduction of Wagner in England, but we may observe that it was the same protagonists, and in the name of the same positions of opening and renewal, who introduced both Wagner and Ibsen. For Shaw, the parallelism was quite clear: as Wagner was his musical hero,[37] so Ibsen was his master in the theatre, an ethical and aesthetic model. Shaw explicitly compared the two battles, recalling in 1913, when both processes of recognition were complete, that Ibsen:

> was treated worse than Wagner, though that seemed impossible. It was, however, easy. We had at least not accused Wagner of obscenity, nor called for the prosecution of Her Majesty's Theatre as a disorderly house after the first performance of *Lohengrin* ... [A]t the moment when he delivered his message to mankind we assured the English nation that he was an illiterate, diseased, half-crazy pornographer, and we intended to prosecute anyone who produced his plays in contravention of the Lord Chamberlain's ban.[38]

To explain the full force of this position, it should be emphasised that, if with his pro-Wagner position Shaw breezily attacked the musical enemy, i.e. the line of 'Mendelssohn–Schumann–Brahms',[39] his support for Ibsen meant a challenge to Pinero and the entire London theatre. His position as an Irishman made him particularly sensitive to the recognition of an author who was peripheral and unrecognised by reason of a similar provincialism. Thus, when *Peer Gynt* was premiered in London in 1889, with Grieg's music, Shaw analysed both the beginning of the international recognition of Norwegian culture, and the English annexationism that recognised foreign productions only in terms of its own cultural vision:

> [E]ven the general public is beginning to understand that the Norwegian people are not simply a poor and wretched lot whose land is prized as a refuge for wealthy foreign hunters and fishermen. They are also commencing to be thought of as a people with a vast modern literature and a remarkably interesting political history. Shakespeare's supremacy in our

own literature has long led us to believe that there is one great dramatist who dominates each national literature. Therefore we are intensely interested in each new word about that "modern Shakespeare" looking in Scandinavia – Henrik Ibsen ...[40]

Shaw's position in support of Ibsen was not simply aesthetic, but also largely political. *The Quintessence of Ibsenism* had been written for a conference of the Fabian Society, of which Shaw had been a co-founder in 1884.[41] Shaw's subversive political positions led him to seek support in Ibsen's 'realist' theatre, which, given his categories of perception, was for him simply an instrument of social criticism. His own plays, which he began to write precisely at this time,[42] follow the same critical line, that of the 'social question', meaning above all a critique of the bourgeoisie. Shaw's use of Ibsen, almost exclusively a 'social' reading of his work, differed both from that of Antoine, concerned above all with the dramatic representation of the 'people', and that of Lugné-Poe, whose interest lay in the aesthetic renewal of the principles of dramatic representation.

Ibsen in Dublin: a weapon against English domination

In Ireland at this time, as in many politically emergent countries, theatre held a leading place in the literary world that was coming into being; the majority of literary debates crystallised around theatrical questions. W. B. Yeats founded the Irish Literary Theatre in 1899, with George Moore and Edward Martyn, and, just as in England and France, where most major protagonists of the Irish Renaissance had lived, Ibsen, associated with Antoine's Théâtre-libre, was first explicitly claimed as a model for the future Irish national theatre. Very soon, however, Yeats rejected Ibsen in the name of his break with realism and the bourgeois drama.

Joyce, for his part, was very interested in Ibsen in the late 1890s, between the age of 16 and 18; Shaw's *Quintessence of Ibsenism*, which he read at an early age, played an important role in his formation. Very soon, he 'used' Ibsen as an anti-nationalist weapon in the Irish literary and theatrical battle. His defence of the Norwegian dramatist was both a way of claiming an autonomous position in the literary field and of proclaiming the importance of an author already famous throughout Europe but still marginal in Dublin.

He made a comparison between Ibsen and Parnell, giving Ibsen the central place in art that he gave Parnell in politics.[43] The great leader of Irish nationalism had committed suicide in 1891, when Joyce was 9. Parnell was one of the mythic heroes of his childhood and adolescence; his father had been a fervent supporter of Parnell, and the young James saw himself as following in the wake of the Irish leader.

This identification with Parnell and Ibsen is essential to understand the origins of Joyce's work, and assumed a very particular reading of the Norwegian dramatist: as a politically dominated writer, Joyce used the Norwegian theatrical innovations as specific weapons in a struggle against both the literary and theatrical domination of London, and against the aesthetic presuppositions imposed by the Irish Renaissance, and Yeats in particular. It seemed as if Joyce shifted his admiration for Parnell on to Ibsen, and chose to struggle politically by the indirect means of literature, rather than in a directly political mode. The young Joyce thus sought out at a very early age the weapons needed to combat the English literary stranglehold, i.e. the imposition of criteria of literary stature dictated from England. He praised Dante against Milton,[44] and above all Ibsen against Shakespeare, this representing a very violent assault on the British pantheon. Joyce's fascination for Ibsen was such that, in order to read him in the original, he learned Norwegian Danish. He also developed a passion for Gerhart Hauptmann, seeing the German dramatist as Ibsen's best disciple; and as Hauptmann's most recent plays had not been translated, he also studied German.[45] Between 1898 and 1901, i.e. the age of 16 and 19, Joyce wrote four important texts, three of these being devoted to the theatre, and two specifically to Ibsen.

One of the first texts of Joyce's to have survived dates from 1898,[46] and deals with the question of 'subjugation' (the term is used several times) in all its forms, especially political subjugation. 'Some things there are no subjugation can repress', Joyce wrote at the age of 16. This text sketches out his entire posture: that of an Irishman in revolt against English colonisation, very politicised, but rejecting direct political struggle in favour of a combat with the weapons of literature.

Joyce went on to deliver a lecture, in early 1900, at the Literary and Historical Society of University College Dublin, on 'Drama and Life',[47] in which, in the name of an abstract defence of the modernity of the 'new' playwrights, and an opposition between the 'defenders of the old school' and the 'New School', he supported Ibsenian drama against that of Shakespeare, who represented the values of the past. This was thus also a manifesto in support of an independent Irish literature: 'Let us criticize in the manner of free people', Joyce wrote, 'as a free race, recking little of ferula and formula.'[48] Joyce was soon greatly influenced by Shaw, but never completely followed his elder compatriot in his own interpretation of Ibsen. Shaw waged a battle that was both literary and political, but in politics he was concerned with society, and in literature with content. For Joyce, on the other hand, Ibsen was above all an effective instrument of struggle against English literary domination, as well as against the aestheticisation and de-realisation effected by the symbolist national theatre that Yeats developed at the Irish Literary Theatre. And it is quite extraordinary to read in this conference of 1900 (just one year after Yeats founded the Irish Literary Theatre) phrases that already sound a sharp critique of the pastoral and legendary aesthetic championed by the intellectuals of the Irish Renaissance:

> It is a sinful foolishness to sigh back for the good old times ... Life we must accept as we see it before our eyes, men and women as we meet them in the real world, not as we apprehend them in the world of faery.[49]

The second text that Joyce devoted to Ibsen, 'Ibsen's New Drama',[50] was also his first published writing. This is a critique of Ibsen's last play, which Joyce had just read in French translation (it seems that he was unwilling to read Ibsen in English translation, and had a systematic preference for the French): *When We Dead Awaken*. His review appeared in the *Fortnightly Review* in April 1900. In a somewhat laboured article (for which he was asked to quote Ibsen, not in French, but in Archer's translation, and to suppress two critical references to the famous Pinero), what is striking is how Joyce understands precisely how Ibsen's writing was a point-by-point response to the neo-romantic aesthetic. What was supposed to be a simple review became an implicit criticism of Yeats, who brought a mythological or legendary world on to the stage in versified and de-realised forms:

> Ibsen has chosen the average lives in their uncompromising truth for the groundwork of all this later plays. He has abandoned the verse form, and has never sought to embellish his work after the conventional fashion ... How easy it would have been to have written *An Enemy of the People* on a speciously loftier level – to have replaced the *bourgeois* by the legitimate hero! Critics might then have extolled as grand what they have so often condemned as banal.[51]

It is clear that from Joyce's point of view – and his intention at this time was to write plays himself – Ibsen had carried out a revolution in the theatre very close to what Manet had achieved in painting.[52] Just as Manet, repudiating thematic painting and the mythological pretext that the academic painters invoked, painted the 'reality' of singular individuals, the world as it is, so Ibsen's realism was an antidote to the Irish neo-romanticism that erected legends, fairy-tales and poems, drawn from a re-evaluated popular culture, into a standard for the entire Irish national literature.

The Ibsen model was so powerful for Joyce that, recalling how the Norwegian dramatist had been claimed by Moore and Martyn, the two other founders of the Irish Literary Theatre in 1899, he was very favourable to Martyn's play *The Heather Field*, given the day after the first scandalous performance of Yeats's *The Countess Cathleen* on 8 May 1899. He remembered this once more in 1919, when he wrote: 'As a dramatist [Martyn] follows the school of Ibsen and therefore occupies a unique position in Ireland, as the dramatists writing for the National Theatre have chiefly devoted their energies to peasant dramas.'[53] The same Norwegian references enabled Joyce somewhat later to depict, not idealised and de-realised peasants, but modern and everyday inhabitants of Dublin.

The last of these texts of Joyce's youth devoted to the theatre was even more violent and magisterial. Titled 'The Day of the Rabblement',[54] this was printed and distributed in October 1901, following the publication of the programme for the new season of the Irish Literary Theatre. An Irish-language play by Douglas Hyde, *Casadh-an-tSugain* (*The Stretched Cord*), was announced, as well as *Diarmuid and Grania*, based on an Irish legend and adapted by W. B. Yeats and George Moore. Joyce saw this as confirming his fears of the direction of the Literary Theatre being both too nationalist and too provincial. Provocative and arrogant, this pamphlet by a young man of 19 dared to publicly question the genius of Yeats, the unanimously respected national poet. ('It is equally unsafe at present to say of Mr Yeats that he has or has not genius.')[55] It also takes a radical position of its own. Once again, to give his diatribe the violence required, Joyce invoked Ibsen:

> The Irish Literary Theatre is the latest movement of protest against the sterility and falsehood of the modern stage. Half a century ago the note of protest was uttered in Norway, and since then in several countries long and disheartening battles have been fought. What triumph there has been here and there is due to stubborn conviction, and every movement that has set out heroically has achieved a little. The Irish Literary Theatre gave out that it was the champion of progress, and proclaimed war against commercialism and vulgarity.... Now, your popular devil is more dangerous than your vulgar devil ... He has prevailed once more, and the Irish Literary Theatre must now be considered the property of the rabblement of the most belated race in Europe ... [t]he Irish Literary Theatre by its surrender to the trolls has cut itself adrift from the line of advancement.[56]

The reference to Norwegian history is sufficient to show how Joyce's admiration was also an identification with this playwright issuing from a small country, recently liberated from political domination, which by creating an unprecedented national literature, written in a language almost unknown in Europe, was in the process of becoming a spokesman for the European avant-garde by revolutionising the entire European theatre:

> The official organ of the movement spoke of producing European masterpieces, but the matter went no further. Such a project was absolutely necessary. The censorhip is powerless in Dublin, and the directors could have produced *Ghosts* or *The Dominion of Darkness* if they chose. Nothing can be done until the forces that dictate public judgement are calmly confronted. But, of course, the directors are shy of presenting Ibsen, Tolstoy or Hauptmann, where even *Countess Cathleen* is pronounced vicious and damnable ... A nation which never advanced so far as a miracle-play affords no literary model to the artist, and he must look abroad.[57]

This profession of faith in literary cosmopolitanism was also a position within the Irish literary space. Like Antoine, and especially Shaw, Joyce questions here the dominant aesthetic-political choices of his theatrical world by identifying with a heretical foreigner. But in Ireland at the turn of the century, still under English colonial domination, Joyce chooses to denounce, not the English stranglehold, but Irish conformism, i.e. the neo-romantic aesthetic catering to the political and moral (or even moralizing) expectations of the majority. As well as a demand for autonomy vis-à-vis the demands of the audience, this text also proclaims the desire to modernise Irish theatre in the face of the country's 'backwardness'. Ibsen becomes in Ireland not simply a champion of realism, but another name for the literary modernity, which had been rejected in Dublin, but which Joyce went on to seek and construct in exile.

The translations, adaptations and productions of Ibsen's plays, their critical reception in England and France, were not mere operations of linguistic translation. They presupposed, on the contrary, the transition from one national field to another, the specific interests of the discoverers, the existence of a criticism open to artistic innovation and sufficiently cosmopolitan to accept foreign productions; not to mention artists who were subversive and marginal in their own national field, and made use of a foreign writer to join a game that was closed to them and impose themselves by promoting different literary 'values'. It was Joyce above all, in one of the texts of his extreme youth, who indicated the key importance of Ibsen in Europe at the turn of the century. Isolated in provincial Dublin, amid the ideas and productions of literary nationalism, Joyce best understood the capital role of Ibsen and the manifold theatrical upheavals he had made possible in Europe, and he alone also managed to grasp the innumerable appropriations for which Ibsen's work had served as object and pretext. In 1900, again, Joyce wrote:

> Twenty years have passed since Henrik Ibsen wrote *A Doll's House*, thereby almost marking an epoch in the history of drama. During those years his name has gone abroad through the length and breadth of two continents, and has provoked more discussion and criticism than that of

any other living man. He has been upheld as a religious reformer, a social reformer, a Semitic lover of righteousness, and as a great dramatist. He has been rigorously denounced as a meddlesome intruder, a defective artist, an incomprehensible mystic, and, in the words of a certain English critic, 'a muck-ferreting dog' ... It may be questioned whether any man has held so firm an empire over the thinking world in modern times.[58]

Divergent interpretations show how recognition in literary capitals occurs at the price of an extraordinary annexation of foreign works to the interests of those occupying a 'central' position in the field, both artists and critics. Certainly it is only possible to understand, for example, the arbitrariness of the double French reading – and French criticism imperturbably continued to raise the question of Ibsen's symbolism, reproducing time after time the schemas inherited from Lugné-Poe – by placing oneself at an international level; only in this way can the categories of 'central' understanding, both artistic and critical, be restored in their full complexity. But it is in this apparent interpretative chaos, in this work of appropriation and dehistoricisation that constitutes the international circulation of texts and the operations of translation and annexation, that the collective work of universalisation is accomplished.

One might well imagine that this historical analysis would lead to fragment the very idea of a universal literature, by reducing the processes of adoption of a work to national particularisms and thus leading to the most radical relativism. This very analysis, however, also enables us to understand how and why, within this multiple, complex and transnational history, the work of universalisation occurs despite everything. In the first place, as we see, Ibsen objectively became a writer recognised as an innovator and renovator throughout Europe, even if this was for different reasons, in different contexts and in different ways. The effect of international recognition, despite being the result of a constitutive misunderstanding of the international circulation of texts, permitted the Norwegian playwright to become a universal writer. One should not underestimate, moreover, the essential role of the 'club of international discoverers' that I have sought to describe here. It is because these mediators knew one another, observed each other, referred to, invited and read one another, each drawing support from the others and thus forming a tight network of communication and information, that they were able to 'manufacture' in practice, and in a collective fashion, an author universally recognised as universal.

Notes

1. For an analysis of another case of different interpretations in England and in France of the same author, see chapter 7 of this volume.
2. S. Collini, *Public Moralists: Political Thought and Intellectual Life in Britain, 1850–1930* (Oxford: Clarendon Press, 1991), p. 357.
3. For a study of literary translation at the same period in both countries, see chapter 9 in this volume.
4. C. Charle, *La Crise littéraire à l'époque du naturalisme: roman, théâtre et politique, essai d'histoire sociale des genres et des groupes littéraires* (Paris: Presses de l'Ecole normale supérieure, 1979); in particular, the chapter 'Crise du théâtre et naissance de l'avant-garde', pp. 113–44.
5. J.-M. Rabaté, *James Joyce* (Paris: Hachette, 1993), pp. 71–2.
6. The exception here is Lugné-Poe, who – by making Ibsen into a symbolist playwright – was seemingly the most removed from the author's objective intentions.
7. Y. Chevrel, *Henrik Ibsen–Maison de Poupée* (Paris: Presses Universitaires de France, 1989), p. 11; A. Antoine, *'Mes Souvenirs' sur le Théâtre-libre* (Paris: Fayard, 1921), p. 38.
8. G. B. Shaw, *Sixteen Self Sketches* (London: Constable, 1949), p. 40.
9. Chevrel, *Henrik Ibsen*, pp. 11–16.
10. André Antoine himself acknowledged in *L'Information*, 19 March 1928, that 'The inauguration of the Berlin Freie Bühne founded on the model of the Théâtre-libre in Paris, took place on 29 November 1889 with the production of *Ghosts*', quoted in *Antoine: l'invention de la mise en scène: anthologie des textes d'André Antoine*, ed. Jean-Pierre Sarazac and Philippe Marcerou (Paris: Actes-Sud-Papiers, Centre National du théâtre, 1999), p. 249.
11. Antoine, *'Mes Souvenirs'*, p. 6.
12. J. Robichez, *Le Symbolisme au Théâtre: Lugné-Poe et les débuts de l'Œuvre* (Paris: L'Arche, 1957), pp. 28–32.
13. See J.-P. Sarrazac, 'Reconstruire le réel ou suggérer l'indicible', in *Le Théâtre en France*, vol. 2, *De la révolution à nos jours*, ed. Jacqueline de Jomaron (Paris: Armand Colin, 1992), pp. 192–214.
14. Zola noted, in response to Jules Huret, that theatre 'always lags behind the rest of literature'; J. Huret, *Enquête sur l'évolution littéraire* (Paris: Charpentier, 1891, new edition by D. Grojnowski, Paris: Corti, 1999), p. 194.
15. Critical articles and translations had appeared in various journals since 1887. See Robichez, *Le Symbolisme*, pp. 92–103.
16. F. Sarcey, *Le Temps*, 31 May 1890.
17. R. Boyer, *Histoire des Littératures Scandinaves* (Paris: Fayard, 1996), in particular chapter 5, 'Le *Genombrott*: 1870 à 1890 environ', pp. 135–95.
18. R. Boyer, 'Introduction', in Henrik Ibsen, *Peer Gynt* (Paris: Flammarion, 1994), p. 13–16.
19. Robichez, *Le Symbolisme*, in particular pp. 148–57.
20. Sarrazac, 'Reconstruire le réel ou suggérer l'indicible', p. 212.
21. Robichez, *Le Symbolisme*, p. 155.

22 Sarrazac, 'Reconstruire le réel ou suggérer l'indicible', p. 276.
23 Sarrazac, 'Reconstruire le réel ou suggérer l'indicible', p. 272.
24 Sarrazac, 'Reconstruire le réel ou suggérer l'indicible', p. 288.
25 *Telegraph*, 25 March 1895: 'We prefer Ibsen in English if we must have him.' Cited by J. Robichez, *Le Symbolisme*, p. 329.
26 Shaw, *Saturday Review* of 30 March 1895; vol. 79, no. 2057.
27 Shaw, *Saturday Review* of 30 March 1895; vol. 79, no. 2057.
28 P. Bourdieu, *Les Règles de l'art* (Paris: Le Seuil, 1992), pp. 174–5 and 180.
29 Robichez, *Le Symbolisme*, pp. 285–6.
30 Robichez, *Le Symbolisme*, p. 326.
31 Robichez, *Le Symbolisme*, p. 93.
32 D. H. Lawrence (ed.), *Shaw's Music* (London: Bodley Head, 1981) vol. 1, pp. 582–3. In the late 1880s, Archer's translations already sold very well.
33 He met Shaw in the reading room of the British Museum, 'poring over Deville's French version of Karl Marx's *Capital*, with the orchestral score of Wagner's *Tristan und Isolde* beside it', according to Shaw's own account of their meeting. See Shaw, *Sixteen Self Sketches*, p. 39.
34 Robichez, *Le Symbolisme*, pp. 326–30.
35 The author of successful vaudevilles, who was now embarking on psychological theatre.
36 'Wagner in Bayreuth', in G. B. Shaw, *How to Become a Musical Critic* (London: Rupert Hart-Davis, 1960), p. 169.
37 In 1898 Shaw published *The Perfect Wagnerite*, in which he discussed *The Ring of the Niebelungen* in the light of the anarchist and socialist ideas of the German revolutionary movement to which Wagner had adhered in 1848–9.
38 'A Neglected Moral of the Wagner Centenary', in Shaw, *How to Become a Musical Critic*, pp. 283–4.
39 G. Liebert, 'Avant-propos' to G. B. Shaw, *Ecrits sur la musique 1876–1950* (Paris: Robert Laffont, 1994), p. xxix.
40 'The Performance of Grieg's Peer Gynt in London', in D. H. Lawrence (ed.), *Shaw's Music*, vol. 1, p. 582.
41 J. Hérou, 'George Bernard Shaw homme de théâtre et socialiste', in *G. B. Shaw un dramaturge engagé* (Caen: Presses Universitaires de Caen, 1998), pp. 33–9.
42 It was actually Grein, the first to direct Ibsen in London, who encouraged Shaw to write his first play, *Widowers' Houses*, and directed this in 1892.
43 R. Ellmann, *James Joyce* (New York and Oxford: Oxford University Press, 1959), p. 55.
44 Ellmann, *Joyce*, p. 60.
45 Ellmann, *Joyce*, p. 79.
46 Joyce, 'Force', in E. Mason and R. Ellmann (ed.), *The Critical Writings of James Joyce*, (London: Faber and Faber, 1959), pp. 17–24.
47 Joyce, 'Force', pp. 38–46.
48 Joyce, 'Force', p. 42.
49 Joyce, 'Force', p. 45.
50 Joyce, 'Force', pp. 47–67.

51 J. Joyce, 'Ibsen's New Drama', in Mason and Ellmann (ed.), *The Critical Writings of James Joyce*, p. 63.
52 See also Joyce's letter to Ibsen for his seventy-third birthday (March 1901) in *Letters*, ed. S. Gilbert (London: Faber and Faber, 1957), p. 51.
53 J. Joyce, 'Programme Notes for the English Players (*The Heather Field* by Edward Martyn)', in Mason and Ellmann (ed.), *The Critical Writings of James Joyce*, p. 251.
54 Joyce, 'The Day of the Rabblement', in Mason and Ellmann (ed.), *The Critical Writings of James Joyce*, p. 251.
55 Joyce, 'The Day of the Rabblement', p. 71.
56 Joyce, 'The Day of the Rabblement', pp. 70–1.
57 Joyce, 'The Day of the Rabblement', p. 70.
58 Joyce, 'Ibsen's New Drama', in Mason and Ellmann (eds), *The Critical Writings of James Joyce*, p. 48.

Part V
Intellectuals, national models and the public sphere

12

French intellectuals and the impossible English model (1870–1914)

CHRISTOPHE CHARLE

Whether intellectuals or not, the French like comparisons. Two nations have especially inspired these: up till 1870 it was England above all else; and, after 1870, Germany. But this convenient break masks a continuing underlying presence of the English comparison in French intellectual debate, particularly in regard to social and political questions. The tradition goes back a long way, as we have seen in previous chapters. And this English reference took a new turn in French public debate of the 1880s through the 1900s, as a function of three specific features of the time.

First, though a durable parliamentary system was now established, France had still not succeeded in making this work in a satisfactory fashion, as shown by the Boulanger episode, the Panama scandal and the Dreyfus Affair. Great Britain, for its part, seemed to have made the transition from an aristocratic parliamentarism to a parliamentary democracy by an expansion of the suffrage, without its institutions having had any very great difficulty in adapting. This provided a theme for the champions of this system who were seeking parallel improvements in the French Republic.

Secondly, since the 1880s, republican France had embarked on a large-scale colonial policy, in which it constantly came up against British competition. Some essayists were thus concerned to investigate the reasons for their rival's success and their own difficulty in arousing the colonial spirit within France's elites and its population at large.[1]

Finally, and at a deeper level, France's demographic decline and the German military threat led a number of French intellectuals, imbued with the Social Darwinist notion of the struggle for life, to question the declining vitality of the French population. France seemed to be following the development of the Roman Empire, whose opulence had brought about a stagnation of births and decadence. The United Kingdom, however, though even richer, had maintained a dynamic population, even prepared for emigration. How could this paradox be accounted for, and was there not a lesson here for France?

A common field of study

The first evidence of the importance of this English reference in the French debates just mentioned is the number of works published on England, or analysing French problems through the English mirror.[2] The total number of publications recorded in Otto Lorenz's *Catalogue de la librairie française* that were not historical, not translated from English, and not of a technical nature, comes to 63 new titles between 1876 and 1885, 76 in the decade 1891–99, and 83 for the six years 1900–5. For Germany, the same source shows a similar upward trend: 40 for 1876–85, and 108 for 1900–5. These totals, however, which lump together pamphlets and monographs, ignore the unequal life of books. Some best-sellers remained in print throughout this period, including such classics, several times reissued, such as Hippolyte Taine's *Notes sur l'Angleterre*,[3] first published in 1870 and reaching its ninth edition in 1890. This offered a comparative paradigm repeated by a whole series of writers equally esteemed by the literate public. In 1887, for example, Emile Boutmy, director of the Ecole libre des sciences politiques, a friend and great admirer of Taine, offered a scholarly version, *Le Développement de la Constitution et de la société politique en Angleterre*, based on a course of lectures given at his school.[4] He supplemented this in 1901 with his *Essai d'une psychologie politique du peuple anglais au XIXe siècle*. This latter was in fact a response to a best-seller by Edmond Demolins, *A quoi tient la supériorité des Anglo-Saxons?*, published in 1897.[5] This book launched the great debate at the turn of the century on the decadence of the Latin races. It owed its success in part to its appearance almost simultaneously with the Dreyfus Affair and the Fashoda crisis. These two crises seemed in fact to confirm his diagnosis, while the defeat of Spain by the United States in 1898 expanded the group of supposedly decadent Latin nations. The sharp dissensions in France, and the humiliation felt towards the rival British Empire, gave ample material for the discourse of French decline. The works cited here were all part of the same political and intellectual trend, that of the liberal right or centre-right, heir to the Orleanist tradition. They continued Guizot's vision of England as a parliamentary political model, what I denote in the title of this essay as the 'impossible English model'.[6]

It must be noted, however, that this dominance is in part an illusion generated by the longer lifespan of these works compared with that of the great majority of the more than seventy titles that dealt with the same subject but have since fallen into oblivion. In so far as it is possible to judge from those listed, the other essays on England were written not only by republicans, but also by anti-Semitic and clerical nationalists, who openly flagged their Anglophobia. Republicans tended to confine themselves to the descriptive or analytic register of a quasi-official enquiry into a more advanced country, whereas the Anglophobes recycled old themes refurbished for contemporary taste.

Two different Anglophilias

The Anglophile current that has left its mark in the history of political ideas was thus, in fact, a minority one. It had to defend its standpoint by a battle on two fronts: vis-à-vis the official position, that of distance from a rival power, in so far as the Entente cordiale was still not on the agenda; and vis-à-vis the anti-English vision, popular or even populist, fuelled by the colonial situation and Napoleonic nostalgia. This double distance explains a particular tone that takes care not to fall into hagiography, so as not to appear completely at odds with the distrust of England that prevailed both among the power elites and the public at large.

As the synoptic table 12.1 shows, these writers were bound by close ties. Emile Boutmy was a protégé of Taine, who helped him establish the Ecole libre des sciences politiques in 1871, with the aim of training capable new elites after the model of the English aristocracy, and staying on top of the rising tide of democracy. André Chevrillon was the nephew of the author of the *Origines de la France contemporaine*, and dedicated his *Etudes anglaises* to his uncle's widow. Max Leclerc's book *L'Education des classes moyennes et dirigeantes en Angleterre*[7] had its origins in a travel prize of 5,000 francs awarded by the Ecole des sciences politiques, and came with a preface by the director of the Ecole libre, Boutmy himself. The author was, moreover, a journalist on the *Journal des Débats*, the major organ of the Orleanist bourgeoisie, and the son-in-law of Armand Colin, publisher of his book as well as that of Boutmy.[8] Edmond Demolins, already mentioned, appears as a dissident in this liberal trend, even if his starting point was a racial schema inspired by Taine's *Notes sur l'Angleterre*, which he supplements with family and social typologies borrowed from Le Play, who shared certain of Taine's convictions. With its provocative title, it aroused a certain scandal even in his own camp.

This liberal group that dominated the decades of the 1870s through 1890s was, however, opposed by another and more academic trend. Further to the left, as well as younger, these rejected on principle the naturalist and psychologistic schemas drawn from Taine and taken over by Boutmy. Their inspiration was the sociological and historical methods of the new Sorbonne. In his preface to Paul Mantoux, the Dreyfusard historian Gabriel Monod, though a colleague of Boutmy at the Institut, clearly marked this different approach:

Table 12.1 The two groups of Anglophile authors

	Period of life	Career	Date of publication	Title and publisher
Taine, Hippolyte	1828–93	Alumnus of the Ecole Normale Supérieure, writer, critic, professor at the Ecole libre des sciences politiques	1871	*Notes sur l'Angleterre* Hachette
Boutmy, Emile	1835–1906	Chairman of the Ecole libre des sciences politiques	1887	*Le Développement de la Constitution et de la société politique en Angleterre* Colin
			1901	*Essai d'une psychologie politique du peuple anglais au XIXe siècle* Colin
Leclerc, Max	1864–1932	Alumnus of the Ecole libre des sciences politiques, journalist	1894 Foreword by E. Boutmy	*L'Education des classes moyennes et dirigeantes en Angleterre* Colin
Demolins, Edmond	1852–1907	Alumnus of the Ecole des Chartes, dissenting member of the Le Play group	1897	*A quoi tient la supériorité des Anglo-Saxons?* Firmin-Didot
Chevrillon, André	1864–1957	Former teacher at grammar schools, man of letters	1901 dedicated to Mrs Taine	*Etudes anglaises* Hachette

Even when a mind as profound, wide-ranging and subtle as Emile Boutmy has tried to analyse the *psychology of the English people*, he has had to do serious violence to reality, to simplify or arrange this arbitrarily, in order to fit it into his general conception of the English character.[9]

	Period of Life	Career	Date of publication	Title and Publisher
Halévy, Elie	1870–1937	Alumnus of the Ecole Normale Supérieure, *agrégé* of philosophy, *docteur ès lettres* professor at the Ecole libre des sciences politiques	1905	*L'Angleterre et son empire* 'Pages libres'
Mantoux, Paul	1877–1956	Alumnus of the Ecole normale Supérieure, *agrégé* of history, *docteur ès lettres*.	1909 Foreword by Gabriel Monod	*A travers l'Angleterre contemporaine* Alcan
Cazamian, Louis	1877–1965	Alumnus of the Ecole Normale Supérieure, *agrégé* of English, *docteur ès lettres*, reader at the Sorbonne.	1911	*L'Angleterre moderne et son évolution* Flammarion

These new authors no longer sought across the Channel the critique of the Bonapartist state they had inherited from Taine; they examined the lineaments of a possible future for industrial society through its most advanced European embodiment. England was seen as a society reformed from within by a powerful social movement, in which the reformist French socialists, to whom these writers were close, found arguments against the false revolutionaries of direct-action syndicalism, increasingly present on the French social stage in the years 1906–9. If even England, the homeland of liberalism, was steadily introducing doses of socialism in its political organisation, it might be hoped that one day the French bourgeoisie, still fearful of income tax or old-age pensions, would have to agree to social reforms such as these. All three analysts were former students at the Ecole Normale Supérieure in the rue d'Ulm, and present a more typical academic profile: they had masters' and doctoral titles. If Elie Halévy also gave lectures at the Ecole de la rue Saint-Guillaume (on socialism, which made waves in this temple of liberalism),[10] after voluntarily abandoning a university career opened to him by his prestigious publications in order to be able to travel and work as he saw fit, he kept his main friends from the Ecole Normale and among the former Dreyfusards. (We could mention here, in particular, Célestin Bouglé and the founding group of the *Revue de Métaphysique et de Morale*, a philosophical review founded by the young generation.)[11] Louis Cazamian and Paul Mantoux shared with Halévy the socialistic and Dreyfusard initiatives of the 1890s.[12] All three were interested less in English politics than in the 'great transformation' of society towards a new democracy and new international problems linked with imperialism.

The Anglophile Liberal Group and its Contradictions

Taine and the dream of an impossible elite

Published in 1871, Taine's *Notes sur l'Angleterre*,[13] which soon became a classic work, placed itself in the context of reflections of major French intellectuals on 'intellectual and moral reform', as in the title of Renan's famous book published the previous year. But while Renan and the champions of university reform found themes for French reform in the Prussian example, Taine drew from his observations on England a rather pessimistic diagnosis for the future of his own country. In his book he combined deterministic schemas ('race, milieu, moment'), elaborated in his *Histoire de la littérature anglaise*, with travel notes accumulated over several short visits.[14] These theses, combined with ethnological observations of reportage, could seem irrefutable to the reader, whereas his investigation was in fact strongly biased by a priori assumptions. Thus he sketched certain analyses of the 'French disease' defined by comparison with the English model. This comparativism of denigration and deploring opened up a long series of books, leading up to the fashionable essayists of the late twentieth century, who simply shifted the country of reference from Britain to the United States.[15] Taine's work served as the first draft for his *Origines de la France contemporaine*, as in the passage:

> Poor Frenchmen, so poor and living in squalor. We are a people of yesterday, ruined from father to son, by Louis XIV, by Louis XV, by the Revolution, by the Empire. We have demolished, and everything has had to be built anew. In England, the following generation does not break with the previous: reforms are superimposed on institutions, and the present, based on the past, continues it.[16]

Reform versus revolution, continuity versus rupture, adaptation versus demolition, the themes of enlightened conservatism specific to England find here their reactualisation in the aftermath of a new shock. Taine did not restrict himself to this stylisation; he also described the balance of classes and the role assigned to each in this perpetual English miracle. The aristocracy, the gentry and the resident landowners were presented in a most favourable light; they combined fortune, prestige, authority, devotion to the public good, patronage of the dominated classes and intellectual curiosity, prepared to draw lessons from experience. This ideal portrait is almost word for word that which Boutmy drew in his pamphlet of 1871 on the new ruling class that France needed after its defeat, and that he dreamed of training by opening the Ecole libre des sciences politiques.[17] The renewal of the English elites was also attributed to the rules of inheritance; primogeniture forced younger sons to seek their fortune or embark on new careers, thus avoiding a lazy mediocrity and fuelling the spirit of enterprise, even in the upper classes. The struggle for life was thus the secret wellspring of English society as a whole, from one extreme to the other: 'Man is strengthened by struggle. The elite of a nation renews itself, and wealth floods across the land.'[18]

Paradoxically, Taine, the free-thinker, also portrays the Anglican clergy in an enthusiastic light. He opposes it right down the line to the French Catholic clergy, as he does the English nobility to the French. Taine's contempt here is quite explicit: 'It is not the peasants who are poorly fed by the seminary, filled with outdated theology, removed from the world by their role, their celibacy and their lack of function.'[19]

As a convinced liberal, Taine saw English society in ideal terms as a society almost without the State, in which groups organised themselves on a voluntary basis and delegated a limited but accepted power to their 'natural representatives'. In France, a universal suffrage extended even to the uneducated, and an abstract and non-hereditary administration that stifled society, were both incapable of succeeding in this way. To this extent, Taine remained sceptical and pessimistic about the possibility – in which Guizot still believed a generation earlier – of adapting the English model on the Continent:

> For the last eighty years, our writers have reasoned their heads off over constitutions; some of them, including the most eminent, would like to introduce in France the constitution of England or the United States, and ask only two years to accustom our nation to it. One of them told me: 'It's a locomotive, you only need add water, and it will right away replace the horse-drawn carriage.' In fact, almost the whole of Europe has tried to adopt the English system, i.e. a more or less restricted monarchy, a lower and an upper chamber, elections, etc. In Greece it has had a grotesque effect, in Spain a lamentable one, in France it has been fragile, in Austria and Italy uncertain; in Prussia and the rest of Germany it has been inadequate, though successful in Holland, Belgium and the Scandinavian states. It is not enough to import the locomotive, it also needs rails to travel on.

> Better indeed not to avoid comparisons drawn from mechanical things; the constitution of a state is organic, like a living being; it belongs only to itself; it cannot be simply assimilated, all that can be copied are the externals. Over and above institutions, charters, written laws, the official almanach, there are ideas, habits, character, the condition of classes, their respective positions, their feelings towards one another, in brief a ramified scaffolding of deep and invisible roots under the visible trunk and foliage. It is these that nourish and sustain the tree. If you plant the tree without roots it will languish, and fall at the first stroke of the axe.[20]

This conservative and organicist sociology offered little hope in the short term for the success of the political current favoured by Taine, even if France was still governed by a conservative coalition when he wrote these lines. How could the English tree be made to grow in French soil? In the final rhetorical parallel that he offers by way of conclusion, however, Taine emphasised the superiority of French society in those domains that in his eyes were essential: climate, distribution of wealth, family and social life, the social status of the artist and the man of letters ('The English are stronger, but the French are happier').[21] Like Renan in the same era, the only practical conclusion he draws from his comparative sociology is the urgent need for a reform of elite education. But while Renan, in *La Réforme intellectuelle et morale*, championed the German academic model, Taine, faced with this urgency, committed himself to a project more Anglo-Saxon in inspiration, the Ecole des sciences politiques that Emile Boutmy had just appealed for in a pamphlet of February 1871.[22]

Taine's orthodox disciples, Boutmy and Max Leclerc, as well as his more heterodox disciple Edmond Demolins, likewise sought in education rather than in politics the solution to the French disease.

The impossible educational reform

Despite his original project mentioned above, Boutmy had failed to make 'Sciences-Po' a privileged training ground for the new elites of the conservative republic.[23] What he established was in fact a kind of private school of administration. The essential criticisms that the liberals made of French institutions (the traditional legal culture, the barrack lycées, the academic competitions, the *grandes écoles*, state intervention at every level of the syllabus) remained intact at the turn of the century.[24]

Max Leclerc's enquiry into the education of the middle classes in England was situated in a complementary procedure: to confirm, by deeper empirical observation, the correctness of Taine's analyses, which saw the origin of the French bourgeoisie's inability to durably establish its power over a democratising society as rooted in classical culture and the Napoleonic lycée.[25] Thus for all its defective and archaic features, in the process of reform in the 1890s, English secondary and higher education could provide correctives. Several of these themes were taken up in the same years by Leclerc, Boutmy, Demolins and Pierre de Coubertin,[26] in the debates that led to the reform of secondary education in 1902. But this convergence in the critique of instruction by a state that neglected genuine education, infantilised pupils, overlooked physical culture in favour of swotting for exams and overwork, did not prevent differences of emphasis between moderates and radicals of educational Anglophilia, as we shall go on to see.

Leclerc: for a change in the family

The originality of Leclerc's book was to combine an investigation into different kinds of teaching institutions in England (public and grammar schools, technical institutes and university extension courses) with general comparative chapters in which he drew lessons applicable in France. Contrary to Taine, who selected positive examples that supported his positions, Leclerc also noted the defects, lacks and educational practices that were inapplicable to French society. This gave his conclusions for France all the more weight. His closer focus on the family, on pedagogic relations and on educational establishments, also opened up a practical perspective for introducing in France, on a restricted scale, certain English educational methods that were deemed to be fertile. His first chapter thus stresses the difference in tone of intimate relations within the French and English family; to be sure, only the bourgeois family is at issue here. Leclerc explicitly accuses French mothers of being too close to their children, and not preparing them for the rough life of boarding school or, later on, life:

> The young Englishman learns from infancy a personal familiarity with the dangers of the outside world, the difficulties of life and the character of men, by direct experience at his own expense; the young Frenchman is surrounded by his mother with incessant care, protected from the least perils and the lightest blows. While the young Englishman is hardened, the Frenchman remains immature, frail and timid; and if he does take risks, he lacks at the decisive moment the necessary sang-froid and concentration.[27]

The forms of secondary education strengthened rather than reduced this difference in preparation for practical life. The reform of the public schools, gradually followed by other secondary establishments, stressed personal tutoring, physical training, self-discipline and apprenticeship for social life, whereas in France it was only the needs of the mind that were catered for, and boarding school plunged the adolescent into an artificial milieu – soulless, disciplinary and cut off from the real world. The heir to Napoleonic despotism, it was incapable of forming the free men of the Republic:

> The prefects and officials of the Republic do not have any different conception of their role today than they had under the sabre of Napoleon. In our *lycées*, the same military discipline, the same accumulation of numbered human molecules, which an enormous mill, turning throughout France under the ministerial pedal, crushes and reduces into human dust.[28]

Like Taine, however, Max Leclerc was well aware of the social and administrative obstacles in the way of reform. The English system of close instruction and healthy boarding in the country was reserved for the richest, or at least a minority of stock-jobbers. It was flexible because it was largely independent of the State, controlled by voluntary associations or charitable foundations. And yet Leclerc's conclusions from his study were less pessimistic than those of his mentor. Instead of expecting everything from above, or a comprehensive reform, as did certain enlightened republican theorists of education, what was needed first of all was to change the basic cell that conditioned everything else, the family: 'The impulse must come from without; and the only thing that can provide it is a reform of manners in the family.'[29]

A critical Anglophile, Max Leclerc understood that, as against the conservative parties that trusted too much in State and Church, it was necessary to change the French bourgeoisie prior to changing institutions – that would simply amount to a counter-revolution which two monarchies, an empire and a conservative republic had never succeeded in achieving. This still appeared quite unlikely nearly twenty-five years after Sedan. There first had to be found a new golden mean between pure liberalism in the English style (increasingly questioned even in England itself) and the traditional French statism shared by both Right and Left: the State that Leclerc called for had to be 'moderating, in part auxiliary, in part propelling'.[30] By changing men (through the training of new educators and through new relations in the family), democratic society in France would finally gain the elites required for its renewal.

Demolins: the public school as remedy for decadence

Demolins's work takes up a number of themes from the previous authors. His theoretical framework also lacked originality, abounding in references to *Notes sur l'Angleterre*,[31] to Le Play's theses on the family and other monographs by Le Play's disciples. On the other hand, neither Max Leclerc nor Emile Boutmy are anywhere cited, presumably because of their too critical tone towards the English model, as well as to mask everything that Demolins has borrowed from them without acknowledgement. What made for the remarkable (and international) success of this book,[32] besides the historical conjuncture already noted, was the systematic and provocative tone, the seemingly dialectical presentation in the form of theses easy to sum up, the alternation between concrete examples and arguments with a strong polemical charge against political figures, French customs, institutions and self-satisfaction. A collection of articles that had already been published in a periodical of the Ecole, *La Science Sociale*, the book is organised in the form of a treatise, developing an implacable comparative demonstration:

- Book 1: the French and the Anglo-Saxon school (with four chapters, titled in the form of questions)
- Book 2: the French and the Anglo-Saxon in private life (four chapters in thesis form)
- Book 3: the French and the Anglo-Saxon in public life (six chapters, alternately theses, descriptions and questions)

As against Boutmy's treatises drawn from university courses, enquiries such as Max Leclerc's that were too subtle and overburdened with information, or the mere travel notes of other Anglophiles, Demolins, by cleverly summarising commonplaces that were already broadly diffused, offered the attraction of an easy read, a concrete and journalistic style, simple ideas hammered in by repetition, and a practical conclusion aimed at the bourgeois paterfamilias.

The French bourgeoisie had begun to complain more and more about the lycées, without necessarily being convinced by Catholic education unless they were believers themselves. Their response to Demolins's appeal was beyond the author's own hopes, and his successful book, followed by public lectures, gave rise to a French-style 'public school', the Ecole des Roches, founded in 1898 at Verneuil-sur-Avre in Normandy.[33]

This paradoxical transfer of an institution, the public school – even if reformed and freed from the outdated aspects still present in its most famous examples – did not, however, contradict Taine's thesis on the impossibility of transferring the English model, nor the doubt of Max Leclerc on the prior reform of the French family. In fact, this school had scarcely any imitators, and influenced only a small and privileged milieu, unable by itself to remedy, on its restricted scale, the assembly of ills that French society suffered in Demolins's view. His book, in fact, fitted into a relatively pessimistic Social Darwinist vision, quite widespread at that time, which condemned the Latin and Catholic peoples to decline, for lack of a spirit of enterprise and adventure.[34] Here, for example, are the closing lines of his book:

> The peoples who escape, by all kinds of petty tricks, this law of personal and intense work, experience a depression, a moral inferiority: thus the Redskin in relation to the Oriental, and the Oriental in relation to the Westerner; thus the Latin and Germanic peoples of the West in relation to the Anglo-Saxon peoples.[35]

Malthusian, rentier, poorly governed, France piled up handicaps in the struggle for life between nations. Its population was declining, its economy lacked dynamism, its unambitious elites ritualised inheritance and petty property. Adolescents dreamed of becoming functionaries. England, on the other hand – fertile, well governed and with a taste for risk – dominated the world through its empire, its exports, its emigrants and its sense of enterprise. Even the working class profited from this openness: the English worker was 'very ingenious at seizing a better situation as soon as the opportunity arises. And he does not even recoil at the idea of leaving his country, as shown by the multitude of Anglo-Saxon emigrants.'[36]

This Manichean vision was paradoxical in another sense, since it was precisely in these years that the debate arose across the Channel about the relative decline of the British economy relative to Germany and the United States, before the Boer War revealed in the following years the lack of preparedness of the British army and the poor physical state of volunteers.[37] Demolins was not unaware of this debate, and mentions it in the preface to his second edition. But he maintains his confidence in Anglo-Saxon superiority, and its ability to react to German competition:

> I repeat, German industry and trade owe their present success to selling the same product at a lower price. If the English cannot manage to product an article at the same price, labour being too expensive in their own country, they will rapidly move, indeed they have already done so, to producing it elsewhere, in poorer countries, where English factories are being established.[38]

This anti-French pessimism and the scepticism of German abilities, out of tune with the attitude of the majority of French commentators on Germany at that time,[39] aroused hostile reactions even in the conservative camp to which Demolins belonged.[40]

The 1900s: England between nationalism and social democracy

Demolins, in fact, despite his public and even pedagogic success, marked more the end of an era than the beginning of a new one. The 1900s were a watershed in the perception of England by French intellectuals, for two sets of reasons. On the one hand, the Boer War, the rise of other imperialisms, the Franco-British rapprochement, the working-class and labour impulse, all focused public attention on the scope of these changes in relation to the old images of the country. The commonplaces repeated since Taine's time about the stability of the United Kingdom, its aristocratic domination, the submissiveness of the popular classes and the invincibility of its empire, were partly refuted simply by events related in the press. As Elie Halévy wrote, the balance sheet of the Boer War was a heavy one: 'more than thirty thousand British soldiers died; more than three hundred thousand men had to be kept there; the 1902 budget rose to £180 million, i.e. four and a half billion francs'.[41] English society thus appeared increasingly similar to its rivals: like France, it was threatened by strikes, social discontent, external and internal threats.[42] And, again like France, England was now experiencing a slowdown in population growth.[43]

The second factor in the evolution of French intellectual perceptions was the arrival on stage of a second group of more academic specialists, who had made prolonged study tours in connection with their works, not just hasty visits like their forerunners. Further to the left, as we noted above, they sought more in the 'English model' than the rescue and reform of a ruling class, a bourgeoisie in quest of legitimacy. The liberal Anglophiles had to change their discourse to respond to these competitors, as well as to distinguish themselves from excesses of racism, in an opposite sense to Demolins.

The strength of English nationalism

This inflection is noticeable, already in 1901, in *Etudes anglaises* by André Chevrillon, the nephew of Taine. Chevrillon used a description of the war in Transvaal to explain to his French readers why nationalism was so strong across the Channel. While French opinion had been generally favourable to the Boers (see chapter 13), Chevrillon, without taking a personal stand, tried to give a psychological explanation of British jingoism. In an iconoclastic manner, he sought to account for the English superiority complex by a transposed comparison of the fashion in which the French sometimes themselves justified their civilising mission:[44]

> Each nation has axioms of this kind, lending the dignity of a principle to its particular tendencies, and because it follows these tendencies, it proclaims itself the first of all nations. We have similar formulas in France: the sovereignty of reason, the abstract rights of man, the social equality of all citizens. For a long while the English have projected into a moral absolute the commands of their organizational instincts, and at least a part of this ideal has echoed their love and feeling for concrete reality[45] ... [England] holds itself the leading nation, the vehicle of human progress, the chief

exponent if not the inventor of modern civilization and its missionary. In India, Egypt and South Africa, it preaches this civilization, and wherever it reaches out its hand, lives gain in independence, security, and material prosperity. Every country that falls under a different hand seems to it lost to civilization or at least compromised. It is for humanity that England works; such is its particular function, which give its special rights.'[46]

This minimalist defence made it possible to avoid making a clear judgement (whether or not the English cause against the Boers had right on its side), which would have come up against prevailing opinion. On the other hand, it suggested that English nationalism, by its strength and the virtual absence of internal challenge (whereas in France, nationalists and Dreyfusard intellectuals had at this point been embattled for more than two years), could serve as an example for a France deeply divided by the sequels of the Dreyfus Affair.

Elie Halévy and the age of empire

The first work that dismantled the liberal orthodoxy, and even more so the Social Darwinist prejudices of Demolins, was that of Elie Halévy. This was written for a small activist publisher inspired by socialistic Dreyfusards: *Pages Libres*.[47] After a deliberately objective presentation of British foreign policy during the nineteenth century, the writer drew moderate conclusions, but criticised the pro-Boer Anglophobes as well as the Anglophile liberals. Against the demonising of Albion by the former, he showed the contradictory interests that divided the British parties and elites, the impossibility of a brutal imperialism, the limits of which had been shown by the difficulties of the Boer War, and the equal inappropriateness of anti-imperialist liberalism of the Hobsonian kind. Halévy denied the imminent decline of England and its empire which his opponents had already announced, but emphasised the parallel vanity of the superiority complex that Demolins claimed to put on a scientific basis. Like other empires, the British one had to adapt to the new international competition and come to terms with former adversaries who were now too numerous, as illustrated the previous year by its rapprochement with France. Halévy risked, therefore, a social diagnosis that contradicted the theories of Demolins. Outward expansion, overseas emigration, and the taste for conquest, far from being the expression of any British superiority, risked opening an age of degeneration just as much as did French introversion:

> The English, therefore, tend with the growth of their empire and by the very fact of this imperialism to become a nation composed no longer of industrialists, traders and workers, but rather of capitalists and administrators; no longer of men who work, but of men who draw for their living on a

share of the work of others. Is it then not through this laziness, to which the very exercise of command functions condemns them, that the higher races degenerate, and end up one day enabling inferior races to shake off their prolonged subjugation?[48]

Halévy takes up here the schema of Demolins, even his very words, reversing Demolins's conclusions by drawing in part on the ideas put forward by Hobson in his famous *Imperialism: A Study* (1902). But after this passage in which he seems to have become contaminated by the ambient ideology, he recovers himself very quickly and ends up with a much more balanced conclusion. For him, neither the superiority of the English people, nor their decadence, were either natural or ineluctable. A philosopher nourished on English and German thinking, who was now transforming himself into a historian, Elie Halévy rejected the naturalist and Darwinian schemas of his predecessors: it was the struggle of nations and the competition of empires, as well as the adaptive capacities of the peoples, that would decide the future of England as well as of the other powers. He concluded with a prophecy that 'the twentieth century will be the century of empires',[49] sufficiently vague to reconcile opposing positions.

Mantoux: England as a school of socialist reform

Four years later, Paul Mantoux inscribed himself still more clearly in this social and nonconformist approach in opposition to the liberal doctrine and the school of Le Play. The new England no longer represented either a miracle of conservatism, as with Taine, nor the genius of adaptation, as with Boutmy. Still less was it the infallible product of racial selection, as with Demolins. It was painted, rather, as a laboratory of reforms, a centre of conflicts and contradictions, perhaps more deeply disturbed at bottom than was contemporary France. In any case, England was an example of multiple attempts of adaptation, the model now of a change from which France would do well to draw an example of progress.[50]

His first two chapters, devoted to the Boer War and jingoism, saw a similar pathology to the nationalism of the Dreyfus Affair, and not this positive patriotic super-ego that Chevrillon exalted in the extract cited above. It was a kind of 'delirium tremens', based on a contempt for other nations to be found throughout Europe. It had been strengthened by pseudo-scientific racial theories that 'have given a philosophical and modern air to the most primitive, absurd and ferocious prejudices'. Almost always victorious, and free from military service, the English population cultivated a falsely positive image of war, as against those continental nations that had suffered from it themselves.[51]

For all that, Mantoux does draw from his comparison of conflicting nationalisms lessons that are valid for other European countries:

> England in 1895 was healthy, despite a few alarming symptoms. Even today,[52] it is a large and robust body, but in the grip of a dangerous fever that it is not trying to cure. If these reflections applied only to England, they would still invite us to beware of ourselves. But unfortunately they can be applied to other countries, our own above all. Our neighbours have a beam in their eye; are we sure that we have only a mote?'[53]

This critical view of foreign policy is largely offset by the four final chapters, in which Mantoux praises the attempts at social reform at a local level (municipal socialism in London, 1890–1900), educational reforms, and the growing working-class pressure. This had led to the emergence of a new force in Parliament, which had managed to make a breach in Conservative policy and the anti-working-class legislation passed at the turn of the century. Through this praise of working-class reformism and the new liberalism that broke with the laissez-faire of the nineteenth century, Mantoux outlined a counter-model of a negotiated social democracy that he hoped would serve as a model for French socialism, once again at that time prey to deep dissensions between moderates and revolutionaries, between the Socialist Party and the Confédération Générale du Travail. Mutatis mutandis, these chapters – in which objective information, direct evidence and political programmes which it was suggested should be transferred (cf. 'an image, or at least a sketch of the socialist state')[54] – recall the use of the impossible English model upheld in the previous generation by the Anglophile liberals, even if Paul Mantoux denounces in passing the analyses of these predecessors:

> British individualism has been the object of countless dissertations. Those who have found it convenient to invent, for their purpose, a theoretical England, have spoken of it in broadly similar terms. The trade unions have often been cited as one of the most remarkable examples of this trust in free association, this repugnance for state intervention, that distinguish the Anglo-Saxon ideal. But the most absolute individualism – which is certainly not that of the unions – supposes, in our state of society, certain guarantees of freedom, established by law.
>
> At a time when the legal conquest of public power in France, the goal assigned to its supporters by classic socialism, is giving way to *direct action*, when syndicalists allied to anarchists preach the defiance of politics, contempt for the ballot (a 'cowards' weapon') and hatred for democracy ('the latest invention of the privileged to deceive the people'), it is not without interest to see in a neighbouring country a no less strong movement in the opposite direction. England, which does not have syndicalists in the recent French sense of the word, but has trade unions that can smile with

pity if they look at ours, sees today these disciplined forces, on a common slogan, take part in political struggle from which they formerly stood apart, systematically and over a long period of years ....[55]

Despite this iconoclastic discourse against the stereotypes of the French liberals, Mantoux still remained unable to escape from the schemas of national psychology that pervaded all social thought of the time, as his conclusion demonstrates:

> Let us take it as assured, however, that if the House of Commons becomes still more democratic, the monarchical and aristocratic elements of the constitution will not thereby be condemned to disappear. For this the whole character of the nation would have to be changed. Tomorrow as yesterday, the spirit of concession and compromise will govern English politics: it is in this way that conservative England maintains its traditions, and in this way that liberal England carries out its reforms.'[56]

Conclusion

This examination of the biased uses of the French–English comparison by intellectuals in the years before 1914 suggests a fourfold conclusion.

Whatever its aim, praising or pejorative, the comparison between nations effects a dual and displaced reading: a reading of the neighbouring society and opinion as a function of the underlying theses held about the writer's own society, and that of the place the writer occupies in his own intellectual field, whether he adopts a position of continuity or dissidence in relation to the dominant conception of the country in question.[57]

As an authoritative argument, this comparison succeeds in producing effects, compared with a mere internal sociological discourse, middlebrow or scholarly, on its own society. This explains the constancy of genre, lasting over centuries, in the case of the two longest unified European nations, while the growing social sciences made it into one of their fetishised methods, by analogy with experimental reasoning.

The delay in representations or modes of explanation in relation to the considered society, though a constant feature, forces (in an inverse sense) more sudden reactualisations than the self-centred view, when a series of massive facts finally brings home the inadequacy of previous analytical categories. But once the new *doxa* is established, it takes many years until it can again be challenged.

Finally, for those of us who practise this exercise, in this book, in a different way, analysis of the biases and question-begging of our predecessors, in pursuit of political ends, should help us guard against similar involuntary errors made by the comparative exercise, even in its scholarly form, which lie in wait for us, as they lie in wait for them.

Notes

1 See P. Leroy-Beaulieu, *De la colonisation chez les peuples modernes* (5th edition, Paris: Guillaumin, 1902), vol. 2, pp. 308–320.
2 See Christophe Prochasson's study of periodicals in this volume (chapter 13). We should also mention the existence of the *Revue Britannique*, compiled from extracts from the major English periodicals. See also Blaise Wilfert's chapter (chapter 9) about literary relations between France and England.
3 7th edition 1883; 8th edition 1885; 9th edition, Paris: Hachette, 1890.
4 Paris: Plon, Chevalier Maresq, 1887; new revised and expanded edition, A. Colin, 1898; 5th edition: 1907.
5 Paris: Didot, 1897; I shall refer here to the recent reissue of this book (Paris: Anthropos, 1998).
6 'Two great states, England and the United States, offer the world in our day the spectacle of this new fact in the world, an established free government and its conditions accomplished through thoroughly different forms and institutions. ... However different they may be, these means, put to the test, have proved equally effective: in each of the two states, the responsibility of the executive is real and public liberties are guaranteed'; F. Guizot, *Mémoires pour servir à l'histoire de mon temps* (Paris: Michel Lévy, 1867), vol. 8, pp. 3 and 6; English: *Memoirs to Illustrate the History of My Time*, trans. by J. W. Cole (London: 1858–67).
7 Paris: A. Colin, 1894.
8 See A. Savoye, 'Max Leclerc (1864–1932), un éditeur engagé', in C. Chambelland (ed.), *Le Musée social en son temps* (Paris: Presses de l'Ecole Normale Supérieure, 1998), pp. 119–34, especially pp. 122–6.
9 G. Monod, foreword to P. Mantoux, *A travers l'Angleterre contemporaine* (Paris: Alcan, 1909).
10 See his letter of 18 January 1902, in E. Halévy, *Correspondance 1891–1937* (Paris: de Fallois, 1996), p. 320. For an English perspective on Halévy, see M. Chase, *Elie Halévy: An Intellectual Biography* (New York: Columbia University Press, 1980), as well as S. Collini, 'Idealizing England: Elie Halévy and Lewis Namier', in S. Collini, *English Pasts: Essays in History and Culture* (Oxford: Oxford University Press, 1999), pp. 67–77.
11 See E. Halévy, *Correspondance*, throughout.
12 Though Elie Halévy was not a socialist, his brother Daniel was at this time, and so were Mantoux and Cazamian, both of these taking part in the political activity around L. Herr, the Société nouvelle d'édition and the movement of *universités populaires*; Sébastien Laurent, *Daniel Halévy: du libéralisme au traditionalisme* (Paris: Grasset, 2001), p. 124ff., and C. Charle, 'Avant-garde intellectuelle et avant-garde politique, les normaliens et le socialisme', in *Paris fin de siècle, culture et politique* (Paris: Le Seuil, 1998), pp. 227–74.
13 Simultaneously published in England: *Notes on England,* translated, with an introductory chapter, by W. F. Rae (London: 1871).
14 In 1861, 1862 and May 1871. He had published these notes previously in *Le Temps* (19 August 1871, 29 October 1871). The first edition of his book

appeared in late December 1871; the second revised edition is referred to here (Paris: Hachette, 1871). On Taine and England, see F. Léger, 'Taine et l'Angleterre', in S. Michaud and M. Le Pavec (eds), *Taine au carrefour des cultures du XIXe siècle* (Paris: Bibliothèque nationale de France, 1996), pp. 25–34.

15 This transition from one model to another was effected in the course of his work by André Siegfried, another eminent member of the Ecole libre des sciences politiques.

16 Taine, *Notes sur l'Angleterre* (Paris: Hachette, 1871), p. 169.

17 Taine, *Notes sur l'Angleterre*, pp. 194–5; the French nobility is on the contrary denigrated, as it would also be in his *Origines de la France contemporaine*; C. Charle, 'Sciences-Po entre l'élite et le pouvoir', *Le Débat*, 64 (March–April 1991), 93–108.

18 Taine, *Notes sur l'Angleterre*, p. 207.

19 Taine, *Notes sur l'Angleterre*, p. 214.

20 Taine, *Notes sur l'Angleterre*, pp. 216–17.

21 Taine, *Notes sur l'Angleterre*, p. 394.

22 E. Boutmy, *Quelques Idées sur la création d'une faculté libre d'enseignement supérieure* (Paris: Imprimerie Laîné, 25 February 1871).

23 See D. Dammame, 'Histoire des sciences morales et politiques des Lumières au scientisme' (thèse d'Etat en science politique, Université de Paris-I, 1982), 2 vols, and 'Genèse sociale d'une institution scolaire, l'Ecole libre des sciences politiques', *Actes de la Recherche en Sciences Sociales*, 70 (November 1987), 31–46; also P. Favre, *Naissances de la science politique en France 1870–1914* (Paris: Fayard, 1989), chapter 1.

24 On this double defeat, see C. Charle, 'Science-Po entre l'élite et le pouvoir', 96 and *La République des universitaires (1870–1940)* (Paris: Le Seuil, 1994), and G. Thuillier, *L'ENA avant l'ENA* (Paris: Presses Universitaire de France, 1983).

25 Max Leclerc explicitly quotes Taine in *L'Education des classes moyennes et dirigeantes en Angleterre* (Paris: Colin, 1894), p. 64, referring to his *Origines de la France contemporaine: le régime moderne*, vol. 2, book 2, chapter 3.

26 P. de Coubertin, *L'Education anglaise* (Paris: Société d'économie sociale, 1887) and *L'Education en Angleterre: collèges et universités* (Paris: Hachette, 1888).

27 Leclerc, *L'Education des classes moyennes et dirigeantes en Angleterre*, p. 28.

28 Leclerc, *L'Education des classes moyennes et dirigeantes en Angleterre*, p. 65.

29 Leclerc, *L'Education des classes moyennes et dirigeantes en Angleterre*, p. 71.

30 Leclerc, *L'Education des classes moyennes et dirigeantes en Angleterre*, p. 365.

31 See E. Demolins, *A quoi tient la supériorité des Anglo-Saxons?* (Paris: Anthropos, 1998), p. 122 and p. 175: 'One must read, in *Notes sur l'Angleterre*, the remarkable pages in which Taine explains how it has arisen that the majority of the English find the landed proprietors are their "natural representatives" and send them to parliament by the ballot ...'

32 Demolins's work reached a printrun of 17,000 copies, and was translated

into English, German, Italian, Spanish, Polish and Arabic.
33 See N. Duval, 'L'adolescence des élites à l'Ecole des Roches: capitanat, sport et spiritualité (de 1899 à 1965)', in J.-P. Bardet, J.-N. Luc, I. Robin-Romero and C. Rollet (eds), *Lorsque l'enfant grandit: entre dépendance et autonomie* (Paris: Presses de l'Université de Paris-Sorbonne, 2003), pp. 559–72 ; E. Demolins, *L'Education nouvelle, l'école des Roches* (Paris: Didot, 1898); L. Colin and R. Hess, 'Préface' to the new edition of *A quoi tient la supériorité des Anglo-Saxons?*, p. xv. It is ironic how English and German historians have debated the responsibility of the public schools for the origins of British decline: for an update on this, see H. Berghoff, 'Public Schools and the Decline of the British Economy 1870–1914', *Past and Present*, 129 (1990), 148–67.
34 See A. Fouillée, 'Dégénérescence? Le passé et l'avenir de notre race', *Revue des Deux Mondes* (15 October 1895), 793–824, and F. Brunetière, 'La lutte des races et la philosophie de l'histoire', *Revue des Deux Mondes*,(15 January 1893), 428–48, referring to Ludwik Gumplowicz, *La Lutte des races* (Paris: Guillaumin, 1893); A. Fouillée, 'Races latines', *Revue des Deux Mondes* (1 December 1899), 561–90, on G. Le Bon and Vacher de Lapouge. On these ideological currents, see J.-M. Bernardini, *Le Darwinisme social en France (1859–1918): fascination et rejet d'une idéologie* (Paris: CNRS-Editions, 1997); and Anne Carol, *Histoire de l'eugénisme en France* (Paris: Le Seuil, 1995).
35 Demolins, *A quoi tient la supériorité des Anglo-Saxons?*, p. 299.
36 Demolins, *A quoi tient la supériorité des Anglo-Saxons?*, p. 132.
37 See E. E. Williams, *Made in Germany* (4th edition; London: Heinemann, 1896; reissued Brighton: Harvester Press, 1973); J. E. Barker, 'The Economic Decay of Great Britain', *Contemporary Review* 79 (1901), 781–812; A. Shadwell, *Industrial Efficiency: A Comparative Study of Industrial Life in England, Germany and America* (London: Longmans, 1906; reissued London: Routledge, 1999); G. R. Searle, *The Quest for National Efficiency* (Oxford: Basil Blackwell, 1971).
38 E. Demolins, *A quoi tient la supériorité des Anglo-Saxons?*, p. 9.
39 See C. Digeon, *La Crise allemande de la pensée française* (Paris: Presses Universitaire de France, 1959), and H. Barbey-Say, *Le Voyage de France en Allemagne (1871–1914)* (Nancy: Presses Universitaires de Nancy, 1994).
40 G. Valbert, 'La supériorité des Anglo-Saxons et le livre de M. Demolins', *Revue des Deux Mondes* (1 October 1897), 697–708. 'G. Valbert' was the pseudonym of the novelist Victor Cherbuliez, a member of the Académie française; see T. Loué, '*La Revue des Deux Mondes du Buloz à Brunetière: de la belle époque de la revue à la revue de la Belle Epoque*', Ph.D., Université de Paris-I, supervised by Alain Corbin, 1998, vol. 1, p. 382. We end up with the paradoxical situation in which a naturalised Swiss Protestant is charged with defending the symbolic image of Catholic-culture France against a traditionalist Catholic panegyrist of the Protestant countries!
41 E. Halévy, *L'Angleterre et son empire* (Paris: Pages Libres, 1905), p. 115.
42 See R. Savary, 'La détérioration physique du peuple anglais (a propos d'une

enquête récente)', *Annales des Sciences Politiques*, 20 (1905), 578–91. For all the alarming statistics drawn from a number of English social investigations, the writer's conclusion optimistically conforms to the English liberal credo.
43 L. Cazamian, *L'Angleterre moderne et son évolution* (Paris: Flammarion, 1911), p. 306.
44 'L'opinion anglaise et la guerre du Transvaal', dated 18 February 1900, in *Etudes anglaises* (Paris: Hachette, 1901), pp. 276–7.
45 Chevrillon, *Etudes anglaises*, p. 298.
46 Chevrillon, *Etudes anglaises*, p. 302.
47 The magazine *Pages Libres* (3,000 subscribers in 1906, with a readership of teachers and trade unionists) was inspired by these Dreyfusard intellectuals – among them Elie's brother, Daniel Halévy – who set themselves an educational task. It also published a collection of popularising works on history and foreign policy. See S. Laurent, *Daniel Halévy: du libéralisme au traditionalisme*, pp. 150–1, and E. Halévy, *Correspondance*, p. 306.
48 Halévy, *L'Angleterre et son empire*, p. 122.
49 Halévy, *L'Angleterre et son empire*, p. 123.
50 As G. Monod wrote in his preface, 'The English have had a tax on income for a century now, without every believing that this was the start of a despoliation of the capitalists. They have made a series of experiments with municipal socialism, of which M. Mantoux describes the most significant, in London itself, without believing that collectivism was about to take over' (*A travers l'Angleterre contemporaine*, p. ix). Louis Cazamian upheld quite similar positions, which is why I have not analysed his book in any detail.
51 Mantoux, *A travers l'Angleterre contemporaine*, pp. 21, 26, 32.
52 In 1902, as Mantoux notes.
53 Mantoux, *A travers l'Angleterre contemporaine*, p. 53.
54 Mantoux, *A travers l'Angleterre contemporaine*, p. 101.
55 Mantoux, *A travers l'Angleterre contemporaine*, pp. 225–6.
56 Mantoux, *A travers l'Angleterre contemporaine*, pp. 281–2.
57 We could compare here the analyses of Alexander Schmidt on the German view of America in the same era: *Reisen in die Moderne: der Amerika-Diskurs des deutschen Bürgertums vor dem Ersten Weltkrieg im europäischen Vergleich* (Berlin: Akademie-Verlag, 1997).

13

An English crisis in French thought? French intellectuals confront England at the time of Fashoda and the Boer War

CHRISTOPHE PROCHASSON

In the novel by Léon Werth, *Clavel soldat*, written in 1916–17 and published in 1919, French *'poilus'* discover old newspapers describing the war in Transvaal: 'An illustration represented drunken soldiers at a station who were beating old men, women and children with their rifle butts. Another showed the surrender of a hundred and eighty English to a handful of Boers. They had their arms in the air. It was the very image of the *Kamerad* and twenty-seven lancers surrendering to the seven dragoons.' The English at that time had occupied the place that a few years later was assigned to the Germans. The culture of war had reshuffled the cards, on the basis of cultural elaborations worked out before the conflict broke out. It effected transpositions, transfers, shifts and translations, in the context of a *triangle of comparison* between the three nations: France, Germany and England. In observing French intellectual life before 1914, the third figure is often lost from sight. Germany is wrongly taken to have polarised all attention. Indeed, it was an indispensable element in the construction of French national identity. And it was also with Germany that personal ties had been long established, especially in the academic field. But Germany was not alone. Throughout the nineteenth century French intellectuals had also been in a dialogue with England. The international crises at the turn of the century, between 1898 and 1901 (Spanish–American war, colonial competition in Africa, Boer War and Boxer rebellion), favoured a renewal of interest and a work of re-reading of English culture.

Analysis of a stereotype

Anyone interested in national stereotypes as these were elaborated in the second half of the nineteenth century cannot but be struck by the permeability that existed between scholarly and journalistic culture. Science seized on commonplace observations and gave them a force that played a role in politics. In this way intellectuals had an influence on the history of international relations by contributing to the construction of 'imagined communities'.

The characters ascribed to a nation by the cultural elites of other nations depend in the first place on the state of political relations between the two countries. The Franco-German relationship, which clearly took a new turn after the war of 1870, has been well defined. But this relationship also had an influence on that between France and England, certainly in so far as this found expression in the public sites of French culture. From Taine to a Demolins who continued to defend the English during the Boer War,[1] a noticeable Anglomania ruled the majority of minds. It played a well-known part in the foundation of the Ecole libre des sciences politiques. England was a great nation: its colonial empire intimidated even more than it irritated, its power and its economic and financial[2] organisation were an example to the liberal elites, while its literature,[3] and in particular its poetry, were flowers of European culture on the same level as German philosophy. The vitality of this Anglophilia, though doubtless qualified by other factors, especially those pertaining to political sensibilities, was all the more active in the last third of the century in that it found itself in opposition to a basis of popular anglophobia. This favourable attitude to England thus contained elements of a distinctive practice working to detach the intellectuals from the rest of the nation.[4]

This has a particular significance as soon as we seek to go beyond the Franco-English opposition and introduce the third term of Germany. In the period we are concerned with here, it seems that this sentiment in favour of England resisted much that might have aroused national passion, because Germany was the natural horizon and the institutional adversary. Until Fashoda, everything happened as if the appeasement line of the Quai d'Orsay towards England, despite the incidents that opposed the two countries on the River Niger, was echoed in positive representations. Certain writers even prioritised the future of (Western) civilisation over and above the wound inflicted on national feeling: was not Fashoda first and foremost a triumph of 'civilisation' over 'barbarism'.[5] The Jubilee of 1897, an occasion to celebrate British imperialism, in no way put an end to this situation, no more than in more restrained intellectual circles did the translation of the book by the great theorist of English imperialism, Sir J. R. Seeley, *L'Expansion coloniale de l'Angleterre*. One of its reviewers, Auguste Filon, acknowledged its 'originality', while noting: 'Not only has he composed his book with German documents, German ideas and German hatreds, he has assimilated all these things and has written a German book in English.'[6] But England was in some respects a good Germany, stripped of the worst features of the nation beyond the Rhine. We can read, for example, in a critical note from Théodore de Wyzewa, introducing the publication of one of the Englishmen most admired by French intellectuals at the end of the nineteenth century (if of an Italian father, as Wyzewa himself points out): Dante Gabriel Rossetti. This epistolatory exchange between Rossetti and Allingham, Wyzewa underlines, is full of humour and displays great erudition.[7] In the *Revue des Deux Mondes*, Francis Charmes constantly defended this line of friendship, based on a natural complicity between two cultures both vowed to defend 'civilisation and culture'.[8]

To speak of England and define its characteristics meant not just working to find an ally in the cultural war between France and Germany, but also, as in any system depicting the other and constructing alterity, speaking of oneself. In a series of articles, part travel story, part ethno-political considerations on England in the midst of the Boer War, André Chevrillon, an *angliciste* at the University of Lille, eagerly compared the London crowd with that of Paris. Contemplating the first, the second came readily to his mind:

> Imagine making the impossible experiment of assembling alongside an English multitude like this a hundred Parisians, so as to note the two types at once. How we would understand things then! How the past, present and future of the two countries would be illuminated! I look at them: what is apparent before all else is the peace, strength and simplicity of the faces: the features are energetic and solid, but not incomplete and crude like those of German or Russian plebeians – in good relief, regularly sculpted, the physiognomies speaking of family calm, stable life, durable sentiments, persistent attitudes of mind, with very rare disturbances of heart and brain. I try and depict to myself the image of a Parisian crowd, and as I find this engraved in my memory, it appears to me softer and more grey, more changeable and nuanced, more feminine and far more intellectual – I do not say intelligent – more differentiated as well, less homogeneous, the individuals less clearly shaped in the same mould, less surely marked by the same powerful national stamp.[9]

The keys to understanding this lie in the observing nation. To understand the other, one has to mobilise all the powers of cultural transfer to reveal the secrets of the translation. The encounter with a young Baptist minister calls for the conversion of an indigenous social type into another that is easier to grasp: 'Of this dissenting minister, the social equivalent in France would be a petty anticlerical employee of fifteen years ago, today a nationalist.' Still better, cohesive social formulas also find their translations. In England, people readily say: 'God wants Man to turn the World to use; England is the chief worker at this task.' In France, Chevrillon immediately adds, 'we have similar formulae, the sovereignty of Reason, the abstract rights of Man, the social equality of all citizens.'[10] The reception of John Bodley's book *France* also offers a fine example of self-definition through comparison. This observer, who had visited every corner of France between 1890 and 1897, displays the natural bond linking the two nations while at the same time attacking France's bad points. This British perspective, denouncing the excessive administration and the Russian alliance, offered a good point of support for the liberals, who gave it good reviews.[11] It also allowed a comparison of the two patriotisms:

> [in England] patriotism is essentially different from our own; through constantly seeking the improvement of humanity, we have come to the negation of a fatherland; and without discussing here whether we are right or wrong, it is well to state that with the Anglo-Saxons there is a kind of racial solidarity, directed at goals that are exclusively practical, that is to say profitable for the individual and the British community. Never mind humanity – all that is not *British* is inferior by definition, and consequently is wrong not to be so.[12]

This is all the more clear with Alfred Fouillée, the philosopher who in October 1898 published a long article proposing a social psychology of England at a time dominated by two major events. The first of these was the Dreyfus Affair; the second, the colonial quarrels between France and England (Fashoda, Tunis, Nikki and Waima, Zanzibar and Madagascar, Siam and Newfoundland).

How can we not see in Fouillée's article a contribution to the debate opened by Durkheim in his article 'L'individualisme et les intellectuels', published in the *Revue Bleue* in July 1898? Durkheim opposed here a 'Latin individualism' which was simply 'negative', consisting above all in lack of respect for rules, to a 'positive' individualism anchored in Anglo-Saxon values and based on respect for rules and for other people. This, according to Fouillée, was the secret of the contemporary admiration for the Anglo-Saxons that he detected among very many essayists (Gustave Le Bon, Vacher de Lapouge, Jacques Bardoux, etc.). There followed an analysis in anthropological vein, in which Fouillée defended English singularity, which he placed at the heart of a dual Franco-German (or, in scholarly terms, Latino-Germanic) polarity. The Englishman was 'a superb specimen of phlegmatic and neuro-motor sanguinity', resolving the contradiction thanks to a subtle mixture of 'Celtic-Ligurian' and Germanic blood. This mixture helped to account for an apparently contradictory characteristic (reversibility is a useful law in establishing national stereotypes, coping with the future and leaving space for possible changes of sign): 'In practical activity and the domain of pure intelligence, the Englishman has remained positive; in poetry, we see him maintain the Germanic sense of the ideal, without however losing that of the real.'[13] The Celtic connection, which makes the English quasi-Gauls, tempers the undesirable aspects of Germanity and 'prevents the Englishman from falling as readily into pessimism as the dreaming and contemplative German,'[14] while his 'taste for reality' makes him an inductive spirit and thus that much more removed from Germanic[15] or even French deductions. The English language itself had profited from the beneficial influences of Latin: 'Instead of remaining closed in on itself like German, the English language was penetrated by logic and relative clarity, especially in prose.'[16] Caught in this double determinism, physical and social, the 'Germanic' qualities of the British, which handicapped the development of sensibility and limited the fineness of spirit, were largely explained as responses to the severe climatic conditions:

> What can certainly be agreed on first of all is that the damp and cold atmosphere of England has reinforced the influences making the acquisition of a certain individual well-being the most necessary goal of all. It has been calculated that the food for a single Englishman would be sufficient for a family of eight people in Greece.[17]

The German dimension of the English character – and it was not quite forgotten that Wilhelm I was the grandson of Victoria – provided an argument that a possible war culture would be in a position to mobilise.

For the moment, however, the English character had many virtues. A happy mix of races enabled it to transcend the weaknesses of each component. The sense of solidarity, the superiority of the 'Anglo-Germanic marriage of inclination' over the 'French marriage of convenience'[18] (which, though it weakened the family spirit, strengthened the qualities of wife over those of mother, and thus discouraged adultery), the acute sense of religion and public morality such as a lay republican – haunted by the recomposition of a public space much disturbed by the Revolution – might envy, England was an example without ever having had the same role 'for the elevation of the human race as a whole'[19] played by France, Italy, and even Germany.

New England versus old

This Anglophilia, shared by the great majority of the French intelligentsia right across the political spectrum, reached a turning point in the years 1898–1901; this was signalled in autumn 1898 with the combined effect of Fashoda and – even more important – the Boer War. With a greater or lesser degree of inertia depending on the milieu, the positive signs turned to negative. The inevitable ambivalences of national stereotypes swung round to serve a different discourse. A theory of two Englands, similar to that of two Germanies – so useful to French intellectuals during the Great War – suddenly erupted. One England, that of George Eliot, John Stuart Mill, John Ruskin, Dante Gabriel Rossetti and Edward Burne-Jones, was good, and explained the fascination that the country had exercised on the majority of French intellectuals. The other, that of Byron, Emily and Charlotte Brontë and Rudyard Kipling, was bad, had been working underground for many years and now carried the day.[20] A pseudo-culture of war inspired this new reading of England. It explains the operation of what was to found, some years later – the new cultural relations between France and Germany – at a time when the signs were once more reversed in favour of England.

Everything is said in an article in a nationalist newspaper in the midst of the Boer War:

> There will thus soon be a year when the English people commit the imprudence of ceding to Chamberlain's propositions, more tempting than honest: this people agreed to sacrifice its fine reputation for liberalism, abandoned the generous tradition of humanity and civilization left by Gladstone, and threw itself behind a few freebooters on the gold of the Transvaal mines.[21]

This theme is repeated in every possible variation in the most Anglophile intellectual milieus. The plasticity of national stereotypes made easy enough a work of reversal to which those most familiar with England now applied themselves. The Boer War marked a moment of crisis not just in Franco-British diplomatic relations, but also in the perspective of the majority of French intellectuals, who experienced the advent of this bad England as a kind of lover's betrayal. The deterioration of representations was extremely fast and thus required an intense cultural mobilisation. If, in February 1899, right under the blow of Fashoda, Ernest Lavisse in his controversy with Charles Dilke could still recall, despite everything, the ties uniting 'two ancient great peoples, free, civilized, and humane',[22] he came round a few months later to desire a rapprochement with Germany.[23]

The old England, he argued, had perished under the blows of the new political culture:

> For those who knew the English people around 1885 and try to find them in the England of today, it seems they have completely disappeared. It is no longer the same nation. They are no longer the same individuals. Everything appears changed, ideas and words, feelings and gestures. This liberal and peace-loving people, who trusted in personal effort, in peace and law, and seemed to have found their eternal gospel in the Manchester doctrine, the people of Cobden and John Bright, are soon going to demand measures of protection, which they previously took thirty years to abolish, and shout

with joy at the announcement of a great war, which Joseph Chamberlain has been promising for five years. Peace-loving England is dead. Liberal England is dying.[24]

The violence of the anti-French press campaign, launched at the time of the Spanish–American War, ended up by wearing out the patience of the most far-sighted. In liberal milieus, England ended up being seen as worse than Germany. At the time of the evacuation of Fashoda, in early November 1898, if the common cultural heritage of France and England was still stressed, this relationship was noticeably transformed. Georges Valbert, in a review of the memoirs of Henry Reeve, titled – almost nostalgically – 'Un Anglais qui aimait la France', emphasised 'the prodigious difference in temperament'[25] between the two peoples. In December again, Francis Charmes, very Anglophile, declared that France was ready to forget everything if British opinion put an end to its anti-French attacks: 'It will find on our part the same spirit as in the past. Recent circumstances, however unpleasant they have been for us, have not altered our dispositions.'[26] This same Charmes, moreover, was still able a few months to acknowledge the faults of the South African republics in their diplomatic handling of the conflict with England, and, initially at least, refrain from blaming England.[27] There is no better way of illustrating this attitude than by Charmes's gesture in November 1899, a year after Fashoda, which put an end to his long indulgence: at the head of his customary 'Chronique', he placed a quotation from the tenth Canto of Byron's *Don Juan*:

> Alas! could She [England] but fully, truly know
> How her great name is now throughout abhorred;
> How eager all the earth is for the blow
> Which shall lay bare her bosom to the sword;
> How all the nations deem her their worst foe.[28]

The birth of this new imperialism, depicted in so many articles and books, is often seen as embodied in the emergence of two individuals who attracted particular attention: J. Chamberlain and R. Kipling. The first of these was constructed as the anti-Gladstone. He was the first person responsible for awakening the passions of the bad England, whereas Gladstone was presented by Francis de Pressensé as 'the most illustrious son of political England in this century'.[29] To attack Chamberlain, and profit from the weakening of Lord Salisbury, was to try and rescue the good England, rather than reject out of hand the entire people. But it was Kipling who most held the attention of French observers. They were fascinated by the young author, and astonished that this writer, a pure product of the new England, could be the nephew of an artist like

Burne-Jones, so tied to the old England. Both the *Revue de Paris* and the *Mercure de France* paid great attention to Kipling, either publishing him in translation or devoting articles and critical notes to his work. Though incontestably renewing English literature, Kipling had swung his country into a new culture of complete brutality, based on vitalist values apparently foreign to the old culture. But did not Kipling's success reside in the reconciliation of the two Englands, and display the absolutely heterogeneous character of French and British cultures? This was the position championed by André Chevrillon:

> Thus the apparent antagonism between the two great characteristics distinguishing the English mind has evaporated. Both of them, the sense of reality and the faculty for intensive dreaming, depend on the same cause: the concrete imagination that reproduces the sensible elements of things – more or less exactly, with their true connections, and more or less dissociated, assembled anew in arbitrary arrangements. And this close relationship is so true that it can be established by an inverse and complementary observation. The French spirit, for its part, which possesses only a mediocre degree of this kind of imagination, has been less well able to adapt its works to reality in the practical domain, at the same time as in the realm of dreams it proved incapable of adventuring very far. Proceeding above all by way of reduced signs, abbreviations, and convenient notations for analysis and reasoning, its special function has been to depict the laws that assemble groups, extract their directing lines, bring them to awareness by way of simple plans in which the deep structure of things appears with clarity, precisely because nothing remains there of the infinite entangled detail.[30]

Here we have the theory of the whole development. The Anglophile intellectuals, caught in an unforeseen current of hostility to England, had to find a way of explaining this turn. Many of them stubbornly continued to draw from existing stereotypes the elements of a rationalisation. We have seen how the dialectic of 'two Englands' filled this function by justifying possible admiration, collaboration and cultural proximity, even while creating a space for a possible war culture. Other approaches sought to display a posteriori what was already foreseeable.

A number of indications long since emitted were now signalled. The new imperialism was born without mystery. A more careful observation of the ties linking commerce and industry to the English political class should have led to more vigilance,[31] so we read here. Alfred Fouillée, in a study this time devoted to the 'Latin races', returns to the character of the 'Anglo-Saxon race' to emphasise an aspect he had neglected in his study devoted to it only a few months previously:

The great Anglo-Saxon people have for a whole century raised the love of money to the dignity of a cult. This love is doubtless as old as the world, but if riches were always honoured, the love of riches itself was not so; nobility of birth, nobility of situation, talent, virtue and health were raised far above fortune. Contemporary England, accepting the new economic and financial order as a deeper political order and, by extension, as a providential one, has too often, and in an open fashion, adored money. This is certainly not the best thing that the Anglo-Saxons have introduced in the modern world, nor the best example they have given to the Latins.[32]

Other aspects of British culture could be reversed in similar fashion: empiricism and the religious spirit had led to political cynicism and the mind of a chosen people, too assured of its right to civilise peoples against their wishes. Everyone could read this for themselves, said most commentators. The new imperialist doctrines had invaded newspapers and magazines. Whole books had been devoted to its triumph: 'All those who have closely followed the history of English ideas and letters for the last two or three years could foresee the explosion of jingoism that today surprises so many people.'[33] Victor Bérard, for example, claimed that more attention should have been paid to the young Dilke, who, 'fresh out of the university mould', put forward around 1868 his dream of a 'Greater Britain'.[34] Everything was prepared for the iniquitous crushing of a small people...

A Dreyfus counter-affair

We have seen how the reading and appreciation of a foreign culture, far from being stable, depends on the political conditions from which it proceeds. Stereotypes are not rigid frames. It is enough, therefore, to recall that the crisis depicted above took place at the very moment at which French intellectuals found themselves caught up in a national crisis. The Dreyfus Affair explains many of its aspects. Nationalist intellectuals took advantage of the Boer War to invent their own Dreyfus Affair and catch out Dreyfusard intellectuals, often indulgent towards England, in their own values.

They profited from a virtual national agreement on how to analyse the conflict between England and the Boers. No one failed to emphasise that this war operated a singular reversal of the situation: 'A great atrocity is about to be committed in the name of civilization,' Francis Charmes announced at the start of the conflict.[35] A people that had been heralds of civilisation, in the vanguard of Western modernity, were falling into barbarism. Civilised people became barbarians, while a small rural nation seemed to represent Right and Justice. This denunciation, sometimes supported by accounts of atrocities, was, however, based first of all on a question of principles. Compassion was more important than information (new weapons, massacres, even the theme of torture, to which only the intelligentsia of a future postwar era would be sensitive). Even those who, like André Chevrillon, maintained their full sympathy for the old civilisation that England had embodied in the eyes of the world, wrote a good number of texts, speeches and proclamations of all kinds, to extol the heroic courage of a small nation whose simplicity of life and insufficient civilisation had preserved it from the evils of Western decadence and corruption. It is not hard to imagine all that French nationalist discourse managed to embroider on this theme. Everyone knew that President Kruger and General Kronje spat on the ground,[36] and that in Transvaal, as Pierre Mille remarked,[37] there was 'neither painting nor sculpture nor national literature nor music', that 'three-quarters' of European mental life was absent there; yet it was no less true that England, in trampling over the rights of this small nation, had sunk to a morally inferior rank. An anonymous contributor to the *Revue de Paris*, most likely an officer or high functionary, even took advantage of this moral degradation that had noticeably altered the degree of British civilisation to maliciously recall the fine lessons in morality that England had offered France at the high points of the *Affaire*: 'Quite recently, we received lessons in justice from the English people; abusing our moral crisis, they reminded us scornfully that above interests there is law, and above prejudices and animosities of caste there is humanity.'[38]

Scarcely was the Dreyfus Affair at an end when the defeated party launched a new combat, seizing the weapons of their adversaries with a view to obtaining a revenge that would at least be symbolic. This mobilisation has been somewhat obscured. But it was no less important, despite a situation very noticeably different from that dominated by the unfolding of the Affair. There were few adversaries to oppose the commitment of nationalist intellectuals in support of the cause of the South African republics. On 3 November 1899, the Paris municipal council adopted a proposal of Roger Lambelin, and a further one of John Labusquière, expressing its full sympathy for the Boers. Other municipal councils, such as those of Vannes and Rennes, likewise voted addresses and resolutions in support of the Boers.[39] Several committees and associations were formed, or turned their attention to supporting these heroic people. A students' committee was established in autumn 1899 to prepare to send reinforcements to the Boers and help to organise international military brigades.[40] A 'Committee for the South African Republics' was also established on 24 October 1899. Chaired by Lieutenant-Colonel Monteil, this attracted the entire elite of the anti-Dreyfusard intelligentsia, whose anglophobia in this case had a clear political significance. This time round, F. Coppée, P. Déroulède, E. Drumont, H. Rochefort, E. Judet and J. Lemaître praised everything they had been accustomed to denouncing in Dreyfusism: democracy, individualism and, more broadly, the modern world. On 15 December, a festival organised under the aegis at the Folies-Marigny theatre was the occasion of a triumph for General Mercier. Other demonstrations also took place, sometimes marked by physical confrontations. This was the Dreyfus Affair continued by other means, with a singular reappropriation of Dreyfusard values by the nationalists in the service of the Boer interest. After one of these meetings, organised at the Tivoli-Vaux-Hall, which was violently disrupted by 'anarchists' and at which M. Barrès and F. Coppée were star speakers, H. Rochefort even agreed to take internationalist values into account:

> What was at issue there was not, for some 'forty pieces of silver', to cancel by terror the acquittal of their Dreyfus, to whom these prefectural assassins owed such rich fare: the traitor of Rennes, of Devil's Island and elsewhere had no part in this affair. The chief argument that these guilty men used against us was their internationalism. Now, the meeting two days ago showed that we can be just as internationalist as them, since the evening's programme was to be completely devoted to a discussion not of the interests of France, but of the struggle under way between England and the South African republics.[41]

The year 1900 saw the high point of all these initiatives. Meetings in support of the Boers, subscriptions and petitions, all flourished as never before. On 5 March, according to a police report, a 'Comité français du Transwaal', very close to the nationalists, managed to attract five hundred people. The 'savages', it was declared, were 'not on the side of the Boers' but on the other side, and the meeting dispersed to cries of 'Vivent les Boers!' and 'Vive la République!' along with 'Down with the Jews!' and 'Down with Loubet!'[42] On 1 April, so-called 'Femmes françaises' published beneath a petition 'for the Boers' an initial list of signatures of women, under the names of their husbands: Victor Bérard, Paul Bert, Armand Colin, Albert Dumont, Victor Duruy, Pierre Foncin, Ernest Lavisse, etc. This engagement of women, a very sensitive point, came in response to the publicity there had been on the participation of Boer women in the fighting and their decisive role in the war. At the end of May, the 'Alliance des savants et philanthropes', chaired by Emile Burnouf, demanded that Delcassé should intervene with England. The resurgence of the Dreyfus Affair was again shown very clearly in the style of subscription launched by L'Intransigeant in March 1900 with the aim of presenting a sword to General Kronje. As with the 'Monument Henry', the subscribers accompanied their gift with a phrase justifying their gesture.[43] The English now occupied the place of the Jew (without the Jew having completely disappeared), and every possible combination and formula of hatred was represented, just as with the 'Monument Henry'.

We have seen how speaking of the other is often to refer to oneself. The crisis in relations between France and England at the turn of the century is an example of this. It enabled accounts to be settled, especially those of the Dreyfus Affair. It also served as an argument for other causes: the initial success of the Boers, for example, could be adduced in favour of a militia army. Comparison is stretched here. With all these limitations, as a former colonel of the second Irish brigade in Transvaal remarked, making his own contribution to this French debate:

> What an absurdity in this reasoning: the Boer militias have done such great things, so a militia would be sufficient for the defence of France! The Boer militia, by their education and their whole style of life, of which we have the equivalent neither in France nor elsewhere, are better trained for essential parts of the soldier's profession than are soldiers in regular armies. A European militiaman could never compare with a Boer militiaman.[44]

The second interest of a crisis like this is that it enables an active cultural model of conflict situations to be put to the test. During these four years, French intellectuals worked to construct an enemy figure, a procedure they employed again a few years later against a different enemy. But with one slight difference. The absence of military confrontation, even if for a few months this seemed to be close, lowered the stakes. Relations were never broken off, and disagreement did not put an end to civility: André Chevrillon insisted on this point, keeping his English 'friends'.[45] It was thus possible to rapidly emerge from the crisis and re-establish a normal regime of relations once the need for this was felt. In the German case, of course, the outcome was quite different.

Notes

1 Cf. E. Demolins, *Boers et Anglais: où est le droit?* (Paris: Firmin Didot, 1900).
2 For example: 'Great Britain is worth taking as an example for us in financial matters. There is no better proof of the support of this than the story of the English debt. Though the oldest of those weighing on civilised peoples today, it is none the less diminishing more rapidly than any other in Europe'; R.-G. Lévy, 'La dette anglaise', *Revue des Deux Mondes* (15 September 1898), 277.
3 See F. Brunetière, 'La littérature européenne au XIXe siècle', *Revue des Deux Mondes* (1 December 1899), 643: 'They are in the history of modern literature the "first poets of nature", as the Dutch were the first painters.' See Henry Davray, in his column 'Lettres anglaises' in *Mercure de France* (February 1900), 549: 'How can those who know its literature not have a deep and faithful sympathy for England? Is there not, over and above political circum-

stances, a domain in which minds that are neither narrow nor superficial can meet each other?'

4 Such as this song, 'Lettre de Marianne à Félix: vive la Russie, milord!', first published in September 1895 in 2,000 copies, according to police sources (Archives de la Préfecture de Police: APP, BA/1071):

'Oh my dear husband
I have to tell you
That you're about to do
Something really stupid.
For it'll make me mad
To see you accept
The invitation (*twice*)
Of perfidious Albion.

'The Englishman has always been
The enemy of France,
Rejoicing secretly
Whenever I'm in pain.
Far from helping us
He'd be glad to kill us off (*twice*)
You mustn't go!

'Don't you have enough
With the whole of France,
Without looking for success
As far away as England.
My heart would grieve
If you made eyes
At Victoria (*twice*)
Yes! You can do better than that!

'Don't you see, the Englishman
Is only a false friend.
I beg you to let them go,
Them and their lord mayor,
Their funny ambassador
Who comes with his baton
To secretly sound you out (*twice*)
Before inviting you!

'If you find things
Too hot here
Go to Nevsky
For a change of scene.
Despite the long journey
It's a nice idea
For surely Nicholas (*twice*)
Will open his arms wide.

> 'Felix, my dear
> Since our marriage
> In our single sky
> There's not been a cloud.
> But if you do me wrong
> Though I love you very much
> I warn you, old man (*twice*)
> It's all over with us!'

5 F. Charmes, 'Chronique de la quinzaine', *Revue des Deux Mondes* (1 October 1898), 715–16.
6 A. Filon, 'Le théoricien de l'impérialisme anglais: Sir J. R. Seeley', *Revue des Deux Mondes* (1 June 1898), 594.
7 Théodore de Wyzewa, 'La correspondance d'un préraphaélite anglais', *Revue des Deux Mondes* (15 February 1898).
8 'Chronique de la Quinzaine', *Revue des Deux Mondes* (1 March 1898), 240.
9 A. Chevrillon, 'L'opinion anglaise et la guerre', *Revue de Paris* (15 August 1900), 681.
10 A. Chevrillon, 'L'opinion anglaise et la guerre', *Revue de Paris* (1 September 1900), 151–2.
11 For example, G. Valbert, 'Le jugement d'un Anglais sur la France politique', *Revue des Deux Mondes* (1 June 1898).
12 H. Davray, 'Lettres anglaises', *Mercure de France* (September 1898), 861.
13 A. Fouillée, 'L'individualisme et le sentiment social en Angleterre', *Revue des Deux Mondes* (1 October 1898), 528.
14 A. Fouillée, 'L'individualisme et le sentiment social', p. 530.
15 A. Fouillée, 'L'individualisme et le sentiment social', p. 532.
16 A. Fouillée, 'L'individualisme et le sentiment social', p. 542.
17 A. Fouillée, 'L'individualisme et le sentiment social', p. 527.
18 A. Fouillée, 'L'individualisme et le sentiment social', p. 537–8.
19 A. Fouillée, 'L'individualisme et le sentiment social', p. 554.
20 A. Chevrillon, 'L'opinion anglaise et la guerre', *Revue de Paris* (1 September 1900), 147.
21 Editorial in *Le Rappel*, 29 August 1900, 'L'anniversaire'.
22 E. Lavisse, 'France et Angleterre: à Sir Charles Dilke', *Revue de Paris* (1 February 1899), 481.
23 E. Lavisse, 'Précautions contre l'Angleterre', *Revue de Paris* (1 January 1900) 211–24.
24 V. Bérard, 'L'Angleterre et l'empire du monde', *Revue de Paris* (15 January 1899), 370.
25 G. Valbert, 'Un Anglais qui aimait la France', *Revue des Deux Mondes* (1 November 1898), 224.
26 F. Charmes, 'Chronique de la quinzaine', *Revue des Deux Mondes* (15 December 1899), 953.
27 F. Charmes, 'Chronique de la quinzaine', *Revue des Deux Mondes* (1 August 1899), 708.

28 F. Charmes, 'Chronique de la quinzaine', *Revue des Deux Mondes* (15 November 1899), 468.
29 F. de Pressensé, 'Gladstone', *Revue des Deux Mondes* (1 July 1898), 48.
30 A. Chevrillon, 'Rudyard Kipling', *Revue de Paris* (1 April 1899), 623.
31 Anonymous, 'Les descentes en Angleterre', *Revue des Deux Mondes* (15 March 1899).
32 A. Fouillée, 'Races latines', *Revue des Deux Mondes* (1 December 1899), 580–1.
33 A. Chevalley, 'La poésie belliqueuse en Angleterre', *Revue de Paris* (1 December 1898), 675.
34 V. Bérard, 'L'Angleterre et le panbritannisme', *Revue de Paris* (15 December 1899), 871–2.
35 F. Charmes, 'Chronique de la quinzaine', *Revue des Deux Mondes* (15 October 1899), 957.
36 A. Chevrillon, 'L'opinion anglaise et la Guerre', *Revue de Paris* (1 September 1900), 161.
37 P. Mille, 'Les Boers: essai de psychologie sociale', *Revue de Paris* (15 June 1900), 695.
38 Anonymous, 'L'Angleterre et le Transvaal', *Revue de Paris* (1 November 1899), 1.
39 *L'Eclair*, 28 November 1899.
40 G. Bourdon, 'Pour les Boers', *Le Figaro*, 9 November 1899.
41 *L'Intransigeant*, 24 December 1899.
42 Police report of 6 March 1900, APP, BA /1551. According to another report of 30 November 1900 (BA/ 54), the visit of President Loubet to President Kruger, while the latter was staying in France, led to cries of 'Vive Loubet!' when the French president arrived.
43 'Down with the hypocritical and grasping English!', 'A group of friends of the Boers who would like to see the last Englishman strangled with the entrails of the last Jewish financier!', '40,000 English, 4,000 men' (*L'Intransigeant*, 1 March 1900); likewise, 'For a Republic without Jews!', 'Several anglophobes from Crie', 'Transvaal for the Boers, France for the French!', 'Shame on the gin drinkers', 'Let's go to Transvaal to revenge Fashoda', 'Belaygue, an old anti-Dreyfusard socialist', 'Long live Rochefort! Down with Jaurès', 'Two anti-Semites, friends of the Boers', 'An enemy of the English since Fashoda', 'Long live Déroulède! Down with Shameful Loubet', 'A group of Bon Marché workers, admirers of the Boers', 'Alexandre F., grandson of an Englishman', 'An anti-Dreyfusard Alsatian', 'Three anglophobe cyclists', 'A French patriot and admirer of the Boers', 'An Alsatian and a Savoyard anglophobe', 'Down with government Yiddery' (11th list, *L'Intransigeant*, 17 March 1900).
44 S. Wilson, 'The Henry Subscription 1898–99', in *Ideology and Experience: Antisemitism in France at the Time of the Dreyfus Affair* (Rutherford: Fairleigh Dickinson University Press, 1982), pp. 125–78 and C. Prochasson, 'Un retour aux sources: l'antisémitisme au temps de l'Affaire', *Jean Jaurès: Cahiers trimestriels*, 137 (July–September 1995), 53–8.
45 André Chevrillon, 'L'opinion anglaise et la guerre', *Revue de Paris* (1 September 1900), 698.

14

Homosexual networks and activist strategies from the late nineteenth century to 1939

FLORENCE TAMAGNE

In the late nineteenth century, when the first activist homosexual movements got under way in Germany, homosexual demands in France and Great Britain were essentially confined to certain intellectual circles, which helped open the debate on homosexuality by speech and writing, as well as by the example of their lifestyle; it was in this way that they sought to influence public opinion in a more liberal direction. The situation, however, was not the same in France, where homosexuality had no longer been a legal offence since the Revolution and the penal code of 1810, and in England, where repression had been intensified following the Labouchère amendment of 1885.[1]

Any study of the commitment of 'homosexual' intellectuals, however, raises a number of methodological problems, in terms of how to approach intellectual milieus, and the specific features of the field of gay and lesbian studies. Unable to expand on these here, I would at least like to mention two such problems. The first concerns the use of the term 'intellectuals', which I use here in a broad sense, choosing to define them, in a perspective more Anglo-Saxon than French, as professional creators or distributors of cultural goods, although figures such as André Gide fall more into the French model of the committed intellectual. The second concerns the use of the term 'homosexual' (male or female), from both a historical and a philosophical perspective. Chronologically, we should recall that the term was only coined in 1869,[2] and took a long time to enter general usage, having to compete with other terms whose origins were variously historical ('pederast'), scientific ('invert'), activist ('Uranian') or slang ('queen'). From the philosophical angle, and in the light of queer theory as particularly initiated by the works of Michel Foucault,[3] it appears that the designation 'homosexual' may be perceived as limitative and judgemental, even plain wrong. It should be evident that in referring to André Gide, for example, as a 'homosexual' intellectual, we have no intention of reducing his life, work and political commitment simply to a sexual dimension. In the same way, such a designation does not necessarily imply the acknowledgement of a particular identity or self-awareness as a 'homosexual'. Care must accordingly be taken not to see in the use of the term, which I prefer to employ as adjective rather than noun, more than a formal usage, intended to indicate the actuality of individuals' sexual practices at a particular moment, and the discourse that may have referred to them.[4]

In this perspective, I have chosen to study the forms of homosexual commitment in intellectual circles from three underlying angles. Can we distinguish forms of sociability that are specific to homosexual intellectuals? Are there particular models of homosexual commitment in France and in Britain? Can a link be made between homosexuality and political commitment?

Homosexual intellectual networks: generational examples and cultural transfer

The figure of the homosexual intellectual was forged, in the late nineteenth century, with reference to two traditions: on the one hand, that of the decadent aesthete; on the other, that of the pederast.

The decadent tradition, with roots not just in France and England, but also in Austria, has frequently been associated with homosexuality. The parallel, however, is not without a certain ambiguity. Certainly, in avant-garde circles, the idea of decadence was associated with artistic and literary modernity, and became the symbol of a heightened sensitivity and refined aestheticism: this is 'Sappho 1900', the imagined and eroticised lesbian deriving both from Théophile Gautier's *Mademoiselle de Maupin* and Baudelaire's *Femmes damnées*, finding its embodiment in the 'muse of the violets', the poet Renée Vivien; on the male side, it is the feminised homosexual, the precious poseur, the deranged dandy always seeking new pleasures – Oscar Wilde, Aubrey Beardsley and Simeon Solomon in England, Jean Lorrain and Robert de Montesquiou in France. But the term 'decadent', carrying also negative connotations, was also often associated with the idea of degeneration. Medical literature denounced homosexuality as a debilitating perversion, along with neurosis and hysteria.[5] Cesare Lombroso, professor of psychiatry at Turin, equated homosexuality with criminality, while Max Nordau, one of his Hungarian disciples, linked together 'egomaniacs, decadents and aesthetes' in his book *Entartung* (*Degeneration*, 1895), as forming a menace to society and the power of the nation. In fact, as Alan Sinfield notes, the representations of homosexuality constructed at this time drew on notions that were highlighted by the Oscar Wilde trial: 'effeminacy, leisure, idleness, immorality, luxury, insouciance, decadence and aestheticism'.[6]

The pederastic tradition, on the other hand, harked back to antiquity, with more recent echoes in the Renaissance and Winckelmann. If reference to 'Socratic love' could be found well before the nineteenth century, it was in Hellenist circles, especially at the University of Oxford, that the process of justification and affirmation of homosexual desire came to be constructed. Walter Pater, in his *Studies in the History of the Renaissance* (1873), opened the way, albeit in a veiled fashion, to a specific homosexual culture, by reclaiming the cult of beauty and of masculine youth as an artistic ideal. John Addington Symonds, likewise, in his *Studies of the Greek Poets* (also 1873), whose few homosexual allusions cost him the Chair of Poetry at Oxford, developed his analysis of pederasty in ancient Greece in *A Problem in Greek Ethics* (1883), privately printed in an edition of ten copies. He was particularly eager to distinguish virile comradeship and noble love, which elevated both lover and beloved and formed the basis of national unity, from sensual love concerned only with the satisfaction of the needs of the flesh.

This distinction, which recalls Plutarch's *Dialogue on Love*, found a further echo on the eve of the First World War, with the secret society of the Apostles which had been founded in Cambridge in 1820, and counted among its members such illustrious names as Bertrand Russell, Lytton Strachey, E. M. Forster and John Maynard Keynes. The Apostles, in a neo-Platonic perspective, defined the love of boys as the highest form of love that could be experienced (the so-called 'higher sodomy'), and proclaimed a link between homosexuality and intelligence. Their reflections – not, of course, devoid of elitism or misogyny – were taken up and developed by the Bloomsbury Group. These theories of sexuality and human relationships, proclaimed in opposition to Victorian morality, had further origins in the group of Neo-Pagans, young people who gathered before the First World War around the poet Rupert Brooke, and at the home of Edward Carpenter, theorist of socialism and homosexuality, as well as in the philosophy of G. E. Moore. The main contribution Bloomsbury brought to the question of homosexuality, however, was a new freedom of language and lifestyle: homosexuality and bisexuality were the norm, and both change of lovers and exchange of partners were perfectly tolerated.[7] If a certain caution still remained – the homosexuality of Forster or Keynes was not publicly bruited about[8] – Bloomsbury nonetheless served as a model for a second generation of homosexual intellectuals born between 1900 and 1910. Including such major figures as W. H. Auden, Christopher Isherwood and Stephen Spender in England, and René Crevel and Daniel Guérin in France, these were distinguished by their greater sexual freedom and their more political approach to homosexuality.[9]

Generational encounters, cultural exchanges and interactions were common at this time between homosexual intellectual networks in France and Britain. London and Paris – but above all Berlin – were at the heart of such cultural transfers.[10]

In the early years of the century, it was Paris that especially formed a centre of attraction for the homosexual and lesbian elite, gathered in the salon of Winnaretta Singer, princesse de Polignac, a lesbian married to Edmond de Polignac, who was likewise homosexual. Of American origin, Winnaretta Singer knew the Anglo-Saxon world very well: at her home, the comte de Montesquiou and Marcel Proust rubbed shoulders with Oscar Wilde, Lord Alfred Douglas and Henry James. In this cosmopolitan milieu, scandals had major repercussions that show the limited unity of these homosexual networks: the Polignac salon suffered the blows of the Oscar Wilde trial in 1895, the suicide of Alfred Krupp in 1903, and the Eulenburg affair in 1907.[11] Another American, the poet Natalie Barney, received 'Left Bank amazons' at 20 rue Jacob,[12] bringing together several generations of lesbians who included Colette, Renée Vivien, the courtesan Liane de Pougy, Romaine Brooks, Marguerite Yourcenar, Sylvia Beach and Adrienne Monnier. Radclyffe Hall and Una Troubridge also visited, even though Hall – who recognised herself in the definition of 'congenital inversion' developed by Havelock Ellis in his book *Sexual Inversion* (1898) and laid claim to her masculinity – scarcely matched the myth of the decadent, fragile and feminine lesbian cultivated by Natalie Barney.

After Paris, it was Berlin in the interwar years that became a pole of attraction for French and, above all, for British homosexuals on account of the abundance of meeting-places and the relative police tolerance there.[13] This provided the opportunity for some of their number to discover the German homosexual movement: André Gide, René Crevel and Christopher Isherwood visited Magnus Hirschfeld's celebrated Institute for Sexual Research, founded in 1919. But, for all that, the German model found only a limited echo, and still less so in France, where the attempt by Gustave Beyria and Gaston Lestrade (an office worker and a postal employee respectively) to establish a homosexual magazine – *Inversions*, in 1924 – met with scarcely any support at all from intellectual and literary circles, with rare exceptions such as the Surrealist artist Claude Cahun.

Awareness and identity: the intellectual as homosexual activist

Whereas in Germany the defence of homosexual rights was based on mass activism, in France and Britain the homosexual voice was borne by intellectuals who, to a greater or lesser extent, chose to affirm their singularity through their work or their personal experience.

This message could be individual or collective. In France, homosexual affirmation took the form of individual commitment, and the debate on homosexuality was almost entirely confined within the literary sphere, a situation that is partly explained by the absence of police repression,[14] as well as by the French intellectual tradition, in which the writer is a privileged conduit for public and private passions. The publication of Marcel Proust's *Sodome et Gomorrhe* in 1921, therefore, could appear as the point of departure for this debate, especially in the press.[15] Scattered homosexual allusions were already to be found in *Du côté de chez Swann*, *A l'ombre des jeunes filles en fleur* and *Le Côté de Guermantes*, though these were fairly muted. But by disclosing the homosexuality of his hero, baron de Charlus, Proust forced the critic to tackle head-on a subject that many at the time still viewed with repugnance. Besides, by offering a regular collation of medical theories of his time, Proust revealed to an ignorant readership the various research that had already been popularised in Germany by the sexologist and activist Magnus Hirschfeld. However, by presenting 'inverts' as an 'accursed race' descending from the Sodomites of old, Proust perpetuated the image of a homosexual subculture haunted by shame and secrecy, linked by mysterious bonds that were invisible to the uninitiated, very similar indeed to certain homophobic stereotypes. The 'self-hatred' that some have read in his work,[16] even if it should be seen in perspective, was singularly denounced by another herald of the homosexual cause in France, André Gide, whose writings were to be decisive for several generations of homosexuals.[17] Gide's own homosexual activism, however, was not without its hesitations and reserves. It was the publication of his *Corydon*, in 1924,[18] that made him into the spokesman of French homosexuals, a situation that he had neither foreseen nor really desired. Wanting to reply both to Proust and to Rémy de Gourmont, who had devoted a chapter to 'the question of aberrations' in his book *Physique de l'amour: essai sur l'instinct sexuel* (1903), Gide's book should be read above all as a defence of pederasty, as inscribed in the Greek tradition, and an attempt to place homosexuality in a cultural perspective, opposing the masculine aesthetic of Sparta to the artificial and 'counterfeit' attraction of woman, and associating it with the most glorious epochs of artistic creation. By this means, if it offered homosexuals the possibility of constructing a positive self-image, it excluded a section of them – the 'shameful Uranians' – who could not recognise themselves in this aristocratic and virile reading of homosexuality. Following *Corydon* in 1926 with his novel *Les Faux-monnayeurs* and in 1928 his autobiographical *Si le grain ne meurt*, Gide took a further step forward in homosexual commitment: in this last book, he abandoned the mask – however transparent – of *Corydon* and confessed his own homosexuality, analysing the path he had taken and reflecting on his assumption of a specific identity. Though it can be read as both justification and provocation – Gide taking pleasure in shocking the reader by describing his gratifying sexual encounters with young boys – and though Gide has been criticised for his blindness in respect of both class and racial inequalities in a context of sexual tourism,[19] *Si le grain ne meurt* had the merit, nonetheless, of showing that homosexuality was neither a burden nor a sickness, and that it was possible to live one's homosexuality in a very different fashion to shame and silence.

A favourite target of the reactionaries,[20] Gide was indignant at the lack of courage shown by his contemporaries, who let him battle alone in the front line: 'X. and Y. go about repeating that they are fed up with pretense, that they have made up their mind to speak frankly henceforth, to brave opinion, to burn their bridges behind them, etc. But they are not burning anything at all; they are very careful not to. The courage of which they boast costs them nothing of what they continue to cling on to. And in the new book they have just produced they have taken great care that their confessions should be of such a sort and so speciously hidden that only the most alert readers can read them between the lines; of such a sort that they will have nothing to retract if later on they become converted or aim at the Academy'.[21] In actual fact, the new visibility of homosexuals in literature had triggered a wave of debate in the French press. After an angry article by the literary critic Paul Souday in *Le Temps*, the magazine *Les Marges* published an investigation into 'homosexuality in literature' on 15 March 1926.[22] Some contributors indicated, with regret, the emancipatory role played by writers: Gérard Bauer, for example, wrote that 'Marcel Proust was like a Messiah for this little people, and through a kind of magic wand, freed them from their slavery.' Others, such as the Communist writer Henri Barbusse, saw only a proof of social degeneration, which he attributed significantly enough to a 'decadent phalanx of intellectuals'.

This denunciation of intellectuals as a class, rather than certain individuals, links up in a striking way with the British position, even if it is possible, as in France, to highlight some emblematic figures, Oscar Wilde being particularly symbolic.[23] If we have already indicated the role of the Bloomsbury Group, it is necessary to stress its moral commitment in the great scandals of English puritanism of the interwar period. In 1928, for example, when a homophobic campaign was launched against the publication of Radclyffe Hall's book *The Well of Loneliness*, a number of homosexual intellectuals including E. M. Forster and Virginia Woolf agreed to give evidence in support of the author, despite their reservations about the work's literary quality.[24] Bertrand Russell discussed the trial at the third congress of the World League for Sexual Reform, held in London in 1928, in a paper titled 'The Taboo on Sex Knowledge', in which he denounced the hypocrisy of British censorship. The debate was also taken up in the British Society for the Study of Sex Psychology, an association inspired by Magnus Hirschfeld, whose honorary president was Edward Carpenter. The BSSP, which had some two hundred members, played no more than a marginal role in the country's social and political life, but its influence was far from negligible, especially in progressive intellectual circles. Its members included G. B. Shaw, E. M. Forster, Maurice Eden and Cedar Paul, Vyvyan Holland, and the playwright Harley Granville-Barker. Radclyffe Hall and Una Troubridge, Bertrand and Dora Russell, were also closely connected with it.

In fact, while the influence of homosexual intellectuals is difficult to quantify, its presence is shown by the repeated attacks made on them. The diffusion of a regular 'cult of homosexuality'[25] in the 1920s, from its origins in the culture of the public schools[26] and great universities, and popularised after the Second World War in the autobiographical novels of Christopher Isherwood (*Down There on a Visit*) and Evelyn Waugh (*Brideshead Revisited*), aroused strong reaction from certain pamphleteers (echoed, of course, in the daily press), who happily denounced Oxford as a nest of 'degenerates' and 'effeminates': 'Perverts' Parties are a University feature. Details are unprintable and I hope to publish them shortly. Homosexuality and lesbianism ... flourish especially among the super-intelligentsia.'[27] In similar fashion, the visibility of homosexuals in certain professions, such as publishing, radio and diplomacy, helped sharpen a feeling of distrust and jealousy towards intellectuals, who were accused of setting up an informal network of influence designed to help young homosexuals on the social ladder. John Lehmann, who published William Plomer, E. M. Forster, Christopher Isherwood and Stephen Spender, and J. R. Ackerley, who as literary and art editor of the *Listener* had helped the career of various lovers, were favourite targets of such criticisms: 'You see how it is that these elegant unemployables get into the higher journalism, and even the academic world, and how reputations are made – you have only to get the right people, whom you already know or can get introductions to, to write the right kind of thing about you in the right places. ... We who are in the habit of asking how such evidently unqualified reviewers as fill the literary weeklies ever got into the profession need ask no longer. They turn out to have been "the most fashionable boy in the school", or to have had a feline charm or a sensual mouth and long eye-lashes.'[28]

Fantasies about the existence of a 'freemasonery of vice' were not born in the 1920s, and the existence of any real homosexual solidarity is a moot point. In reality, it was by coming from the same social background, having studied together, frequenting the same families and having the same friends, that these intellectuals were able to help one another. What struck outside observers, however, was the sexual specificity and the sometimes tendentious character of recruitment, which they believed was not always conducted on the basis of professional criteria. The ties that certain of these intellectuals had with the parties of the Left, moreover, raised the question of their political commitment.

Homosexuality and political commitment

Should one suppose there is any link between sexual and political orientation? It is impossible, in the absence of sources, to answer such a question. The statistics kept by political parties do not mention the sexual character of their members, no more than homosexual organisations ever tried to analyse their own members' political tendencies. The German movements, which were the most well organised, presented themselves as apolitical, though their leaderships at least were close to the Sozialdemokratisches Partei Deutschlands (SPD) and Kommunistische Partei Deutschlands (KPD). This does not imply, however, that all of their members voted for the Left, even if the movement's slogans requested them to do so. In analysing the relationship of homosexuals to politics, therefore, all we have to go on is individual testimony, basically that of intellectuals, who in their majority came from the middle and upper classes. One possible angle of approach would be to study the reasons for the commitment of certain intellectuals in the 1920s and 1930s to the Socialist and Communist parties,[29] a commitment that they justified in part on the basis of their homosexual identity.

One of the arguments frequently invoked is the existence of a sense of solidarity with the working class, perceived both as oppressed minority and object of desire. The working-class fantasy that is a recurrent theme of homosexual literature between the two wars, can be interpreted simultaneously as the rejection of a puritanical upbringing, the desire to flout the social and sexual conventions of the bourgeoisie, and an attempt to rehabilitate the body through the valorisation of virile strength and manual work. If the quest for sexual partners outside one's own class was not something specific to the 1920s (nor indeed to homosexual relations),[30] the theme of the 'ideal friend' that plays so notable a part in *Maurice*[31] and implies a relationship of equality between the intellectual and his companion, would seem characteristic of the period, despite its illusory aspect. The attraction of the working-class boy derives both from an idealisation of the working-class world, and from the hope that love will be able to overcome class obstacles. The homosexual intellectual often thinks of himself as an outsider, and by this choice of partner places himself deliberately outside the pale. Stephen Spender thus recalls: 'I was able to speak to outcasts as one who had made himself an outcast',[32] while in France, Daniel Guérin wrote: 'It was not just from amorous considerations that I invited Marcel; also involved in this was an appetite for social transgression. I launched a challenge to my class.'[33] In the same way, the predilection for working-class partners of German origin, to be found in Auden, Isherwood and Spender, functioned as a manifesto against a puritanical and rigid England: if this fraternisation with the former enemy also betrayed the guilt felt at having been too young for the Great War, it had as corollary a declared pacifism that had its roots in the demand for a homosexual relationship. Christopher Isherwood's reasoning here is enlightening on the influence that the homosexual variable could play in the formation of political consciousness: 'Suppose, Christopher now said to himself, I have a Nazi army at my mercy. I can blow it up by pressing a button. The men in that army are notorious for torturing and murdering civilians – all except for one of them, Heinz. Will I press the button? No – wait: Suppose I know that Heinz himself, out of cowardice or moral infection, has become as bad as they are and takes part in all their crimes? Will I press the button, even so? Christopher's answer, given without the slightest hesitation, was: Of course not. That was a purely emotional reaction. But it helped Christopher think his way through to the next proposition. Suppose that army goes into action and has just one casuality, Heinz himself. Will I press the button now and destroy his fellow-criminals? No emotional reaction this time, but a clear answer, not to be evaded: Once I have refused to press that button because of Heinz, I can never press it. Because every man in that army could be somebody's Heinz and I have no right to play favourites. Thus Christopher was forced to recognize himself as a pacifist – although by an argument which he could only admit to with the greatest reluctance.'[34]

As a 'deviant' sexuality, homosexuality justified a stand at odds with the mainstream, since, to be homosexual meant being outside the pale, to support a party of the far Left was simply to push this logic of exclusion to its limit, to take up the accusations of right-thinking people who saw homosexuality as a potential danger, a foreign body in the heart of the nation. 'I came to socialism via phallicism,'[35] Daniel Guérin symbolically wrote. The hopes raised by Soviet legislation[36] helped cultivate the myth of a natural communion between homosexuality and revolution, and explain to a certain degree the support that intellectuals such as Auden and Spender gave to the Communist Party. The unpleasant term 'Homintern'[37] applied to the Auden group is symbolic in this sense: simultaneously stigmatisation of a network of homosexual sociability and denunciation of its left-wing sympathies, the expression served to reveal the fantasies of plotting and treason that fuelled homophobic prejudice.[38]

Sympathy for Communism declined after 1934, following the recriminalisation of homosexuality in the USSR and its denunciation as a 'fascist perversion'. Christopher Isherwood recalls how, along with his friends, he tried to minimise the importance of this development, on the grounds that similar laws existed in Britain and the United States.[39] But the socialist myth had been shattered: 'Yes – but if Communists claim that their system is juster than capitalism, doesn't that make their injustice to homosexuals less excusable and their hypocrisy even viler? [Christopher] now realized he must dissociate himself from the Communists, even as a fellow-traveller. He might, in certain situations, accept them as allies but he could never regard them as comrades. He must never again give way to embarrassment, never deny the rights of his tribe, never apologize for its existence, never think of sacrificing himself masochistically on the altar of that false god of totalitarians, the Greatest Good of the Greatest Number – whose priests are alone empowered to decide what "good" is.'[40]

From now on, homosexual identity was clearly proclaimed. If it had been strong enough to affect political choices, and able to modify class behaviour, it defined before all else its own survival. Hitler's seizure of power in 1933 and the establishment of Stalinism in the USSR were both fundamental threats for homosexuals, putting an end to their hopes of emancipation. For certain intellectuals, such as Christopher Isherwood, political commitment now also had to follow from homosexual commitment: 'As a homosexual, [Christopher] had been wavering between embarrassment and defiance. He became embarrassed when he felt that he was making a selfish demand for his individual rights at a time when only group action mattered. He became defiant when he made the treatment of the homosexual a test by which every political party and government must be judged. His challenge to each one of them was: "All right, we've heard your liberty speech. Does that include us or doesn't it?"'[41]

Study of homosexual intellectual circles lends itself particularly well to comparative analysis. Homosexual networks were often cosmopolitan, operating in fact via transfers – migration, exile, travel – which gave the occasion for both encounters and discussions, indeed beyond just France and Great Britain. If it is possible to distinguish a French model that is fundamentally individualistic from a English homosocial model, each different again from a German model that is more communitarian, there was much interaction, including in the political field: the interest of left parties for homosexual intellectuals is symptomatic in this respect.

The rise of Nazism, then the Second World War, contributed to new cultural transfers. Faced with the destruction of the German homosexual scene and the lifelessness of the English, France became the pole of attraction for homosexuals. Others chose to emigrate to the United States: the route taken by W. H. Auden, Christopher Isherwood, and Benjamin Britten. After the war, the destruction of the European homosexual scene and the return to order of the Cold War years made the United States into the new centre of gravity of homosexual activism. Christopher Isherwood became in the 1970s a very active member of the homosexual liberation movement in America, serving as a link between the intellectual commitment of the 1920s and 30s, and communitarian activism.

Notes

1 'Buggery' was punishable by a death sentence until 1861, when this was replaced by imprisonment from ten years to life. In 1885, the Criminal Law Amendment Act, incorporating the so-called 'Labouchère amendment', provided for a penalty of up to two years' imprisonment for 'gross indecency' between two males. Conviction for homosexual offences was now far more systematic, with a notable rise in numbers.
2 'Homosexual' was used for the first time by the Hungarian writer Karoly Maria Kertbeny, in a memoir addressed to the Prussian Ministry of Justice, demanding the abolition of penal laws on 'unnatural acts'.
3 See M. Foucault, *The History of Sexuality*, vol. 1, *An Introduction* (Harmondsworth: Penguin, 1981); also J. Butler, *Bodies that Matter: On the Discursive Limits of 'Sex'* (Routledge: London and New York, 1993).
4 For convenience, I will stop putting 'homosexual' in apostrophes at this point.
5 See, for example, A. Tardieu, 'La Pédérastie' (1857), in François Cartier, *La Prostitution antiphysique* (Paris: Le Sycomore, 1981); and Richard von Krafft-Ebing, *Psychopathia Sexualis: eine klinische-forensische Studie* (Stuttgart: F. Euke, 1887).
6 A. Sinfield, *The Wilde Century* (London: Cassell, 1994), pp. 11–12.
7 On these questions, see, for example, R. Skidelsky, *J. M. Keynes, Hopes Betrayed 1883–1920* (London: Macmillan, 1983).
8 As is well-known, Forster was unwilling to publish his most explicit works during his lifetime, the novel *Maurice* as well as certain short stories. As a general rule, homosexuals of this generation, born in the 1870s and 1880s, still found it hard to affirm their sexuality positively. In France, Marcel

Jouhandeau never managed to reconcile his spiritual aspirations and his sexual life; his book *De l'abjection* (1939) is a frightful testimony of this self-refusal.

9 See 'Homosexuality and political commitment' later in this chapter.
10 See F. Tamagne, *Histoire de l'homosexualité en Europe: Berlin, Londres, Paris, 1919–1939* (Paris: Le Seuil, 2000).
11 See M. de Cossart, *Une Américaine à Paris, la princesse de Polignac et son salon 1865–1943* (Paris: Plon, 1979).
12 See S. Benstock, *Women of the Left Bank: Paris 1900–1940* (Austin: University of Texas Press, 1986).
13 See M. Bolle (ed.), *Eldorado: homosexuelle Frauen und Männer in Berlin 1850–1950, Geschichte, Alltag und Kultur* (Berlin: Frölich und Kaufmann, 1984), exhibition held at the Berlin Museum, 26 May–8 July 1984.
14 Though homosexuality as such was not a crime in French law, homosexuals could be subjected to formal police surveillance if they were suspected of endangering national security or undermining military honour. They could also be arrested under the charge of public offense against decency and immoral behaviour, notably in cases that involved minors. See Tamagne, *Histoire de l'homosexualité en Europe*.
15 See E. Ahlstedt, *La Pudeur en crise, un aspect de l'accueil d'A la recherche du temps perdu de Marcel Proust 1913–1930* (Paris: Jean Touzot Librairie, 1985).
16 See G. D. Painter, *Marcel Proust* (London: Chatto & Windus, 1989), 2 vols.
17 According to Gaston Gallimard, Gide supposedly said to Proust, 'You have set the question back fifty years,' to which Proust replied: 'I don't see any question, for me there are only individuals.' Cited by M. Erman, *Marcel Proust* (Paris: Fayard, 1994), p. 227.
18 A first version of *Corydon*, containing the two first dialogues and a section of the third, was printed anonymously in Bruges on 22 May 1911, under the name of C. R. D. N., in twelve copies. On 5 March 1920, a further twenty-one copies were printed. Only in May 1924 did *Corydon* appear publicly and in definitive form.
19 See H. Khelil, *Sens, Jouissance, tourisme, érotisme, argent dans deux fictions coloniales d'André Gide* (Tunis: La Nef, 1988).
20 Publications that attacked Gide's commitment to the homosexual cause included François Nazier's *L'Anti-Corydon* (1924) and an article by Marcel Réja titled 'La révolte des hannetons', published in *Mercure de France* on 1 March 1928 (these 'maybugs' supposedly representing the homosexuals multiplying in literature). 'Far from being sterile as we were led to believe,' Réja wrote, 'their unions seem remarkably prolific.'
21 8 December 1929; André Gide, *Journals*, ed. and trans. J. O'Brien (London: Secker & Warburg, vol. 2 (1947–51)), p. 85.
22 The magazine's editorial committee had drawn up a questionnaire, which was sent to several writers of the time. They were asked in particular if 'the homosexual preoccupation developed after the war of 1914–18' and whether 'the introduction of homosexual characters in literature could have

a damaging effect on morals and art'.
23 It is interesting to note that the French press, preferring to treat supposedly controversial topics by way of euphemism, was fond of using literary references. The critic Paul Souday, for example, wrote in *Le Temps* on 21 February 1924, reviewing the Lord Chelsea cycle by Abel Hermant: 'Lord Chelsea is thus a kind of English Charlus or an Oscar Wilde.'
24 The case was, however, lost in advance. Only Desmond MacCarthy was called to give evidence, and the book was banned in Britain. It was published in the United States, and in French translation by Gallimard. A play inspired by the book was staged in Paris in September 1928.
25 The expression was used by Noel Annan, in *Our Age: English Intellectuals Between the Wars, A Group Portrait* (New York: Random House, 1991).
26 See, for example, J. Gathorne-Hardy, *The Public School Phenomenon 1597–1977* (London: Hodder & Stoughton, 1977).
27 T. H. Harrisson, *Letter to Oxford* (Wyck: The Hate Press, 1933), p. 28.
28 Q. D. Leavis, cited by V. Cunningham, *British Writers in the Thirties* (Oxford: Oxford University Press, 1988), p. 149.
29 For want of space, I shall deal here only with homosexual commitment to the left in these decades. It is necessary to recall, however, that a certain number of homosexual intellectuals (male and female), such as Maurice Sachs, Radclyffe Hall and Natalie Barney, were close to fascism at this time. On these questions, see Tamagne, *Histoire de l'homosexualité en Europe*, and S. Benstock, 'Paris Lesbianism and the Politics of Reaction, 1900–1940', in M. B. Duberman, M. Vicinus and G. Chauncey Jr (eds), *Hidden from History: Reclaiming the Gay and Lesbian Past* (London: Penguin, 1991).
30 Oscar Wilde described the pleasure, tinged with sadomasochism, of 'feasting with panthers', and young errand boys (telegraph boys in particular), regularly fed the scandals of the Victorian age.
31 Forster's short stories 'Ansell' and 'Dr Woolacoot' are in the same vein.
32 S. Spender, *World Within World* (London: Faber & Faber, 1991), p. 119.
33 D. Guérin, *Autobiographie de jeunesse* (Paris: Belfond, 1972), p. 167.
34 C. Isherwood, *Christopher and His Kind* (London: Methuen, 1977), pp. 249–50.
35 D. Guérin, *Homosexualité et révolution* (Saint-Denis: Vent du ch'min, 1983), p. 44.
36 Homosexuality was decriminalised in Soviet Russia in 1918.
37 The expression was coined by Cyril Connolly and Maurice Bowra.
38 Similar accusations were relaunched, with increased violence, after the Second World War, in connection with the 'Cambridge spies'.
39 Isherwood's memoirs have to be treated with caution. By the time they were written, he was engaged in the homosexual rights movement, and perhaps unconsciously sought to justify former positions that might subsequently appear too timid.
40 Isherwood, *Christopher*, pp. 248–9.
41 Isherwood, *Christopher*, p. 248.

15

Ironies of war: intellectual styles and responses to the Great War in Britain and France

Jay Winter

I want to address a problem in comparative intellectual history. Why is it that the imaginative language in which most British intellectuals, writers and artists addressed the Great War was fundamentally different from that used by their French counterparts?[1] In this chapter, I want to summarise these differences and to provide a sketch of some of their origins. The basic argument is that British intellectuals privileged irony in a way that has informed the construction of a canon of war literature. This emphasis on irony is at the heart of war poetry and the war memoirs of the two postwar decades.

While irony is in no sense uniquely British in origin or nuance, it is nonetheless the dominant style of British thinking about the war, informing a set of attitudes which has been passed down to later generations. Nothing of the kind exists in France. This contrast is evident in the simple fact that the poetry of Wilfred Owen has never been translated en bloc into French.[2] The first translation of Siegfried Sassoon's poetry was rendered in French in 1987,[3] though a French edition of *Memoirs of a Fox-Hunting Man* was published in 1938.[4]

The absence of French versions of canonical British imaginative works on the war has led to a further deepening of the conceptual distance between later British and French versions of the cultural history of the conflict. It is hardly surprising that a country whose publishing industry found no place for the poetry of Owen and Sassoon would find no place for translations of the path-breaking works of Paul Fussell on *The Great War and Modern Memory*,[5] or of Samuel Hynes on *A War Imagined*,[6] both of which deal at length with the ironies of British war writing.

Another Anglo-Saxon work of scholarship has made it across the Channel. Modris Ekstein's *Rites of Spring* was translated into French a few years after its publication in English.[7] But this fact reinforces my overall argument, for Ekstein's book is primarily about the avant-garde. Think about Stravinsky's *Rites of Spring* or Diaghilev's choreography, or the uproar they created in Paris. No irony here.

In sum, I want to explore the landscape of a kind of cognitive dissonance between British and French imaginings of the Great War, imaginings whose differences persist to this day but whose origins lie at the beginning of the twentieth century. Layer upon layer of ironic meaning has been placed on the Great War, a war endured but not quite shared imaginatively by these two Allies. It is through an understanding of this aspect of what Raymond Williams called structures of feeling[8] that we can begin to appreciate how in very different ways the 1914–18 war became a crucial part of the distinctive cultural histories of Britain and France in the twentieth century.

The ironic temperament

The literature on the subject of irony is vast, but I want to focus here on two levels on which scholarly writing operates. The first deals with textual strategies which impart a tone to a conversation or a text; the second uses a more generalised sense of the term 'irony' as suggesting a temperament or a form of reflection. Another way of putting the point is to suggest that one location of irony is within literary history as a device central to certain representational practices, certain narrative strategies in prose or poetry. But, in addition, the notion of 'irony' implies an attitude, a stance – what Samuel Hynes calls a 'turn of mind'.[9]

Literary scholars have produced rich and learned works on the forms of ironic prose – the juxtaposition of anticipation and outcome, the existence of more than one meaning to a phrase or action, and the implicit bond between author and reader – over the heads of the characters – as to what those meanings are. There is much of importance here in the study of comparative intellectual history.[10]

I would like to focus on the second usage of the term 'irony', one that suggests its disruptive and disturbing playfulness. This interpretive strategy in no sense reduces irony to but one level of meaning or power; highlighting one facet of the subject simply helps frame a necessarily complicated set of issues in cultural history. Hutchens has put the point well about the kind of irony I would like to trace: irony as a certain kind of play. She urges us 'to see it as a sport, a game played for its own sake', but a game in which the ironist exhibits a 'curious detached enjoyment, even in the midst of making a serious case'.[11]

> Irony, though it may be directed toward an end, is in itself a sport – a sport the neat trickiness of which is felt to be enjoyed by the ironist for its own sake, quite apart from his purpose in employing it. (Here, incidentally, may be the reason why detachment is generally held to be a necessary element of irony, even though the ironist may be quite evidently making a case.)

Irony may therefore be seen as basically *the sport of bringing about a conclusion by indicating its opposite.*[12]

The difference between irony and deception is that the ironist has no advantage to gain by saying one thing and meaning another. The gain, so to speak, in the pose is that the ironist avoids seeing the world as a site of action where justice reigns, or could operate. Irony is an antidote to zealotry, to chauvinism, or even to moral certainty. No categorical imperatives here. On the contrary – *pace* Kant, lying is entirely justifiable. Why? Because something or someone is making a sport of human existence, and the language appropriate to that sport is irony.

This notion of irony is not merely verbal. Understood as a temperament, irony is always the work of an agent: someone expresses it, breathes it, lives it. It is both a grammar and a condition of existence. It is a way of representing both the self and the world, at some distance from each.

The importance of being earnest about the war: British responses

How did this sense of destiny as a sport, a game played for its own sake, translate into a stance central to many British representations of the Great War? Partly, the answer may be found in the structures of classical education and sport which moulded the British middle and upper classes in the second half of the nineteenth century and beyond. Partly the answer lay in the world of sociability that British men of all classes enjoyed in football leagues and the like in the prewar period. In part it was to defend that world of clubs and pubs and small solidarities that many of them joined up in the first place.

It is, therefore, hardly surprising that sporting metaphors litter soldiers' correspondence. After all, even though the Football League suspended its schedule in 1915, football continued on the other side of the Channel. A civilian army brought its civilian entertainments with it to the Western Front. Football leagues mushroomed in the base areas behind the lines, and offered some semblance of normality and physical exertion without the risk to life and limb that soldiers faced further up the line. There was nothing in the French army like this.

The conceit of turning war into sport and sport into war turned darker as the war went on. The 1st Battalion of the eighteenth London Regiment 'kicked off' the Battle of Loos with a football in 1915. A year later it was the 8th East Surreys turn to 'play the game'. Each of the four platoons of the company commanded by Captain W. P. Nevill went over the top with a football. He offered a prize to the first unit to reach the German lines. A neighboring battalion witnessed what happened. 'As the gunfire died away', recalled Private L. S. Price, 'I saw an infantryman climb onto the parapet into No Man's Land, beckoning others to follow. As he did so he kicked off a football; a good kick, the ball rose and traveled well towards the German line. That seemed to be the signal to advance.' Captain Nevill never got to hand over the prize: he was killed, but two of the footballs made it. One is in the National Army Museum in London; the other, at the Queen's Regiment Museum in Canterbury.[13]

Even a cursory glance at British intellectuals' responses to the war indicates how much literary accounts of the conflict deeply coloured by such sporting images. Sport created a familiar space in which the incongruities of war could be imagined. 'Have you forgotten yet', Siegfried Sassoon asked, 'that war's a bloody game?' Just the sort of thing for 'a fox-hunting man' turned into another kind of hunter by the outbreak of war. Irony riddles his account of the incident which won him the Military Cross, an honour he was later to hurl into the Mersey in protest at the never-ending character of the war. He encountered a squad of German infantrymen in a trench, hurled his grenades at them, and mused over the fact that they never knew they were fleeing from 'a single fool'. This kind of physical prowess and deception would not have been out of place on a playing field, but it became odd and even alarming when the stakes were dismemberment or mutilation. Irony here explodes heroic pretensions and the prose (and honours) that conventionally (and obscenely) accompany them.

Further ironies in Sassoon's war emerged directly out of his celebrated protest against it. Here the game pitted one well-connected junior officer against the entire general staff. Once more the 'single, solitary fool', Sassoon kicked off with a letter to his superior explaining why he couldn't return to his unit at the end of his leave. The war was insane and its continuation a crime. Through well-placed friends, the letter was printed in *The Times* and read into *Hansard*. The Army parried by declaring him mad. When he was posted to Craiglockhart Hospital outside of Edinburgh, he fought another duel, this time against a more sympathetic adversary, his attendant physician and psychologist, W. H. R. Rivers. Rivers tried to convince Sassoon that his duty lay in France, not in futile protest in Britain. To refuse to go back was selfish, not selfless; it was too close to cowardice for comfort. This got to Sassoon, who finally saw that the only way for him to protest further against the war was to go back to it, to stand alongside of the men he led, 'and in their tortured eyes/To find forgiveness'.

Consider the irony of Rivers's double-bind. A physician, honour-bound to do the sick no harm, was entrusted with the task of curing shell-shocked men and thereby returning them to the site of their injuries, where they were almost certain to face the horrors that had broken them in the first place. By healing men, he was killing them. What kind of sport is that? Rivers is neither a fool nor a charlatan. He is trapped in a game not of his making. And, together with Sassoon – who refers to Rivers by his real name in *Memoirs of an Infantry Officer* – Rivers is forced to confront the fact that someone or something is making a sport of their lives, their sense of honour, their common decencies, and those of the millions of men with whom they served or against whom they fought.

Sassoon's protest and Rivers's dilemma share one crucial feature. They have in common a deep sense of irony, which enables Sassoon to frame dissent, and Rivers to contain it. When all is said and done, they both play by the rules of the game. A game, after all, is a stylised encounter after which nothing happens; it is self-contained. When the game is over, life begins again, as it did for Sassoon and other patients in Craiglockhart, like the poet Wilfred Owen. He did not survive the war, but was killed a week before the Armistice. Another irony.

Other kinds of gamesmanship mark the irony in Robert Graves's approach to reality in his celebrated war memoir, *Goodbye to All That*: 'in 1916, when on leave in England after being wounded, I began an account of my first few months in France. Having stupidly written it as a novel, I have now to re-translate it into history.'[14] Real documents jostle with imaginary ones in the book in such a way as to mock anyone who tries to read it to find out 'what the war was really like', in a phrase which would have been perfectly at home in the language of his great-uncle, the German historian Leopold van Ranke. Captain Robert von Ranke Graves, proud British warrior against the Hun, is an irony in and of himself. Surely this lies behind his famous epigram that 'The memoirs of a man who went through some of the worst experiences of trench warfare are not truthful if they do not contain a high proportion of falsities'; only those who tell lies about the war can actually tell the truth. His ironic detachment, his status as a 'trickster', subverts the notion that any kind of history can be written about the war.[15]

There is irony and much more in these scattered instances of gallows humour, of laughter from the graveyards, which are repeated in many other British accounts of the war. It is their ironic tone which gives so many of them their detached and ambivalent character. The men who wrote them were soldier pacifists, men who told tales of war with pride, but did so in order to eviscerate the lies of those who had no idea how ugly war is. Robert Graves was proud of the regimental traditions of the Royal Welsh Fusiliers, but his memoir is hardly a celebration of its fate. By saying 'goodbye to all that', he was stating the opposite, and insisting that echoes of 'the game' would never vanish from their lives. Charles Carrington called this attitude 'the 1916 fixation'.[16] If anyone wrote memoirs for the purpose of putting memory to rest, he was in for a surprise. The war just wouldn't let you go. 'Once you have lain in her embrace,' Guy Chapman wrote, 'you can admit no other mistress'.[17]

The question as to whether the war was justified produced very mixed answers in the works of most British soldier memoirists. Most believed that it had started out meaning something and yet wound up meaning nothing. It was a game with rules, and then someone tore up the rule book. The game we call 'war' never came to an end; it began to devour or dominate everything around it, and even years or decades after the Armistice, the soldiers of the Great War were still trapped, in their minds, still going over the ground again, still at the front.

The importance of being earnest about the war: French responses

Much of this sense of war as a setting never to fade away is also evident in French intellectuals' responses to the Great War. But there are powerful distinctions to be drawn between such writings and those of British intellectuals. These contrasts arise from different subject positions of the writers. Some of these stances are straightforwardly political, in representing a point of view associated with a party or parties. Others are more indirect, in voicing a kind of anti-political stance based on the moral authority of the trench soldier. Both are missing by and large in Britain.

Henri Barbusse's *Le Feu*, published in 1916 and quickly translated into a dozen languages, set a standard for soldiers' memoirs which was recognised by many who did not share his political outlook. Céline, for once, was in the mainstream when he wrote that Barbusse's book was valuable for puncturing the bloated prose of *les embusqués*, the shirkers who dreamed of war without risking their necks. Barbusse's style of rustic populism fitted in well with the political position he came to adopt as a leading Communist intellectual. But that very fact indicates a politicised context which took the problem of how to represent the war into an arena in which irony didn't fit easily.

The same is true for those writers in the political centre, like Genevoix, whose voice reverberated throughout the veterans' movement of the interwar years.[18] These were men, as Antoine Prost has shown magisterially, who saw it as their moral mission to make a future war unthinkable.[19] The central motif of their discursive practice was based upon a juxtaposition of a world of human values, which the *génération du feu* knew in their bones, to the world of 'politics', understood as the arena of those who literally wallow in shit. To read their letters or their journals is to appreciate the depths of this hatred of the politicians. The wrath of these men extended to fantastic rhetorical gymnastics. What they did was to concoct a whole vocabulary of insults surrounding the notion that politicians were beneath contempt. One set of terms is derived from *'politique'* by adding a suffix: *'politicards'*, *'politiqueux'*, associated with *'bistrot'* and *'boor'*, *politicaille*, *'politicailler'*, *'politicaillerie'*, *'politicaillon'*, all referring to the world of hangers-on, pigs around the trough, old-stagers, windbags.

The ferocity of this indictment of politics is stunning. It also accounts for the political weakness of the veterans' movement itself. Drawing its strength from small market towns, and from small businessmen, petty tradesmen and farmers remote from the capital, this was the politics of *la France profonde*, trying to go above the heads of the partisan crowd in Paris, to speak to the people of France.

The failure of this crusade was built into its mode of operation. Their aim was a kind of moral disarmament, a message to children and to the world at large that war was an abomination. But even anti-politics is a kind of politics, whose contours developed in an entirely unanticipated direction. Some even followed their general, Pétain, into collaboration in 1940.[20]

If the political road taken by Barbusse described one form of response to the war, then that of the mainstream of the veterans' movement, and many intellectuals among them, described another. What they shared was a set of moral convictions which ruled out irony and displaced it with righteous anger.

It is important to note the variety of French literary responses to the war. A mere glance at the writing of Barrès, Cendrars, Drieu de la Rochelle, Giono and Céline disturbs any effort to unify French intellectual responses under a single rubric. Let me just say that the cadences and forms of French war literature are strikingly and consistently different from its British counterpart. Recourse to irony is certainly not absent, but it is less dominant, less ubiquitous, than it is in the imaginative landscape of British war writers.

In this difference in style, it is tempting to see the reason for a fundamental distinction in genre as being between French and British writing on the war. It has been evident for decades that, when anyone refers to war literature in Britain, a central part of this reference is to war poetry. Gurney, Rosenberg, Thomas, Owen and many others brought to their verse an intensity and a clarity of phrase which has made their work endure. It is now part of the National Curriculum that every British child studies. There is nothing comparable in France. It is not that poetry was unknown in France. On the contrary – it is that French poetry did not capture a fundamental facet of the 'structure of sentiment' of soldiers who fought and who told the yet-unknowing world about these matters. Prose did the job in France. What made the difference? Perhaps the ironic temperament is necessary for what we now call war poetry. It provides a distance, a suspension of values, a form of affectionate mockery or masked anger which distils into a concentrate the overwhelming sense experience of war. The Second World War did not inspire such an ironic cloudburst among either British or French writers. The political character of the war was different; the stakes were different, and the men of 1914–18 had already been over the ground.

Poetry in Britain also captured some of the cadences of the sacred. Without the conflict between Republic and Roman Catholicism, British reference to the music of the King James Bible was uncontroversial and ubiquitous. Poetry could approach the sacred without being sanctimonious or parti pris. War poets like Owen, and others, could minister rather than instruct, and one way they did so was to take an ironic stance, to ask readers no longer to tell 'the old lie' that it is noble and fitting to die for one's country. French poets and writers never reached this point. To them, the war was either sacred or a sin; irony inhabits the space between the two.

Giraudoux and the theatre of ambivalence

Now for the exception, and what an exception he was. One way of highlighting the divide that separates the majority of British and French commentators on the Great War is to draw attention to one figure who, in terms of sensibility and style, managed to bridge the gap. Jean Giraudoux was that rare intellectual equally at home in entirely different cultural milieus, a *cosmopolite* without any trace of Jewishness, which in many eyes converted the word *cosmopolite* into a light insult. His internationalism in outlook and manner was more than a diplomatic façade; Giraudoux created a space where a kind of worldly, pan-European irony framed one of the enduring French masterpieces of the twentieth-century theatre of war.

I refer to *La Guerre de Troie n'aura pas lieu*, first performed in Paris in 1935.[21] The title itself announces the game, which emerges in the very first exchange of the play. Andromache, Hector's wife, tells Cassandra that there will be no Trojan War. Cassandra bets her that she is wrong. We know that Cassandra will win the bet, and so does the author, but Andromache is in the dark. Thus we see the different communities of understanding which irony describes, all in a wager about destiny.

But right from the start Giraudoux offers us an even greater irony. The opening lines spoken by Andromache are impossible. At the moment she speaks, Andromache cannot have heard of the Trojan War, since it was called that only after the fact. Hence, for her to say before its outbreak that it won't take place is to evidence knowledge – there will be a Trojan War – that undermines the content of her flat claim that it won't take place. What wicked game is Giraudoux playing here?

The subject of the play, and the choices it describes, are no laughing matter. Indeed, Giraudoux employs irony as a powerful defensive strategy in a world where war threatens. In the play, irony is the last shield that Andromache and Hector wear to protect them and all of Troy from the scourge of war, and from those among them who turn bloodshed into poetry and carnage into heroism. Irony is the way they try to disarm the dangerous fools among them from triggering war. After the patriotic poet Demokos, the quintessential bellicose civilian, announces that killing a man gives a warrior the right to a woman, Andromache begs to differ. She tells him and her father-in-law Priam that women really love cowards, who are men who stay alive. Priam cautions her by saying she should be careful not to prove 'the very opposite of what you want to prove'. Priam doesn't see that she is speaking the direct truth: What is more honourable than dishonourable conduct in the pursuit of peace? 'But which is the worse cowardice', she asks: 'To appear cowardly to others, and make sure of peace? Or to be cowardly in your own eyes, and let loose a war?'

Her husband repeats this anti-heroic principle time and again. In this respect, Giraudoux's Hector is not Homer's. In this play, Hector believes that 'honour' is a word which describes an inner state. To cast it off in public as the price of averting war is to lose only the outer trappings of true honour which remains within. Here is the central strategy of the game he plays in this prewar period: the game of persuading the Greeks that there is no cause for war in the presence in Troy of Helen, snatched by Paris from her royal Greek husband. Ajax comes to take her home and finds that Hector invites him to have her. Ajax taunts Hector: 'What if I call you a coward,' he asks. 'That is a name I accept,' is Hector's reply. 'What if I spit,' says Ajax. 'Go ahead,' says Hector. 'What if I slap?' 'Go ahead,' says Hector, and Ajax does. The slap leaves its mark, but Hector claims that the swelling shows he is healthier on that side of his face. Then the poet Demokos challenges Ajax; and, to prevent them from conjuring up the casus belli they both are itching to find, Hector slaps Demokos himself, and then denies that anything has happened. War is averted, but in light of the general insouciance around him about the prospects of bloodshed, Hector has a sense that all these minor victories still do not add up to much: 'I win every round. But still with each victory, the prize [peace] eludes me.'

The next round is even more deliciously ironic. In negotiations with Ulysses, Hector declares that 'Paris has not touched Helen'. He is clearly lying, as the sailors aboard Paris's ship attest willingly. But Helen, whose heart is made of stone, is quite literally untouchable; Hector is speaking the truth, but not the one his companions think he is. Ulysses goes along with this conceit, and sees peace accomplished for a very paltry price: he will tell Menelaus that nothing had happened to Helen in Troy. 'I have more than enough eloquence to convince a husband of his wife's virtue.'

The soldier/diplomats withdraw and peace seems assured, until the very last moment, when the heroic fool Demokos shouts 'Treachery, and to arms' when he realises that Helen is returning to Greece. Significantly enough, Hector kills Demokos, who in his last breath lies, and says that Ajax had killed him. This lie provokes the Trojans to kill Ajax, setting the war in motion. Hector is defeated, and the doom of his people is assured. The Trojan poet Demokos is dead, says Cassandra. 'And now the Grecian poet will have his word,' Homer's Trojan War, sung five centuries after the events in the play, is about to begin.

What a game Giraudoux has described. But its playfulness only masks the deadly seriousness of the drama. In a way, irony is the vehicle for a battle of representations, in which heroic notions of war collide with heroes stripped of those very beliefs. *La Guerre de Troie n'aura pas lieu* is a duel between pacifism, represented by Hector, and heroism, expressed by Demokos. The poet is one of the old men who praise war without knowing it. He is a pale imitation of Barrès and others, whose heroic aggression somehow had survived the carnage of Verdun and the Somme and had come to threaten the world again.

What the play describes is an ironic ambiguity familiar to anyone who – like Giraudoux – surveyed the French veterans' movement in the inter-war years. As Prost has shown, they were men whose heroism could not be challenged; now, in the aftermath of war, they were determined to make war on facile notions of heroism. If they did not speak out, it would return. Like Hector, they had a sense of a mission constantly eluding them. The corrupt politicians and poets and propagandists were still there. To ex-soldiers like Giraudoux, who knew what combat was, another war was both unthinkable and it was just around the corner. That is what the inter-war phrase *'entre-deux-guerres'* is all about.

It would be an injustice to an ironist of the stature of Giraudoux to limit his play to this single frame of reference. Yes, he had fought both on the Western Front and at Gallipoli; yes he had been wounded twice and decorated with the Legion of Honour.[22] Yes, he was a diplomat who knew from many of his superiors and his adversaries what cheap, overblown language looked like. But his art is hardly autobiography; to assume so is to fall into a trap much cruder than his prose. I suggest that it is the tone of his voice which sets him aside from most French writers of the war generation as well as from the didactic cadences of the veterans' movement in inter-war France. Irony sets him apart, and drew him sympathetically, temperamentally, to those other ironists across the Channel who meditated on the war. His ironic detachment, mixed with moral purpose, made his reactions to the 1914–18 war closer to Owen and Sassoon than to Barbusse and Genevoix.

It would be pointless to try to explain completely the complexity of Giraudoux's voice through his biography. The elegance of his prose would shrivel under such heavy-handedness. We know that his reach was European, and indeed extra-European. At the Ecole Normale Supérieure, he wrote his thesis on the following subject: 'Quel but poursuit l'Allemagne en développant sa marine de guerre?' Not much irony there. Nor was there anything unusual in a French intellectual's deep acquaintance with and admiration for German language and literature. What was somewhat more unusual was that Giraudoux's sympathies extended to the Anglo-Saxon world as well.

Here he benefited from a current of Francophilia deeply entrenched at Harvard. In part funded by James Hazen Hyde, son of an insurance tycoon, Harvard launched an exchange programme which brought Giraudoux to Cambridge, Massachusetts, in 1907. When the professor of French was struck down with typhoid fever, Giraudoux delivered his lectures on eighteenth-century French literature. He was active in theatrical productions there, too. After a tour around America, he was introduced to the President, Theodore Roosevelt. It was at this time that Giraudoux decided to bypass the *Agrégation* in German and a future academic career, and to concentrate on diplomacy.

That career would take him to the highest levels of the French diplomatic service. In the 1920s and 1930s, he travelled extensively, as inspector of French diplomatic missions. Naturally, the Franco-German dialogue was of major concern to him, as it was to all diplomats, but his gaze was not fixed on this one issue. His interests, as well as the sources of his vision, were multiple. The ironic voice he found was truly European, and through it he expressed without sentimentality the Sisyphean struggle towards a European peace always just out of reach.

All his adult life, Giraudoux struggled with the duality of war and peace, and found in irony a way of expressing the tragedy of his generation, scarred by one war and unable to avoid another. That ironic voice was both distinctive and echoed others like it outside of France. In this sense he was a poet of the sentiments at the heart of the inter-war French veterans' movement. But he was a poet with a voice of his own, one with ironic cadences with clear affinities to other literary responses to the war.[23]

If it is true that British and French intellectual responses to the Great War were different, and that irony is one facet of that distinction, the question remains as to why this should be so? In brief, it may be useful in this book to draw on some conjectures which move intellectual history outside an older tradition that privileged the pure study of style and sensibility over cultural and political contexts.

My aim is to point to some disparities, some differences in emphasis and location, which may be of interest in situating these materials. First, the notion of irony rests more easily with those further removed from the battlefields of the war. France was invaded; the bloodshed occurred on French soil, and the outcome of those battles determined the outcome of the war. There is not much room for irony on these points. But there are other longer-term contrasts which may lie behind the different tone and emphases in these two countries' intellectual responses to the war. Some of these arose from the very different role played by ex-soldiers in postwar society. There was nothing in Britain remotely like the French veterans' movement. The proportion of ex-soldiers who joined veterans' groups in France was four times greater than in Britain. The absence of conscription before the war, added to the controversy over conscription during it, provided few supports for making veterans' experience a centrepiece of postwar political discourse. There wasn't even a minister for veterans' affairs in Britain, that business being handled by the Ministry of Pensions, set up initially in 1908 to help the elderly. Individual veterans became prominent in inter-war politics, but when they tried (like Oswald Mosley) to introduce military forms into British political life, they failed miserably, consigned to an obscurity from which they never escaped.

It was not only veterans politics that differed in the two countries. It was that the distance between intellectual groups and the political world in France and Britain was pronounced. Years ago, in doing some work on the French war economy, I was struck with the way the Minister of Commerce, Etienne Clémentel, would excuse himself from ministerial meetings so that he could walk over to the rue de Varenne, where he was conducting experiments in optics in Rodin's house. Could that have happened in London? Perhaps, but I don't believe it ever did. And Clémentel was not exceptional: others, like Clemenceau, crossed the line between the arts and public affairs time and again. British and French intellectuals live in a different proximity to the institutions of the State, and this positioning might reinforce different structures of feeling, different styles of expression. One aspect of that difference is what I have called the ironic temperament, especially its utility as a distancing device.

A word or two should be added about the structuring effects of irony on political protest. Irony both enabled it and contained it. The British recourse to an imagery of games and gamesmanship, to fair play and decency, built into that irony a kind of limiting force. Games suspend time. When they come to an end, nothing in the real world has changed. Could the same be said for irony as a sport, a game played for its own sake? Ironists could have their say, and then just fade away. In this sense, irony is both the fate of an intellectual class without a direct political or social function and a means of ensuring that this remains the case. Distance has its price alongside it privileges.

Above all, irony destabilises. It rules out certain kinds of certainty. It is a mirror in which the gaze confronts something which is not quite what it seems to be. Confronting it means admitting that all interpretations, including this one, must remain up in the air.

The war in France was very much down to earth. Fighting on, and for, one's land makes detachment appear either dangerous or frivolous. Céline was both, and that was precisely the point. His evisceration of moral rectitude is a rude response to two decades of unironic French writing on the war. But his reply was that of the *picaro*, the bandit on the run, just one step ahead of the law. His savage wit and uncanny ear for ordinary language created a fictional landscape utterly remote from irony. For irony remains embedded in the classical tradition; it is detached humanism with a wry smile. Céline defecated on it, and, indeed, on us all.

Just as there is nothing in French like British war poetry, so there is nothing in English like Céline or Barbusse or Genevoix, and the list could go on. Writing about war discloses much more than literary patterns or fashions. It provides a window on the social situation of writers as much as on their audiences. A British upper middle class, by and large educated in public schools, came into the war with one canonical language: that of Edwardian pastoral romance. They left the war with another language – one which we now call ironic. Anticipation versus outcome. Irony traverses the space between the two. French verse forms largely survived the war: the cause was too close to home; the bloody price too high. In France, the public celebrated the victory, but staggered under the weight of its butchery. Only in the hands of a detached genius like Giraudoux could there be a marriage of the intellectual styles of these distant partners, these uneasy allies, these incompatible survivors of the slaughter. And, even in his hands, irony comes to an end. In *La Guerre de Troie n'aura pas lieu*, Hector loses his battle to make war impossible. The rest, as they say, is history.

Notes

1 Thanks are due to Fritz Stern, Annette Becker and Sarah Cole for their comments on this chapter.
2 I am grateful to Helen MacPhail for her advice on this matter.
3 Bernard Le Floch has kindly provided me with his edition of these poems: Siegfried Sassoon, *Poèmes de guerre,* trans. Bernard Le Floch (Paris: Caractères, 1987).
4 Siegfried Sassoon, *Mémoires d'un chasseur de renards,* trans. Antoinette Sémeziès and Jacques Elsey (Paris: Gallimard, 1938).
5 Paul Fussell, *The Great War and Modern Memory* (New York: Oxford, 1985).
6 Samuel Hynes, *A War Imagined: the First World War and English Culture* (New York: Athaeneum, 1991).
7 Modris Ekstein, *Le Sacre du printemps: la Grande Guerre et la naissance de la modernité* (Paris: Plon, 1991).
8 Raymond Williams, *The Long Revolution* (New York: Columbia University Press, 1961).
9 Samuel Hynes, *The Edwardian Turn of Mind* (London: Jonathan Cape, 1970).
10 For a survey of some of this vast literature, see D. C. Muecke, *Irony,* (London: Methuen & Co, 1970); Cleanth Brooks, *Modern Poetry and the Tradition* (Chapel Hill: University of North Carolina Press, 1939); Wayne Booth, *A Rhetoric of Irony* (Chicago: University of Chicago Press, 1974); and, more recently, Birgit Baldwin, 'Irony, That "Little Invisible Personnage": A Reading of Kierkegaard's Ghosts', *MLN Comparative Literature,* 104:5 (1989), 124–41, and Alan Wilde, *Horizons of Assent: Modernism, Postmodernism, and the Ironic Imagination* (Baltimore: Johns Hopkins University Press, 1981). I am grateful to Sarah Cole for her guidance in this literature.
11 Eleanor N. Hutchens, 'The Identification of Irony', *English Literary History,* 27:4 (1960), 363.
12 Hutchens, 'The Identification of Irony', p. 358, author's italics.
13 Martin Middlebrook, *The First Day on the Somme* (London: Fontana, 1975), pp. 124, 254.
14 Robert Graves, *Goodbye to All That* (London: Penguin, 1930), p. 79.
15 As cited in Fussell, *Great War and Modern Memory,* p. 203.
16 Charles Carrington, *Soldiers from the Wars Returning* (London: Methuen, 1965), pp. 252–3.
17 Guy Chapman, *A Passionate Prodigality* (London: Heinemann, 1933), p. 277.
18 Maurice Genevoix, *Ceux de 14* (Paris: Le Seuil, 1984).
19 Antoine Prost, 'Combattants et politiciens: le discours mythologique sur la politique entre les deux guerres', *Mouvement Social,* 85 (1973), 117–49. I am grateful to Antoine Prost for many discussions of this theme.
20 Antoine Prost, *Les Anciens combattants et la société française* (Paris: Presses de la Fondation nationale des sciences politiques, 1977), 3 vols.

21 On the play, see Roy Lewis, *Giraudoux: la guerre de Troie n'aura pas lieu* (London: Edward Arnold, 1971); Gunnar Graumann, *'La Guerre de Troie' aura lieu: la préparation de la pièce de Giraudoux* (Lund: C. W. K. Gleerup, 1979); Michel Maillard, *Giraudoux: des repères pour situer l'auteur* (Paris: Nathan, 1997); and Chris Marker, *Giraudoux* (Paris: Le Seuil, 1978).

22 See Jean Giraudoux, *Campaigns and Intervals*, trans. Elizabeth S. Sergeant. (Boston: Houghton Mifflin, 1918).

23 On Giraudoux, among many other works, see Jacques Body, *Giraudoux et l'Allemagne* (Paris: Publications de la Sorbonne, Littératures 7, 1975, reprinted 2003); and *Jean Giraudoux: la légende et le secret* (Paris: Presses Universitaires de France, 1986).

16

Conclusions and perspectives
Christophe Charle

The confrontation and occasional combination of historical and sociological methodologies from the two countries, as practised in this book, has aimed at escaping from a certain number of false debates and ritual objections to Franco-British comparison in intellectual history and the history of intellectuals. Do the opposing religious and subsequently political paths followed by France and England since the Reformation and the French Revolution not prevent any valid contextualised comparison? And do the correlative contrasting developments in their systems of secondary and higher education not prejudge, right from the start, any counterposing of the styles of intervention and mental horizons of the two countries' cultural elites? Does not the rivalry, real or symbolic, political and religious, national and international, between the two nations, block any direct transfer or dialogue of an intellectual or cultural nature?

Each of the chapters in this book shows that both analogies and differences, exchanges and refusals, are based on a common foundation that is far more solid than initial oppositions would suggest. This resonance has made it possible, following the precepts put forward by Marc Bloch in his foundational article on comparative history,[1] to raise questions left in shadow by an a priori refusal of comparison, or by exclusive recourse to normative comparison, specific to the two historiographies. Above all, it challenges the major obstacle to any comprehensive and comparative analysis: the arbitrary division of labour between university disciplines, specific to each academic universe, that prevents the same questions being raised on each side of the Channel.

As the historic trajectory of the various contributions gathered here indicates, this divided situation is neither a constant phenomenon nor an eternal truth. At other times (the eighteenth century, the Victorian age and the July monarchy, the late nineteenth century), intellectual circulation and political debate between the two countries, as well as knowledge of the neighbouring land, seem to have been far more intense than they are today, and sometimes even directly integrated into internal national debate. A complete analysis of the causes for this non-dialogue between French and English intellectuals since the inter-war period would require lengthy development and a specific study.[2] Here we can only try and sketch this in broad lines, to aid a better understanding of the origins of the resistance to intellectual comparativism.

Cross-Channel or transatlantic?

It is well-known how in philosophy the majority of influential French thinkers since the nineteenth century have chiefly constructed their doctrines by reference to the works of classical philosophy or German phenomenology, whereas so-called 'analytic' or Anglo-Saxon philosophy has only recently begun to penetrate the field of French philosophical study. In the social sciences, the balanced equilibrium of the founding fathers between German and English theories was replaced, after 1945, by a special relationship, according to different schools, with either the United States or Germany, or with both. In history, the connections formed early on between Marc Bloch and English historiography hardly survived after his death.[3] The heirs of the '*Annales* school' in modern and contemporary history turned, rather, towards Italy and Spain or, more recently, to Germany and the United States.[4] Even the important influence of Marxism in the historiography of both countries in the 1950s and 1960s, instead of creating an intellectual tie, erected an additional frontier. Paradoxically, in fact, the various Marxisms – English and French – adopted strongly national colours and concentrated on questions specific to the interpretation of national and political history, to which intellectual and cultural dimensions, without exception, were subordinated, precisely as a function of the dominant economistic vision, to economic problematics or to questions of strategy bound up with the political conjuncture.[5] Such conjunctures, however, were clearly very different in each country, given the very unequal weight of the Communist Party or Marxist groups on either side of the Channel.

The absence or delay in translation of certain major works of historiography or social science into the neighbouring language is not explained only by the fallacious idea that knowledge of either English or French was sufficiently widespread among academics of the respective country to make this costly undertaking one that publishers could avoid. At a deeper level, it derives from the absence of a possibility of reception for the other's discourse, hence a lack of intermediaries sufficiently stubborn to convince a publisher of the necessity of the enterprise. To take even such an esteemed figure as Marc Bloch (himself, moreover, greatly given to comparison, especially with England), the translation dates of his major works owe less to their intrinsic importance than to external overdeterminations indicating to a publisher the kind of reception they might expect. Thus *Strange Defeat*, published in France in 1946, was translated into English as early as 1949, as its topicality and link with recent British experience clearly made it a work able to reach a relatively broad public.[6] *Feudal Society*, on the other hand, originally published in 1939 and generally seen as the author's mature masterpiece, had to wait until published by an American university press in 1961,[7] while *The Royal Touch* remained in the waiting room until 1973, even though its original French edition dated from 1924 and the book was based on a Franco-English comparison.[8]

As Blaise Wilfert and Pascale Casanova have also shown in this book, on questions of literature and theatre, this sealing of intellectual frontiers between the two countries is not simply a function of economic obstacles, or the existence of other invisible modes of connection that the frequency of translations grasps only imperfectly. The dominant poles in each disciplinary or intellectual field are, in general, themselves involved in the national closure of the two linguistic spaces. Conversely, it is the outsiders or the dominated poles who make use of foreign works and authors as symbolic allies, in order to make their own voices heard and challenge the official national vision. If this process can be seen in many cultural fields up to the Second World War, it seems since then to have disappeared in favour of a privileged interaction between the French and British intellectual fields on the one hand, and the ascendant American field on the other. Both British and French academics, intellectuals, scholars and writers now generally form direct relations with America, no longer bothering so much with their immediate neighbours. On the British side, this privileged relationship has also been facilitated by the common language and ensuing 'brain drain', accelerated since 1980 by the brutal educational policy of Prime Minister Margaret Thatcher. On the French side, the Franco-American intellectual dialogue was based on a first wave of migration during the war,[9] then on the transatlantic fashion for existentialism in the 1950s, for the '*nouveau roman*' in the 1960s, and subsequently for 'structuralism' and 'post-structuralism', transformed into 'French theory' by the French departments of certain major universities.[10]

The disciplinary specialisation and very marked spatial differentiation characteristic of the American academic and intellectual field contributed to the disappearance of those factors that at certain moments facilitated direct relations between British and French intellectuals: the model of generalised liberal intellectual inherited from the Enlightenment and the marked centralisation of intellectual resources in the two capitals, London and Paris, or their immediate periphery (Oxford and Cambridge).[11] Specialisation, which resulted in works only being read if they dealt with one's own subject, and all the more so as they were written in a foreign language, did not just result from the academic intraversion of French and British intellectuals in the postwar decades, but also from new demands for expertise on the part of the State. These demands, especially in the social sciences, contributed to reinforcing national problematics, or selecting at the international level only references that agreed with these, most often taken from American literature, given the relations of force in publishing.

These national problematics, for their part, despite the apparent, though far less real, internationalisation of intellectual life in the second half of the twentieth century, may well have exerted their influence on both sides of the Channel to a greater extent than before the war. Certain national themes, however, continued to offer analogies between the intellectual debates of both countries: the end of Empire and decolonisation, the various effects of the war, economic modernisation and the advent of a consumer society in Europe along American lines, the emergence of a mass culture,[12] the obsession with the decline of the two old nations in the face of the two superpowers, then of the new and rebuilt nations (Germany, Japan, the emergent countries of Asia), the enquiry into national identity and the relation to the past.[13]

These apparently similar thematics relate to the geopolitical earthquake that the two former imperial societies, allied as they were in the twentieth century for better and for worse, had experienced in less than forty years.[14] They were formulated, however, in two different political and intellectual spaces, and in terms sufficiently different for the intellectuals of each nation not to experience the need to interest themselves in their neighbour's debate, differently therefore from the situation in the nineteenth century, as shown in this book. An influence is demonstrable from the commitment of French intellectuals against the Algerian war to the forms of activity of American intellectuals against the Vietnam War. But it would be hard to find such casual connections between the postcolonial conflicts of Britain and France.[15] In the same way, while the two educational systems each experienced the most rapid transformation in their history, pedagogic and institutional debates continued in splendid ignorance of one another, or viewed each other through caricaturing stereotypes that contrasted with the investigative spirit of the nineteenth-century educational reformers in Britain and on the Continent.

All these gaps summarily recalled here explain the drifting apart of the French and English intellectual continents at the time when the analyses of this book end, and the difficulty we have experienced in trying to re-tie the threads for periods in which interaction, dialogue and reciprocal knowledge (of a world that might have been very small, but occupied controlling positions) of French and British intellectuals understood in the broadest sense were undoubtedly at their peak.

Reconciling historiographies

As a function of these considerations, it is easier to understand why British and French historiographies nourished themselves until very recently on self-referential stereotypes, something that reinforced the privileged study of certain periods that backed up these stereotypes, and the silence they maintained on various questions that were deemed incongruous: on the British side, the history of intellectuals continues to have, on the whole, a bad press, despite the recent efforts of publications inspired by French practices;[16] on the French side, the history of intellectuals is too exclusively dominated by the political approach, too often in fact a 'religious history' or a polemical history inspired by current concerns, cut off from a genuine intellectual history in the sense this is given by Stefan Collini in the introduction to his *History, Religion and Culture*.[17] The two historiographies each emphasised certain figures of the intellectual to the detriment of others, amounting to just another manner of adopting a truncated perspective and falsifying comparison. In England, attention was focused on the great scholarly figures of Oxford and Cambridge, on non-conformist intellectuals with an aristocratic detachment, or, to a lesser extent, on outsiders who managed to force the establishment doors – for instance, Sidney Webb a century ago, or Richard Hoggart and Eric Hobsbawm more recently. In France, a privileged status was given to generalist men of letters, to activist intellectuals, those linked with extremist parties, or scholars who strayed into politics. Critical analysis of the works of Noel Annan and Perry Anderson, proposed here by Stefan Collini in chapter 3, shows in the British case how these two writers, so often cited, still retained at the basis of their theses these simplifying figures, giving their conclusions a systematic bias. The symmetrical demonstration could easily be extended, and applied to the French case or to certain periods of English intellectual history that are not depicted by Collini.

Even the very kind of work preferentially conducted by each of these historiographies contributes to making the transfer of problematics or results a hazardous thing at best. We know the power and importance of the tradition of intellectual biography, or the commented publication of personal writings (autobiographies, diaries, letters) of the major British intellectual and political figures. If these kinds of monographs and sources are not unknown in France, they are far less common, by reason of the discredit cast on event-type history or biography by the historiographic tradition of *Annales*, without the ensuing gap always being made up by works of collective biography or histories of broader intellectual groups. On the French side, moreover, intensive works of the same genre have been, above all, the work of specialists in neighbouring disciplines who have not always had the englobing perspective of historians. In particular, they have tended to adopt a genealogical approach that privileges the most visible individuals, whereas English biographical works offer trustworthy information well beyond leading intellectuals, scholars or women of letters. In the opposite sense, the approach by way of collective biographies, which has been one of the major characteristics of recent cultural and intellectual history in France, has scarcely aroused emulation across the Channel, despite the wealth of available biographical material. Some of the chapters in this book illustrate the interest of this tool of comparison in the British case as in the French, and it is to be hoped that they will be a spur to new work.

It is, in fact, only by reconstituting the space of debate by synchronic sections – as is done in the chapters by Julien Vincent, Pascale Casanova and myself – that it is possible to grasp the full variety of categories of intellectuals competing in each field or sub-field, and explain why relations of exchange were or were not established between the different poles of the two national intellectual fields. Only in this way is it possible to reach a comprehensive and explanatory comparison that does not boil down to a biased confrontation of historical stereotypes and episodes, contemporary with each other but in actual fact separated by the specific rhythms of each intellectual field.

Proposals for a study of imperial intellectual societies

It is important in any case to expand the perspective in order to deal with a historical dimension that is too often overlooked. In the course of the period in question, both countries acquired the status I have defined elsewhere as that of 'imperial societies'. This term should be understood as meaning far more than the presently renewed debate over empires and imperialisms. Both France and the United Kingdom were imperial societies in the nineteenth century in the sense that they each presented themselves, in Europe and indeed throughout the world, as cultural models, sui generis but each with a universal vocation that justified their conquests and the diffusion of their culture to the world as a whole. Intellectuals, understood in the broadest sense, were precisely the bearers (or critics) and beneficiaries (or victims when they challenged it)[18] of this project. This specificity – which subsequently appeared also in Germany and Italy at the end of the nineteenth century – explains the appearance of new and unprecedented interactions between the intellectuals of the two countries. This, however, was also full of new incomprehensions, misrecognitions and divergences, illustrated here by most of the chapters on the late nineteenth and early twentieth centuries, or by intensive historiographic productions in the standard bibliography.[19] Starting from this common problematic of imperial societies and its effects on the intellectual life and intellectuals of the two countries, it should be possible to avoid in future the aporias that block this field of study. Part of the dynamic of these questions, in fact, is not uniquely national and internal, as both historiographies believe. Precisely because the stakes are imperial and those of cultural hegemony, they are defined or transformed as a function of the rivalry, avowed or not, with the nearest other imperial power, i.e. most of the time France or the United Kingdom, and, as far as the intellectual and cultural domain is concerned, with the neighbouring intellectuals. There is no doubt, as certain chapters here demonstrate, that these relationships are not always direct, immediate or homogeneous. The situation of rivalry and proximity leads to censorship, masking and disguise – all the more so in that, by virtue of being imperial, the two cultures do not measure themselves by the same standard, going so far as to claim exclusive hegemony in certain specialist domains (British 'sport', French 'taste', etc.), a pretension that the intellectuals of each country abundantly develop with a view to avoiding comparison or standardisation, a reductive treatment that they abhor for themselves, as for all symbolic goods.

The other advantage of this perspective is to escape the equally reductive alternatives between internal and external study, approach through discourse or approach through networks and collective biographies. To understand why one or other intellectual was led in these transnational debates to choose this or that position, an individual intellectual biography or a cartography of the terms of debate at a given moment remains at the phenomenological level. The terms of debate are not only intellectual, they involve visions of internal and external relations of domination. The positions adopted are not just the fruit of an individual logic; they refer to relations of force produced by the specific capital deployed or not by particular individuals in a given intellectual field. These do not have a permanently fixed value. By the play of misrecognitions facilitated by a change in the frame of reference, disadvantaged intellectuals are able to conquer a new status, authorising a different discourse for the conquest of new positions. In France as in Britain, the social networks of peripheral regions invested more than those of central regions in the imperial project, both at the practical level and in its ideological defence. There is a whole field of study for comparison here.[20]

The effects of imperial status in the two nations can be compared in the opposite sense in the attractive capacity of their intellectual fields on the elites and intellectuals of the dominated countries. Various works in progress have demonstrated the existence of international academic 'markets' defining spaces polarised around a principal metropolis, and overlapping only to a very limited extent.[21] But a simply global and statistical analysis is not able to resolve all questions as to the origin of these preferential attractions and their effects on both the culture of reception and the culture of origin of these intellectual emigrants. The best-documented case is the great forced migration of German and Central European intellectuals to the West in the wake of the advent of Nazism and other dictatorial regimes. Despite the anti-fascist solidarity that existed in both France and Britain, these two countries did not equally receive the same kind of intellectuals, and there is here a secret affinity with the dominant cultural image of the two imperial societies. The relatively successful integration of many German and Austrian academics in Britain contrasts with their almost total rejection in France: 112 German academics settled first in the United Kingdom (19 per cent of the total number of academic refugees), as against 162 in the United States (27 per cent) but only 56 in France (9 per cent). After a few years, only 2 per cent of their number remained in France.[22] In contrast to this, a far greater proportion of refugee artists, writers and journalists arrived in Paris or the south of France, even if they went on to experience a difficult life or a tragic fate after 1940.[23] This asymmetry reflects the sclerosis of university life in inter-war France, in contrast with the continuing radiance of artistic and literary life, at least in the national and international imaginary.[24]

External factors of this kind, the detailed study of which needs to be further pursued, function as revealing reagents of masked structures, hidden customs or implicit rules defining cultures with a hegemonic vocation, even when these proclaim themselves open and universalist. This double decentring can also be practised on a different scale, while maintaining the perspective of comparisons and transfers. Presenting the trajectories of intellectual or artistic figures who, despite a foreign origin managed to reach the highest possible level of apparent integration, should not be used (as it habitually is) to illustrate and praise the integrationist virtues that each imperial cultural model, despite everything, displays. Even these successes, which contradict the sociological pessimism suggested by the statistically dominant trajectories, enable us to grasp the more or less effective braking mechanisms, the alliances and circumstances that triggered these, the toll that had to be paid. In the British case, the recently published memoirs of an outsider in the informal British Empire, Eric Hobsbawm, offer a glimpse into the mechanisms of transgression and adaptation to the new context and new practices that determine whether the new arrival succeeds or fails in acclimatising himself or herself in the new intellectual milieu.[25]

We have equally rich sources to hand on émigré intellectuals such as Ludwig Wittgenstein, Norbert Elias and Karl Popper in Great Britain,[26] Alexandre Koyré, B. Groethuysen and Picasso in France, to take some examples that are well-known though heterogeneous. Beyond the purely individual approach predominant in historiography, which wraps itself in a towering erudition fascinated by its hero, we should construct comparative series of trajectories of integration and rejection, to provide keys to the underlying circulation or impossible transplantation in both French and British intellectual fields.

Such perspectives therefore demand, as has been attempted in this book, an effective cooperation between historians of both countries and, more globally, between specialists in the social sciences, as well as the desire to break free of the false divisions born of an excessive historical specialisation into autonomous subsidiary branches. They also require the will to transfer problematics and methods from one national context to the other, and above all a refusal to forget that the two cultures are themselves each part of wider frames of reference (European and imperial), which weigh on the internal issues at stake far more than contemporaries are aware.

Notes

1 M. Bloch, 'Pour une histoire comparée des sociétés européennes' (1928), reprinted in *Mélanges Historiques* (Paris: A. Colin, 1963), pp. 16–40.
2 The radically divided attitudes of French and British writers in relation to the First World War, as analysed by Jay Winter in chapter 15, are a first indication of this growing gulf. Another would certainly be the debate aroused by J. M. Keynes with his famous book *The Economic Consequences of the Peace* (first English edition, London, 1919; French translation Paris: Gallimard, 1920).
3 E. J. Hobsbawm, 'A Life in History', *Past and Present*, 177 (November 2000), 3–16, which depicts the role of M. M. Postan (a professor of Russian origin) in spreading the ideas of Marc Bloch and *Annales* at Cambridge.
4 Institutional factors also promoted the intensification of connections between French and German historians: the foundation of the Mission historique française in Germany by Robert Mandrou (1977), then of the Centre Marc Bloch in Berlin (1992) under the direction of Etienne François. Although

older (1946), the Maison française at Oxford did not play an equivalent role. Moreover, the late entry of the UK into the European Community and the Gaullist mistrust of Britain explain why successive governments hardly encouraged Franco-British academic exchange on the same scale.

5 L. Kolakowsky, *Main Current of Marxism* (1978; English translation: Oxford: Oxford University Press, 1981–5).

6 M. Bloch, *Strange Defeat, a Statement of Evidence Written in 1940*, introduction by Sir Maurice Powicke, foreword by Georges Altman, translated from the French by Gerard Hopkins (London and New York: Oxford University Press, 1949).

7 M. Bloch, *Feudal Society*, translated from the French by L. A. Manyon, foreword by M. M. Postan (Chicago: University of Chicago Press, 1961).

8 *The Royal Touch: Sacred Monarchy and Scrofula in England and France*, trans. J. E. Anderson (London: Routledge & Kegan Paul, 1973).

9 This led to the encounter between Claude Lévi-Strauss, then a refugee in New York, American anthropology in the persons of Franz Boas, Ralph Linton and Ruth Benedict, and Russian linguistic structuralism (Roman Jakobson). It was in New York that Lévi-Strauss drafted the first version of his *Elementary Structures of Kinship* (published 1948). See L. Jeanpierre, 'Des hommes entre plusieurs mondes: étude sur une situation d'exil. Intellectuels français réfugiés aux Etats-Unis pendant la deuxième guerre mondiale', Ph.D. dissertation, Ecole des Hautes Etudes en Sciences Sociales, 2004. In a previous generation, Marcel Mauss had formed a close and direct connection with English anthropology; see M. Fournier, *Marcel Mauss* (Paris: Fayard, 1994), pp. 123ff., 635ff.,p. 650.

10 F. Cusset, *French Theory: Foucault, Derrida, Deleuze et Cie, et les mutations de la vie intellectuelle aux Etats-Unis* (Paris: La Découverte, 2003); G. Pestureau, 'Sartre et les Etats-Unis', in M. Rybalka and G. Idt (eds), *Etudes Sartriennes* II–III, *Cahiers de Sémiotique Textuelle,* 5–6, Université Paris-X, 1986. When these works were re-imported via the US to Britain, they aroused anger on two fronts: rejection of American tutelage, and reticence towards French writers who had already been reinterpreted by certain American university departments to the point of making them unrecognisable to those familiar with the originals.

11 H. Liebersohn, 'The American Academic Community before the First World War: A Comparison with the German "Bildungsbürgertum"', in W. Conze and J. Kocka (eds), *Bildungsbürgertum im 19. Jahrhundert* (Stuttgart: Klett-Cotta, 1985), vol. 1, pp. 163–85; R. L. Geiger, *To Advance Knowledge: The Growth of American Research Universities, 1900–1940* (new edition, New Brunswick: Transaction Publishers, 2004), and *Research and Relevant Knowledge: American Research University Since World War II* (New York and Oxford: Oxford University Press, 1993); T. Bender and C. Schorske (eds), *American Academic Culture in Transformation* (Princeton: Princeton University Press, 1997).

12 This explains the translation, if with certain distortions in relation to the author's actual project, of Richard Hoggart's book *The Uses of Literacy* (*La*

Culture du pauvre; Paris: Minuit, 1970). This was inscribed in the perspective of the struggle by Bourdieu and Passeron for a sociology of culture, against the invading sociology of mass media of American inspiration. See P. Bourdieu and J.-C. Passeron, 'Sociologues des mythologies et mythologies des sociologues', *Les Temps Modernes,* 211 (December 1963), 998–1021, and J.-C. Passeron (ed.), *Richard Hoggart en France* (Paris: Bibliothèque publique d'information, 1999), especially pp. 222ff.

13 See, in particular, S. Collini, *English Pasts: Essays in History and Culture* (Oxford: Oxford University Press, 1999), and P. Nora (ed.), *Les Lieux de mémoire* (Paris: Gallimard, 1984–92), 7 vols; partial American translation: *Realms of Memory: Rethinking the French Past*, edited and with a foreword by Lawrence D. Kritzman (New York: Columbia University Press, 1996–1998), 3 vols.

14 C. Charle, *La Crise des sociétés impériales (1900–1940), Allemagne, France, Grande-Bretagne, essai d'histoire sociale comparée* (Paris: Le Seuil, 2001).

15 D. L. Schalk, *War and the Ivory Tower: Algeria and Vietnam* (New York: Oxford University Press, 1991).

16 S. Collini, 'Intellectuals in Britain and France in the Twentieth Century: Confusions, Contrasts and Convergence?', in J. Jennings (ed.), *Intellectuals in Twentieth-Century France, Mandarins and Samurais* (London and New York: St Martin's Press, 1993), pp. 199–225; T. W. Heyck, 'Myths and Meanings of Intellectuals in Twentieth-Century British National Identity', *Journal of British Studies*, 37:2 (1998), 192–221.

17 S. Collini, R. Whatmore and B. Young (eds), *History, Religion and Culture. British Intellectual History 1750–1950* (Cambridge: Cambridge University Press, 2000), p. 3: 'an "intellectual history" which tries to recover the thought of the past in its complexity and, in a sense, which is neither self-contradictory nor trivial, as far as possible in its own terms.'

18 For instance, the fate of English radical intellectuals, or regional and ethnic minorities in the two countries that reject integration. On the imperial debate among British intellectuals in the nineteenth century, see J. Stapleton, *Political Intellectuals and Public Identities in Britain since 1850* (Manchester: Manchester University Press, 2001), pp. 24–31.

19 For a recent account of Anglo-French cultural relations, see also R. and I. Tombs, *That Sweet Enemy: The French and the British from the Sun King to the Present* (London: W. Heinemann, 2006).

20 See E. Sibeud, *Une Science impériale pour l'Afrique? La construction des savoirs africanistes en France 1878–1930* (Paris: Editions de l'Ecole des Hautes Etudes en Sciences Sociales, 2002); P. Singaravélou, *L'Ecole française d'Extrême-Orient ou l'institution des marges (1898–1956): Essai d'histoire sociale et politique de la science coloniale* (Paris: L'Harmattan, 1999); J. Schneer, *London 1900: The Imperial Metropolis* (New Haven and London: Yale University Press), 1999; *The Oxford History of the British Empire*, ed. W. Roger Louis (Oxford and New York: Oxford University Press, 1999), vols 3–5. Edward Saïd's work *Culture and Imperialism* (New York: Knopf, 1993) certainly tackles these questions, but his approach, too global as well

as too monographic, leads to incomplete and biased conclusions.
21 V. Karady, 'Students' Mobility in Western Universities: Patterns of Unequal Exchange in the European Academic Market, 1880–1939', in C. Charle, J. Schriewer and P. Wagner (eds), *Transnational Intellectual Networks: Forms of Academic Knowledge and the Search for Cultural Identities* (Frankfurt: Campus Verlag, 2004), pp. 361–400, and 'La migration internationale d'étudiants en Europe', *Actes de la Recherche en Sciences Sociales*, 145 (December 2002), 47–60.
22 See H. A. Strauss, 'The Migration of Academic Intellectuals', in H. A. Strauss and W. Röder, with H. Caplan, E. Radvany, H. Möller and D. M. Schneider (eds), *International Biographical Dictionary of Central European Emigrés 1933–1945*, vol. 2, part 1, A–K, *The Arts Sciences and Literature General* (Munich, New York, London and Paris: K. G. Saur, 1983), p. lxxxii.
23 J.-M. Palmier, *Weimar en exil: le destin de l'émigration intellectuelle allemande antinazie en Europe et aux Etats-Unis* (Paris: Payot, 1988).
24 C. Charle, *La République des universitaires (1870–1940)* (Paris: Le Seuil, 1994); E. Cohen, *Paris dans l'imaginaire national de l'entre-deux-guerres* (Paris: Publications de la Sorbonne, 1999).
25 'I have been attached to and felt at home in several countries and seen something of many others. However, in all of them, including the one into whose citizenship I was born, I have been, not necessarily an outsider, but someone who does not wholly belong to where he finds himself, whether as an Englishman among the Central Europeans, a continental immigrant in Britain, a Jew everywhere – even indeed particularly in Israel – an anti-specialist in a world of specialists, a polyglot cosmopolitan, an intellectual whose politics and academic work were devoted to non-intellectual, even, for much of my life, an anomaly among communists, themselves a minority of political humanity in the countries I have known. This has complicated my life as private human being, but it has been a professional asset for the historian', Eric J. Hobsbawm, *Interesting Times: A Twentieth-Century Life* (London: Allen Lane, 2002), p. 416.
26 K. R. Popper, *Unended Quest: An Intellectual Autobiography*, (1st edition, 1974; Glasgow: W. Collins, 1978); L. Wittgenstein, *Cambridge Letters: Correspondence with Russell, Keynes, Moore, Ramsey and Sraffa 1912–1948*, ed. B. McGuinness and G. H. von Wright (Oxford and Cambridge, MA: Blackwell, 1996); R. Monk, *Ludwig Wittgenstein: The Duty of Genius* (London: Cape, 1990); N. Elias, *Reflections on a Life* (Cambridge: Polity Press, 1994); J.-F. Stoffel, *Bibliographie d'Alexandre Koyré* (Florence: L. S. Olschki, 2000); P. Daix and A. Israël, *Pablo Picasso: dossiers de la Préfecture de police: 1901–1940* (Paris: Editions. des catalogues raisonnés; Moudon, Switzerland: Acatos, 2003); K. Grosse Kracht, *Zwischen Berlin und Paris: Bernhard Groethuysen (1880–1946): eine intellektuelle Biographie* (Tübingen: Niemeyer, 2002).

Index

Abélard, P. 27
Achard, Cl. Fr. 100
Ackerley, J. R. 277
Ainslye, Sir 87
d'Aguesseau, H. F. 71
Albert the Great 29
Albert, H. 181
Albert, Prince, of Saxe-Coburg and Gotha 158
D'Alembert, Jean Le Rond 68–9, 76, 88, 90
Alexander the Great 106
Allingham, W. 258
Amos, A. 158, 161, 162
Anderson, P. 3, 9, 46, 51, 52–4, 56–7, 58, 303
Annan, N. 3, 9, 15, 46–51, 52, 54, 303
D'Annunzio, G., 177, 179, 182
Antoine, A. 16, 216–22, 224, 228
Apollinaire, G. 189
Aquinas 26, 29
Archer, W. 178, 180, 187, 218, 221–2, 226
d'Argenson, family 84
Arlympale, Colonel 85
Arnold, M. 183
Auden, W. H. 273, 279–81
Augier, E. 218–19
Austin, A. 184
Austin, J. 157

Babbage Ch. 157
Bacon, F. 39, 76

Bagehot, W. 197
Baldick 57
Bale 36
Balfour 55
Balzac, H. de 115, 178
Banks, J. 102
Banville, T. de 175
Barbusse, H. 276, 289–90, 294, 296
Barclay, R. 103
Bardoux, J. 259
Baretti 83
Barine, A. 181
Barney, N. 274
Baron, H.-T. 107
Barrès, M. 174, 175, 186, 266, 290, 293
Baudelaire, C. 184, 272
Baudet, J. J. J. 100
Bauer, G. 276
Baux II, P. 107
Bax, E. B. 187
Bayle, P. 35
Beach, S. 217, 274
Beardsley, A. 55, 272
Beauchamp, Lord 85
Beaumont de la Bonninière, G. A. 157
Becque, H. 219
Bedos 100
Belayse, C. 109
Bellessort, A. 181
Belloc, H. 183, 184
Bentham, J. 88
Bérard, V. 264, 266
Beraud, L. (S. J.) 100

Berkeley, G. 106
Berkeley, Lord 85
Bernouilli, D. 69
Berry, Duke of 34
Bert, P. 266
Bertholon, P. N. (abbé) 100
Berwick (family) 87
Beyria, G. 274
Bible, K. J. 291
Bignon 66
Bjørnson, B. 178, 179, 180, 182
Blake, W. 58, 131
Blanqui, L. A. 157, 201
Bloch, M. 25, 299, 300
Boccaccio, G. 30
Bodley, J. 259
Boerhaave, H. 110
Böhm-Bawerk, E. von 202
Bohun 85
Bonar, J. 202
Bonnet, A. 208
Bos, C. du 181
Boswell, J. 91
Boucher de la Richarderie, G. 87
Boufflers, Mme de 89, 90
Bouger, P. 69
Bouglé, C. 240
Boulanger, G. (general) 235
Bourbon, Duke of 34
Bourdieu, P. 1, 15, 18, 28, 30, 199, 217
Boutmy, E. 236–8, 240, 242–5, 249
Boutroux, E. 179
Brabant, Siger de 29
Brahms, J. 223
Brandes, G. 220
Brémont, de 71
Brentano, L. 203
Bright, J. 261
Brioist, P. 7, 8, 10–13,
Bristol, F. A. Hervey (lord) 88
Britten, B. 281
Brockliss, L. 6, 8, 10, 12–13, 201
Broglie, Victor (duc) 157
Brontë, C. 261
Brontë, E. 261
Brook Taylor 103

Brooke, R. 273
Brooks, R. 274
Brougham, H. P. 157, 161
Broughton, T. 134
Broussais, F. 157
Broussonnet, P. M. A. 88, 90
Brunetière, F. 189
Buccleuch, Duke of 89
Buchan, W. 105
Buchanan, R. 179
Buchez, P. 208
Buffon, G.-L., (comte) 68, 69, 88
Buissière 74
Buracy, C. 92
Burdette 134
Burgundy, Duke of 34
Burke, E. 139
Burne-Jones, E. 261, 263
Burnouf, E. 266
Bute, J. S. (lord) 109
Butler, M. 131
Byron (admiral) 103
Byron, G. G. N. (lord) 129, 131, 261–2
Byron, I. 103

Cahun, C. 274
Caird, E. 202
Calais 45
Calvet, E. P. F. 12, 13, 98, 99, 102–3, 107, 108, 109, 110, 111, 112, 113, 114, 115
Calvière, Ch. Fr. (marquis de) 100
Camden, W. 36
Campbell-Bannerman, H. 175
Campos, C. 176
Cannan, E. 201
Cantillon, R. 196
Carlile, R. 131, 136
Carmontelle (Louis Carrogis) 90
Carpenter, E. 273, 277
Carrington, C. 288
Carter, J. 209–10
Cartwright, J. 134
Casanova, P. 6–8, 10, 15, 135, 200, 202, 301, 304

Index 313

Cassini de Thury, C.-F. 68, 75
Cassini, J. 74
Castel, L. B. 69
Caylus, A. C. P. (comte de) 88, 99–100
Cazamian, L. 239–40
Céline, L.-F. 289–90, 296
Celsius 75
Cendrars, B. 290
Chalmers, T. 157
Chamberlain, J. 223, 261–2
Chambers 91
Chandler, R. 106
Chandler, S. 29
Chapman, G. 289
Charle, C. 7–8, 10, 14, 16, 26–9, 48, 151, 182, 217
Charlemond, J. Caulfield (lord) 90
Charles, Duke of Orleans 31
Charles I 39, 78, 112
Charles II 63
Charmes, F. 258, 262, 264
Chartier, A. 31–4
Chartier, R. 11
Chateaubriand, F. R. 113, 115, 129
Châtelet, E. (marquise) 69, 71, 75
Chaucer, G. 32, 33, 34
Chekhov, A. 178
Cheselden 70
Chevrillon, A. 237–8, 247, 249, 258, 263, 265, 267
Clairaut, A. L. 69, 71
Claret de La Tourrette, A.-L. 99
Clarke 74
Clemenceau, G. 179, 295
Clémentel, E. 295
Clifford, H. (Lord) 109
Cloots, A. 135
Cobbett 134
Cobden, R. 261
Cochin, C. N. 90
Colbert, J.-B. 63
Coleridge, S. T. 153
Colet, J. 35
Colette 274
Colin, A. 237, 266
Colley, L. 16

Collini, S. 2–3, 6, 9, 214, 303
Colson, J. 71
Comestor, P. 29
Comte, A. 152
Comte, C. 157
Condamine, C. M. de la 69, 74
Condorcet, A.-N. 14, 75, 135, 147–8, 150, 152–6, 158, 162
Contantin (abbé) 100
Cook, A. 7, 8, 10, 14,
Cook, J. 106
Coppée, F. 266
Corbière, T. 189
Cossa, L. 197–9, 204, 210
Coste 104
Côte, père 74, 106
Cotton, R. 39
Coubertin, P. de 243
Couplet 66
Couptet de Tantreaux 66
Cournot, A. 202
Courtois, J. Fr. B. 100
Cousin, V. 157
Craddock, Mrs 82
Crevel, R. 273–4
Cudworth, R. 106
Cullen, W. 104
Cunningham, W. 201
Curzon, G. N. (lord) 175

Dante, D. A. 30
Daudet, A. 178
Daudet, L. 174
Daunou, F. 148, 157
Davison, T. 131
Davray, H. 181, 182, 188
Deffand, du 90
Defoe, D. 114
De La Bletterie, J. P. R. (abbé) 88
Delcassé, T. 266
Deledda, G. 179
De l'Espinasse, Mlle 89, 90
De l'Isle 73
Demolins, E. 236–8, 242–6, 248–9, 257
Déroulède, P. 266

Desaguliers, J. T. 68, 71, 75
Descartes, R. 69, 74, 75
Deschamps, E. 31, 33, 34
Destutt de Tracy, A. L. C. 157
Diaghilev, S. 284
Dickens, C. 178
Diderot, D. 68, 91–3, 104, 105, 113, 134
Didier 74
Digby, K. 105
Digeon, C. 16, 206
Dilke, Ch. 261, 264
Dillon 87
Ditton 71
Dostoyevsky, F. 181, 189
Douglas, A. (lord) 274
Doumic, R. 189
Dreyfus Affair 4, 6, 10, 27, 174, 221, 235–7, 240, 248–9, 259, 264–7
Drieu de la Rochelle, P. 290
Drummond, W. 87, 132
Drumont, E. 266
Du Bos, Ch. 181
Duchatel, T. 157
Duclos, C. P. 88, 90
Du Deffand, Mme 90
Dumas, A. 178, 218–19
Dumas, A. (the younger) 219
Dumont, A. 266
Dupin, A. 157
Dupin, C. 157
Dupont de Nemours, P. S. 89
Dupré de Saint-Maur, Mme 89
Dupuis, C. 132
Dupuit, J. 202
Durkheim, E. 54, 259
Duruy, V. 266
Dutens 80

Eagleton, T. 57
Eckhart, Master 29
Eden, M. 277
Eden, W. (lord) 84, 87
Edgeworth, F. Y. 204, 206
Edward, C. 82
Ekstein, M. 284

Elias, N. 307
Eliot, G. 178, 261
Eliot, T. S. 55, 182, 184, 188
Elizabeth I 36, 37, 39
Ellis, H. 274
Enville, Duchess of 189
D'Ennery, M. 99, 100, 103
Erasmus 31, 34, 35
Espagne, M. 7, 40, 151, 196

Fabulet, L. 183
Faujas de St Fond, B. 99, 100, 102
Fawcett, H. 210
Fénelon, F. 130
Ferguson, A. 106
Ferguson 106
Feuillet, O. 157
Filon, A. 257
Fitz-James (family) 87
Fitz-Maurier, Lord 92
Flaubert, G. 178, 181
Fogazzaro, A. 179
Folkes, M. 66
Foncemagne, E. 88
Foncin, P. 266
Fontenelle, B. Le Bovier de 66, 74
Ford, F. M. 184, 188
Forster, E. M. 273, 276–7
Forth, Mr 84–5
Foucault, M. 181, 271
Fouchy, J. P., Grandjean de 66, 70
Fouillée, A. 179, 259, 263
Fouquier, H. 179
Foville, A. de 194
Fox, family 88
Foxe, J. 36
France, A. 178
Franck, A. 157
Franklin, B. 87, 91–2
Freind, J. 105
Fuller, T. 105
Fussell, P. 284

Gaillard 102
Gaillard (bailli) 100, 102
Gaillard, C. 100

Gallois 66
Garnett, C. 178, 181
Garrick, D. 92
Gascoigne, J. 11
Gaul, R. 159
Gautier, T. 272
Genet, J.-P. 2, 9, 13
Genevoix, M. 289, 294, 296
Geoffrin, M. T. G. (madame) 90
Geoffroy, E. F. 68
George I 86
George II 86
George III 108
George, H. 201–2
Gérouin (abbé) 100
Gibbon, E. 11, 88, 91, 104
Gide, A. 175, 271, 274–6
Gide, C. 208–9
Giono, J. 290
Giraud, Ch. 157
Giraudoux, J. 17, 291–4, 296
Gissing, G. 51
Gladstone, W. E. 183, 261–2
Godin, L. 73, 74
Goethe, J. W. von 7
Goldsmith, O. 80, 88, 106
Goncourt, J. and E. 219
Goodman, D. 11
Gordon 106
Gosse, E. 175, 176, 178, 181, 186, 188, 189, 222
Gossen, H. H. 202
Gourmont, R. de 182, 184, 187, 189, 275
Gower, J. 32, 33
Grafton, R. 88
Gramsci, A. 4
Graves, R. 288
Graville 88
Greet, T. 109
Grein, J. T. 221–2
Grieg, E. 223
Grimm, S. H. 90
Groethuysen, B. 307
Grote, J. 157, 159
Guérin, D. 273, 279

Guillaumin, A. 209
Guizot, F. 14, 114, 153, 154–8, 159, 162–3, 236, 241
Gurney, I. 290
Guyot, Y. 210
Gyles, F. 196

Haaksonsen, K. 11
Habermas, J. 32
Hacking, I. 148, 154
Hails, W. 135
Hakluyt, R. 36
Halévy, E. 16, 179, 239–40, 247–9
Hall, R. 274, 276
Hallam, H. 157, 159
Haller, A. von 112
Halley, E. 66, 72, 73
Halley, Thomas 69
Hanover, Augustus-Frederick of 108
Hamilton, A. 157
Hardy, T. 178
Harney, G. J. 131
Harris, J. 66
Harrison, P. 11
Harvey, W. 105
Hauksbee, F. 105
Hauptmann, G. 178, 225, 228
Hazard, P. 10
Heinemann, W. 178, 181, 182
Helvétius, C.-A. 88, 89, 90–2, 107, 129, 134
Henault, C. J. F. 89
Henley, W. 185, 186
Henri IV 112
Henry VIII 35
Herder, G. 7
Herford, H. 186
Hertford, F. S. Conway (lord) 85, 88–9
Hervey, Lord 88
Higgs, H. 194
Hirschfeld, M. 274–5, 277
Hobbes, T. 104
Hobhouse, L. T. 54
Hobsbawm, E. 1, 54, 303, 307
Hobson, J. 249

Hoccleve, T. 32, 33
Hoggart, R. 51, 303
d'Holbach 89–93, 129, 134
Holinshed, R. 36
Holland (family) 88
Holland, V. 277
Homer 292–3
Hugo, V. 178
Hulme, T. E. 189
Hume, D. 11, 12, 13, 85, 92, 104, 106
Humphreys, J. 161
Hunt, H. 134
Hunter, J. 104
Hunter, W. 104
Hurlock, Mr 109
Hutchens, E. N. 285
Hutcheson, F. 106
Hutchinson, T. W. 202–3
Huxley, A. 50
Hyde, D. 227
Hynes, S. 284–5

Ibsen, H. 15, 16, 173, 175, 177, 178, 179, 180, 185, 187, 200, 214–29
Inge, W. R. 208
Isherwood, C. 273–4, 277, 279–81
l'Isle, de 73

James I 112
James, H. 178, 274
James, R. 103, 105
Jaurès, J. 179
Jennings, J. 10
Jevons, W. S. 147, 196, 200, 202
Johnson, J. 136
Johnson, S. 91, 109
Jouffroy, T. 157
Jouhaud, C. 35
Joyce, J. 16, 189, 216–18, 222, 224–8
Judet, E. 266
Jurin, J. 66, 73
Jusserand, L. 188
Jussieu, A. de 68

Kaminsky, H. 181

Kant, I. 286
Kay, J. 152
Keill, J. 105
Kemble, J. M. 158
Keynes, J. M. 56, 273
Keynes, J. N. 197, 199, 204
Kingsborough, Lord 109
Kingston, Duchess of 85
Kipling, R. 175, 178, 183, 185, 261–3
Knight, J. (Admiral) 109
Knight, P. (Lady) 109
Knight, R. P. 132
Koyré, A. 307
Kronje, P. (general) 265–6
Kruger, P. (president) 265
Krupp, A. 274

La Condamine, C. M. de 68, 69, 74
La Hire 66
La Rochefoucauld (family) 84–5, 89–90
La Tourrette, M. A. 100, 102, 110
La Vallière, duchesse de 89
Laborde, A., comte de 157
Labouchère, H. 271
Labusquière, J. 265
Lacurne de Sainte-Palaye J.-B. 88
Laforgue, J. 184, 189
Lalande 88
Lamartine, A. de 114
Lambelain, R. 265
Lamennais, F. de 115, 208
Lang, A. 180
Langland 32
Lanson, G. 189
Larbaud, V. 183, 188
Laski, H. 57
Lasserre, P. 179
Lavisse, E. 261, 266
Lavoisier, A. L. de 88, 90
Lazowski 90
Le Bon, G. 259
Le Galienne, R. 186
Le Goff, J. 9, 26, 27, 29
Le Play, F. 237, 244, 249
Le Tourneur, P. 107

Leavis, F. R. 56, 57
Leblanc (abbé) 93
Lecky, W. E. H. 210
Leclerc, G. L. 69
Leclerc, M. 237–8, 242–5
Lee, S. 186
Lehmann, J. 277
Leland, J. 36
Lemaître, J. 179, 266
Leroy-Beaulieu, P. 210
Lespinasse, J. de 89, 90
Lestrade, G. 274
Leterrier, A. S. 153–4
Lilley, A. L. 208
Lilti, A. 11
Lingard, J. 157
Locke, J. 35, 80, 104, 106, 148
Lombard, P. 29
Lombroso, C. 272
Lorenz, O. 236
Lorrain, J. 272
Lorris, G. de 31
Louis XIV 36, 37, 63, 113, 189
Louis XV 82
Louis XVI 82, 114
Louvois 66
Lucian 34
Ludlow, J. M. 208
Lugné-Poe, A. 16, 216–17, 220–2, 224, 229
Lydgate, J. 32, 33

Macartney, G. 106
Macaulay, T. B. 157
McCulloch, J. R. 157
Machaut, G. de 31
Machin, J. 66
Mackay, T. 209
McLaurin, C. 73, 74
Macpherson, J. 107
Maeterlinck, M. 177, 220–1
Maffei, F. S. 99
Maihows, Dr 88
Maine, H. 161–2
Mairan, J. J., Dortous de 66, 74
Malebranches 69

Mallarmé, S. 175, 178
Mallock, W. H. 179
Malthus, T. 157, 159
Manet, E. 226
Manners, J. 111
Mantoux, P. 78, 237, 239–40, 249–51
Marett, R. R. 208
Mariotte, E. 71
Marmontel, J. F. 90, 92
Marshall, A. 197, 203–4, 206
Marshall, squire 88
Martyn, E. 224, 226
Marx, E. 181
Mauclair, C. 187
Maupassant, G. de 178, 182
Maupertuis, P. L. Moreau de 69, 71, 74, 76
Maurras, Ch. 174, 175, 188
Mayow, J. 105
Mead, R. 105
Meller, A. 89
Mendelssohn, F. 223
Mendes da Costa, E. 102
Menger, C. 200
Mercier, A., (general) 266
Mercier, L.-S. 80, 94
Meredith, G. 178
Meung, J. de 31
Micciari, J. 98, 101
Michelet, J. 157
Mignet, F. 157
Mill, J. S. 147, 152–3, 157–9, 197, 261
Mille, P. 265
Milton, J. 106, 225
Mitford, W. 109
Moivre, A. de 68–71, 74
Molin, X. de 101, 111
Monnier, A. 274
Monod, G. 237
Montaigne, M. de 35
Montalembert, C. (comte) de 87
Monteil, P.-L., (colonel) 265
Montesquieu, C. de Secondat 11, 68, 79, 196
Montesquiou, R. de 272, 274
Montmor, P. R. de 69–71

Moore 87
Moore, G. 224 226–7
Moore, G. E. 150, 273
Moore, T. 131
Morand, S.-F. 70, 107
More, T. 34
Moreau de Maupertuis, P. L. 69
Moreau de Vérone 102
Moreau de Vicq d'Azyr, F. 101
Morellet, abbé 92, 93
Moretti, F. 174, 176
Morice, Ch. 182
Morley, J. 51
Morris, Governor 92
Morris, W. 51, 55, 58, 183
Mortimer, C. 66, 70
Morton, R. 105
Mosley, O. 295
Mulhern, F. 57
Murray, G. 183

Nairn, T. 52
Napoleon I 113, 114, 149, 159
Naudet, P. (abbé) 157
Necker, J. 114
Needham, W. 68
Nevill, W. P. (captain) 286–7
Newton, I. 66, 69, 70, 71, 74, 76, 106, 148
Nicholson, J. S. 197
Niel, J. G. 101, 115
Nietzche, F. 173, 178, 179, 187
Nivernais, Duke of 88
Noiriel, G. 81
Nolet, J.-A. (abbé) 75
Nordau, M. 272
Norman, E. 210
Nugent 80

O'Connor, F. 131
Oakeshott, M. J. 55
Ockham, W. of 29
Oldenburg 72
Orage, A. O. 178, 189
Orleans, Duke of 85, 89
Owen, W. 284, 288, 290–1

Paine, T. 130, 134
Palante, G. 179
Palfrey, D. 8, 10, 14
Pankhurst, C. 50
Park, J. J. 152
Parnell, C. S. 224–5
Parsons, J. 68
Passinges 99, 100
Passy, H. 157
Pater, W. 178, 273
Paul, A. (S. J.) 101
Paul, C. 277
Paul, F. 101
Peacock, T. L. 131
Pease, E. 50, 51
Peckham 88
Pellerin, J. 101
Pemberton, H. 74, 106
Pennant, T. 88
Perrin, E. 219
Perrot, J.-C. 12
Pétain, P., (general) 290
Petit de Julleville, L. 189
Petrarch 30
Pézenas, E. 71, 108
Phelps, L. R. 210
Picasso, P. 307
Pinero, A. 175, 222–3, 226
Pinkerton, J. 87
Piranesi 130
Pisan, C. de 31, 33
Pitcairne, A. 105
Pitt 113
Plomer, W. 277
Plowden, C. 109
Plutarch 273
Pocock, J. 5, 6, 7, 11
Polignac, E. de 274
Pompadour, J. A. de (marquise) 89
Pope, A. 104, 107
Popper, K. 54, 307
Pougy, L. de 274
Pound, E. 182, 184, 189
Pownall, T. 111
Praslin, Duke of 89
Pressensé, F. de 262

Prévost, A.-F. 104
Prévost, M. 178
Price, L. S. 286
Priestley, J. 88, 107, 136
Pringle, J. 104, 112
Pritchard, C. 157
Privat de Molières, J. 69, 74
Prochasson C. 8, 10, 16, 17
Prost, A. 289, 293
Proust, M. 274–6
Pryme, G. 158, 160

Quesnay, F. 89
Quételet, A. 152

Racine, J. 114, 177
Ramsay, A. of Kinkell 92
Ranke, L. von 288
Rawley, W. 39
Raynal, G. (abbé) 129, 134
Réamur 66
Reeve, H. 262
Régis, P. S. 74
Reinwald, C. 208
Réjane 221
Rémusat, C. F. M. de (comte) 157
Renan, E. 240, 242
Ricardo, D. 197
Richardson, S. 91, 107
Richmond, C. L. (lord) 75, 92
Rieder, F. 182
Rigby, Dr 88
Rimbaud, A. 184
Rivers, W. H. R. 287–8
Rivoire, A. (S. J.) 101, 103
Robartes, F. 70
Robert, H. 130
Robertson 106
Robertson, W. 104
Roche, D. 8, 10–13
Rochefort, H. 266
Rohault, J. 74
Roosevelt, T. 294
Roscher, W. 194, 197, 201
Rose, H. J. 151
Rosenberg, I. 290

Rossetti, G. D. 258, 261
Rothblatt, S. 150
Rousseau, J.-J. 90, 98, 103
Roustan, J. B. 101
Ruskin, J. 51, 261
Russell, B. 48, 51, 273, 277
Russell, D. 277
Rust 92
Rutty, W. 66

Sacquin, M. 87
Sade, J.-F.-P.-A. de 111
Sainte-Beuve, C. A. 129
Sainte-Croix, G. E. J. (baron) 101, 106, 107
Saint-Hilaire, B. 157
Saintsbury, G. 179, 181, 182, 186, 189
Saint-Véran, J. D. (abbé) 101
Saint-Vincens, J. Fr. P. 101, 111
Salisbury, Lord 262
Sand, George 12, 95
Sandricourt, Ch. Fr. S. (baron) 101
Sarcey, F. 179, 219
Sardou, V. 218–19
Sassoon, S. 284, 287–8, 294
Saurin 74
Savine, A. 181, 182
Say, J. B. 160
Schlegel (brothers) 114
Schmoller, G. von 194, 197
Schopenhauer, A. 187
Schumann, R. 223
Schumpeter, J. 194
Scott, C. 179
Scott, W. 114, 178, 182
Scotus, D. 29
Scribe, E. 218
Sedgwick, A. 149
Seeley, J. R. 257
Séguier, J.-F. 99, 102–3, 105, 106, 107, 108, 109
Senior, N. W. 157
Serao, M. 179
Shakespeare, W. 107, 114, 222–5
Shaw, G. B. 16, 180, 187, 216–18, 221–5, 228, 277

Shelburn, Lord 92
Shelley, P. B. 131
Sher, R. B. 11
Sidgwick, H. 55, 57, 147, 148, 150, 154, 162–3, 203
Sienckiewicz, H. 179
Sims, J. 105
Sinfield, A. 272
Singer, W. 274
Sirven 35
Skinner, Q. 2
Sloane, H. 66, 68, 70, 72, 102–3, 110
Smart, W. 202
Smith, A. 12, 88–9, 91–2, 155, 197
Smollett, T. G. 80, 94, 111
Smyth, W. 159
Snow, C. P. 51
Solomon, S. 272
Sorel, G. 179
Souday, P. 276
Spence, T. 131
Spencer (family) 88
Spencer, H. 51, 209
Spencer, H. J., first Earl 109
Spender, S. 273, 277, 279-80
Staël, G. (madame de) 11, 114, 159, 196
Stanley, H. 88
Stapleton, J. 10
Stendhal 114
Stephen, J. 158, 159, 160
Sterne 80, 85, 88, 92, 94
Stewart, L. 75
Stock, P. V. 181
Stormont, D. Murray (lord) 84
Stowe, J. 36
Strachey, L. 50, 273
Stravinsky, I. 284
Stuart, J. 109, 157
Suard, J.-B.-A. 106
Sudermann, H. 178
Suffolk, Earl of 91
Swift, J. 107
Swinburne, A. C. 178, 184
Sydenham, T. 105

Symonds, J. A. 273
Symons A. 182

Taggart 88
Tailhade, L. 189
Taine, H. 236–45, 247, 249, 257
Tallyrand, C. A. 148
Tamagne, F. 7, 10, 17
Tawney, R. H. 57
Taylor, B. 66, 103
Taylor, R. 131, 136
Tennyson, A. 178, 184
Thackeray, W. M. 178
Thatcher, M. 301
Thral (family) 84
Thickeness, P. 93
Thiers, L. A. 157
Thomas, E. 290
Thompson, E. P. 14, 58, 137
Thompson, J. 203
Thünen, J. H. von 202
Tickell 109
Tocqueville, A. 115, 157
Tolstoy, L. 173, 178, 181, 228
Tooke, W. 157
Topalov, C. 208
Trevelyan, G. M. 47
Trevor-Roper 4, 112
Troubridge, U. 274
Turgot, A. R. J. 81, 89, 105
Turner 105
Turquet de Mayerne, T. 112

Vacher de Lapouge, G. 259
Valbert, G. 262
Varignon, P. 69
Vaugelas, L. J. Lagier de 101
Verger, J. 26, 28
Vérone, M. J. B. 101
Vicq d'Azyr, F. 101
Victoria (Queen of England) 260
Villemot 74
Villon, F. 175
Vincent, J. 8, 10, 15, 151, 304
Vivien, R. 272, 274
Vizetelly, H. 175, 179, 182

Vogüé E. M. de 181, 184, 186, 187, 188
Volney, C. 14, 125–8, 131, 132, 134, 136–39
Voltaire 11, 35, 37, 63, 66, 68, 71, 74, 76, 79, 98, 178

Wade, J. 131
Wagner, R. 184, 223
Walker, A. 88
Waller, R. 66
Walpole, H. 82, 88
Walras, L. 200, 202
Walsh, J. 88
Warsley 68
Watson, J. 131
Waugh, E. 277
Webb, S. 303
Weber, M. 54
Wedgwood, J. 109
Wells, H. G. 51
Werner, M. 7, 40
Werth, L. 256
Wetherell, N. 109
Whately, R. 157
Whewell, W. 153, 154, 157–61, 163

Whytt, R. 104, 105
Wieser, F. von 202
Wilde, O. 178, 185, 272, 274, 276
Wilfert, B. 7, 8, 10, 14–15, 135, 200, 202, 301
Wilhelm I 260
Wilkes 88, 92
Wilkinson, J. 109
Williams, R. 285
Willis, T. 105
Winter, J. 7, 8, 10, 17
Wittgenstein, L. 307
Wolff, H. W. 208
Woodhouse, T. 73
Wooler, T. J. 131
Woolf, V. 276
Wyclif, J. 29
Wyzewa, T. de 181, 187, 258

Yeats, W. B. 16, 224–7
Young, A. 12, 85, 88–90
Young, B. W. 11
Yourcenar, M. 274

Zola, E. 173, 175, 177, 179, 185, 219, 222